PROMPT CORRECTIVE ACTION IN BANKING: 10 YEARS LATER

RESEARCH IN FINANCIAL SERVICES: PRIVATE AND PUBLIC POLICY

Series Editor: George G. Kaufman

PROMPT CORRECTIVE ACTION IN BANKING: 10 YEARS LATER

RESEARCH IN FINANCIAL SERVICES: PRIVATE AND PUBLIC POLICY

Series Editor: George G. Kaufman

RESEARCH IN FINANCIAL SERVICES:
PRIVATE AND PUBLIC POLICY VOLUME 14

PROMPT CORRECTIVE ACTION IN BANKING: 10 YEARS LATER

EDITED BY

GEORGE G. KAUFMAN
Loyola University Chicago, Chicago, IL, USA

Emerald

United Kingdom – North America – Japan –
India – Malaysia – China

Emerald Group Publishing Limited
Howard House, Wagon Lane, Bingley BD16 1WA, UK

Third edition 2008. Previous editions 1982, 1988

Reprints and permission service
Contact: books@emeraldinsight.com

British Library Cataloguing in Publication Data
A catalogue record for this book is available from the British Library

ISBN: 978-0-7623-0987-0

Printed and bound in Great Britain by
CPI Antony Rowe, Chippenham and Eastbourne

CONTENTS

LIST OF CONTRIBUTORS

Urs W. Birchler	Director, Systemic Stability Research, Swiss National Bank, Switzerland
Sarah Bohn	Division of Insurance and Research, Federal Deposit Insurance Corporation, USA
Timothy Critchfield	Division of Insurance and Research, Federal Deposit Insurance Corporation, USA
Aristóbulo de Juan	President, Aristobulo de Juan and Associates, Spain
Robert A. Eisenbeis	Director of Research and Senior Vice-President, Federal Reserve Bank of Atlanta, USA
Douglas D. Evanoff	Vice-President, Research Department, Federal Reserve Bank of Chicago, USA
R. Alton Gilbert	Vice-President, Research Department, Federal Reserve Bank of St. Louis, USA
William Gruben	Senior Economist and Vice-President, Federal Reserve Bank of Dallas, USA
Benton E. Gup	Chair of Banking, University of Alabama, USA
John R. Hall	Department of Economics and Finance, University of Arkansas at Little Rock, USA
Gerald A. Hanweck	Professor of Finance, George Mason University, USA
Alan C. Hess	Professor of Finance and Business Economics, University of Washington, USA

W. Curt Hunter	Director of Research and Senior Vice-President, Federal Reserve Bank of Chicago, USA
George G. Kaufman	John F. Smith Professor of Finance and Economics, Loyola University Chicago, USA
Thomas B. King	Banking Supervision and Regulation, Federal Reserve Bank of St. Louis, USA
Jahyeong Koo	Research Department, Federal Reserve Bank of Dallas, USA
David T. Llewellyn	Professor of Money and Banking, Loughbourough University, UK
Andrea M. Maechler	African Department, International Monetary Fund, USA
Andrew P. Meyer	Banking Supervision and Regulation, Federal Reserve Bank of St. Louis, USA
Larry Mote	Policy Analysis Division, Comptroller of the Currency, USA
Robert R. Moore	Financial Industry Studies Department, Federal Reserve Bank of Dallas, USA
Harvey Rosenblum	Director of Research and Senior Vice-President Federal Reserve Bank of Dallas, USA
Lynn Shibut	Division of Insurance and Research, Federal Deposit Insurance Corporation, USA
Lewis J. Spellman	Department of Finance, The University of Texas at Austin, USA
Mark D. Vaughan	Supervisory Policy Officer and Economist, Federal Reserve Bank of St. Louis, USA
Larry D. Wall	Financial Economist and Policy Advisor, Federal Reserve Bank of Atlanta, USA

INTRODUCTION

In December 1991, the U.S. Congress enacted and President George Bush signed the Federal Deposit Insurance Corporation Improvement Act (FDICIA). The Act was motivated by the severity of the U.S. banking and thrift crisis of the 1980s and represented the most important banking legislation since the Banking (Glass-Steagall) Act, which was enacted in 1933 at the depth of the previous most severe banking crisis in U.S. history. Between 1980 and 1991, some 1,500 commercial and savings banks, representing 10% of the industry in 1980, failed and more than 1,000 savings and loan associations (S&Ls), representing 25% of the industry, failed. In addition, delays in resolving the S&L failures helped to increase the cost beyond the resources of the then Federal Savings and Loan Insurance Corporation (FSLIC) and required the taxpayers to pay some $150 billion to insured depositors at these institutions. The large number and high cost of the failures were in large measure attributable to serious flaws in the extant government-sponsored deposit insurance program that encouraged insured institutions to assume excessive credit and interest rate risks and bank regulators to delay imposing corrective sanctions on troubled institutions and resolving economically insolvent institutions.

FDICIA attempted to correct these flaws by reforming the deposit insurance structure through requiring regulatory prompt corrective actions (PCA) and least cost resolution (LCR). PCA mandated a series of both discretionary and mandatory sanctions that the regulators first may and then must apply as an institution's financial health progressively deteriorates as reflected in a number of lower capital-to-asset ratios. These sanctions are intended to encourage the institutions to reverse their deterioration before it is too late. But if they fail to do so, PCA requires resolution of the institutions before their book-value capital is fully depleted. This is intended to minimize any losses from failure.

The designated PCA sanctions are modelled after the actual sanctions that the private market typically imposes on troubled firms in noninsured industries and that are distorted in banking by the government-provided insurance. Thus, FDICIA attempts to supplement regulatory and supervisory discipline with simulated market discipline.

Since its introduction in the United States in 1991, PCA been has been explicitly or implicity adopted in word if not spirit in many developed and developing countries with greatly different banking and regulatory structures.

How well has it worked or could it work? The papers collected in this volume attempt to answer these questions for both the U.S. and other countries by authors and discussants from a number of different countries. The papers also consider reinforcing or alternative prudential techniques. Thus, they add to our storehouse of knowledge on improving the performance of banking systems and should prove useful to researchers, practioners, and policy-makers both in evaluating extant regulatory structures and in designing new or modified structures.

All the papers were presented by the authors and commented on by the discussants at invited sessions at the annual meeting of the Western Economic Association in Seattle, Washington in July 2002. Maia Pykina (Loyola University Chicago) provided assistance both in arranging the session programs and in preparing the papers for publication.

George G. Kaufman
Series Editor
August, 2002

PART I:
MARKET DISCIPLINE BY BANK CREDITORS

SUBORDINATED DEBT AND PROMPT CORRECTIVE REGULATORY ACTION

Douglas D. Evanoff and Larry D. Wall

ABSTRACT

Several recent studies have recommended greater reliance on subordinated debt as a tool to discipline bank risk taking. Some of these proposals recommend using subordinated debt yield spreads as additional triggers for supervisory discipline under prompt corrective action (PCA); action that is currently prompted by capital adequacy measures. This paper provides a theoretical model describing how use of a second market-measure of bank risk, in addition to the supervisors own internalized information, could improve bank discipline. We then empirically evaluate the implications of the model. The evidence suggests that subordinated debt spreads dominate the current capital measures used to trigger PCA and consideration should be given to using spreads to complement supervisory discipline. The evidence also suggests that spreads over corporate bonds may be preferred to using spreads over U.S. Treasuries.

I. INTRODUCTION AND OVERVIEW

Prompt corrective action is based on a simple mandate directed toward bank supervisors: "resolve the problems of insured depository institutions at the least possible long-term cost to the deposit insurance fund."[1] The central provisions of prompt corrective action (PCA) aim to provide a series of interventions as a bank's financial condition deteriorates. Moreover, rather than relying solely

Prompt Corrective Action in Banking: 10 Years Later, Volume 14, pages 3–29.

ISBN: 0-7623-0987-3

on supervisory judgment about a troubled bank's financial condition, PCA focuses on quantifiable measures of a bank's financial condition. In particular, supervisory intervention is currently triggered by bank capital adequacy ratios.

Although quantifiable measures have a variety of advantages, probably the most important advantage in the context of PCA is that their use reduces the scope for supervisors to exercise forbearance. The measure used, however, needs to be closely associated with the financial condition of the bank if it is to effectively achieve this purpose. A limitation of focusing almost exclusively on capital adequacy ratios is that banks and supervisors have substantial influence over the calculation of the numerator (capital) and denominator (a proxy for risk) of these ratios. The Basel Bank Supervisors Committee is currently trying to address problems in the calculation of the denominator (see BIS, 2001). Yet the more serious problem lies with the measurement of capital. Whether capital is measured using historical cost accounting (as is currently the case) or economic value accounting, a bank's capital will reflect declines only if the bank voluntarily recognizes the losses or the supervisors force recognition. Given that banks usually resist recognition of losses that would result in their being undercapitalized under PCA, responsibility for accurate capital measurement rests with the supervisors. This is to say, if the supervisors want to exercise forbearance, all they need do is acquiesce to a bank's refusal to recognize losses. Prominent examples of such acquiescence by supervisors include recognition of losses at U.S. banks due to loans to less-developed-countries (mostly in Latin America) in the 1980s and recognition of domestic loan losses by Japanese regulators throughout the later 1990s.

An alternative to exclusive reliance on capital adequacy ratios would be to use some market-based risk measure as a trigger for supervisory action. Examples of such measures would include the spread of subordinated debt obligations over comparable maturity Treasury obligations as proposed by Evanoff and Wall (2000a) and probabilities of default calculated using stock returns, such as is done by KMV (see Gunther, Levonian & Moore, 2001).[2] The advantage of using a market-based risk measure is that market participants have a strong incentive to base their valuations on the expected payouts for their claim, whether or not a particular price is the one desired by banks and their regulators. The disadvantage of using a market-based risk measure is that the prices may incorporate more than the credit risk of the issuer. For example, the price of a bank's debt depends in part on factors such as the term structure of interest rates and the liquidity of the debt obligation.

The fact that the pricing of market obligations depends on more than the credit risk of the obligation is one of the primary arguments raised against plans

to use market-based risk measures. Supervisors, it is argued, should not be forced to discipline a bank based on a market-based measure when they know that the bank is in good financial condition.[3]

This paper addresses the criticism of using market-based risk measures in two ways. First, it provides a simple model to illustrate the underlying wisdom of PCA, that the use of a quantitative risk measure may produce better outcomes even if the quantitative risk measure is on average less accurate than supervisory evaluations. The model considers two cases. The first is one where the supervisor knows the true condition of some banks, but not others. In this case the quantitative risk measure may improve the evaluation of banks about which the supervisor is uncertain. In the second case, the supervisor knows the condition of all banks with certainty and the condition of the bank is measured with error by the quantitative measure. However, in this situation the supervisor exercises forbearance toward banks that should be disciplined with positive probability. The use of a quantitative measure may improve outcomes in this second case by reducing the probability of forbearance, even though it may result in the disciplining of a healthy bank.

The second part of the paper provides empirical evidence on the potential use of subordinated debt yield spreads as a trigger for PCA. This paper extends Evanoff and Wall (2001) which provided evidence that subordinated debt spreads over both Treasury and corporate bond indices are better predictors of supervisory ratings than are the risk-based capital adequacy ratios. Evanoff and Wall (2002) focus on banks that have high subordinated debt spreads over Baa yields, but are rated satisfactory by the bank supervisors. That analysis finds that almost all of the banks with high spreads have some indication that they are indeed higher risk. In a few cases, the supervisors appeared to be substituting frequency of exams for reductions in CAMEL or BOPEC ratings. Other measures of risk considered that indicate that the high spread banks were indeed higher risk include regulatory early warning scores, market-to-book ratios, credit agency ratings and recent supervisory ratings.

This paper extends Evanoff and Wall (2002) to examine banks with high subordinated debt spreads over U.S. Treasury rates. The focus is on spreads over Treasuries for a couple of reasons. First, spreads over Treasuries may provide more accurate, albeit more procyclical, measures of banks' risk than spreads over Baa debt. The average spread of Baa securities over Treasury securities increases as credit defaults increase, providing an automatic relaxation of any standard that uses subordinated debt spreads over a Baa index. The use of a Treasury index may provide a more consistent test through time. Second, Evanoff and Wall (2002) used spreads over Baa in part for a practical reason that may no longer be relevant. At the time of their analysis, the stock of publicly traded Treasury securities was forecast to disappear due to federal government surpluses. Budgetary developments since the terrorist incidents of September 11, 2001 suggest that the stock of publicly traded Treasury securities may remain substantial. Evanoff and Wall (2002) discuss the theoretical advantages and disadvantages of the alternative spreads.[4] The empirical analysis in this paper may highlight the actual differences during the sample period.

The paper is organized as follows. The next section contains the theoretical model describing how use of a second "market measure" of bank risk to initiate PCA may be beneficial. The third section discusses the data and empirical methodology used to test the implications of the theory. The fourth presents the results and the final section summarizes and provides concluding remarks.

II. DISCIPLINING BANKS WITH TWO RISK SIGNALS

This section develops a model of optimal bank discipline when two risk signals are available. The first subsection lays out the assumptions of the model. The second analyzes optimal solutions under the assumption that supervisors act in a socially optimal manner. The third subsection analyzes the solutions under the assumption that supervisors sometimes exercise forbearance on weak banks even though the social welfare would be enhanced if the banks were disciplined. The fourth subsection discusses the implications of the results.

Model Assumptions

The objective of the social planner is to establish rules that minimize the cost of errors in the disciplining of banks. Banks are assumed to be of two quality types $Q \in \{H, L\}$. Type L banks are low quality and should be disciplined by the regulators. Type H banks are high quality and should not be disciplined. Given that the null hypothesis is that a bank is solvent, then disciplining a type H bank is a type-1 error that generates total social costs of $T1$. Conversely, failure to discipline a type L bank is a type-2 error that generates total social costs of $T2$.

Bank types are not directly observable but bank examiners receive a signal of each bank's quality at the end of their examination. The signal to the examiners, R, may take one of three forms: $R \in \{A, B, C\}$. If the examiner receives signals A or C then the bank's type is revealed with certainty: signal A signifies a type H bank and signal C signifies a type L bank. If the signal to the examiner is B, however, then the examiner knows only that the bank is type H with probability q and type L with probability $(1 - q)$.

A second, independent signal of a bank's quality, *IS*, may also be observed: $\infty < IS < \infty$.[5] For example, bank capital adequacy ratios are currently used as an independent signal to prompt PCA. For this second signal, the probability that a bank is of high quality is $p(H \mid IS)$ and the probability that it is of low quality is $(1 - p(H \mid IS))$. The probability that a bank is of high quality is an increasing function of *IS*:

$$p'(H \mid IS) > 0.$$

This general formulation allows, but does not require that the independent signal be perfectly correlated with a bank's condition.

Model Solution Without Agency Problems

If there are no agency problems, the examiner always uses his signal optimally, and no other signal exists then the decision rule is straightforward. The examiner:

(1) never disciplines banks when the signal is *A*;
(2) always disciplines banks when the signal is *C*; and
(3) disciplines banks when the signal is *B*

only if the expected cost of incorrectly disciplining type *H* banks that are rated *B* is less than the cost of incorrectly failing to discipline type *L* banks:

$$qT1 < (1 - q)T2.$$

If an alternative signal, *IS*, is available then its use may reduce the social costs of incorrectly disciplining banks. One way of incorporating *IS* into the discipline process, along the lines of PCA, would be to establish a single trigger score for disciplining all banks, *t*. That is, all banks with *IS* values less than *t* would be disciplined. In addition, any bank with an *IS* value greater than *t*, but that received an examination rating of *C* would also be disciplined. In this case the social planner would solve for the value of *t* that minimizes the costs of disciplining all banks.

$$\min_t SC = \int_{-\infty}^{t} T1p(H \mid IS, R = A)dIS + \int_{-\infty}^{t} T1p(H \mid IS, R = B)dIS$$
$$+ \int_{-\infty}^{t} T2(1 - p(H \mid IS, R = B))dIS. \qquad (1)$$

The use of a single trigger score for all banks would result in the cost of Type-1 errors arising from disciplining some banks that received an examination rating

$R=A$. There would also be costs associated with the classification errors of some high and low quality banks that receive an examination rating of B. There would not be errors associated with failing to discipline banks that received an examination rating of C because all of these banks would be disciplined.

The strict adherence to a single trigger point with the IS signal for all banks is inefficient in the absence of agency costs. The examiners know with certainty that type A banks should not be disciplined and type C banks should be disciplined. Thus, the independent signal could be applied only to those banks receiving an examination rating of B, where the banks may be of high or low quality. In this case, the social planner first finds the optimal trigger point:

$$\min_t SC = \int_{-\infty}^{t} T1p(H|IS, R=B)dIS + \int_{-\infty}^{t} T2(1-p(H|IS, R=B))dIS. \quad (2)$$

The social planner then selects the strategy with the lowest cost:

(1) disciplining all type B banks;
(2) disciplining none of the type B banks; and
(3) disciplining only those banks with examination ratings of B and an $IS>t$.

Model Solution With Agency Problems

Although the application of a single trigger point to all banks may be suboptimal in the absence of agency problems, PCA was explicitly developed to address agency problems; see Benston et al. (1986). Thus, a more thorough analysis of PCA requires an environment in which supervisors do not always impose discipline on banks even when examination results indicate that discipline is appropriate. In order to focus on this agency problem, in this section we assume that the examination signal observed by the supervisor contains no error, that is all banks receive an examination rating of A or C. Furthermore, assume that the examiners do not always forbear on banks with an examination rating of C, but rather exercise forbearance (or leniency) with a probability of l where $0<l\leq 1$. Moreover, supervisors know that if they rate a bank C and fail to discipline the bank then Congress may learn of the forbearance and impose a penalty on them. Thus, in those cases where the supervisors exercise forbearance, they will also claim that the examination of the bank returned a signal of A.

For a given probability of forbearance, l, the social planner's problem is to pick a PCA trigger rate that minimizes the following social costs:

$$\min_t SC = \int_{-\infty}^{t} T1p(H|IS, R=A)dIS + \int_{-\infty}^{t} T2(l)(1-p(H|IS, R=C))dIS. \quad (3)$$

The first order condition for a solution of Eq. (3) is

$$\partial SC/\partial t = T1p(H|t, R=A) + T2l - T2(l)p(H|t, R=C) = 0. \quad (4)$$

Let the value of t that solves Eq. (4) be t^*. Then the effect of an increase in the proportion of C rated banks that receive forbearance, l, on t^* is

$$\frac{\partial t}{\partial l}|F.O.C.=0 = -[T2 - T2p(H|t,R=C)]/[T1p'(H|t,R=A) - T2lp'(H|t,R=C)] > 0. \quad (5)$$

That is, an increase in the proportion of banks receiving forbearance leads to a decrease in t^*. Given that t is directly related to bank quality, this suggests that an increase in forbearance leads to more banks being disciplined.

Implications

The results in the case with no agency costs have implications for the use of an independent signal. First, a single trigger point for all banks is inefficient. Thus, absent agency costs, the current structure of PCA with a set of trigger points that applies to all banks is inefficient if examiners sole goal is to minimize social costs from incorrectly disciplining banks. Second, the use of an independent signal may improve social welfare even if it is not always very accurate. The signal need only be better than imposing a uniform discipline policy for all banks with examination ratings of B in order to improve social welfare. The proportion of banks with examination ratings of A and C that would be misclassified by the independent signal is irrelevant if the independent signal is only applied to banks with examination ratings of B.

The results in the case allowing for agency costs also have important implications for the situation where agency costs are relevant. First, the independent signal need not be more accurate than the signal observed by examiners. The signal to the examiners in the model with agency costs does not contain any error, but the use of an independent signal may, depending on parameter values, nevertheless be preferred from a societal perspective because supervisors do not always discipline banks with low examination signals.

Second, an increase in the rate of forbearance will lead to a lower trigger point, t^*, for the independent signal. Thus, if the trigger point for PCA using the independent signal is t^* then ex post evaluations of the accuracy of the PCA measure will be biased down if the probability of forbearance is greater than zero. The optimal trigger point is set with the intention that supervisors will sometimes act before the trigger forces supervisory action.

A general implication for the empirical analysis is that we should pay special attention to cases where the independent signal says the bank is high risk, but the examination signal says it is low risk – this is where both the costs and benefits of the independent signal arise. If the independent signal is incorrect then using it generates costs, if the independent signal is correct then using it generates benefits.

III. MEASURING BANK RISK

The empirical analysis below focuses on the cases where subordinated debt yield spreads are high but supervisory ratings are satisfactory. However, to motivate the potential use of subordinated debt yield spreads as a PCA trigger, we contrast the relative accuracy of alternative capital ratios and subordinated debt spreads in predicting bank condition. We measure bank condition as subsequent CAMEL or BOPEC ratings.[6] Evanoff and Wall (2001) found that subordinated debt spreads outperformed most of the capital measures, including the measure currently used to trigger PCA, in predicting bank condition. Capital measures were shown to add very little predictive power once the debt spread was accounted for.[7] Below we summarize those findings.

For the current analysis we introduce results from the estimation of alternative single-variable logit models in Evanoff and Wall (2001) and use them as a starting point to more fully evaluate observations where predictions from debt markets do not coincide with supervisory ratings.[8] As emphasized in our theory section, these are the very observations where adding a second signal to the PCA process could have the most impact.

Data

We use the data developed in Evanoff and Wall (2001). It includes a sample of bank subordinated debt yields between 1985 and 1999 that satisfy two criteria:

(1) the issuer must be among the 100 largest domestic banking organizations in the United States; and
(2) the bond must be listed on Bloomberg with quarterly yield data.

If sufficient trading occurs in a bond, then Bloomberg reports volume-weighted average transaction prices. If trading is not sufficient, then matrix-generated prices based on price quotes from informed market traders are reported. Prices are weighted averages based on a minimum of two price sources and they must be within an "acceptable" tight range.[9]

Much of the analysis in Evanoff and Wall (2002) uses subordinated debt yield spreads over maturity matched Baa corporate bonds. The current analysis evaluates spreads over maturity matched Treasury security yields. Treasury yields are obtained from the Board of Governors of the Federal Reserve System's web site and the spread over Treasuries is calculated as the difference between the subordinated debt yield and the calculated yield on a comparable maturity Treasury security.[10]

We also obtained confidential supervisory ratings from the Federal Reserve Supervision Department database. The ratings are the composite CAMEL(S) rating for banks and the composite BOPEC rating for bank holding companies. About 70% of the observations are at the bank holding company level. Capital adequacy ratios are calculated using data from the Reports of Condition and Income filed by banks (Call Reports) and bank holding companies (FR Y-9C) with their respective federal supervisor.

We examine a subsample of 452 observations from the data in Evanoff and Wall (2001) that contains complete information on the bond spreads over Treasuries. Within this subsample there are 13 banks with a supervisory rating of 3 or lower.

Results

The results of estimating logit models to predict supervisory examination ratings are presented in Table 1 and are from Evanoff and Wall (2001). They indicate that subordinated debt spreads over Treasuries (*Sub-debt spread over Treasuries*) provide greater predictive power than the current PCA capital adequacy standard (*PCA capital adequacy status*). Although the "percentage correct" is relatively high for the *PCA capital adequacy status*, the high level of "tied" observations suggests the model is not very confident of its assignment of individual observations and the low percentage of correct 3–4 classifications suggests the model is doing very poorly in identifying problem banks. The rather low concordance found using the alternative capital measures raise concerns about their usefulness to forecast future problem banks. Therefore, with one exception, the alternative capital adequacy ratios are generally inferior to the spread measures at predicting supervisory rating; the exception being the *Tier-1 leverage ratio*. Evanoff and Wall (2001), Table 3,

Table 1. Binomial Model Predicting CAMEL Ratings as a Function of Capital Ratios and Debenture Spreads Over the Treasury Rate.

Variable	Parameter Estimate (1)	Parameter Estimate (2)	Parameter Estimate (3)	Parameter Estimate (4)	Parameter Estimate (5)
Intercept	–5.2195 (0.0001)	–3.0839 (0.1008)	1.2028 (0.5061)	–1.3070 (0.4499)	–4.5877 (0.0001)
Sub-debt spread over Treasuries					1.1047 (0.0038)
PCA capital adequacy status	1.5700 (0.0525)				
Total risk based capital ratio		–0.0352 (0.8155)			
Tier 1 leverage ratio			–0.7052 (0.0119)		
Tier 1 capital to risk-weighted exposure				–0.2622 (0.2083)	
Association of Predicted Probabilities and Observed Responses					
Concordant	14.8%	43.2%	65.9%	54.8%	76.8%
Discordant	3.1%	35.4%	30.8%	40.3%	19.0%
Tied	82.1%	21.4%	3.3%	4.9%	4.2%
Gamma	0.656	0.099	0.363	0.152	0.604
% Correct	94.0%	23.2%	55.3%	38.9%	58.0%
% 3–4 Correct	15.4%	0%	69.2%	53.8%	69.2%
% 1–2 Correct	96.4%	23.9%	54.9%	38.5%	57.6%
Chi-square for covariates (p-value)	2.259 (0.0967)	0.058 (0.8098)	6.402 (0.0114)	1.797 (0.1801)	6.475 (0.0109)

The results are from Evanoff and Wall (2001). The dependent variable takes a value of 0 for CAMEL (or BOPEC) ratings 1 and 2, and a value of 1 for ratings 3 and higher. The PCA capital adequacy status ranges from 1 for the best capitalized banks (well capitalized) to 5 for the least well capitalized (critically undercapitalized). The p values for the maximum likelihood parameter estimates are in parentheses below the coefficients. The "Chi square for covariates" statistic is based on the log likelihood statistic, and tests the marginal explanatory power of the independent variables relative to a model with only a constant term. The associated p values are included in parentheses.

Concordance is a measure of the correlation between the observed and predicted probabilities of the dependent variable. A pair of observations is said to be concordant if, based on the model, the observation that has a particular rating has a sufficiently higher probability of receiving that rating than does the other observation. A pair is discordant if the reverse is true. A pair is tied if the probability interval between the two observations is sufficiently small, 0.002. A correlation index, the Goodman-Kruskal Gamma index, is also included for assessing the predictive power of the model and for making comparisons across models. If nc is the number of concordant pairs and nd the number of discordant pairs, then the Goodman-Kruskal Gamma $= (nc - nd)/(nc + nd)$. See Goodman and Kruskal (1972). Generally, the index approaches zero as independence between the two measures increases. Number of observations = 452.

present further results from estimating models that include both the debt spreads and capital adequacy measures. Their results indicate that inclusion of the capital measures appear to add little to the explanatory power of the models. The performance of subordinated debt spreads satisfies an important prerequisite for tying PCA to debt market information.

While the spread measures perform better than the current PCA triggers at predicting troubled banks, as discussed below, they still result in a number of misclassifications; i.e. the spread suggests the bank is high-risk while the supervisory rating suggests otherwise. As discussed earlier, these differences are a prerequisite for generating cost and/or benefits from initiating PCA with debt spreads. Additional analysis is therefore needed to associate the spread and risk measures and to determine the extent of the potential gains from such a program.

IV. A MORE DETAILED ANALYSIS OF "MISCLASSIFICATIONS"

This section discusses the empirical methodology used to analyze the misclassifications resulting from using the debt spreads to predict risk levels as proxied by supervisory ratings. Can we delineate the source of the differences in bank classification between debt spreads and supervisory ratings?[11] In particular, we consider a priori reasons for expecting that in certain circumstances the spread may be a poor indicator of bank condition. We also evaluate situations in which subordinated debt spreads may be a better indicator of bank risk than the model projects.

Misclassifications and Liquidity Issues

The spread on a bank's subordinated debt over comparable maturity Treasury securities may depend on a variety of factors, perhaps the largest of which is the reduced liquidity of bank issues, see Hancock and Kwast (2001). If this premium is approximately the same for all banks, its presence simply requires an adjustment to the spread used to trigger supervisory action. However, if it varies across banks, some additional adjustment needs to be made. Most subordinated debt proposals recognize that bond issues by smaller banks are likely to have higher liquidity premiums because the issue size is smaller and may attract less attention from bond analysts. Hence, smaller banking organizations are typically excluded from mandatory subordinated debt issuance requirements.[12] As a rough first approximation, we consider any debt issue by a bank not among the largest thirty in that year to be likely to have a relatively high liquidity premium. These banks are then excluded from further analysis.[13]

Additional Factors to Consider in Evaluating the Accuracy of the Yield Spreads and Examination Ratings

After accounting for the above mentioned liquidity concerns, the remaining observations will be evaluated to determine when the debt yields identified a problem that was apparently not being reflected in the examination ratings. This part of the empirical analysis is made more complicated by our inability to objectively determine the true condition of the bank. Unfortunately, the problem of not having the true measure of a bank's condition is unavoidable in analyzing an independent signal of bank risk. Thus, we examine a variety of measures while being careful to note any limitations on the conclusions that can be drawn from the results. Our procedure is to use supervisory information and a variety of accounting and financial market measures to identify banks that appear to be financially distressed around the time of the examination although the regulatory rating suggests the bank is low risk.

We use two measures of supervisory concern about the bank. The first is whether the bank has been re-examined within a six-month period. While bank supervisors ordinarily go at least one year between examinations, in some cases in our sample the supervisors appeared to be substituting frequent exams for lower CAMEL ratings. Discussions with examiners indicate that this procedure has been followed for some banks at certain times in the past.[14] The second measure of supervisory concern is whether the bank has been or will be rated less than satisfactory within one year of the current rating.

We also consider alternative accounting measures of the condition of the bank. Accounting ratios are accounted for via parameter estimates from econometric forecasting models aimed at identifying problem banks – early warning models. The econometric model approach is more likely to yield an objective risk measure. The models were created to use accounting data to identify potential problem institutions to help guide the use of examination resources.[15] If these models indicate that the banks identified by the yield spreads had a higher probability of failure or were good candidates for a rating downgrade, that result would be consistent with debt yield spreads correctly signaling that the bank is high risk.

We use two early warning models to identify banking organizations that were good candidates for downgrades both at the time of the examination and over several subsequent quarters. The first is that of Gilbert, Meyer and Vaughan (GMV, 2000). The model is designed to predict future bank supervisory rating downgrades to less than satisfactory condition (i.e. CAMEL 3, 4 or 5) based on accounting data. It is more flexible than other early warning models commonly used by supervisors in that it emphasizes the potential for deterioration in bank condition rather than bank failure; downgrades being a much more common phenomenon during our sample period. As such, parameter estimates are allowed to vary through time to more accurately account for changing influences on bank condition. Where appropriate, we also augment the results of the GMV model with those of the Federal Reserve's "System to Estimate Examination Ratings," or SEER risk rank model, which is used to predict the probability of bank failure.[16] The GMV ratings are obtained from the authors and the SEER risk rankings are obtained from confidential Federal Reserve supervision files.

Common stock prices may also yield information on the financial condition of banking organizations. As a rather crude proxy for bank condition we consider a market-to-book ratio of less than one as being indicative of the equity market's concern about the financial condition of a bank. An alternative measure would be market-adjusted equity returns. We do not include this measure in our analysis, however, because negative equity returns may be caused merely by a firm's transition from having great earnings prospects to having mild difficulties that should not be sufficient to trigger PCA. Another alternative is the price-to-earnings ratio, but the interpretation of this ratio is less clear when a bank suffers losses. Thus, results consistent with the supervisors exercising forbearance would be:

(1) low debt ratings;
(2) the equity market measure indicating problems before the satisfactory examination rating is assigned; and
(3) the equity market measure indicating a problem after the examination rating is assigned.

The bond ratings are obtained from *Moody's Banking and Finance Manual, various issues*. Market-to-book ratios are obtained from the *American Banker* for the last business day in each quarter.

V. EMPIRICAL RESULTS

Based on the model presented in column 5 of Table 1, and employing probability assumptions similar to those employed in Evanoff and Wall (2002), the analysis correctly predicts 288 observations, misclassifies (misses) three high risk institutions and misclassifies (erroneously classifies as high risk) 183 observations. The 183 type-2 errors can be significantly improved upon by raising the spread threshold from an 84 basis point spread to 90 or 100 basis points.[17] However, we base our analysis on the 84 basis point spread to approximately match the cut-off point suggested by the logit estimation results in column 5 of Table 1 and to enable us to compare results using spreads over alternative debt instruments.

The cut-off point of 84 basis points correctly classifies 10 of the 13 banks with CAMEL ratings of 3 or 4. The bulk of the following analysis emphasizes the 183 additional banks (35% of the highly rated banks) classified as problem institutions although the supervisory rating suggested otherwise. As mentioned above, the misclassification may occur for a number of reasons including the possibility that subordinated debt markets simply incorrectly classify low-risk institutions as high-risk. We evaluate this possibility. The first subsection compares the high-spread banks with the remainder of the sample, the next subsection further analyzes the characteristics of the high-spread banks and the final subsection summarizes the lessons learned from the empirical analysis.

Contrasting High- and Low-spread Banks

A comparison of certain characteristics of banks with high spreads vs. those with low spreads is found in Table 2. The results presented in the first three rows suggest there is little difference in capital adequacy ratios between the high-and low-spread groups, in either a statistical or economic sense. We also found that there was essentially no difference in an ordinal PCA capital

Table 2. Means of Bank Capital and Downgrade Probabilities Across Subsamples.

	Predicted "good" banks (1)	Predicted "problem" banks* (2)
Risk based capital	12.5%	12.2%
Tier-1 leverage	7.08%	6.99%
Tier-1 risk-based	8.85%	8.56%
Early-warning model: GMV-1	1.0	4.77
Early-warning model: GMV-2	1.0	7.9

* A "problem bank" is one which has a subordinated debt issue trading at a yield spread equal to or greater than 84 basis points over a maturity matched Treasury bond. The early warning model measure is normalized to one for the predicted "good" banks; thus the other measures are relative to the normalized category.

adequacy measure taking on values from 1 to 5 depending on whether the bank is considered Well Capitalized, Adequately Capitalized, Under Capitalized, Significantly Undercapitalized or Critically Undercapitalized, respectively, under the guidelines introduced in the early 1990s. This index is of particular interest since it is the measure currently being used to trigger PCA.

Substantial differences exist, however, across the two subgroups using alternative criteria to measure potential bank problems. To incorporate information from early warning models, two alternative measures based on the GMV (2000) regulatory downgrade model are presented in Table 2. The first, GMV-1, is a measure of the probability of a downgrade based on beginning of year projections. GMV-2 is based on end-of-year data; thus it measures conditions realized during the year and can be considered more of a current-condition measure while the GMV-1 measure is more forward looking. Each measure is indexed to the mean of the non-problem bank subsample.

The GMV-1 measure of bank condition for our high-yield spread subsample is over four times that for the other group, suggesting a substantial difference in the potential for downgrades to less than satisfactory status across the two groups.[18] Results using the GMV-2 measure suggests even greater differences. There are also differences using the regulator's SEER model. Thus, there is some evidence that the "misclassified" observations may be different from satisfactory rated banks.

Analysis of High Spread Banks

In this section we further delineate the high spread banks. We first separate the banks with high spreads into three groups: those that we can explain as either being in agreement with supervisory ratings, those that may have significant noise in their yield spread measures, and the remaining banks. This remaining group, the "unexplained" observations, is then further investigated.

The observations that are easily explained are summarized in Table 3. The 193 observations are first ranked by spread with a ranking of 1 assigned to the highest spread and a ranking of 193 assigned to the lowest spread (but greater than 84 basis points). The observations are then separated by these rankings into eight sets of 25, with the last set including the 17 observations with the smallest spreads (but greater than 84 basis points). This procedure allows an evaluation of the accuracy of the spread measure as yield spreads decline while at the same time providing ample protection for the confidentiality of individual bank examination ratings.

The second column contains the number of observations in each set where the bank is rated less than satisfactory (i.e. a CAMEL or BOPEC rating of 3

Table 3. Analysis of Projected Problem Banks Based on Subordinated Debt Yields: Identification of Banks With Clear Reasons for High Spreads.

Ranking by spread (1)	Less than satisfactory examine rating (2)	Potentially noisy data (3)	Unexplained observations with satisfactory regulatory ratings and no noisy data (type-2 error) (4)
1–25	2	14	9
26–50	4	8	13
51–75	0	8	17
76–100	2	6	17
101–125	1	7	17
126–150	0	12	13
151–175	1	7	17
176–193	0	5	13

or 4). These are the observations where the yield spreads and the supervisors appear to be reaching similar conclusions. For example, among the banks with the largest 25 yield spreads, two banks were rated less than satisfactory by the supervisors.

The third column contains the number of observations with potentially noisy data because the observations came from a smaller bank. For example, eight banks with spreads ranked between 26 and 50 in our sample fall into the category of banks with potentially noisy data. The fourth column contains the unexplained observations where the bank received a satisfactory rating and there is no obvious indication that the spread measure contains unusual noise.

Table 4 provides an analysis of the unexplained misclassifications. Columns 3 through 7 of Table 4 provide information on the extent to which other risk measures suggest the bank was high-risk. A high early warning score is defined as one at least four times the mean value of the GMV-1 model, GMV-2 model or SEER model. In some cases there may be multiple reasons for classifying the bank as potentially high-risk, thus a bank may be included in more than one of the columns. For example, a bank that was re-examined within six months and had a high early warning score would be included in both of those columns. Column 8 gives the number of banks for which, after accounting or these additional factors, there is still no indication of higher risk.

The results in Table 4 suggest that a significant proportion of the unexplained observations with high yield spreads had one or more indicators that the

Table 4. Analysis of Projected Problem Banks Based on SubordiNated Debt Yields: Debt Spreads of at Least 84 Basis Points Over Treasury Yields.

Ranking by spread	Unexplained observations*	Remaining observations with one or more indicators of a problem (All relevant categories noted)					No indicator of a problem or data noise
		Re-examined within 6 months	Rated less than satisfactory within 1 year	High early warning score	Market-to-book less than 1.0	Rated Baa	
(1)	(2)	(3)	(4)	(5)	(6)	(7)	(8)
1–25	9	3	1	9	2	2	3
26–50	13	1	1	3	2	1	7
51–75	17	5	2	4	0	4	8
76–100	17	4	0	7	1	5	8
101–125	17	6	0	5	0	2	7
126–150	13	7	0	5	1	3	5
151–174	17	5	1	4	1	4	6
176–193	13	6	2	3	1	3	3

* Observations remaining after deleting observations with unsatisfactory examine ratings and those observations from banking organizations not among the largest 30 by asset size in the year of the observation.

bank was actually high risk. Combined with the banks that were assigned less-than-satisfactory regulatory ratings, this suggests that many of the banks that subordinated debt markets suggested were high-risk, were also banks about which the supervisors or market had some concerns.

After accounting for these indicators of above-average risk, we are left with thirty-nine bank observations with no obvious indication of problems; from an original 183 misclassifications. While a number of these would have been eliminated if we had adjusted our threshold criteria to 90 or 100 basis points, whether one chooses to do that depends on how one weighs the costs of disciplining a sound bank vs. the costs of failing to discipline a weak bank. However, we still would have been left with some banks misclassified as risky banks as a result of their relatively high spreads.

Comparisons of these results with those found using a spread over Baa rated debt (Evanoff & Wall, 2002) indicates that use of the spread over Treasuries results in more misclassifications as type-2 errors. In the analysis using spreads over Baa yields, 21% of the unexplained observations (after accounting for thin market trading and data concerns) showed no indication of having higher risk characteristics. In the current analysis (after accounting for thin market trading) 40% of the observations showed no indication of having higher risk characteristics – i.e. contrasting columns 2 and 8 of Table 4. Additionally, the unexplained observations using the Baa spreads were generally bunched near the threshold; that is these observations had relatively low spreads in the group of misclassified observations. In the current analysis, the misclassifications are more evenly spread across various spread-groupings (rows in Table 4) instead of being bunched at or near the threshold. Thus, the spread over Treasuries does not appear to perform as well as the spread over Baa rated corporate debt in identifying high-risk banks.

One important difference between the sample used in this study and that in Evanoff and Wall (2002) is that the current study incorporates a longer sample period. The earlier study was limited to the 1990 to mid-1998 period due to limitations of their corporate bond yield spread data. The longer sample period used in this study incorporates the collapse and restructuring of Long-Term Capital Management (LTCM) in September 1998. An important part of LTCM's strategy was to earn profits by supplying liquidity to a number of relatively illiquid markets. LTCM's positions were unwound and its operations were ultimately shut down after September 1998, resulting in a reduction in liquidity and an increase in liquidity premiums in a number of markets (see President's Working Group, 1999). If the collapse and restructuring of LTCM caused an overall increase in liquidity premiums in corporate bond markets, the spread of bank subordinated debt issues over Treasury securities during this period would also have increased. Such an increase would be mistaken as an increase in credit risk premiums for the post-LTCM sample of bank subordinated debt in Tables 3 and 4.

Post Long-Term Capital Management

This section explores the possible impact of LTCM on the information content of subordinated debt yield spreads by dropping those observations from September 1998 to the end of the sample period. If the collapse and restructuring of LTCM increased liquidity premiums then deleting observations after its collapse should reduce the proportion of unexplained observations for which there are no obvious indicators of risk.

Deleting all of the observations from September 1998 to the end of the sample reduces the number of high-spread observations by 75 to 118. The results from the pre-LTCM period are presented in Tables 5 and 6 in a format similar to that of the entire sample in Tables 3 and 4.

In contrast to the results for the entire sample, most of the observations in Table 5 with less than satisfactory supervisory ratings are in the group of banks with the highest spreads. Also, the number with less than satisfactory ratings declines uniformly as the spread increases.

The number of observations with no indicator of problems in Table 6 (row 8) is less than the number with no indicator in Table 4 for each of the rows. The number with no indication of problems in the group of banks with the highest spreads drops from 3 to 1, the number in the group ranked from 26–50 drops from 7 to 5, and the remaining declines are even more dramatic. The fall also occurs as a proportion of the unexplained observations (contrasting columns 2 and 8 of Tables 4 and 6). The proportion of unexplained observations with no indicator of risk drops to 23% (14/62), which is essentially the same as Evanoff and Wall (2002) found using Baa spreads. However, the results in Table 6 differ from those obtained using spreads over Baa debt in that over one-third of the observations with no indicator or risk are in a category of banks with relatively high spreads (see the row for banks with the 26–50 highest spreads in Table 6). Taking a closer look at observations in this row, however, a majority of them were obtained from a single quarter in 1987. This suggests that closer analysis of these observations may yield additional insight into potential issues surrounding market disruptions that need to be considered when using subordinated debt yield spreads; particularly spreads over Treasuries.

While the collapse and restructuring of LTCM appears to have influenced the liquidity premiums on corporate bonds, its collapse and restructuring may also have influenced the credit risk spreads on these bonds. The collapse may have

Table 5. Subsample Analysis of Projected Problem Banks Based on Subordinated Debt Yields: Identification of Banks With Clear Reasons for the High Spread – Excluding the Post-Long-Term Capital Management Period.

Ranking by spread	Less than satisfactory examine rating	Potentially noisy data	Unexplained observations with satisfactory regulatory ratings and no noisy data (type-2 error)
(1)	(2)	(3)	(4)
1–25	6	10	9
26–50	2	6	17
51–75	1	9	15
76–100	1	16	8
101–118	0	5	13

Table 6. Subsample Analysis of Projected Problem Banks Based on Subordinated Debt Yields: Debt Spreads of at Least 84 Basis Points Over Treasury Yields – Excluding the Post-Long-Term Capital Management Period.

Ranking by spread	Unexplained observations*	Remaining observations with one or more indicators of a problem (All relevant categories noted)					No indicator of a problem or data noise
		Re-examined within 6 months	Rated less than satisfactory within 1 year	High early warning score	Market-to-book less than 1.0	Rated Baa	
(1)	(2)	(3)	(4)	(5)	(6)	(7)	(8)
1–25	9	1	2	5	4	1	1
26–50	17	5	2	6	1	4	5
51–75	15	9	0	8	1	4	3
76–100	8	4	0	3	3	2	1
101–118	13	5	1	2	1	4	4

* Observations remaining after deleting observations with unsatisfactory examine ratings and those observations from banking organizations not among the largest 30 by asset size in the year of the observation.

increased credit risk premiums to the major banks that were LTCM's creditors and counterparties in over-the-counter (OTC) derivative transactions due to the risk that LTCM would not be able to honor these debts. The collapse may also have threatened the value of the trading and investment portfolios of banks that held positions similar to LTCM if portfolios had to be liquidated at distressed prices. While such a credit risk increase in spreads is potentially important for some banks, it appears not to be very important for our sample. The banks that were most exposed to LTCM were the money center banks that had credit exposure to LTCM and may also have had similar trading positions. Given that LTCM was restructured without major losses to creditors and its positions unwound in an orderly manner, its creditors suffered, at most, minor losses. If some bank's subordinated debt yields experienced large increases in credit risk premiums due to LTCM, the jump in yields should have happened to the largest banks in the September or possibly December 1998 periods. Yet, looking at our sample during this period, there is only one large bank that could have experienced such an increase in credit spreads.[19]

A second way in which LTCM may have influenced credit spreads is by reinforcing market perceptions that some financial firms are too-big-to-fail. In LTCM's case, the Federal Reserve Bank of New York organized the meetings to restructure LTCM. While the Reserve Bank did not provide any direct support to LTCM, its role in facilitating the meetings might lead some market participants to expect Federal Reserve intervention should a large bank encounter financial problems. This may be a particular concern given that LTCM was a hedge fund, not a bank, and accordingly did not have a federal supervisor or an important role in the payments system. If credit spreads declined due to a strengthening in the conjectural value of a too-big-to-fail policy, that effect is swamped in our data by the liquidity impact of LTCM.

Thus, the finding that LTCM may have increased the liquidity spreads on bank subordinated debt tends to support the recommendation of Evanoff and Wall (2000a, c) to set the threshold for supervisory action based on the Baa spread.[20] However, as discussed in those studies, there are data issues that should be further evaluated and further work looking at the Baa spread during this period would be necessary to confirm the benefits of using the Baa spread.

VI. SUMMARY AND POLICY IMPLICATIONS

The ability of PCA to limit supervisory forbearance is substantially weakened by its reliance on capital adequacy ratios where the measure of capital is under the control of banks and their supervisors. One potential complement to capital adequacy ratios would be to use a risk measure extracted from market prices. Perhaps the biggest objection from supervisors to the use of a market-based risk measure is that the measure may signal that a bank should be disciplined even though the supervisor's information suggests the bank is low risk. The risk measures extracted from market prices may contain such errors, largely because financial market prices incorporate more than the credit riskiness of the issuer.

This study addresses the concern with using market risk measures both theoretically and empirically. The theoretical section of the paper shows that the use of an imperfect risk measure for PCA can improve outcomes even if the supervisor has perfect information. The reason for the improvement is that the benefits from limiting forbearance may more than offset the gains from the supervisor's superior information.

The empirical analysis focuses on one particular risk measure, the yield spread of subordinated debt securities over comparable maturity Treasury securities. This part of the study uses the methodology that Evanoff and Wall (2002) applied to subordinated debt spreads over Baa bonds. The advantage of using spreads over Treasury securities is that the spread over Treasuries may more accurately capture the probability of failure over the business cycle, albeit at the cost of potentially making the standard more pro-cyclical. The current quality of the data may also be superior when Treasury spreads are considered. A potential cost of using the spread over Treasuries is that short-term market disruptions may affect private debt yields differently than that of Government debt. Thus, spreads over Treasuries may be more sensitive to short-term changes in liquidity and credit risk than would spreads over private debt yields (e.g. Baa bonds).

The results of examining spreads over Treasury securities suggest that subordinated debt yield spreads have substantial predictive power. However, the results also suggest that the spreads are an imperfect indicator, some high spreads were not accompanied by any other signs that the bank was high risk. Further analysis suggested that a substantial fraction of the apparent classification errors from using spreads over Treasury securities may be due to an increase in the liquidity premiums on corporate bond issues in the wake of the collapse of LTCM. This finding suggests that not only do subordinated debt spreads appear to dominate the current capital measures used to trigger PCA, but that careful consideration should be given to determining which spread to use. The findings suggest that the merits of using a spread over a corporate bond index, such as Baa bonds, may exceed those of using alternative spreads and therefore deserves further consideration.

NOTES

1. Section 131 of FDICIA, titled "Prompt Regulatory Action," creates a new Section 38 of the Federal Deposit Insurance Act.

2. For discussions of the benefits of introducing a mandatory subordinated debt program for large commercial banks see Evanoff and Wall (2000a, b, c), Kwast, et al. (1999), and Flannery (2001). While subordinated debt proposals are frequently associated with U.S. banking markets, there is evidence from European markets suggesting similar potential benefits: see Sironi (2001) and Benink and Wihlborg (2002).

3. Evanoff and Wall (2002, p. 1007) discuss alternative means to incorporate subordinated debt yields in PCA which some may find less Draconian and more palatable.

4. One of the major differences being the extent to which the different spreads 'bind' over the business cycle.

5. This second signal could be any one of a number of signals including those that are the focus of this study: a capital adequacy ratio and the yield on a bank's subordinated debt. In the following model we incorporate a signal that is assumed to be increasing in the quality of the bank, e.g. capital ratios. If the quality of the bank is *decreasing* as the signal increases (e.g. as with debt spreads) the model would need to be adjusted accordingly.

6. These are measures of the composite financial condition of the bank or bank holding company, respectively, as summarized by the federal banking agencies.

7. It could be argued that one limitation of this analysis is the possibility that capital ratios, debt spreads and supervisory ratings may not be independent. Investors in subordinated debt certainly care about supervisor's evaluations and supervisors have demonstrated a strong interest in capital ratios. Supervisors may also care about subordinated debt spreads. Evanoff and Wall (2001) attempted to minimize the potential for supervisory evaluations to influence capital ratios and yield spreads by using the risk measures to predict supervisory ratings in the *following* quarter. Whether spreads influenced examiners is impossible to determine without additional information; however, discussions with examiners suggest that supervisors were not placing much weight on subordinated debt spreads in the late 1990s. However, since we are analyzing observations where the two measures *differ*, whether the two measures are independent is less important.

8. Readers interested in a more thorough critical analysis of the use of capital ratios for triggering PCA are referred to Tables 1–4 of Evanoff and Wall (2001).

9. For a more detailed description of the data see Evanoff and Wall (2001, 2002).

10. Comparable maturity Treasury obligations are obtained via linear interpolations of the term structure across 3 month, 6 month, 1 year, 2 year, 3 year, 5 year, 7 year, 10 year and 30 year securities.

11. Evanoff and Wall (2002) address the issue of whether debt spreads and supervisory ratings are measuring the same risk. The concern is that subordinated debt yields reflect only expected losses to the holders of the debt while the primary concern

of supervisors is the probability of failure. Thus, any misclassifications may simply result from measuring different risks.

12. For example, Evanoff and Wall's (2000a) proposal would require only the largest 25 banks to issue subordinated debt. Similarly, most of the discussion in Kwast et al. stresses the debt of the top 50 U.S. banking organizations.

13. While this partially addresses the liquidity issue there may still be a time dimension to liquidity (e.g. ad hoc events or cyclical effects) that we are not capturing. In earlier work we attempted to account for this by allowing for fixed time effects in the empirical analysis and the results were not appreciably changed. However, this is an important issue that merits future work to develop a more accurate signal of firm condition.

14. This indicator is not perfect. A follow-up examination may occur for other reasons such as to evaluate the safety and soundness implications of a proposed takeover. However, in most cases in our sample there appears to be confirmation of supervisory concern in the form of repeated re-examinations over the same time period, or signals from one or more of our other indicators. In addition, the fact that the supervisors are substituting examination frequency for lower CAMEL ratings does not necessarily imply that the supervisors are failing to impose adequate discipline. We do not have information on the recommendations made by supervisors to these banks or on what action the supervisors threatened to take if their recommendations were not followed.

15. Krainer and Lopez (2001) augment these models with information from equity markets and find the additional information to be of value in predicting future regulatory ratings.

16. For a discussion of the model see Cole and Gunther (1995) and GMV (2000). The SEER model is less flexible in that bank failures have been so rare during the 1990s that the parameter estimates have been frozen throughout the period.

17. The type-2 errors decline to 153 and 97 for a 90 and 100 basis points spread, respectively. One's choice of the appropriate threshold depends on the relative trade off in unnecessarily disciplining problem banks vs. failing to discipline troubled institutions (i.e. the relative cost of type-2 and type-1 errors).

18. This forward-looking measure best serves the intended role of the model: to predict future downgrades. The alternative measure (GMV-2) is included for robustness since the actual date of the examination information may be closer to the end of the year. Individual year subsamples were also analyzed since the period could be divided into particularly tranquil and less-tranquil subperiods. There was still a consistent difference across subsamples. One caveat, however, concerns the population of U.S. banks used to generate the GMV (and SEER discussed later) prediction model. Although it includes larger banks, the sample is dominated by smaller institutions. Thus, our sample of debt-issuing banks would not be a representative sample of banks from which the model parameter estimates were generated.

19. Recall that in order for a subordinated debt issue to be included in our sample, the issuer must have received a CAMEL(S) (or BOPEC) rating from its federal supervisor in the following calendar quarter. Thus, many potentially relevant debt issues are not included because the bond issuer did not receive a rating during the quarter.

20. For a discussion of data concerns see Evanoff and Wall (2002).

ACKNOWLEDGMENTS

The authors wish to thank Mark Flannery, Xavier Freixas, Joe Haubrich, George Kaufman, and William Perraudin for helpful comments and suggestions in earlier discussions about the topic. The authors also acknowledge the input and help of Nancy Andrews, Mark Murawski and George Simler in developing the database used in the study, Andy Meyer, Alton Gilbert, and Mark Vaughan for graciously providing detailed information about their "early warning model," and our discussants – Ben Gup and Alan Hess – for their comments at the special session on market discipline and prompt corrective action in banking at the 2002 Western Economic Association meetings in Seattle. The opinions expressed, however, are the authors' and not necessarily those of the people mentioned above, the Federal Reserve Bank of Chicago, Federal Reserve Bank of Atlanta or the Federal Reserve System.

REFERENCES

Bank for International Settlement (2001). The New Basel Capital Accord. Consultative Paper Issued by the Basel Committee on Banking Supervision, June.

Benink, H. A., & Wihlborg, C. (2002). The New Basel Capital Accord: Making it Effective with Stronger Market Discipline. *European Financial Management, 8*, 103–115.

Cole, R. A., & Gunther, J. W. (1995). FIMS: A New Monitoring System for Banking Institutions. *Federal Reserve Bulletin, 81*, 1–15.

Evanoff, D. D., & Wall, L. D. (2000a). Subordinated Debt as Bank Capital: A Proposal for Regulatory Reform. Economic Perspectives, Federal Reserve Bank of Chicago, Second Quarter, pp. 40–53.

Evanoff, D. D., & Wall, L. D. (2000b). The Role of SND in Bank Safety and Soundness Regulations. Proceedings of a Conference on Bank Structure and Competition, Federal Reserve Bank of Chicago, pp. 480–493.

Evanoff, D. D., & Wall, L. D. (2000c). Subordinated Debt and Bank Capital Reform. In: G. Kaufman (Ed.), *Research in Financial Services: Private and Public Policy* (vol. 12, pp. 53–120). JAI Press.

Evanoff, D. D., & Wall, L. D. (2001). SND Yield Spreads as Bank Risk Measures. *Journal of Financial Services Research, 20*, 121–146.

Evanoff, D. D., & Wall, L. D. (2002). Measures of the Riskiness of Banking Organizations: Subordinated Debt Yields, Risk-based Capital, and Examination Ratings. *Journal of Banking and Finance, 26*, 989–1010.

Flannery, M. J. (2001). The Faces of 'Market Discipline'. *Journal of Financial Services Research, 20*, 107–120.

Gilbert, R. A., Meyer, A. P., & Vaughan, M. D. (2000). The Role of a CAMEL Downgrade Model in Bank Surveillance. In: G. Kaufman (Ed.), *Research in Financial Services: Private and Public Policy* (vol. 12, pp. 265–86). JAI Press.

Gunther, J. W., Levonian, M. E., & Moore, R. R. (2001). Can the Stock Market Tell Bank Supervisors Anything They Don't Already Know? Economic and Financial Review, Federal Reserve Bank of New York, pp. 1–9.

Hancock, D., & Kwast, M. L. (2001). Using Subordinated Debt to Monitor Bank Holding Companies: Is it Feasible? *Journal of Financial Services Research, 20*, 147–188.

Krainer, J., & Lopez, J. A. (2001). Incorporating Equity Market Information into Supervisory Monitoring Models. Presented at a Conference on Banks and Systemic Risk, sponsored by the Bank of England, London (May 24).

Kwast, M. L., Covitz, D. M., Hancock, D., Houpt, J. V., Adkins, D. P., Barger, N., Bouchard, B., Connolly, J. F., Brady, T. F., English, W. B., Evanoff, D. D., & Wall, L. D. (1999). Using SND as an Instrument of Market Discipline. Report of a study group on subordinated notes and debentures. Board of Governors of the Federal Reserve System, M. Kwast (chair), Staff Study No. 172, December.

President's Working Group on Financial Markets (1999). Hedge Funds, Leverage, and the Lessons of Long-Term Capital Management.

Sironi, A. (2001). An Analysis of European Bank's SND Issues and its Implications for the Design of a Mandatory Subordinated Debt Policy. *Journal of Financial Services Research, 19*, 233–266.

CAN FEEDBACK FROM THE JUMBO-CD MARKET IMPROVE OFF-SITE SURVEILLANCE OF COMMUNITY BANKS?

R. Alton Gilbert, Andrew P. Meyer and Mark D. Vaughan

ABSTRACT

We examine the value of feedback from the jumbo-certificate-of-deposit (CD) market in the off-site surveillance of community banks. Using accounting data, we construct proxies for default premiums on jumbo CDs and produce rank orderings of community banks – defined as institutions holding less than $500 million in assets (constant 1999 dollars) – based on these proxies. Next, we use an econometric surveillance model to generate rank orderings based on the probability of encountering financial distress. Finally, we compare these rank orderings as tools for flagging emerging problems. Our comparisons include eight out-of-sample test windows during the 1990s. We find that feedback from the jumbo-CD market would have added little value in community-bank surveillance during our sample period. Taken together, our findings validate current surveillance practices. We conclude by arguing that the robust economic environment of the 1990s probably plays a large role in our results.

Prompt Corrective Action in Banking: 10 Years Later, Volume 14, pages 31–62.

ISBN: 0-7623-0987-3

I. INTRODUCTION

In recent years, bank supervisors around the developed world have explored strategies for harnessing market pressure to contain bank risk. Indeed, the new Basel capital accord counts market discipline as an explicit pillar of bank supervision – along with supervisory review and capital requirements. In the United States, one popular proposal for enhancing market discipline involves requiring large banks to issue a standardized form of subordinated debt (Board of Governors, 1999, 2000; Meyer, 1999). Advocates of this proposal argue that high-powered performance incentives in the sub-debt market will lead to accurate assessments of bank risk. And, in turn, these assessments – expressed for high-risk institutions as rising yields or difficulties rolling over maturing debt – will pressure bank managers to maintain safety and soundness (Lang & Robertson, 2000).

Even if financial markets provide little direct pressure to contain bank risk, market-generated risk assessments could still contribute to one component of supervisory review – off-site surveillance. Off-site surveillance involves the use of accounting data and anecdotal evidence to schedule on-site exams and to monitor bank progress in addressing previously identified deficiencies. Risk assessments from financial markets could contribute to surveillance in two ways. First, market signals about risk might flag troubled banks missed by conventional surveillance tools. Second, market signals might point to emerging problems before conventional surveillance tools. In the U.S., off-site surveillance relies heavily on financial statements that banks must file quarterly with their principal supervisor. Markets, in contrast, render risk verdicts at a much higher frequency, in some cases even daily.

To date, discussions about harnessing financial markets for supervisory purposes have centered on large, complex banking organizations. Discussions have centered on larger banks because the supervisory benefits would be highest and the compliance costs lowest for these institutions (Emmons, Gilbert & Vaughan, 2001). The benefits would be highest for large banks because of their complexity; these institutions engage in non-bank activities frequently and use derivative instruments heavily. Large banks also account for the lion's share of U.S. banking assets, making the stability of the financial system dependent on their safety and soundness. The compliance cost would be lowest because most of these institutions already tap national financial markets routinely. For example, at the end of 2000, 44 of the largest 50 commercial banks, and 46 of the 50 largest bank holding companies, had subordinated debt outstanding.

Financial markets could play a useful role in the supervision of community banks. Community banks do fund most of their operations with core deposits (Bassett & Brady, 2001). And the prices and quantities of these deposits – typically checking accounts, passbook savings deposits, and small time deposits – tend to be "sticky" (Flannery, 1982). Still, community banks face one form of market discipline – they compete in the national market for jumbo certificates of deposit, that is time deposits with balances exceeding the $100,000 ceiling for deposit insurance coverage. At year-end 2000, banks holding less than $500 million in assets – the definition of community banks set forth in the Financial Modernization Act of 1999 – funded 13.2% of their assets with jumbo CDs, up from 9.1% at year-end 1990. Academic research has repeatedly confirmed that jumbo-CD holders react to bank-specific risk. [See Hall, King, Meyer and Vaughan (2002) for recent evidence as well as a review of previous research.] This reaction could pressure community bankers to contain risk or signal community-bank supervisors to take action.

Supplementary information from the jumbo-CD market might prove particularly useful in community-bank surveillance. Many community banks operate under extended exam schedules, with up to 18 months elapsing between full-scope examinations. This extended schedule may reduce the information content of community bank financial statements, thereby reducing the effectiveness of off-site supervisory monitoring. Verification of financials is one important source of value created by examinations (Berger & Davies, 1998; Flannery & Houston, 1999); indeed, recent research has documented large adjustments in asset quality measures following examinations, particularly for institutions with emerging problems (Gunther & Moore, 2000). It is possible that the holders of a community bank's jumbo CDs, because their own money is at stake, supplement published income statements and balance sheets with independent research. Another possibility is that information about safety and soundness leaks to uninsured depositors through the bank's board of directors, a body that typically includes prominent local businesspeople. Thus, sudden changes in jumbo-CD yields or withdrawal patterns might signal impending trouble more quickly or more reliably than surveillance tools based on quarterly financial statements.

Another reason to consult the jumbo-CD market for help in community-bank surveillance is that these banks represent a disproportionate threat to the deposit insurance fund. Community banks fail more often than larger banks. From 1984 through 1998, for example, the average failure rate for banks with less than $500 million in assets (1998 constant dollars) was 0.73%; the failure rate for banks holding over $500 million in assets was 0.33%. In addition, community banks have accounted for a disproportionately large share of assets at risk in failures. At year-end 2000, the U.S. banking sector contained 7,570 banks holding less than $500 million in assets. These banks accounted for 91.7% of U.S. banks and 12.9% of U.S. banking assets. Between 1984 and 1998, community banks accounted for 40% of the assets of failed U.S. banks. Finally, losses to the FDIC from community-bank failures, per dollar of assets, have exceeded losses from large-bank failures. Losses have been higher because community banks are top-heavy with assets that are expensive to liquidate – fewer securities and more fixed assets – and because community banks have fewer uninsured and unsecured claimants to absorb failure costs (James, 1991). More timely or more accurate warning about emerging problems would help supervisors reduce the costs of community bank failures to the FDIC.

Although the jumbo-CD market could, in theory, provide supervisors with useful information, available data permit only the construction of crude proxies for the desired signals about community-bank risk. Just a handful of large banks issue jumbo CDs that are actively traded in secondary markets, so real-time, market-generated yields are not available for small institutions (Morris & Walter, 1993). It is possible, however, to use quarterly financial data to construct average jumbo-CD yields for almost every bank in the country. These yields can then be combined with data from the Treasury market to produce proxies for default premiums on jumbo CDs. Other researchers have successfully used this approach to test hypotheses about bank risk (for example, James, 1988; Keeley 1990; and, more recently, Martinez-Peria & Schmukler, 2001). Still, proxies based on these yields suffer from two related types of measurement error. First, they are average rather than marginal measures and, therefore, somewhat backward looking. Second, they are quarterly accounting measures rather than real-time economic measures. How much value default-premium proxies add in community-bank surveillance is ultimately an empirical question. Answering this question is important as a validation exercise for current surveillance practices. Answering this question is also important because proxies for jumbo-CD default premiums offer the only real hope for integrating market feedback into community-bank surveillance.

Assessing the supervisory value of feedback from the jumbo-CD market requires establishing a benchmark with output from current surveillance tools. It is not enough to note that jumbo-CD measures react to bank risk contemporaneously or forecast emerging safety-and-soundness problems successfully because supervisors already have systems in place for these purposes. The acid test of the jumbo-CD measures, or of any potential off-site tool for that matter, is whether it improves materially upon current practice.

Four recent papers evaluate market signals with a "best-practices-in-surveillance" benchmark. Evanoff and Wall (2001) compare regulatory-capital ratios and subordinated-debt yields as predictors of supervisory ratings; they find that sub-debt yields modestly outperform capital ratios in one-quarter-ahead tests. Gunther, Levonian, and Moore (2001) add estimated default frequencies from the KMV model – a risk measure drawn from the equity market – to an econometric model designed to predict holding-company supervisory ratings with accounting data. They find that the KMV data improve in-sample fit. Krainer and Lopez (2001) also include equity-market variables – in this case, cumulative abnormal stock returns and KMV default probabilities – in a model of holding-company ratings. Unlike Gunther, Levonian, and Moore, they assess the value added by equity-market variables by measuring improvement in one-quarter-ahead forecasts. Like Evanoff and Wall, they find that market variables provide only a modest boost to out-of-sample performance. Curry, Elmer and Fissel (2001) investigate whether market signals derived from the prices of bank shares improve the accuracy of a model designed to predict CAMELS ratings four quarters ahead. They estimate the basic models with ratios derived from the call reports, and their expanded models include variables derived from the prices of bank shares. They find evidence that including the variables derived from the prices of bank shares improves the fit of the equations.[1]

We compare the performance of jumbo-CD signals and econometric models in the off-site surveillance of community banks. Specifically, we combine our yield measure with Treasury yields to obtain proxies for jumbo-CD default premiums. We then compile rank orderings of the sample banks based on these proxies. Next, we estimate a probit model with financial and supervisory data to predict the likelihood that each sample bank will encounter financial distress in the next eight quarters. We then compile a rank ordering based on estimated distress probabilities. Finally, we track the out-of-sample prediction records of the default-premium orderings and the distress-probability orderings over an eight-quarter horizon. Because uninsured depositors may react to risk by withdrawing their money rather than demanding a higher yield, we also examine the performance of rank orderings based on jumbo-CD runoff. As robustness checks, we evaluate the predictive power of jumbo-CD orderings extracted with a more sophisticated technique and with different cuts of the sample banks. We also assess orderings obtained when jumbo-CD default premiums are added to the econometric surveillance model. All these tests are designed to build on the emerging literature on the value of market signals in bank surveillance.

Our empirical tests indicate that feedback from the jumbo-CD market would have contributed little to community-bank surveillance in the 1990s. In all eight out-of-sample test windows, rank orderings based on output from the econometric surveillance model significantly outperform rank orderings based on jumbo-CD default premiums or runoffs. More important, the jumbo-CD orderings improve little on random orderings. These findings prove robust to different extraction techniques and sample cuts. Finally, including jumbo-CD default premiums in the early warning model does not enhance its out-of-sample performance. Collectively, our findings validate current surveillance practices. We argue that the robust economic environment of the 1990s probably plays a large role in our results.

II. A PRIMER ON OFF-SITE SURVEILLANCE

The cornerstone of supervisory review is thorough, regularly scheduled, on-site examinations. Under rules set forth in the Federal Deposit Insurance Corporation Improvement Act of 1991 (FDICIA), most U.S. banks must submit to a full-scope federal or state examination every 12 months; small, well-capitalized banks must be examined every 18 months. These examinations focus on six components of safety and soundness – capital protection (C), asset quality (A), management competence (M), earnings strength (E), liquidity risk exposure (L), and market risk sensitivity (S). At the close of each exam, examiners award a grade of one (best) through five (worst) to each component. Supervisors then draw on these six component ratings to assign a composite CAMELS rating, which is also expressed on a one through five scale. In general, banks with "one" or "two" composite ratings are considered safe and sound while banks with "three," "four," or "five" ratings are considered unsatisfactory. As of March 31, 2000, supervisors classified just over 6% of U.S. banks as unsatisfactory.

Bank supervisors support on-site examinations with off-site surveillance. Off-site surveillance refers to the use of quarterly accounting data and anecdotal evidence to monitor the condition of supervised banks between scheduled exams. Although on-site examination is the most effective tool for spotting safety-and-soundness problems, it is costly and burdensome. On-site examination is costly to supervisors because of the examiner resources required and burdensome to bankers because of the intrusion into daily operations. Off-site surveillance reduces the need for unscheduled exams. Off-site surveillance also helps supervisors plan exams by highlighting risk exposures at specific institutions. For example, if pre-exam surveillance reports indicate that a bank has significant exposure to interest-rate fluctuations, then supervisors will add interest-rate-risk specialists to the exam team.

Two commonly used off-site tools are supervisory screens and econometric models. Supervisory screens are combinations of financial ratios, derived from quarterly balance sheets and income statements, that have given warning in the past about developing safety-and-soundness problems. Supervisors draw on their experience to weigh the joint information content of these ratios. Econometric models also combine information from financial ratios. These models rely on statistical tests rather than human judgment to combine ratios, boiling information from financial statements down to an index number that summarizes bank condition. In past comparisons, econometric models have outperformed supervisory screens as early warning tools (Gilbert, Meyer & Vaughan, 1999; Cole, Cornyn & Gunther, 1995). Nonetheless, screens still play an important role in off-site surveillance. Supervisors can develop screens quickly to monitor emerging sources of risk; econometric models can be modified only after new risks have produced a sufficient number of safety-and-soundness problems to allow re-specification and out-of-sample testing.

The Federal Reserve uses two econometric models in off-site surveillance. These models are collectively known as SEER, the System for Estimating Examination Ratings. One model, the SEER risk-rank model, uses the latest quarterly accounting data to estimate the probability that each Fed-supervised bank will fail within the next two years. The other model, the SEER rating model, uses the latest data to produce a "shadow" CAMELS rating for each supervised institution – that is, the rating that would have been assigned had the bank been examined using its most recent financial statements. Every quarter, analysts at the Board of Governors feed the latest financial data into the SEER models and forward the results to the 12 Reserve Banks. The surveillance section at each Reserve Bank, in turn, follows up on each "red-flagged" institutions. The Federal Deposit Insurance Corporation (FDIC) and the Office of the Comptroller of the Currency (OCC) also use econometric models as a part of the off-site surveillance regimen for the banks they supervise (Reidhill & O'Keefe, 1997).

To assess the marginal value of feedback from the jumbo-CD market, we use a downgrade-prediction model to "benchmark" the performance of econometric surveillance models. A downgrade-prediction model is designed to flag banks headed for financial distress. More specifically, it estimates the likelihood of tumbling from "satisfactory" condition (CAMELS "one" or "two" ratings) into "unsatisfactory" condition (composite CAMELS "three," "four," or "five") in the coming quarters. In theory, a model designed to predict downgrades could improve upon the SEER framework. Downgrades to

Table 1. How Common Were Downgrades to "Unsatisfactory" Condition in the 1990s?

This table demonstrates that downgrades from safe-and-sound to unsatisfactory status were common in the 1990s, thereby allowing re-estimation of a downgrade-prediction model on a yearly basis. Specifically, the far right column shows the number of sample banks rated as safe and sound (composite CAMELS of "one" or "two") at each year-end that were downgraded to unsatisfactory status (composite CAMELS of "three," "four," or "five") in the following 12 months. The data reveal that two-rated banks were much more likely to tumble into unsatisfactory condition than one-rated banks. Although downgrades to unsatisfactory condition were common throughout the decade, they became less frequent in the mid-1990s as overall banking conditions improved.

Year of Downgrade	CAMELS Rating at Beginning of Year	Number of Banks	Number of Banks Downgraded to Unsatisfactory Status	Percentage of Banks Downgraded to Unsatisfactory Status	Total Number of Downgrades to Unsatisfactory Status
1990	1	2,190	34	1.55	699
	2	5,482	665	12.13	
1991	1	1,959	22	1.12	424
	2	5,277	402	7.62	
1992	1	2,291	7	0.31	182
	2	5,980	175	2.93	
1993	1	2,911	9	0.31	162
	2	5,726	153	2.67	
1994	1	3,091	8	0.26	102
	2	4,885	94	1.92	
1995	1	3,284	10	0.30	127
	2	4,522	117	2.59	
1996	1	3,242	7	0.22	125
	2	3,741	118	3.15	
1997	1	3,022	19	0.63	152
	2	3,105	133	4.28	
1998	1	3,067	19	0.62	201
	2	3,047	182	5.97	
1999	1	3,088	12	0.39	190
	2	3,320	178	5.36	
2000	1	3,226	3	0.09	49
	2	3,684	46	1.25	

unsatisfactory condition were common throughout the 1990s (see Table 1), whereas few banks failed during this period. Thus, a downgrade-prediction model can be re-estimated quarterly.

The SEER risk-rank model, in contrast, was estimated during the years 1985–1991, and model coefficients have been "frozen" since the estimation period. More important, a downgrade-prediction model may flag banks not currently under close scrutiny that need watching. Institutions with "three," "four," or "five" composite ratings fail at a much higher rate than institutions with "one" or "two" ratings, so "unsatisfactory" institutions already receive scrutiny between exams. Recent research suggests that a downgrade-prediction model would have improved slightly over the SEER framework in the 1990s in flagging emerging distress (Gilbert, Meyer & Vaughan, 2002). Because of the downgrade-prediction model's theoretical appeal and slight performance edge on 1990s data, we use it to produce risk rankings that will benchmark current surveillance practices.

In essence, we compare the performance of a single supervisory screen with the performance of an econometric model as early warning tools. The supervisory screen used here – measures of jumbo-CD default premiums or runoffs – differs from other screens by summarizing overall bank risk, not just one type of exposure such as liquidity or credit risk. Previous evidence from the jumbo-CD market confirms risk pricing. (See Table 2 for a summary of published findings).

The effect should be stronger in the wake of FDICIA – an act designed in part to shift failure costs from the FDIC to uninsured depositors (Benston & Kaufman, 1998). As a check, we regressed our measures of jumbo-CD yields and runoffs on SEER failure probabilities and a host of control variables. These results – reported in Table 3 – confirm responsiveness to bank-specific risk, though this response is economically small.

The economically small response suggests that jumbo-CD default premiums and runoffs put little direct pressure on banks to contain risk. It does not suggest, however, that ordinal rankings based on these measures lack information about bank condition. Again, only out-of-sample performance tests can determine whether these rankings improve upon rankings obtained with current surveillance tools.

III. THE DATA

Our data set includes quarterly accounting data for most U.S. community banks as well as confidential supervisory assessments of these banks, beginning with the late 1980s and continuing through the 1990s. Specifically, we use

Table 2. Does Published Evidence Point to "Risk Pricing" by U.S. Jumbo-CD Holders?

This table summarizes research on risk pricing by jumbo-CD holders in the U.S. (We use the term "bank" to refer bank holding companies as well as banks.) These studies employed both cross-section and time-series techniques and used a variety of risk proxies and control variables. Overall, the evidence suggests that jumbo-CD holders price bank-specific risk.

Authors	Issuer of Jumbo Certificate of Deposit	Sample Dates	Was Bank-Specific Risk Priced?
Crane (1976)	Bank	1974	Somewhat
Baer and Brewer (1986)	Bank	1979–82	Yes
Hannan and Hanweck (1988)	Bank	1985	Yes
James (1988)	Bank	1984–86	Yes
Cargill (1989)	Bank	1984–86	Yes
James (1990)	Bank	1986–87	Yes
Keeley (1990)	Bank	1984–86	Yes
Ellis and Flannery (1992)	Bank	1982–88	Yes
Cook and Spellman (1994)	Thrift	1987–88	Yes
Brewer and Mondschean (1994)	Thrift	1987–89	Yes
Park (1995)	Bank	1985–92	Yes
Park and Peristiani (1998)	Thrift	1987–91	Yes
Hall, King, Meyer, and Vaughan (2002)	Bank	1988–90, 1993–95	Yes

accounting data from the fourth quarter of each year, beginning in 1989 and ending in 1998; we use confidential supervisory assessments from 1990 through 2000. Following the approach used in the SEER framework, we estimate the downgrade-prediction model on all CAMELS one- and two-rated U.S. banks and then use model coefficients to out-of-sample downgrade-probability estimates for community banks. The number of observations underlying the downgrade-prediction model range from 7,836 (1992–1993 regression) to 8,666 (1995–1996 regression).

The data come from the Federal Financial Institutions Examination Council (FFIEC) and the National Information Center of the Federal Reserve System (NIC). We use income and balance sheet data from the Reports of Condition and Income (the call reports), which are collected under the auspices of the FFIEC. The FFIEC requires that all U.S. commercial banks submit quarterly call reports to their principal supervisors; most reported items are available to

Table 3. Do Our Measures of Jumbo-CD Yields and Runoffs "Price" Bank-specific Risk?

This table displays the results of regressions of jumbo-CD yields and runoffs on failure probability and controls. The failure-probability measure – produced by the SEER risk-rank model – serves as a summary measure of bank-specific risk. The other explanatory variables control for influences on yields and runoffs besides bank-specific risk. These influences include the percentage of the bank's jumbo-CD portfolio with fixed rates, the average maturity of the bank's jumbo-CD portfolio, the bank's asset size, the bank's relationship with a holding company ("1" if a member), the bank's propensity to tap national funding markets ("1" if a user of brokered deposits), and the bank's degree of market power ("1" if in an MSA). State dummies (not reported) control for differences in tax laws and regional economic conditions. Time dummies and maturity-adjusted Treasury yields control for business-cycle effects. The regressions use pooled end-of-year data for 1988 through 1996. Three stars indicate statistical significance at the 1% level; two stars indicate significance at the 5% level; and one star indicates significance at the 10% level.

The SEER failure probability has a statistically significant but economically small impact on yields and runoffs. For example, the coefficient on SEER failure probability is significant at the 1% level in each equation. At the same time, these coefficients imply that jumping from the sample-mean failure probability of 0.545% to 3.522% (one standard deviation higher) would have depressed the average sample bank's return on assets by only one-quarter basis point – from 1.1898% to 1.1873%.

The economically small risk effect suggests that the jumbo-CD market puts little direct pressure on banks to maintain safety and soundness. It does not suggest, however, that ordinal rankings based on jumbo-CD screens lack information content. Again, only out-of-sample performance tests can determine whether these rankings improve upon rankings obtained with current surveillance tools.

		Jumbo-CD Yield Regression			Jumbo-CD Runoff Regression		
	Independent Variable	Coef.	Std. Err.		Coef.	Std. Err.	
	Intercept	–0.4774	0.1337	***	14.9297	1.7430	***
Bank-Specific Risk Variable	SEER failure probability	0.0073	0.0014	***	–0.1568	0.0180	***
Control Variables	Fixed-rate percentage	–0.0024	0.0006	***	0.0212	0.0083	**
	Mty-weighted Treasury yield	1.1126	0.0203	***	–1.9718	0.2643	***
	Maturity	–0.0758	0.0141	***	–0.6689	0.1841	***
	Maturity-Treasury interactive	–0.1915	0.0136	***	–0.2069	0.1769	
	Holding-company dummy	–0.0087	0.0104		–0.0490	0.1357	
	Brokered-deposit dummy	0.1408	0.0159	***	1.1418	0.2067	***
	MSA dummy	–0.0514	0.0088	***	0.2401	0.1143	**
Regression Statistics	Number of observations	109,635			109,635		
	R^2	0.5747			0.0344		

the public. We also rely on CAMELS composite and management ratings from the National Information Center (NIC) database. This database is available to examiners and analysts in the banking supervision function of the Federal Reserve System but not to the public.

To reduce bias in the performance tests, we exclude from the sample any bank with an operating history of less than five years. Financial ratios for these start-up, or de novo, banks often take extreme values that do not imply safety-and-soundness problems (DeYoung, 1999). For example, de novos often lose money in their early years, so their earnings ratios are poor. These extreme values can distort model coefficients and could compromise the relative performance of the downgrade-prediction model. Another reason for excluding de novos is that supervisors already monitor these banks closely. For example, the Federal Reserve examines each of its newly chartered banks every six months. Full-scope exams continue on this schedule until the de novo earns a composite CAMELS rating of "one" or "two" in consecutive exams.

Our calculation of default premiums begins with three items taken from each sample bank's quarterly call report submissions. These items are interest expense paid on jumbo CDs, dollar volume of jumbo CDs outstanding, and the distribution of remaining maturities on jumbo CDs. To generate quarterly yield observations for each bank, we divide jumbo-CD interest expense by average jumbo-CD balances. We use distributions of remaining maturities to control for term-structure effects. From 1989 through 1996, the FFIEC required banks to slot jumbo CDs in one of four buckets based on time remaining to maturity – "less than three months remaining," "three months to one year remaining," "one year to five years remaining," and "over five years remaining." In 1997, the two longest maturity buckets changed to "one year to three years remaining" and "over three years remaining." These reporting conventions allow only a crude adjustment for maturity. For example, jumbo CDs in the "less than three months remaining" bucket may include long-term instruments issued several years ago that are about to mature. Nevertheless, these data offer the only available means of controlling for the impact of maturity on yields.

We use two distinct methods to turn these call-report items into default-risk premiums – a yield-spread method and a simple-residuals method. We use two methods to insure that subsequent performance tests are not biased by reliance on only one, possibly poor proxy for default premiums. Admittedly, both methods control only for term-to-maturity. Later in Section VI, we try to isolate default premiums with a more sophisticated approach that controls for influences on yields besides maturity. We begin with simple methods because the resulting proxies are similar to screens commonly used by surveillance analysts. The default-premium measures obtained from the two methods are highly correlated; the correlation coefficient over all the sample years is 0.92.

The yield-spread method generates default-premiums by subtracting risk-free yields from jumbo-CD yields. Specifically, we start with the dollar volume of jumbo CDs in each maturity class for each sample bank. We then multiply each of these dollar figures by that quarter's rate of return on Treasury issues with comparable maturity. The sum of these resulting values, divided by the total jumbo-CD balances, approximates each bank's risk-free yield. Next, we obtain a default-premium series by subtracting – for every quarter in the sample – each bank's risk-free yield from its average jumbo-CD yield.

The simple-residuals method proxies default premiums with residuals from year-by-year yield regressions. The dependent variable in each regression is fourth-quarter jumbo-CD interest expense divided by average fourth-quarter jumbo-CD balances. The independent variables include an intercept term and the percentage of the jumbo-CD portfolio in each of the four maturity buckets. Tables 4a and 4b contain the regression results.

Overall model fit is poor – perhaps because other factors play important roles in determining yields – but the combined explanatory power of the maturity variables is statistically significant for each year's regression. The estimated intercepts – which approximate the yield on "less than three months to maturity" instruments – change in concert with market rates on three-month jumbo CDs, though adjustments take place with a lag. For instance, the intercept for the 1991 equation (5.72%) is well above the secondary-market yield on three-month CDs in the fourth quarter of 1991 (4.91%). Because interest rates were lower that quarter (1991, Q:IV) than in prior quarters, jumbo CDs about to mature included higher-yield instruments issued in prior quarters. Still, for each year, coefficient signs and magnitudes for the maturity variables reveal that yields rose with time-to-maturity, implying that the equation residuals may serve as acceptable proxies for default premiums.

IV. THE SURVEILLANCE BENCHMARK – A CAMELS-DOWNGRADE-PREDICTION MODEL

The CAMELS-downgrade-prediction model transforms available accounting and supervisory data into distress probabilities. Specifically, the model is a probit regression. The dependent variable equals one for any sample bank whose composite CAMELS rating slips from one/two status to three/four/five status in the following eight quarters; the variable equals zero for banks that are examined but not downgraded in the eight-quarter window. The explanatory variables include the financial-performance ratios and bank size measure used

Table 4a. Are Residuals from the "Jumbo-CD Yield on Remaining Maturity" Regressions Potentially Good Proxies for Default Premiums?

As one measure of default premiums, we use residuals from year-by-year regressions of jumbo-CD yields on remaining maturities. This table displays the results for the 1991 through 1996 regressions. Regression coefficients appear on top; standard errors appear below in parentheses. Three stars indicate statistical significance at the 1% level; two stars indicate significance at the 5% level; and one star indicates significance at the 10% level. The intercept estimates approximate the average fourth-quarter yields on jumbo CDs maturing in less than three months. The intercept estimate plus the coefficient estimate on "3 TO 12" approximates the average yield on instruments maturing in three months to one year. The intercept estimate plus the coefficient estimate on "12 TO 60" approximates the yield on jumbo CDs maturing in the next 12 months to five years. The coefficient on OVER 60 has a comparable interpretation. Coefficient signs and magnitudes for the maturity variables reveal that in each year yields rose with time-to-maturity, implying that the equation residuals may serve as good proxies for default premiums.

	Fourth quarter of:					
Independent variables	1991	1992	1993	1994	1995	1996
Intercept	0.0572*** (0.0006)	0.0367*** (0.0005)	0.0332*** (0.0004)	0.0433*** (0.0004)	0.0538*** (0.0006)	0.0512*** (0.0005)
3 to 12	0.0090*** (0.0013)	0.0122*** (0.0009)	0.0060*** (0.0008)	0.0012 (0.0008)	0.0051*** (0.0010)	0.0041*** (0.0009)
12 to 60	0.0256*** (0.0021)	0.0276*** (0.0012)	0.0253*** (0.0009)	0.0117*** (0.0009)	0.0091*** (0.0012)	0.0107*** (0.0011)
Over 60	0.0137 (0.0113)	0.0470*** (0.0065)	0.0290*** (0.0045)	0.0085* (0.0047)	0.0182** (0.0082)	0.0024 (0.0078)
Adjusted R^2	0.0149	0.0531	0.0690	0.0164	0.0070	0.0099
F-statistic for significance of the three independent variables	59.338***	208.245***	264.166***	57.65***	23.68***	30.91***

Table 4a. Continued.

Percentage of deposits with remaining maturity:	1991	1992	1993	1994	1995	1996
Within 3 months	53.17%	48.93%	45.90%	45.01%	45.62%	43.55%
3 to 12 months	29.43	30.00	30.38	31.35	33.8	40.92
12 to 60 months	15.99	18.94	21.32	21.88	19.11	15.09
Over 60 months	1.41	2.13	2.41	1.76	1.47	0.44
Yield on three-month CDs in the secondary market	4.91%	3.44%	3.28%	5.86%	5.72%	5.41%

Table 4b. Are Residuals From the "Jumbo-CD Yield on Remaining Maturity" Regressions Potentially Good Proxies for Default Premiums?

This table displays the results from the 1997, 1998, and 1999 regressions. The long-term maturity buckets for these three years differed from the buckets for 1991 through 1996. Again, regression coefficients appear on top; standard errors appear below in parentheses. Three stars indicate statistical significance at the 1% level; two stars indicate significance at the 5% level; and one star indicates significance at the 10% level. Once again, coefficient signs and magnitudes for the maturity variables reveal that in each year yields rose with time-to-maturity, implying that the equation residuals may serve as good proxies for default premiums.

	Fourth quarter of:		
Independent variables	1997	1998	1999
Intercept	0.0531*** (0.0008)	0.0493*** (0.0007)	0.0495*** (0.0004)
3 to 12	0.0044*** (0.0015)	0.0074*** (0.0011)	0.0031*** (0.0007)
12 to 36	0.0084*** (0.0019)	0.0127*** (0.0015)	0.0078*** (0.0010)
Over 36	0.0072 (0.0047)	0.0154*** (0.0031)	0.0135*** (0.0020)
Adjusted R^2	0.0026	0.0127	0.0134
F-statistic for significance of the three independent variables	8.83***	38.11***	39.78***
Percentage of deposits with remaining maturity:	1997	1998	1999
Within 3 months	40.44%	39.69%	38.95%
3 to 12 months	42.80	43.60	45.42
12 to 36 months	13.90	13.36	12.71
Over 36 months	2.85	3.35	2.92
Yield on three-month CDs in the secondary market	5.73%	5.20%	6.06%

in the SEER risk-rank model, as well as two additional CAMELS-related variables. Table 5 describes the explanatory variables and the expected relationship between each variable and the likelihood of a downgrade.

The financial-performance ratios are designed to measure leverage risk, credit risk, and liquidity risk – three risks that have consistently produced financial distress in commercial banks (Putnam, 1983; Cole & Gunther, 1998). The bank size and CAMELS-related variables capture the impact of other factors that may affect downgrade risk.

The downgrade-prediction model relies on six measures of credit risk, the risk that borrowers will fail to make promised interest and principal payments. The credit-risk measures include the ratio of loans 30–89 days past due to total assets (PAST-DUE-30), the ratio of loans over 89 days past due to total assets (PAST-DUE-90), the ratio of loans in non-accrual status to total assets (NONACCRUING), the ratio of other-real-estate-owned to total assets (OREO), the ratio of commercial-and-industrial loans to total assets (COMMERCIAL-LOANS), and the ratio of residential-real-estate loans to total assets (RESIDENTIAL-LOANS). The model relies on six measures of credit risk because this risk was the driving force behind bank failures in the late 1980s and early 1990s (Hanc, 1997). We include the past-due and non-accruing loan ratios because banks tend to charge off higher percentages of these loans than loans in current status. We include "other real estate owned" (OREO), which consists primarily of collateral seized after loan defaults, because a high OREO ratio often signals poor credit-risk management – either because a bank had to foreclose on a large number of loans or because it had trouble disposing of seized collateral. PAST-DUE-30, PAST-DUE-90, NONACCRUING, and OREO are backward-looking because they register asset quality problems that have already emerged (Morgan & Stiroh, 2001). To give the model a forward-looking dimension, we add the commercial-and-industrial-loan ratio because, historically, the charge-off rate for these loans has been higher than for other loans. Similarly, we include the residential real estate ratio because, historically, losses on these loans have been relatively low. With the exception of the residential-loan ratio, we expect a positive relationship between the credit-risk measures and downgrade probability.

The model contains two measures of leverage risk, the risk that losses will exceed capital and produce insolvency. The leverage-risk measures include total equity minus goodwill as a percentage of total assets (NET-WORTH) and net income as a percentage of total assets (or, return on assets, ROA). We expect higher levels of capital (lower leverage risk) to reduce the likelihood of CAMELS downgrades. Return on assets bears on leverage risk because retained earnings are an important source of additional capital for many banks

Table 5. Which Factors Help Predict Downgrades to Unsatisfactory Status?

This table lists the independent variables used in the downgrade-prediction model. The signs indicate the hypothesized relationship between each variable and the likelihood of a downgrade from satisfactory status (a CAMELS one or two composite rating) to unsatisfactory status (a CAMELS "three," "four," or "five" rating). For example, the negative sign for the net worth ratio indicates that, other things equal, higher net worth reduces the likelihood of a downgrade over the next two years.

	Independent Variables	Symbol	Hypothesized Relationship
Credit Risk	Loans past due 30–89 days as a percentage of total assets.	PAST-DUE–30	+
	Loans past due 90+ days as a percentage of total assets.	PAST-DUE–90	+
	Nonaccrual loans as a percentage of total assets.	NONACCRUING	+
	Other real estate owned as a percentage of total assets.	OREO	+
	Commercial-and-industrial loans as a percentage of total assets.	COMMERCIAL-LOANS	+
	Residential-real-estate loans as a percentage of total assets.	RESIDENTIAL-LOANS	–
Leverage Risk	Total net worth (equity capital minus goodwill) as a percentage of total assets.	NET-WORTH	–
	Net income as a percentage of average assets (return on average assets).	ROA	–
Liquidity Risk	Book value of investment securities as a percentage of total assets.	SECURITIES	–
	Deposits > $100M (jumbo CDs) as a percentage of total assets.	LARGE-TIME-DEPOSITS	+
Control Variables	Natural logarithm of total assets, in thousands of dollars.	SIZE	?
	Dummy variable equal to 1 if bank has a CAMELS rating of 2.	CAMELS–2	+
	Dummy variable equal to 1 if the bank's management rating is worse than its composite CAMELS rating.	BAD-MANAGE	+

and because higher earnings provide a larger cushion for withstanding adverse economic shocks (Berger, 1995). We expect higher earnings to reduce the risk of downgrade.

The downgrade-prediction model uses two ratios to capture liquidity risk, the risk that loan commitments cannot be funded or withdrawal demands met at a reasonable cost. The liquidity-risk measures include investment securities as a percentage of total assets (SECURITIES) and jumbo-CD balances as a percentage of total assets (LARGE-TIME-DEPOSITS). A larger stock of liquid assets – such as investment securities – indicates a greater ability to meet unexpected funding needs and should, therefore, translate into a lower downgrade probability. Liquidity risk also depends on a bank's reliance on non-core funding. Non-core funding – which includes jumbo CDs – can be quite sensitive to the difference between the interest rate paid by the bank and the market rate. All other things equal, greater reliance on jumbo CDs implies a greater likelihood of a funding runoff or an interest-expense shock and, hence, a CAMELS downgrade.

In addition to financial ratios, the model includes variables designed to capture the impact of asset size, CAMELS differences, and management competence on downgrade risk. We add the natural logarithm of total assets (SIZE) because large banks can reduce risk by diversifying across product lines and geographic regions. As Demsetz and Strahan (1997) have noted, however, geographic diversification relaxes a constraint, enabling bankers to assume more risk, so we make no prediction about the relationship between size and downgrade probability. We include a dummy variable equal to one if a bank's composite CAMELS rating is a "two" because two-rated banks tumble into unsatisfactory status more often than one-rated banks. (See Table 1 for downgrade rates for one- and two-rated institutions in the 1990s.) Finally we employ a dummy variable (BAD-MANAGE) equal to one if the management component of the CAMELS rating is higher (weaker) than the composite rating. In these cases, examiners have registered concerns about management's competence, even though these problems have yet to produce financial consequences.

We estimate the downgrade-prediction model for eight separate sample windows. In each equation, downgrade status (1 = downgrade, 0 = no downgrade) in years $t+1$ and $t+2$ is regressed on accounting and supervisory data for banks rated CAMELS "one" or "two" in the fourth quarter of year t. For example, to produce the first downgrade equation (reported as the "1990–91" equation in Table 6), we use all non-de novo, U.S. community banks with one or two composite ratings as of December 31, 1989.

Table 6. How Well Does the Downgrade-prediction Model Fit the Data?

This table presents the results of probit regressions of downgrade status on financial performance ratios and control variables. The dependent variable equals "1" for a downgrade and "0" for no downgrade in calendar year $t+1$ and $t+2$. Values for independent variables are taken from the fourth quarter of year t. Standard errors appear in parentheses below the coefficients. One asterisk denotes statistical significance at the 10% level, two asterisks at the 5% level, and three at the 1% level. The pseudo-R^2 indicates the approximate proportion of the variance in downgrade status that is explained by the model.

Overall, the downgrade-prediction model fits the data relatively well. For each of the eight regressions, the log-likelihood test statistic allows rejection of the hypothesis that all model coefficients equal zero. In addition, eight of the independent variables are significant with the predicted sign in all eight years, and all of the variables were significant in at least some years. Although model performance for the decade is good overall, in-sample fit does deteriorate slightly in later years due to the decline in downgrade frequency.

		Period of Downgrade in CAMELS rating			
	Independent Variable	1990–91	1991–92	1992–93	1993–94
	Intercept	-2.087***	–0.957***	–0.081	0.048
		(0.246)	(0.264)	(0.318)	(0.375)
Credit Risk	PAST-DUE–30	0.112***	0.150***	0.136***	0.174***
		(0.021)	(0.022)	(0.026)	(0.033)
	PAST-DUE–90	0.376***	0.328***	0.239***	0.304***
		(0.039)	(0.040)	(0.047)	(0.060)
	NONACCRUING	0.235***	0.199***	0.291***	0.178***
		(0.029)	(0.030)	(0.036)	(0.045)
	OREO	0.220***	0.216***	0.145***	0.167***
		(0.030)	(0.032)	(0.031)	(0.043)
	COMMERCIAL-LOANS	0.009***	0.013***	0.009**	0.002
		(0.003)	(0.003)	(0.004)	(0.005)
	RESIDENTIAL-LOANS	–0.005**	–0.004	–0.004	–0.005
		(0.002)	(0.002)	(0.003)	(0.003)
Leverage Risk	NET-WORTH	–0.054***	–0.048***	–0.073***	–0.074***
		(0.010)	(0.011)	(0.013)	(0.013)
	ROA	–0.241***	–0.318***	–0.200***	–0.263***
		(0.035)	(0.039)	(0.043)	(0.051)
Liquidity Risk	SECURITIES	–0.016***	–0.017***	–0.013***	–0.009***
		(0.002)	(0.002)	(0.002)	(0.003)
	LARGE-TIME-DEPOSITS	0.017***	0.019***	0.015***	0.017***
		(0.003)	(0.003)	(0.004)	(0.005)
Control Variables	SIZE	0.079***	–0.029	–0.125***	–0.147***
		(0.017)	(0.019)	(0.024)	(0.030)
	CAMELS–2	0.633***	0.517***	0.509***	0.432***
		(0.062)	(0.068)	(0.087)	(0.102)
	BAD-MANAGE	0.488***	0.401***	0.478***	0.466***
		(0.051)	(0.054)	(0.061)	(0.069)
	Number of Observations	8,494	8,065	7,836	8,058
	Pseudo-R^2	0.219	0.226	0.208	0.161
	–2 log likelihood testing whether all coefficients (except the intercept) = 0	7211.785***	6053.423***	3946.413***	2444.832***

Table 6. (Continued).

	Independent Variable	Period of Downgrade in CAMELS rating			
		1994–95	1995–96	1996–97	1997–98
	Intercept	–0.780*	–0.011	–0.162	–1.371***
		(0.402)	(0.436)	(0.415)	(0.388)
Credit Risk	PAST-DUE–30	0.119***	0.164***	0.189***	0.093***
		(0.035)	(0.035)	(0.033)	(0.029)
	PAST-DUE–90	0.296***	0.322***	0.399***	0.347***
		(0.064)	(0.074)	(0.064)	(0.057)
	NONACCRUING	0.192***	0.145***	0.157***	0.187***
		(0.046)	(0.051)	(0.046)	(0.044)
	OREO	0.192***	0.153***	0.091	0.156**
		(0.044)	(0.052)	(0.059)	(0.067)
	COMMERCIAL-LOANS	0.007	0.013***	0.010**	0.005
		(0.005)	(0.005)	(0.005)	(0.005)
	RESIDENTIAL-LOANS	–0.002	–0.013***	–0.009***	0.000
		(0.004)	(0.004)	(0.003)	(0.003)
Leverage Risk	NET-WORTH	–0.032**	–0.034***	–0.036***	–0.020*
		(0.014)	(0.013)	(0.014)	(0.012)
	ROA	–0.229***	–0.164***	–0.393***	–0.110**
		(0.052)	(0.038)	(0.063)	(0.044)
Liquidity Risk	SECURITIES	–0.002	–0.010***	–0.015***	–0.011***
		(0.003)	(0.003)	(0.003)	(0.003)
	LARGE-TIME-DEPOSITS	0.024***	0.020***	0.023***	0.019***
		(0.005)	(0.005)	(0.005)	(0.004)
Control Variables	SIZE	–0.150***	–0.202***	–0.150***	–0.101***
		(0.033)	(0.035)	(0.032)	(0.030)
	CAMELS–2	0.594***	0.589***	0.501***	0.760***
		(0.104)	(0.103)	(0.099)	(0.093)
	BAD-MANAGE	0.389***	0.510***	0.406***	0.535***
		(0.075)	(0.078)	(0.083)	(0.081)
	Number of Observations	8,664	8,666	8,574	8,306
	Pseudo-R^2	0.150	0.188	0.223	0.182
	–2 log likelihood testing whether all coefficients (except the intercept) = 0	2130.311***	1977.293***	2189.627***	2347.306***

PAST-DUE–30	Loans over 30 days past due as a percentage of total assets	NET-WORTH	Equity less goodwill as a percentage of total assets
PAST-DUE–90	Loans over 89 days past due as a percentage of total assets	ROA	Net income as a percentage of total assets.
		SECURITIES	Book value of securities as a percentage of total assets
NONACCRUING	Loans on nonaccrual status as a percentage of total assets	LARGE-TIME-DEPOSITS	Large denomination time deposit liabilities as a percentage of total assets.
OREO	Other real estate owned as a percentage of total assets	SIZE	Natural logarithm of total assets, in thousands of dollars.
COMMERCIAL-LOANS	Commercial and industrial loans as a percentage of total assets	CAMELS–2	Dummy variable equal to 1 if bank has a CAMELS rating of 2.
RESIDENTIAL-LOANS	Residential real-estate loans as a percentage of total assets	BAD-MANAGE	Dummy variable equal to 1 if the bank's management rating is worse than composite CAMELS rating.

We then regress downgrade status during 1990 and 1991 on fourth quarter 1989 (1989, Q:IV) data. We continue with this timing convention through a regression of downgrade status in 1997 and 1998 on 1996, Q:IV data.

The downgrade-prediction model fits the data relatively well. (Table 6 contains these regression results.) For all eight regressions, the log-likelihood test statistic allows rejection of the hypothesis that the model coefficients jointly equal zero at the one-percent level of significance. The pseudo-R^2, which indicates the approximate proportion of the variance of downgrade/no downgrade status explained by the model, ranges from a low of 15.0% for the 1994–1995 equation to a high of 22.6% for the 1991–1992 equation. The estimated coefficients on eight explanatory variables – the jumbo-CD-to-total asset ratio, the net worth-to-total asset ratio, the past due and non-accruing loan ratios, the net income-to-total asset ratio, and the two CAMELS dummy variables – are statistically significant with the expected sign in all eight equations. The coefficient on the size variable has a mixed-sign pattern, which is not unexpected, given the theoretical ambiguity about the relationship between size and risk. The coefficients on the other five explanatory variables are statistically significant with the expected sign in at least three of the eight equations. Although model performance for the decade is good overall, in-sample fit does deteriorate slightly in later years due to the decline in downgrade frequency.

V. OUT-OF-SAMPLE PERFORMANCE TESTS – JUMBO-CD VERSUS THE DOWNGRADE RANKINGS

Next, we conduct performance tests of the risk rankings drawn from downgrade probabilities and jumbo-CD default premiums. For each year, we use the probit model to estimate the likelihood that each sample bank will suffer a downgrade in the next eight quarters, and then we rank banks from highest downgrade probability to lowest. Similarly, for each year we rank the banks from highest to lowest default premium. We obtain separate rankings for the yield-spread measure and the simple-residuals measure. Although each approach produces a different index number, they may all lead to similar ordinal rankings. Only out-of-sample testing can determine whether the default-premium rankings differ from the downgrade-probability rankings and whether differences in rankings favor default premiums as a surveillance tool. Out-of-sample tests – which use an evaluation period subsequent to the estimation period – are crucial because they mimic the way supervisors actually conduct off-site surveillance. Also, as has been demonstrated in the "profitability-of-trading rules" literature, superior in-sample performance often fails to translate into superior out-of-sample performance (Roll, 1994; Sullivan, Timmermann & White, 1999).

We assess out-of-sample performance using the type-one and type-two error rates for each risk ranking. Each type of forecast error is costly. A missed downgrade – a type-one error – is costly because accurate downgrade predictions give supervisors more warning about emerging problems, and early intervention reduces the likelihood of failure. A predicted downgrade that does not materialize – a type-two error – is costly because it wastes scarce supervisory resources and imposes unnecessary regulatory burdens. A trade-off exists between the two types of error; supervisors can eliminate over-predicted downgrades, for example, by assuming that no banks are downgrade risks.

For each risk ranking, power curves can be drawn to indicate the minimum achievable type-one error rates for any desired type-two error rate (Cole, Cornyn & Gunther, 1995). For example, the yield-spread power curve shows the type-one and type-two error rates when an ordinal ranking based on spread-over-Treasuries is interpreted as a rank ordering of downgrade risk. We trace out the curve by starting with the assumption that no sample bank is a downgrade risk. This assumption implies that all subsequent downgrades are surprises – a 100% type-one error rate. Because no banks are incorrectly classified as downgrade risks, the type-two error rate is zero. We obtain the next point on the curve by selecting the bank with the highest spread. If that bank suffers a downgrade in the following eight quarters, then the type-one error rate for the yield-spread ordering decreases slightly. The type-two error rate remains at zero because, again, no institutions are incorrectly classified as downgrade risks. If the selected bank does not suffer a downgrade, then the type-one error rate remains at 100%, and the type-two error rate increases slightly. By selecting banks in order of yield spread and re-calculating type-one and type-two error rates, we can trace out a power curve. At the lower right extreme of the curve, all banks are considered at risk of a downgrade. At this extreme, the type-one error rate is 0%, and the type-two error rate is 100%. Figure 1 shows 1992–1993 power curves for each risk ranking.

The areas under the power curves provide a basis for comparing the forecast accuracy of each risk ranking. Smaller areas imply lower overall rates of type-one and type-two errors and, hence, more accurate risk rankings. For each ranking, we express the area under the curve as a percentage of the total area in the box. A useful benchmark for evaluating the economic significance of differences in forecast accuracy is the area produced when risk rankings are randomly selected. Random selection, over a large number of trials, produces power curves with an average slope of negative one. Thus, the area under a

1992–93 Downgrade Predictions Using Year-end 1991 Data

This figure shows that the downgrade-prediction model significantly outperforms all three jumbo-CD default premium screens. Indeed, a watch list based on the CD screens hardly improves over a watch list compiled by randomly selecting one- and two-rated banks. (See Table 7.)

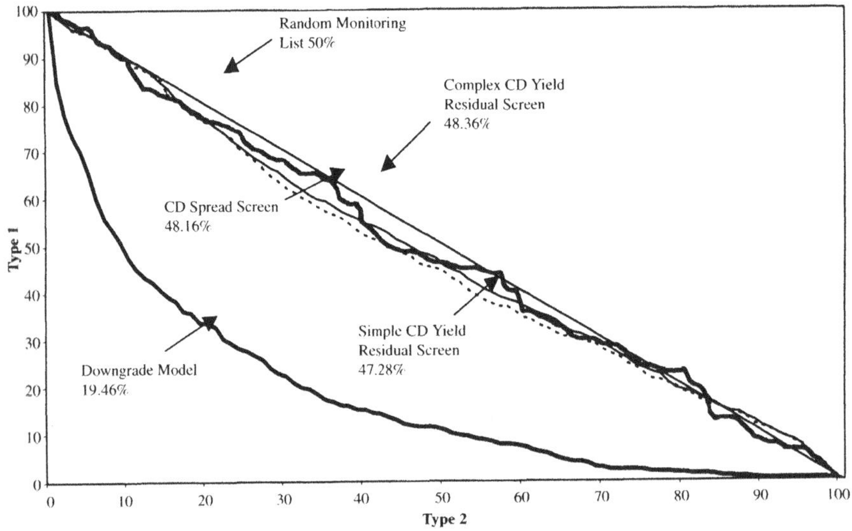

This figure shows the trade-off between type-one and type-two error rates for watch lists based on the downgrade model, the yield-spread screen, and the residuals screen. Here, type-one errors are "missed" downgrades--that is, one- or two-rated banks not flagged as downgrade risks that subsequently suffer CAMELS downgrades. Type-two errors, in contrast, are "over-predicted" downgrades--that is, one- or two-rated banks flagged as downgrade risks that do not suffer subsequent downgrades. A desirable early-warning tool minimizes type-one errors for any given level of type-two error. A convenient way to compare watch list performance is to calculate the area under each list's power curve and express that area as the percentage of the total area in the box. Smaller areas are desired because they imply a simultaneous reduction in both types of errors. The 50% line notes the resulting power curve if banks at risk of downgrade are selected randomly.

Fig. 1. How Well Do the Models Predict Out-of-Sample CAMELS Downgrades?

random-ordering power curve equals, on average, 50% of the area of the entire box.

This method of evaluating relative performance – though somewhat atheoretic – does make the best use of the existing data. A more theoretically appealing approach would start by minimizing a loss function that places an explicit weight on the benefits of early warning about financial distress and the costs of wasted examination resources and unnecessary disruption of bank activities. The relative performance of the rankings could then be assessed for the optimal type-one (or type-two) error rate. Unfortunately, the data necessary to pursue such an approach are unavailable. Without concrete data about supervisor loss functions, we opt for power curves that make no assumptions about the weights that should be placed on type-one and type-two errors. This approach also allows supervisors to use our results to compare performance over any desired range of error rates.

Our out-of-sample tests follow a timing convention that reflects the way supervisors actually conduct surveillance. To test the downgrade-model rankings, we start by regressing 1990–1991 downgrade status on financial and supervisory data from the fourth quarter of 1989. By the end of 1991, supervisors would have possessed coefficient estimates from this regression. We then apply these coefficients to fourth-quarter 1991 data for each sample bank to obtain a downgrade probability for 1992 and 1993. Finally, we rank banks by these probabilities and use the ranking – together with actual downgrade incidence in 1992 and 1993 – to construct a power curve. Downgrade-model curves for the remaining seven test windows reflect the same timing convention. To test the jumbo-CD rankings, we first order banks by their year-end 1991 yield spreads. Next, we derive a power curve for this ranking, assuming that high spreads map into high downgrade probabilities for the 1992–1993 window. We follow this procedure seven more times, each time deriving a new ranking when new call-report data would have become available and drawing a new yield-spread curve for this ranking. To complete the jumbo-CD tests, we rank banks by residuals from the 1991 "yield-on-maturity" regression and derive power curves assuming that a high residual equals a high downgrade risk in the 1992–93 window. Once again, we repeat this procedure seven times, producing eight simple-residuals power curves in all.

The evidence overwhelmingly points to the downgrade-prediction model as the superior surveillance tool. Indeed, the default-premium rankings barely improve on random rankings. In the first test window (1992–1993), for example, the area under the yield-spread power curve (48.16%) and the area under the simple-residuals power curve (47.28%) are close to the random-selection benchmark of 50%. In sharp contrast, the area under the downgrade-model curve is just 19.46%. The power-curve patterns over the next seven test windows are remarkably consistent with the patterns in the first test window. (Fig. 1 contains the power curves for the 1992–1993 test window. Because the power curves for the other test windows are so similar, they were omitted to save space. Table 7 presents power-curve areas for each surveillance tool and each test window, as well as the average area for each tool over all eight tests.)

Table 7. Do Measures of Jumbo-CD Default Premiums and Runoffs Add Value in Community-bank Surveillance?

This table summarizes the out-of-sample performance of risk rankings obtained from the downgrade-prediction model and the jumbo-CD data. Performance comparisons are based on areas under power curves. Power curves illustrate the trade off between type-one errors (the percentage of missed downgrades) and type-two errors (the percentage of over-predicted downgrades) for the risk rankings produced by each surveillance tool. A smaller area under the curve implies a lower rate of both types of errors and, thus, a better surveillance tool. Each cell in columns two through eight contains the area under the power curve for a specific risk ranking over a specific test window.

The evidence suggests that jumbo-CD rankings add little value in community-bank surveillance. Risk rankings produced by the downgrade-prediction model (column two) perform considerably better than a random ranking (area of 50%). At the same time, risk rankings based on jumbo-CD default premiums or runoffs (columns four through eight) perform little better than random risk rankings. Moreover, adding jumbo-CD default premiums to the downgrade-prediction model (column three) did not improve its out-of-sample performance.

Downgrade Years (1)	Downgrade Model (2)	Downgrade Model with Yield Spread (3)	Yield-Spread (4)	Simple Residuals (Yields) (5)	Simple Runoff (6)	Complex Yield Residuals (7)	Complex Runoff Residuals (8)
1992–93	19.46%	20.42%	48.16%	47.28%	49.54%	48.36%	52.06%
1993–94	21.87%	23.34%	47.23%	46.88%	47.77%	39.75%	52.22%
1994–95	23.19%	23.55%	51.01%	50.49%	45.53%	48.27%	47.25%
1995–96	17.85%	18.68%	43.09%	43.32%	47.88%	38.90%	46.12%
1996–97	15.61%	18.03%	47.45%	47.46%	45.87%	42.11%	41.55%
1997–98	18.84%	19.47%	45.61%	46.26%	45.23%	42.31%	44.50%
1998–99	21.12%	21.59%	47.25%	47.21%	47.81%	43.50%	49.28%
1999–00	19.14%	18.80%	46.10%	46.13%	44.09%	46.35%	48.00%
Mean All Years	19.64%	20.49%	46.99%	46.88%	46.72%	43.69%	47.62%

Over all eight tests the average area under the downgrade-model curves is 19.64%, the average area under the yield-spread curves is 46.99%, and the average area under the simple-residuals curves is 46.88%. In the individual test windows, the downgrade-model areas range from 15.61% (1996–1997 test window) to 23.19% (1994–1995). Meanwhile, the areas under the yield-spread rankings range from 43.09% (1995–1996) to 51.01% (1994–1995), and the areas under the simple-residuals rankings range from 43.32% (1995–1996) to 50.49% (1994–1995).

VI. ROBUSTNESS CHECKS

Proxies for default premiums appear to have little value in community-bank surveillance. It is possible, however, that the poor performance of our proxies stems from a poor method of extracting signals from jumbo-CD data. It is also possible that jumbo-CD screens would have proved useful in monitoring a different cut of community banks. Finally, it is possible that jumbo-CD screens would have improved the performance of the downgrade-prediction model. In short, before ruling out a role for jumbo-CD screens in surveillance, we must check our results for robustness.

One potential explanation for the poor performance of our default-premium measures is that risky banks substitute insured for uninsured deposits (Billett, Garfinkel & O'Neal, 1998). If such a "substitution effect" were important, then signals about changing risk exposures would show up in jumbo-CD runoffs rather than default premiums. To explore this possibility, we compute the year-over-year percentage change in outstanding jumbo CDs for each sample bank. Then, we rank banks each year from largest to smallest percentage runoff, assuming that high runoff percentages map into high downgrade probabilities. Finally, as before, we use these rankings, together with observed downgrades, to generate power curves for all eight out-of-sample windows. Column 6 of Table 7, labeled "simple runoffs," contains the power-curve areas for the runoff rankings. The average area over all the out-of-sample tests is 46.72%, on par with the 46.99% average for the yield-spread rankings and 46.88% average for the simple-residuals rankings. This evidence suggests that runoff screens, like the default-premium screens, would contribute little to community bank surveillance.

Our relatively simple approach to computing default premiums and runoff percentages may also account, in part, for our findings. Accordingly, we test jumbo-CD rankings obtained by a more sophisticated method. This method, which we term the "complex residuals" method, involves first regressing yields on a richer set of non-financial explanatory variables, then ranking banks by the residuals, and finally generating power curves with these rankings. We repeat this procedure for runoff percentages. The richer set of explanatory variables was identified through an extensive specification search in related research. See Hall, King, Meyer and Vaughan (2002) for a detailed discussion of this search and the control variables. These explanatory variables include controls for interest-rate levels, regional economic conditions, idiosyncratic aspects of the bank's jumbo-CD portfolio, and idiosyncratic aspects of demand and supply for the bank's jumbo CDs. These controls should reduce noise in the default-premium and runoff measures and, thereby, increase the forecasting power of risk rankings based on these measures. Out-of-sample performance of risk rankings based on "complex" yield residuals (column 7 of Table 7) is slightly better than the performance of the other default-premium rankings – the average area under the eight power curves dips about three percentage points to 43.69%. At the same time, the performance of the risk rankings based on runoff residuals ("complex-runoff residuals" in column 8 of Table 7) worsens slightly – the average area rises nearly one percentage point to 47.62%. More important, these areas are still close to random-selection areas and far from the downgrade-model areas. The evidence implies that even jumbo-CD rankings based on sophisticated measures of default premiums and runoffs contain little information about bank condition.

Although our default-premium and runoff measures turn in poor forecasting performances as single-variable screens, they may add value as regressors in the downgrade-prediction model. Indeed, previous research has identified single-variable surveillance screens with this property (Gilbert, Meyer & Vaughan, 1999). Pursuing this angle, we estimated "enhanced" downgrade-prediction models that include each default-premium proxy and each runoff measure. As before, we rank the sample banks using downgrade probabilities generated by the enhanced model. Column 3 in Table 7 contains the results of out-of-sample tests of the model enhanced by simple yield spreads. In seven of eight test windows, the baseline downgrade model outperforms the enhanced downgrade model. On average, the power-curve area under the enhanced model's risk rankings is 20.49% – slightly worse than the 19.64% area for the baseline model (column 2). The results for the other enhanced downgrade models are similar. In short, proxies for jumbo-CD default premiums or runoffs do not improve surveillance as independent variables in the downgrade-prediction model.

Another possibility is that we define community banks too rigidly. Raising the asset cutoffs, for example, might lead to more informative risk rankings because jumbo CDs at small banks act like core deposits. Also, jumbo-CD holders at larger institutions might be more sophisticated and, hence, more likely to monitor bank condition. To test for an "asset threshold" effect, we conduct all the out-of-sample performance comparisons (default-premium rankings vs. runoff rankings vs. downgrade-model rankings) on non-de novo, U.S. banks holding less than $1 billion (1999 dollars) in assets. Raising the size threshold to $1 billion – or to a variety of thresholds between $500 million and $1 billion for that matter – does not alter our findings. In out-of-sample tests based on a variety of asset thresholds, the downgrade-prediction model still emerges as the superior surveillance tool.

VII. CONCLUSIONS

We find that feedback from the jumbo-CD market would have added little value in community-bank surveillance during the 1990s. Specifically, rank orderings produced by a downgrade-prediction model – a model chosen to benchmark current surveillance practices – would have significantly outperformed rank orderings based on jumbo-CD default premiums and runoffs throughout the decade. And jumbo-CD orderings would have improved little over random orderings. Finally, adding jumbo-CD screens to the downgrade-prediction model did not improve its out-of-sample forecasting record. We see this evidence as a partial validation of current surveillance practices.

Problems with the jumbo-CD data or frictions in the jumbo-CD market could explain the poor performance of the screens. As noted, all of our default-premium proxies are based on a noisy measure of yields. Large degrees of measurement error, due to marginal vs. average problems or accounting data vs. market data problems, would explain the lack of information in the default-premium rankings. Another possibility is that jumbo-CD rates posted by community banks "cluster" around integers and even fractions (Kahn, Pennacchi & Sopranzetti, 1999); such clustering would make rates less responsive to changes in bank risk and risk rankings based on those rates less informative. Still another possibility is that jumbo CDs in community banks are relatively free of default risk – either because balances barely exceed $100,000 or because balances belong mostly to municipalities (and are therefore, by law, collateralized with blue-chip securities). A final possibility is that holders of community-bank jumbo CDs are simply noise traders, giving little thought to default-risk when deciding where to place their funds.

We are not persuaded that data problems and market frictions account solely for our findings; the long business-cycle expansion of the 1990s, no doubt, also plays a role. Over this period, bank profitability ratios, capital ratios, and reserves-to-problem loan ratios soared to near record highs, while failure rates plummeted to near record lows. In such an environment, jumbo-CD screens – no matter how accurately measured or precisely determined – are unlikely to convey information about risk because the benefits of monitoring are so low. Such an explanation would account for the successful use of average yields in bank-risk studies a decade ago – a time when financial distress was fairly common and failures were sharply rising. Such an explanation would also account for the inability of other researchers to find significant supervisory value in real-time, economic data from the 1990s. In short, the peculiarity of the sample period may compromise attempts to assess the supervisory value of any market-based signal. Assessing the supervisory potential of market feedback in bank surveillance may have to await data from all phases of the business cycle.

NOTE

1. Curry, Elmer and Fissel (2001) report results for in-sample estimation and out-of-sample simulations. The results labeled "out-of-sample simulations" actually apply the coefficients of the models to holdout samples, rather than simulating the equations for time periods other than the time periods for which the equations were estimated.

ACKNOWLEDGMENTS

Critical feedback from a number of sources greatly improved this work. Specifically, we would like to thank the following bank supervisors – Carl Anderson, John Block, Joan Cronin, and Kim Nelson – and the following economists – Rosalind Bennett, Doug Evanoff, Mark Flannery, John Jordan, John Hall, Jim Harvey, Tom King, John Krainer, Bill Lang, Jose Lopez, Dan Nuxoll, Evren Ors, Jim Thomson, Sherrill Shaffer, Scott Smart, and Larry Wall – for helpful comments and discussions. We also profited from exchanges with seminar participants at Baylor University, the Federal Reserve System Surveillance Conference, the Federal Reserve System Committee on Financial Structure meetings, the Financial Management Association meetings, the Office of the Comptroller of the Currency, and Washington University in St. Louis. Any remaining errors and omissions are ours alone. The views expressed in this paper do not represent official positions of the Federal Reserve Bank of St. Louis, the Board of Governors, or the Federal Reserve System.

REFERENCES

Baer, H., & Brewer, E., III (1986). Uninsured Deposits as a Source of Market Discipline: Some New Evidence. Federal Reserve Bank of Chicago *Economic Perspectives*, (September/October), 23–31.

Bassett, W. F., & Brady, T. F. (2001). The Economic Performance of Small Banks, 1985–2000. *Federal Reserve Bulletin*, (November), 719–728.

Benston, G. J., & Kaufman, G. G. (1998). Deposit Insurance Reform in the FDIC Improvement Act: The Experience to Date. The Federal Reserve Bank of Chicago *Economic Perspectives*, (2nd Quarter), 2–20.

Berger, A. N. (1995). The Relationship between Capital and Earnings in Banking. *Journal of Money, Credit and Banking*, *27*, 432–456.

Berger, A. N., & Davies, S. M. (1998). The Information Content of Bank Examinations. *Journal of Financial Services Research*, *14*, 117–144.

Billett, M. T., Garfinkel, J. A., & O'Neal, E. S. (1998). The Cost of Market vs. Regulatory Discipline in Banking. *Journal of Financial Economics*, *48*, 333–358.

Board of Governors of the Federal Reserve System (1999). Using Subordinated Debt as an Instrument of Market Discipline. *Staff Study 172* (December).

Board of Governors of the Federal Reserve System and the United States Department of the Treasury (2000). *The Feasibility and Desirability of Mandatory Subordinated Debt*, (December).

Brewer, E., III, & Mondschean, T. H. (1994). An Empirical Test of the Incentive Effects of Deposit Insurance. *Journal of Money, Credit, and Banking, 26*, 146–164.

Cargill, T. F. (1989). CAMEL Ratings and the CD Market. *Journal of Financial Services Research, 3*, 347–358.

Cole, R. A., & Gunther, J. W. (1998). Predicting Bank Failures: A Comparison of On- and Off-Site Monitoring Systems. *Journal of Financial Services Research, 13*, 103–117.

Cole, R. A., Cornyn, B. G., & Gunther, J. W. (1995). FIMS: A New Monitoring System for Banking Institutions. *Federal Reserve Bulletin, 81* (January), 1–15.

Cook, D. O., & Spellman, L. J. (1994). Repudiation Risk and Restitution Costs: Toward an Understanding of Premiums on Insured Deposits. *Journal of Money, Credit and Banking, 26*, 439–459.

Crane, D. B. (1976). A Study of Interest Rate Spreads in the 1974 CD Market. *Journal of Bank Research, 7*, 213–224.

Curry, T. J., Elmer, P. J., & Fissel, G. S. (2001). Regulator Use of Market Data to Improve the Identification of Bank Financial Distress, Federal Deposit Insurance Corporation Working Paper 2001-01, December.

Demsetz, R. S., & Strahan, P. E. (1997). Diversification, Size, and Risk at Bank Holding Companies. *Journal of Money, Credit, and Banking, 29*, 300–313.

DeYoung, R. (1999). Birth, Growth, and Life or Death of Newly Chartered Banks. Federal Reserve Bank of Chicago. *Economic Perspectives*, (3rd Quarter), 18–35.

Ellis, D. M., & Flannery, M. J. (1992). Does the Debt Market Assess Large Banks' Risk? Time Series Evidence from Money Center CDs. *Journal of Monetary Economics, 30*, 481–502.

Emmons, W. R., Gilbert, R. A., & Vaughan, M. D. (2001). Controlling Risk by Big Banks: Can Markets Help? Federal Reserve Bank of St. Louis. *Regional Economist*, (October), 5–9.

Evanoff, D. D., & Wall, L. D. (2001). Sub-debt Yield Spreads as Bank Risk Measures. *Journal of Financial Services Research, 20*, 121–145.

Flannery, M. J. (1982). Retail Bank Deposits as Quasi-Fixed Factors of Production. *American Economic Review, 72*, 527–536.

Flannery, M. J., & Houston, J. F. (1999). The Value of a Government Monitor for U.S. Banking Firms. *Journal of Money, Credit, and Banking, 31*, 14–34.

Gilbert, R. A., Meyer, A. P., & Vaughan, M. D. (2002). Could a CAMELS Downgrade Model Improve Off-Site Surveillance? Federal Reserve Bank of St. Louis. *Review*, (January/February), 47–63.

Gilbert, R. A., Meyer, A. P., & Vaughan, M. D. (1999). The Role of Supervisory Screens and Econometric Models in Off-Site Surveillance. Federal Reserve Bank of St. Louis. *Review*, (November/December), 31–56.

Gunther, J. W., & Moore, R. R. (2000). Financial Statements and Reality: Do Troubled Banks Tell All? Federal Reserve Bank of Dallas. *Economic and Financial Review*, (3rd Quarter), 30–35.

Gunther, J. W., Levonian, M. E., & Moore, R. R. (2001). Can the Stock Market Tell Bank Supervisors Anything They Don't Already Know? Federal Reserve Bank of Dallas. *Economic and Financial Review*, (2nd Quarter), 2–9.

Hall, J. R., King, T., Meyer, A. P., & Vaughan, M. D. (2002). Did FDICIA Improve Market Discipline? A Look at Evidence from the Jumbo-CD Market. Supervisory Policy Analysis working paper, Federal Reserve Bank of St. Louis, June.

Hanc, G. (1997). The Banking Crises of the 1980s and Early 1990s: Summary and Implications. In: *History of the Eighties: Lessons for the Future* (vol. 1). Washington, D.C.: Federal Deposit Insurance Corporation.

Hannan, T., & Hanweck, G. A. (1988). Bank Insolvency Risk and the Market for Large Certificates of Deposit. *Journal of Money, Credit, and Banking*, *20*, 203–211.

James, C. (1991). The Losses Realized in Bank Failures. *Journal of Finance*, *46*, 1223–1242.

James, C. (1990). Heterogeneous Creditors and LDC Lending. *Journal of Monetary Economics*, *25*, 325–346.

James, C. (1988). The Use of Loan Sales and Standby Letters of Credit by Commercial Banks. *Journal of Monetary Economics*, *22*, 395–422.

Kahn, C., Pennacchi, G., & Sopranzetti, B. (1999). Bank Deposit Rate Clustering: Theory and Empirical Evidence. *Journal of Finance*, *56*, 2185–2214.

Keeley, M. C. (1990). Deposit Insurance, Risk, and Market Power in Banking. *American Economic Review*, *80*, 1183–1198.

Krainer, J., & Lopez, J. A. (2001). Incorporating Equity Market Information into Supervisory Monitoring Models. Working Paper, Research Department, Federal Reserve Bank of San Francisco, August 30.

Lang, W. W., & Robertson, D. (2000). Analysis of Proposals for a Minimum Subordinated Debt Requirement. Comptroller of the Currency, Economic and Policy Analysis Working Paper No. 2000-4, March.

Martinez-Peria, M. S., & Schmukler, S. L. (2001). Do Depositors Punish Banks for Bad Behavior? Market Discipline, Deposit Insurance, and Banking Crises. *Journal of Finance*, *56*, 1029–1051.

Meyer, L. H. (1999). Market Discipline as a Complement to Bank Supervision and Regulation, Speech before the Conference on Reforming Bank Capital Standards, Council on Foreign Relations, New York, June 14.

Morgan, D. P., & Stiroh, K. J. (2001). Market Discipline of Banks: The Asset Test. *Journal of Financial Services Research*, *20*, 195–208.

Morris, M. D., & Walter, J. R. (1993). Large Negotiable Certificates of Deposit. In: *Instruments of the Money Market*. Richmond, VA: Federal Reserve Bank of Richmond.

Park, S. (1995). Market Discipline by Depositors: Evidence from Reduced-Form Equations. *Quarterly Review of Economics and Finance*, *35*, 497–514.

Park, S., & Peristiani, S. (1998). Market Discipline by Thrift Depositors. *Journal of Money, Credit, and Banking*, *30*, 347–364.

Putnam, B. H. (1983). Early Warning Systems and Financial Analysis in Bank Monitoring: Concepts of Financial Monitoring. Federal Reserve Bank of Atlanta. *Economic Review*, (November), 6–13.

Reidhill, J., & O'Keefe, J. (1997). Off-Site Surveillance Systems. In: *History of the Eighties: Lessons for the Future* (vol. 1). Washington, D.C., Federal Deposit Insurance Corporation.

Roll, R. (1994). What Every CFO Should Know About Scientific Progress in Financial Economics: What is Known, and What Remains to be Resolved. *Financial Management*, *23*(2), 69–75.

Sullivan, R., Timmermann, A., & White, H. (1999). Data-Snooping, Technical Trading Rule Performance and the Bootstrap. *Journal of Finance*, *54*, 1647–1691.

DID FDICIA ENHANCE MARKET DISCIPLINE ON COMMUNITY BANKS? A LOOK AT EVIDENCE FROM THE JUMBO-CD MARKET

John R. Hall, Thomas B. King, Andrew P. Meyer and Mark D. Vaughan

ABSTRACT

The Federal Deposit Insurance Corporation Improvement Act of 1991 (FDICIA) directed the FDIC to resolve bank failures in the least costly manner, shifting some of the burden of failure resolutions to holders of jumbo certificates of deposit (CDs). Using call report data, we examine the sensitivity of community-bank jumbo-CD yields and runoffs to bank-specific risk before and after FDICIA. We also examine the economic significance of estimated risk sensitivities, looking at the implied impact of risk on community-bank funding costs and profits. The results indicate that while yield and runoff measures were sensitive to bank-specific risk before and after FDICIA, the estimated risk coefficients in both samples were small. Further, these coefficients were not statistically or economically different across the two sample periods. We conclude that the jumbo-CD market provides little pressure on community banks to contain risk.

Prompt Corrective Action in Banking: 10 Years Later, Volume 14, pages 63–94.

ISBN: 0-7623-0987-3

INTRODUCTION

Did the Federal Deposit Insurance Improvement Act of 1991 (FDICIA) increase market discipline on community banks? This research question is important for any cohort of banks because U.S. bank supervisors have devoted such energy to establishing markets as a third pillar of supervision – along with supervisory review and capital requirements. Advocates argue that high-powered performance incentives in financial markets lead to accurate assessments of bank risk. And, in turn, these assessments – expressed for high-risk institutions as rising yields on or difficulties rolling over liabilities – force bank managers to maintain safety and soundness. Although this story has considerable theoretical appeal, empirical research to date offers little evidence that bank managers respond to market assessments (Bliss & Flannery, 2001). Provisions of FDICIA were designed to shift some of the costs of bank failure to uninsured creditors. Evidence about the economic significance of the reaction to the act – for any cohort of banks – would inform the debate about the role for markets in bank supervision. It is possible, for example, that FDICIA increased the price of risk-taking in a way that no bank manager could ignore.

Focusing on the community banks is important because these banks represent a disproportionate threat to the deposit insurance fund. Community banks fail more often than larger banks. From 1984 through 1998, for example, the average failure rate for banks with less than $500 million in assets (1998 constant dollars) was 0.73%; the failure rate for banks holding over $500 million in assets was 0.33%. In addition, community banks have accounted for a disproportionately large share of assets at risk in failures. At year-end 2000, the U.S. banking sector contained 7,570 banks holding less than $500 million in assets. These banks accounted for 91.7% of U.S. banks and 12.9% of U.S. banking assets. Between 1984 and 1998, community banks accounted for 40% of the assets of failed U.S. banks. Finally, losses to the FDIC from community-bank failures, per dollar of assets, have exceeded losses from large-bank failures. Losses have been higher because community banks are top-heavy with assets that are expensive to liquidate – fewer securities and more fixed assets – and because community banks have fewer uninsured, unsecured creditors to absorb failure costs (James, 1991).

Another reason to focus on community banks is that many of these banks operate under extended exam schedules, with up to 18 months elapsing between full-scope examinations. This extended schedule may reduce the accuracy of community bank financial statements, thereby reducing the effectiveness of off-site supervisory monitoring. Verification of financials is one important source of value created by examinations (Berger & Davies, 1998; Flannery & Houston, 1999); indeed, recent research has documented large adjustments in asset quality measures following examinations, particularly for institutions with emerging problems (Gunther & Moore, 2000). It is possible that the uninsured creditors of community banks, because their own money is at stake, supplement published income statements and balance sheets with independent research. Another possibility is that information about safety and soundness leaks to uninsured creditors through the bank's board of directors, a body that typically includes prominent local businesspeople. Thus, pronounced spikes in funding costs or withdrawals could bring pressure to bear on the bank before supervisors spot an emerging problem.

The chief source of financial-market pressure on community banks – indeed, the only pressure for many such banks – is the jumbo certificate-of-deposit market. Jumbo certificates of deposit (CDs) are time deposits with balances above the $100,000 deposit insurance ceiling. Although community banks rely heavily on locally obtained core deposits (Bassett & Brady, 2001) – checking accounts, passbook savings deposits, and small time deposits – whose prices and quantities tend to be "sticky" (Flannery, 1982), they also compete nationally for jumbo CDs. Indeed, jumbo certificates of deposit have become an even more important part of community-bank capital structure in recent years. At year-end 2000, banks holding less than $500 million in assets – the definition of a community bank set forth in the Financial Modernization Act of 1999 – funded 13.2% of their assets with jumbo CDs, up from 9.1% at year-end 1990. The weight of the evidence confirmed that jumbo CDs contained a default-risk premium before FDICIA. [See Table 1 for a review of previous research.] It is possible that FDICIA increased this premium enough to dissuade community bankers from taking risks.

We use a six-step research strategy to evaluate FDICIA's impact on the cost of jumbo-CD funding for community banks. First, we specify clean test windows before and after the act. Second, we identify a suitable sample of community banks for each test window. Third, we draw on income and balance sheet data for the sample banks to construct measures of jumbo-CD yields and runoffs, measures of overall bank risk, and measures of other influences on yields and runoffs that must be held constant. Fourth, for each test window, we estimate pooled regressions of jumbo-CD yields and runoffs on a summary measure of bank-specific risk – holding other influences on yields and runoffs constant with appropriate control variables. Fifth, we use the risk coefficients from these regressions to calculate the impact of a change in risk on bank profitability in each test window. Finally, we use the difference in the price of risk-taking in the pre- and post-FDICIA windows – expressed in terms of the

Table 1. Does Published Evidence Point to "Risk Pricing" by Jumbo-CD Holders?

This table summarizes extant research on risk pricing by jumbo-CD holders. (We use the term "bank" to refer to bank holding companies as well as banks.) These studies employed both cross-section and time-series techniques and used a variety of risk proxies and control variables. Overall, the evidence suggests that jumbo-CD holders price bank-specific risk. Most of this evidence pre-dates FDICIA, however. Unlike previous research, we test risk pricing before and after FDICIA with a consistent research strategy.

Study	Sample Period	Country	Issuer/ Instrument	Number of Institutions	Price or Quantity?	Market Discipline Present?
Crane (1976)	1974	U.S.	Bank jumbo CDs	24	Price	Somewhat
Goldberg and Lloyd-Davies (1985)	1976–82	U.S.	Bank jumbo CDs	25	Price	Yes
Baer and Brewer (1986)	1979–82	U.S.	Bank jumbo CDs	40	Price	Yes
James (1988)	1984–86	U.S.	Bank large time deposits	58	Price	Yes
Hannan and Hanweck (1988)	1980–84	U.S.	Bank jumbo CDs	~200	Price	Yes
Cargill (1989)	1984–86	U.S.	Bank jumbo CDs	58	Price	Yes
Keeley (1990)	1971–86	U.S.	Bank jumbo CDs	85	Price	Yes
Ellis and Flannery (1992)	1982–88	U.S.	Bank jumbo CDs	6	Price	Yes
Cook and Spellman (1994)	1987–88	U.S.	Thrift jumbo CDs	~200	Price	Yes
Crabbe and Post (1994)	1986–91	U.S.	Bank jumbo CDs	41	Quantity	Yes
Brewer and Mondschean (1994)	1987–89	U.S.	Thrift jumbo CDs	4	Price	Yes
Park (1995)	1985–92	U.S.	Bank jumbo CDs	~10,000	Both	Yes
Park and Peristiani (1998)	1986–90	U.S.	Classes of thrift deposits	~3,000	Both	Yes
Jordan (2000)	1989–95	U.S.	Classes of bank deposits	65	Both	Yes
Martinez Peria and Schmuckler (2001)	1981–97	Argentina, Chile, and Mexico	Classes of bank time deposits	~200	Both	Yes
Goldberg and Hudgins (2002)	1984–94	U.S.	Thrift jumbo CDs	619	Quantity	Yes

impact of risk on community-bank profitability –to assess the impact of the act on discipline from the jumbo-CD market.

Taken together, the evidence suggests that the jumbo-CD market applied little pressure on community banks to contain risk – either before or after FDICIA. The results indicate that yield and runoff measures were sensitive to bank-specific risk before and after FDICIA. But the estimated risk coefficients in the pre-act and post-act samples were small. Even more to the point, these coefficients were not statistically or economically different across the two sample periods. Thus, the jumbo-CD market is not apt to be an effective pillar in community-bank supervision in the current environment. We conclude with a cautionary note – the unusual sample period, a period including the longest business-cycle expansion in U.S. history, may play an important role in our findings. Before closing the door on jumbo-CDs as a supervisory tool, we must examine evidence from all phases of the business cycle.

Our research strategy and our evidence about jumbo-CD risk pricing advance the literature in four specific ways. First, we offer the first large-sample test of FDICIA's impact on depositor discipline in banking markets. One paper has hinted at the impact of FDICIA on jumbo-CD funding costs (Jordan, 2000), and only two other papers have examined the impact of a regime shift on market discipline at all – Flannery and Sorescu (1996) looked at the U.S. subordinated-debt market's reaction to the government's retreat from a "too big to fail" policy, and Martinez Peria and Schmukler (2001) studied depositor reaction to banking crises in Argentina, Chile, and Mexico. Second, we analyze the economic importance of changes in risk pricing, thereby providing evidence on the "risk influencing" as opposed to the "risk monitoring" aspects of market discipline for a larger sample of U.S. banks than was used in previous research (Bliss & Flannery, 2001). Third, we provide an expansive list of control variables that nests the controls used in previous studies and that will prove useful in other research on bank liabilities. Fourth, we note an observational equivalence problem that makes interpreting previous market-discipline research difficult. For example, Goldberg and Hudgins (2002) note significant jumbo-CD runoff in failing thrifts both before and after FDICIA; this runoff may very well reflect supervisory discipline rather than market discipline. Our research strategy offers a solution to this observational equivalence problem.

A PRIMER ON FDICIA

FDICIA introduced the most sweeping changes in bank regulation since the 1930s (Benston & Kaufman, 1998). Two of these significant changes were prompt corrective action and annual exam frequency. Of these, prompt corrective action (PCA) has received the most scientific study. The evidence suggests that PCA capital thresholds were set too low and that they would have made little difference in the banking crisis of the 1980s (Peek & Rosengren, 1997; Jones & King, 1995; Gilbert, 1992). Increased exam frequency has also received some scientific attention, with the evidence suggesting that annual exams would have reduced losses to the deposit insurance fund (Gilbert, 1993).

FDICIA mandated one other important change in the regulatory regime – least-cost failure resolution. Before 1991, the FDIC cleaned up most failures with "purchases and assumptions." In these resolutions, the FDIC offered cash to healthy banks to assume the liabilities of failed ones – in effect, shielding uninsured depositors against losses. The new law directed the FDIC to resolve failures in the least expensive fashion, meaning that jumbo-CD holders had to share in the losses. The post-FDICIA numbers point to heightened exposure. In the three years running up to the act – 1988 through 1990 – jumbo-CD holders suffered losses in only 15% of 597 bank failures. But from 1993 to 1995, uninsured depositors lost money in 82% of the 60 failures (FDIC data reported in Benston and Kaufman (1998)). The new resolution procedure, though motivated by a desire to shield taxpayers from the costs of failures, should have also prompted jumbo-CD holders to pay more attention to bank risk. And more attention to risk spells a potential role for jumbo-CD holders in disciplining that risk.

Despite the importance of least-cost resolution to the market discipline debate, little effort has been devoted to analyzing its effects on deposit behavior. Indeed only two papers have addressed this issue explicitly. Jordan (2000) examined depositor discipline at failing New England banks in the late 1980s and early 1990s, but only a handful of his observations come from the post-FDICIA period. Goldberg and Hudgins (2002) look at jumbo-CD runoff for a large sample of failing thrifts, both before and after FDICIA. They find significant runoff as failure approaches, runoff they ascribe to market discipline.

Although Goldberg and Hudgins do investigate for thrifts the same research question we investigate for banks, their study suffers from a serious observational equivalence problem – the observed runoff could be the product of supervisory discipline or market discipline. Banks approaching failure typically operate under enforcement actions that call for improvement in regulatory capital ratios (Gilbert & Vaughan, 2001). One way to improve regulatory capital ratios quickly is to allow high-priced funding – jumbo CDs obtained in the national market, for example – and low-yielding loans to run off. Table 2 provides evidence of this loan and jumbo-CD shrinkage for Fed-supervised banks that failed in the 1990s. Of the 28 banks that failed, 24 operated under enforcement actions in the quarter of failure. The mean age of these actions at failure was 6.8 quarters. Beginning about six quarters before failure, the 24 banks under enforcement actions began to shrink, and, in particular, jumbo CDs began to run off. Indeed, jumbo CDs ran off faster than core deposits so the ratio of jumbo CDs to total deposits declined as well. In short, because jumbo-CD runoff at failing institutions may reflect concerted efforts by bank management to comply with supervisory actions rather than adverse reactions by depositors to bank risk, the Goldberg-Hudgins evidence is hard to interpret. We rely on a sample that is largely free of enforcement actions, so our evidence reflects the interaction of jumbo-CD markets and bank management. Also, unlike Goldberg and Hudgins, we examine the impact of risk on yields as well as runoff.

RESEARCH STRATEGY

We start with quarterly accounting data for all U.S. commercial banks, collected for two test windows – one for three years running up to FDICIA (1988–1990) and another for three years after FDICIA began to take effect (1993–1995). We use income and balance sheet data from the Reports of Condition and Income (the call reports), which are collected under the auspices of the Federal Financial Institutions Examination Council (FFIEC). Most call-report data are available to the public. We also rely on confidential supervisory ratings from the National Information Center (NIC) database of the Federal Reserve System. We define the period running from the first quarter of 1991 to the fourth quarter of 1992 as the event window. Following Goldberg and Hudgins (2002), we begin our pre-FDICIA sample in 1988 and end our post-FDICIA sample in 1995. We use these cut-off dates because changes in the call report make construction of a consistent series of key variables problematic before 1988 or beyond 1995.

To be "suitable" for inclusion in the sample, a bank must meet three criteria – a size test, a jumbo-CD usage test, and an operating-history test. First, the bank must hold less than $500 million in assets (1999 dollars) – the upper bound for a community financial institution set forth in the Financial Modernization Act of 1999. In addition, the bank must hold more than $5,000,000 in jumbo CDs in its deposit portfolio. We used this threshold to eliminate outlier banks; varying the threshold did not alter our results. Also, each bank must have an operating history of at least five years. We excluded de

Table 2. Is Jumbo-CD Runoff at Failing Banks Due to Supervisory Discipline or Market Discipline?

In the quarters running up to failure, troubled banks typically face intense supervisory pressure to improve their capital ratios. Troubled banks can raise capital ratios by allowing high-priced funding – such as jumbo CDs – and low-yield loans to run off. Observed changes in jumbo-CD dependence may, therefore, be the result of supervisor rather than market discipline. This table illustrates this observational equivalence problem for a sample of Fed-supervised banks. In the 1990s, 28 Fed-supervised banks failed; 24 of these banks operated under safety-and-soundness-related enforcement actions in the quarter of failure. The average age of these enforcement actions was 6.8 quarters. The mean and median growth rates show a consistent pattern of high loan and deposit growth two to three years before failure. In the two years running up to failure, however, loan and deposit growth first decline and then turn negative. The final two columns show that the jumbo-CD-to-total-deposit ratio also drops significantly when enforcement actions are imposed on the bank.

Quarters to Failure (1)	Number of Banks (2)	Mean Asset Growth (3)	Median Asset Growth (4)	Mean Loan Growth (5)	Median Loan Growth (6)	Mean Deposit Growth (7)	Median Deposit Growth (8)	Mean Jumbo-CD Growth (9)	Median Jumbo-CD Growth (10)	Mean Jumbo CD/ Deposits Ratio (11)	Median Jumbo CD/ Deposits Ratio (12)
12	22	4.21	1.78	3.65	3.63	4.75	2.54	5.99	1.11	28.29	24.93
11	22	5.64	1.82	1.97	0.75	5.60	2.68	2.57	0.53	19.00	12.12
10	22	3.82	1.37	3.19	3.24	5.04	2.03	7.70	−1.10	15.66	3.95
9	23	6.98	0.91	6.47	1.45	8.39	2.61	7.42	−5.35	29.25	32.32
8	23	2.68	−0.84	9.25	1.02	5.32	−1.04	8.41	0.02	29.34	30.34
7	24	2.16	1.47	11.29	−0.17	2.97	1.78	1.14	−3.66	16.76	8.08
6	24	0.54	0.74	12.98	0.74	1.37	0.42	−3.20	0.23	17.25	15.07
5	24	−0.11	−3.43	3.68	−2.65	0.47	−3.31	−6.62	−10.08	23.74	21.40
4	24	−3.31	−3.37	−1.87	−2.77	−1.96	−2.81	−7.00	−9.09	17.46	9.35
3	24	−2.06	−1.74	−1.79	−3.10	−2.43	−1.95	−5.95	−9.62	14.45	7.24
2	24	−3.38	−3.64	−4.86	−5.01	−2.04	−2.40	−5.00	−6.04	11.99	6.21
1	24	−6.81	−7.77	−7.02	−5.74	−4.33	−4.71	−12.33	−11.36	13.09	7.29
0	17	−10.39	−10.55	−8.99	−9.63	−8.03	−7.83	−17.14	−16.63	8.70	4.98
All State Member Banks[1]	35,606	3.22	1.54	8.27	2.05	4.14	1.31	6.61	0.84	14.23	10.81

novos because their financial ratios tend to take extreme values (DeYoung, 1999).

We impose one additional restriction that differentiates our work from previous empirical work on market discipline – sample banks must boast satisfactory supervisory ratings. All U.S. banks undergo a full-scope federal or state examination every 18 months. Currently, these examinations focus on six components of safety and soundness – capital protection (C), asset quality (A), management competence (M), earnings strength (E), liquidity risk exposure (L), and market risk sensitivity (S). At the close of each exam, examiners award a grade of one (best) through five (worst) to each component. Supervisors then draw on these six component ratings to assign a composite CAMELS rating, which is also expressed on a one through five scale. In general, banks with "one" or "two" composite ratings are considered satisfactory while banks with "three," "four," or "five" ratings are considered unsatisfactory. The "S" component of the CAMELS rating was introduced January 1, 1997, so the supervisory ratings in our analysis are CAMEL composites.

We exclude observations from unsatisfactory banks to eliminate the observational equivalence problem noted earlier – changes in jumbo-CD yields or withdrawal patterns for these banks may be the product of supervisor rather than market discipline. Supervisors typically impose enforcement actions on banks receiving downgrades to unsatisfactory status (Gilbert & Vaughan, 2001). These supervisory actions, in turn, often include directives to improve regulatory capital ratios. Apart from the data presented earlier, other research has documented significant loan and deposit shrinkage at banks subject to enforcement actions (Peek & Rosengren, 1995, for example). To be certain that observed patterns in our sample reflect depositor rather than supervisor discipline, we limit our sample to banks receiving a "one" or "two" CAMEL composite rating on the last full-scope examination. We use satisfactory status as a proxy for the absence of enforcement actions because pre–1990 data on these actions is not available in consistent form from all three Federal bank regulators.

Even with the "satisfactory CAMEL" constraint, our sample was large and heterogeneous in both the pre-FDICIA and the post-FDICIA windows. True, the constraint eliminated 22% of the pre-FDICIA observations and 9% of post-FDICIA observations. Still, the 1988–1990 sample includes 32,134 observations, and the 1993–1995 sample includes 36,168 observations. More important, the remaining banks exhibit significant variation in condition. (See Table 3 for the sample statistics.) For example, the standard deviation of the summary measure of bank risk – the probability of failure in the next 24 months – is 4.41% (mean 1.05%) in the pre-FDICIA sample. Even with the

Table 3. How Do the Pre- and Post-FDICIA Samples Differ?

This table provides summary statistics for the sample banks in the pre- and post-FDICIA periods. Because of the banking crisis of the late 1980s, failure probabilities from the pre-FDICIA period are higher and more variable than in the post-FDICIA period. The measures of exposure to specific types of risk suggest that the higher pre-FDICIA failure probabilities stem from greater reliance on commercial loans, weaker asset quality higher liquidity risk, and weaker capital ratios. Jumbo-CD yields were also 334 basis points higher in the pre-FDICIA period than in the post-FDICIA period; this difference is traceable to higher overall bank risk and higher money market rates. Also of note, post-FDICIA banks were larger than pre-FDICIA banks, reflecting ongoing consolidation in the industry. Post-FDICIA banks were also more inclined to issue jumbo CDs with long maturities, more likely to use brokered deposits, and less likely to operate in a Metropolitan Statistical Area (MSA).

		Pre-FDICIA (1988–90) 32,134 observations		Post-FDICIA (1993–95) 36,168 observations	
Variable		Mean	Standard Deviation	Mean	Standard Deviation
Dependent Variables					
CD Yield		7.97%	1.90%	4.63%	1.26%
Jumbo deposit growth rate		3.56%	18.00%	4.05%	17.61%
Risk Variables – SEER and Its Components					
Probability of failure (SEER)		1.05%	4.41%	0.21%	1.56%
Credit Risk	Commercial and industrial loans/total assets	12.31%	8.27%	9.88%	6.99%
Credit Risk	Residential real estate loans/total assets	15.30%	9.62%	16.96%	10.25%
Credit Risk	Other real estate owned/total assets	0.35%	0.64%	0.23%	0.45%
Credit Risk	Loans 30 to 89 days past due/total assets	1.11%	0.92%	0.81%	0.69%
Credit Risk	Loans over 89 days past due/total assets	0.34%	0.47%	0.17%	0.32%
Credit Risk	Loans on nonaccrual status/total assets	0.54%	0.68%	0.39%	0.50%

Table 3. Continued.

Variable		Pre-FDICIA (1988–90) 32,134 observations Mean	Standard Deviation	Post-FDICIA (1993–95) 36,168 observations Mean	Standard Deviation
Risk Variables – SEER and Its Components – Continued					
Liquidity	Large time deposits/ total assets	14.18%	7.46%	11.10%	6.11%
	Book value of securities/total assets	28.47%	14.67%	32.63%	14.82%
Capital Protection	Tangible net worth/ total assets	8.51%	2.36%	9.37%	2.67%
	Yearly return on average assets	1.07%	0.58%	1.28%	0.55%
Total assets (in thousands)		$123,132	$80,708	$143,438	$94,131
Control Variables					
Percentage of fixed-rate jumbo CDs		99.05%	5.00%	98.18%	7.11%
Maturity-weighted Treasury yield		8.02%	0.58%	4.96%	1.15%
Weighted-average maturity (in years)		0.54	0.30	0.86	0.45
Maturity-Treasury volatility interactive term		0.11	0.55	0.32	0.65
Percentage of banks in holding companies		79.3%		79.9%	
Percentage of banks offering brokered deposits		5.4%		8.5%	
Percentage of banks in MSAs		52.5%		48.8%	

improvement in banking conditions in the 1990s, this summary measure still had a standard deviation of 1.56% (mean 0.21%) in the post-FDICIA sample.

We rely on call-report data to construct our measures of jumbo-CD yields. Only a handful of large money-center banks issue jumbo CDs that are actively traded in secondary markets, so real-time, market-generated yields are not available for community banks (Morris & Walter, 1993). It is possible, however, to use quarterly income-statement and balance-sheet data to construct average yields for almost every bank in the country. These yields can then be combined with data from the Treasury market – and appropriate control variables – to produce proxies for default premiums on jumbo CDs. Other researchers have successfully used this approach to test hypotheses about bank risk (for example, James, 1988; Keeley 1990; and, more recently, Martinez Peria & Schmukler, 2001). Figure 1 shows the quarterly sample mean of our yield measure along with various market interest rates over the sample period. Although derived entirely from accounting data, our measure tracks the market yields closely.

We model jumbo-CD yields and withdrawals as a function of a summary measure of bank risk and a vector of control variables. Specifically, we first estimate the following regression separately for the pre-FDICIA and the post-FDICIA samples:

$$P_{i,t} = \alpha + \beta\pi_{i,t} + \gamma'\chi_{i,t} + \varepsilon_{i,t} \quad (1)$$

where $P_{i,t}$ is the average jumbo-CD yield at bank i in time t, $\pi_{i,t}$ is a summary measure of bank risk, $\chi_{i,t}$ is a vector of control variables, α, β, and the vector γ are ordinary least squares regression coefficients, and $\varepsilon_{i,t}$ is an error term with the standard properties. In an alternate specification we use jumbo-CD growth as the dependent variable because uninsured depositors can react to risk by withdrawing their money rather than demanding a higher yield. Jumbo-CD growth is measured by the quarterly percentage change in outstanding balances, as indicated by each bank's call report. Specifically, we estimate:

$$Q_{i,t} = \delta + \phi\pi_{i,t} + \phi'\chi_{i,t} + \varepsilon_{i,t} \quad (2)$$

where Q_i is the percentage change in dollar volume of jumbo CDs at bank i over quarter t. Our growth equation is similar to growth equations estimated by Park (1995), Park and Peristiani (1998), and Aadland, Dahl and Stephen (2000). Our specification, however, relies on a different summary measure of bank risk and a different vector of control variables.

Following other studies, we use estimated probability of failure as the summary measure of bank risk. Unlike other studies that rely on failure probabilities generated by independently estimated models (Park & Peristiani, 1998, for example), we employ failure probabilities generated by the econometric model the Federal Reserve uses in off-site surveillance – the SEER risk-rank model. The SEER risk-rank model harnesses the latest quarterly call-report data for all U.S. commercial banks to estimate the probability that each Fed-supervised bank will fail within the next two years. The independent variables in the model include proxies for credit risk, liquidity risk, and leverage risk – along with a control variable for bank size. Table 4 describes these variables and notes the expected relationship between each variable and the likelihood of failure. Extensive in- and out-of-sample

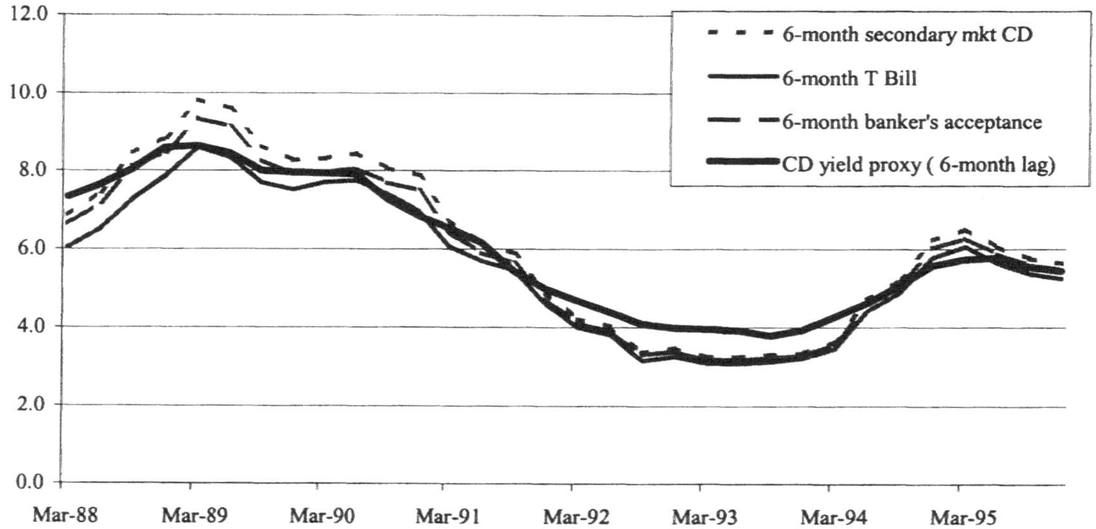

Fig. 1. Yield Proxy Versus Market Rates.

This figure compares the yield proxy that we constructed from the call report data to secondary-market yields on comparable instruments. Generally, the proxy tracks the other interest rates closely although with a lag. *Source: Federal Reserve Statistical Release H.15.*

Table 4. What are the SEER Failure-prediction Variables?

This table lists the independent variables used in the SEER (System to Estimate Examination Ratings) Risk-Rank model. The signs indicate the hypothesized relationship between each variable and the likelihood of failure in the next two years. For example, the negative sign for the net-income (ROA) ratio indicates that an increase in earnings will reduce the likelihood of failure, all other things equal. We use failure probabilities estimated by the SEER risk-rank model as indices of overall bank risk in our yield and runoff regressions.

Variable		Effect on failure probability
Credit Risk	Loans past due 30–90 days/total assets	+
	Loans past due 90+ days/total assets	+
	Nonaccrual loans/total assets	+
	Other real estate owned (OREO)/total assets	+
	Residential real estate loans/total assets	–
	Commercial and industrial loans/total assets	+
Leverage Risk	Tangible capital/total assets	–
	Net income/average assets (ROA)	–
Liquidity Risk	Investment securities/total assets	–
	Large time deposits/total assets	+
Control Variable	Natural log of total assets	–

"+" indicates that higher levels of the variable lead to higher probabilities of failure; "-" indicates the opposite.
Table adapted from Cole, Cornyn, and Gunther (1995).

validation tests were performed on the SEER risk-rank model at the time of its development in the early 1990s (Cole, Cornyn & Gunther, 1995). In addition, the risk-rank model is validated annually by the surveillance section at the Board of Governors. Finally, recent research has validated the risk-rank model in out-of-sample performance tests against other surveillance tools (Gilbert, Meyer & Vaughan, 2002). Figure 2 displays average SEER probabilities over time. Previous work on risk pricing by jumbo-CD holders tested a joint hypothesis:

(1) the failure prediction model estimated for the paper summarizes bank risk; and
(2) jumbo-CD holders price overall bank risk.

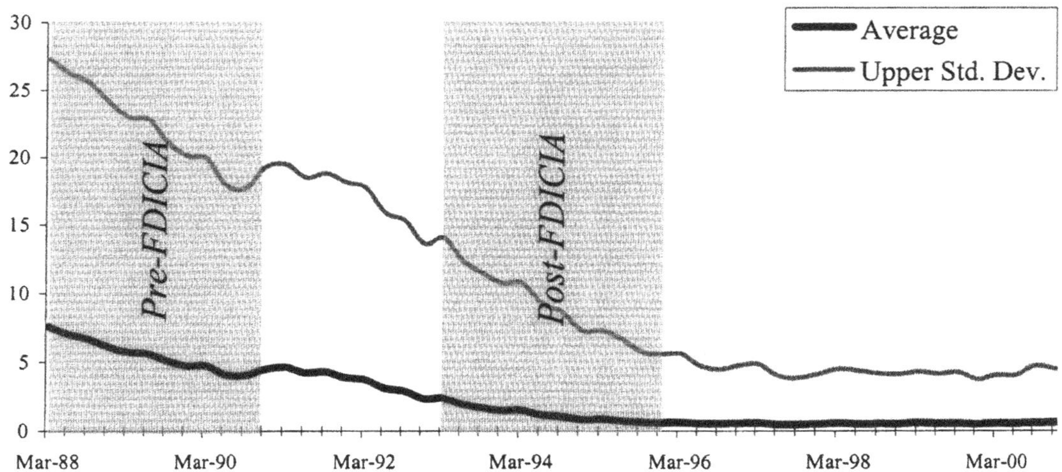

Fig. 2. SEER Failure Probabilities Over Time.

This figure shows how U.S. bank risk, as measured by the Federal Reserve's System to Estimate Examination Ratings, has varied over time. SEER indicates the probability that a bank will fail over a two-year horizon, based on a logistic regression containing eleven risk variables (see Table 4). In the pre-FDICIA period, both the average and the variance of bank risk were higher than in the post-FDICIA period.

By relying on a failure-prediction model that is actually used in bank surveillance, we test the second hypothesis cleanly.

One other problem with existing research is an inconsistent set of control variables in the yield and runoff equations. Broadly speaking, most other work controlled explicitly for idiosyncratic aspects of the jumbo-CD portfolio (such as the percentage of CDs with fixed rates and the average maturity of the portfolio), money market conditions, and market power of the issuing bank. Time dummies were then added to capture the impact of omitted variables. If other neglected variables have important influences on yields or runoff, and the time dummies inadequately capture the impact of these neglected variables, then the risk coefficients will be biased. Because tests of the statistical significance and economic importance of the risk coefficients are central to our work, we conduct an extensive search for appropriate control variables. Candidates for inclusion in the set control variables were drawn from examiner suggestions, previous jumbo-CD research, and other related market-discipline research. The control variables used in all previous work are nested in our vector of controls. After extensive experimentation with various combinations, we settled on a vector that controls for interest-rate levels, regional economic conditions, idiosyncratic aspects of the bank's jumbo-CD portfolio, and idiosyncratic aspects of demand and supply for the bank's jumbo CDs. Although multicollinearity leads to some instability in the coefficients on the control variables, the estimates of the risk coefficients – our principal focus – were remarkably stable across specifications.

Specifically, the "all other things equal" vector ($X_{i,t}$), includes a variable that directly controls for money market conditions and indirect controls for the average maturity of the jumbo-CD portfolio. To control for the general level of interest rates, we compute a maturity-weighted Treasury yield for each quarter using interest-rate data from the Federal Reserve Economic Database (FRED) at the Federal Reserve Bank of St. Louis. For each bank, the call report breaks the jumbo-CD portfolio into maturity ranges (0–3 months, 3–12 months, etc.) and reports the dollar value of jumbo CDs in each range. We then multiply the proportion of each bank's CDs in each maturity pool by the rate on comparable maturity Treasury issues in the same period to obtain the appropriate risk-free rate for calculating default spreads.

We also control for maturity directly by including each bank's average CD maturity in the yield and runoff regressions. This variable controls for term-structure and liquidity effects. An additional maturity-related issue arises from our use of accounting data to proxy for the yield on newly issued CDs. Because our yields are constructed by dividing total quarterly interest expense on jumbo CDs by the average balances, they conflate the rates paid on older CDs that have yet to mature with the rates paid on fresh issues. Banks with shorter average CD maturities will thus produce average yields that adjust more readily to market rates. In an environment in which interest rates are stable, the difference between the yields at banks with relatively short and long maturities will be negligible. When rates are changing rapidly, however, this effect will introduce an additional source of variation to the data. To address this problem, we include an interactive variable computed as the product of the two-quarter lag of each bank's average maturity and the most recent two-quarter change in the maturity-adjusted risk-free rate.

We control for another idiosyncratic aspect of each bank's jumbo-CD portfolio – the percentage of jumbo CDs with fixed as opposed to floating interest rates. This control is necessary because depositors bearing different levels of interest-rate risk may demand different risk premiums. The value of fixed rates to both depositors and banks depends on their individual interest-rate-risk positions, and so we have no prior about the direction of the influence of this variable on average yields.

We also control for the presence of a holding company behind the sample bank. In theory, depositors may perceive banks belonging to bank holding companies differently from institutions with no umbrella organization. For example, in the late 1980s – the period corresponding to our pre-FDICIA sample – Texas holding companies proved to be sources of weakness for subsidiary banks. Dozens of healthy subsidiary banks were shuttered when regulators closed the lead bank in the holding company (Cannella, Fraser & Lee, 1995). More generally, the Financial Institutions Reform, Recovery, and Enforcement Act of 1989 (FIRREA) included formal cross-guarantee provisions that made healthy subsidiary banks in a holding company responsible for losses incurred by the FDIC in connection with failed affiliates of the same holding company. Thus, jumbo-CD holders may look past the condition of an individual bank to the overall condition of the holding company. We control for a holding-company effect with a dummy variable that equals "1" when the given bank is a member of a holding company, and 0 otherwise. We also experimented with the ratio of subsidiary bank assets to total holding company assets (not reported) – on the premise that smaller members of large holding companies can enjoy more "source of strength" benefits from affiliation. Again, the risk coefficients were not sensitive to differences in holding company controls.

In addition, we control for a bank's willingness to tap national markets for funding. Some community banks can satisfy all their funding needs with core deposits and locally obtained jumbo CDs. And yields and runoffs for local jumbo CDs may be sticky because these deposits are essentially core deposits, showing little sensitivity to money market conditions or bank-specific risk either because of market power (Berger & Hannan, 1989) or retail adjustment costs (Flannery, 1982). Going to the national market for funding means paying the going rate. The call report does not distinguish jumbo CDs by the location of the holder, so we proxy with a variable designed to capture a bank's willingness to go outside its local market – a dummy variable equal to "one" for sample banks with brokered deposits. Brokered deposits are blocks of deposits just under the $100,000 insurance ceiling that move around the country in search of the highest yield. The Financial Institutions, Reform, Recovery and Enforcement Act of 1989 (FIRREA) restricted the use of brokered deposits by weakly capitalized institutions; examiners frown on the use of brokered deposits even by healthy banks. Thus, the presence of brokered deposits is a strong signal that a bank's funding needs exceed local supply. We also tried a model with the ratio of brokered deposits to total assets; once again, the signs and magnitudes of the risk coefficients were not affected.

We control directly for the impact of market power on jumbo-CD yields and runoff. Specifically, we use a dummy variable for banks located in Metropolitan Statistical Areas (MSAs) on the premise that banks in urban markets face more competition. Power in the local deposit market could enable a bank to offer less than the going rate on jumbo CDs, given current money market conditions and bank-specific risk. Banks with market power may also be less likely to take risks because of a desire to protect the value of their charter (Keeley, 1990), so in the absence of a proper control variable the risk coefficients could be biased. We also controlled for market power with the state-level Herfindahl-Hirschmann index for each bank (without using the state dummies discussed below). Again, the magnitudes of the risk coefficients did not change appreciably.

The vector of control variables also includes dummies for the state in which each sample bank operates. These dummies control for differences in regional economic conditions, state banking laws, and state income tax laws. We rely on state-level dummies to control for differences in regional economic conditions because recent research indicates that county-level economic conditions are not useful in predicting bank condition (Meyer & Yeager, 2001). We do not use a state-level economic series like the unemployment rate because they would be collinear with the state-dummy variables. (We did try state-level unemployment rates in a model excluding the state dummies. Again, the magnitudes of the failure-probability coefficients did not change appreciably.) State-level controls may also help control for differences in banking concentration not accounted for with the MSA dummy.

Finally, we control for any additional time effects with a dummy variable for each sample quarter. These dummies control for seasonal fluctuations in deposits and money market conditions and for business-cycle fluctuations inside of each sample window. These dummies also control for differences in the perceived condition of the deposit insurance fund. Cook and Spellman (1994) argue that losses on insured deposits are possible if the FDIC lacks the resources to indemnify depositors. Even if the public recognizes that insured deposits carry the full faith and credit of the U.S. government – as has been the case since the Competitive Banking Equality Act of 1987 – they may still fear the transaction costs associated with having funds tied up in a lengthy failure resolution. Cook and Spellman rely on time dummies to make their empirical case for risk premiums on retail deposits. In a similar vein, Cooperman, Lee and Wolfe (1992) use a different sample and a different empirical strategy to generate evidence of risk premiums on insured funds.

EMPIRICAL RESULTS

Overall, the yield and runoff equations fit the data well in both the pre-FDICIA and the post-FDICIA sample periods. (Tables 5 and 6 contain these regression results.) In all four equations, the block of bank-specific control variables is jointly significant; in most cases, the individual bank-specific controls are significant with the anticipated signs as well. The blocks of time and state dummies are also strongly significant. The R^2 are low in all four equations, but not out of line with figures reported in other studies. Particularly noteworthy is the 0.433 R^2 in the post-FDICIA yield regression. This high R^2 stems from the combined effects of greater interest-rate variability in the second period (see Fig. 1) and sluggishness in our measure of average yields. When interest rates are stable, the independent variables that incorporate maturity structure – average maturity, the maturity-weighted risk-free rate, and the interactive maturity variable – account only for term-structure effects, not for the effect of different rates paid on previously issued CDs. When rates fluctuate markedly, however, yields at short-maturity banks align more closely with the market than those at long-maturity banks, and the maturity variables account for most of the total variation in yields. This phenomenon also accounts for the higher statistical significance of the maturity-based variables in the second period.

The signs and magnitudes of the risk coefficients in the yield and runoff equations provide evidence about the extent of any discipline imposed by the jumbo-CD market. Positive, statistically significant risk coefficients for the yield equations and negative statistically significant risk coefficients for the runoff equations in each window would indicate some market discipline in that

Table 5. Do Jumbo-CD Yields React to Failure Probability?

Equation (1) Regression Results

This table reports results for regressions of jumbo-CD yields on estimated probabilities of failure and control variables. Positive and significant coefficients on failure probabilities are evidence of market discipline. Asterisks indicate statistical significance at the 5% (**) and 1% (***) levels. Coefficients on quarterly dummy variables and state dummy variables are not reported. The results indicate that in both periods banks with higher risk paid more for their uninsured deposits, although the economic significance of this discipline was small. In the pre-FDICIA period, a one-percentage-point increase in failure probability led to an average increase of 0.6 basis points in jumbo-CD yields. In the post-FDICIA period, the effect strengthened to 1.0 basis point.

	1988–90 (Pre-FDICIA)		1993–95 (Post-FDICIA)	
Independent Variable	Coefficient (Std. Error)		Coefficient (Std. Error)	
Probability of Failure	0.0061	**	0.0099	***
	(0.002)		(0.003)	
% Fixed Rate	0.0041	**	–0.0051	***
	(0.002)		(0.001)	
Maturity-weighted Treasury Yield	0.8555	***	0.8222	***
	(0.137)		(0.040)	
Maturity	0.0529		0.1136	***
	(0.047)		(0.023)	
Maturity-Treasury Interactive	–0.1695	***	–0.1917	***
	(0.039)		(0.018)	
Holding Company Dummy	0.0632	**	–0.0448	***
	(0.027)		(0.013)	
Brokered Deposit Dummy	0.2497	***	0.1084	***
	(0.048)		(0.018)	
MSA Dummy	–0.011		–0.04	***
	(0.023)		(0.011)	
R^2	0.084		0.433	
F-statistic Controls	16.69	***	284.78	***
F-statistic Time Dummies	42.74	***	248.46	***
F-statistic State Dummies	11.23	***	25.68	***
Observations	32,134		36,168	

window – that is, an increase in failure probability does translate into higher yields and faster runoff. A statistically significant increase in the risk coefficient in the post-FDICIA window relative to the pre-FDICIA window would signal an increase in risk sensitivity (market discipline) following the act. The

Table 6. Do Jumbo-CD Growth Rates React to Failure Probability?

Equation (2) Regression Results

This table reports results for regressions of jumbo-CD growth rates on estimated probabilities of failure and control variables. Positive and significant coefficients on failure probabilities are evidence of market discipline. Asterisks indicate statistical significance at the 5% (**) and 1% (***) levels. Coefficients on quarterly dummy variables and state dummy variables are not reported. The results indicate that in both periods banks with higher risk experienced slower deposit growth, although the economic significance of this discipline was small. In the pre-FDICIA period, a one-percentage-point increase in failure probability led to an average decrease of 15 basis points in jumbo-CD growth. In the post-FDICIA period, the effect strengthened to 16 basis points.

	1988–90 (Pre-FDICIA)		1993–95 (Post-FDICIA)	
Independent Variable	Coefficient (Std. Error)		Coefficient (Std. Error)	
Probability of Failure	–0.1506	***	–0.1617	***
	(0.023)		(0.059)	
% Fixed Rate	0.0461	**	0.0035	
	(0.020)		(0.013)	
Maturity-weighted Treasury Yield	–5.7627	***	–4.9917	***
	(1.337)		(0.737)	
Maturity	–0.5448		–0.5222	
	(0.455)		(0.419)	
Maturity-Treasury Interactive	0.6399	*	4.0265	***
	(0.377)		(0.321)	
Holding Company Dummy	0.0131		0.4901	**
	(0.259)		(0.242)	
Brokered Deposit Dummy	0.5686		0.9599	***
	(0.465)		(0.336)	
MSA Dummy	0.2315		0.5408	***
	(0.226)		(0.198)	
R^2	0.024		0.036	
F-statistic Controls	6.84	***	33.90	***
F-statistic Time Dummies	30.68	***	36.88	***
F-statistic State Dummies	4.98	***	3.41	***
Observations	32,134		36,168	

magnitude of the risk coefficients – in each window and across the two windows – indicates the economic significance of this discipline. Applying estimated risk coefficients to the income statements and balance sheets of the average sample bank in each period offers insight into the economic implications of coefficient magnitudes.

Evidence from the yield and runoff regressions indicates that jumbo-CD holders priced failure risk in both the pre- and post-FDICIA windows, but that little – if any – change in risk sensitivity followed FDICIA. The risk coefficients are significant at the one-percent level in the yield equations for both sample periods. In the pre-FDICIA sample, a one-percentage-point increase in the SEER failure probability boosts jumbo-CD yields by 0.61 basis points; in the post-FDICIA sample, the risk effect is 0.99 basis points for every one-percentage-point increase in failure probability. The p-value for a test of the difference in risk coefficients is 0.4748, however, so we cannot rule out the possibility that risk sensitivities in each period are equal. In the runoff equations, the coefficient on the SEER probability is negative and significant at the one-percent level in the pre-FDICIA sample; the estimated coefficient (–0.1506) implies that a one-percentage-point increase in failure probability produces a 15-basis-point run-off in jumbo-CD holdings for the quarter. In the post-FDICIA sample, the risk coefficient is also negative and significant; the coefficient (–0.1617) implies that a one-percentage point increase in failure probability translates into a 16-basis-point quarterly run-off in jumbo CDs. The difference in the estimated risk coefficients across the two sample periods (–0.0111), though in the anticipated direction, is even smaller than the differences across periods in risk coefficients from the yield regressions. And the p-value for a test of differences in runoff sensitivity is 0.8637.

To sort out the economic meaning of these results, we examine the profitability penalty for risk taking implied by these risk coefficients. Specifically, we compute the difference in return on assets – a common measure of bank profitability – that would have obtained between a safe bank and a risky bank in each window, assuming that the banks conformed to sample averages in every other respect. We define a safe bank and a risky bank with extreme values – zero% failure probability and 100% failure probability – to provide upper bounds for assessments of economic significance. Our regression results show that in both periods the risky bank would have paid a higher CD yield and would have issued fewer CDs. Return on assets would, therefore, have been influenced by four separate effects:

(1) the higher interest expense on newly issued jumbo CDs;
(2) the shift from jumbo CDs to other types of funding;
(3) the foregone revenue from slower asset growth; and
(4) the smaller asset base.

For simplicity, we assume that all jumbo-CD runoff is reflected one-for-one in assets and that yields on other bank assets and liabilities remain constant.

The estimated profitability penalties suggest that the jumbo-CD market imposed little effective discipline on community banks either before or after FDICIA. Under our assumptions, moving from zero-percent failure probability to 100-percent failure probability in the pre-FDICIA period would have reduced ROA by 3.8 basis points – just 3.55% of the mean ROA (1.07%) and 6.55% of the standard deviation of ROA for the period (0.58%). Similarly, in the post-FDICIA sample, ROA would have fallen 4.3 basis points – a figure equal to 3.36% of the mean ROA (1.28%) and 7.82% of the standard deviation of ROA for the period (0.55%). Under more plausible definitions of safe and risky banks – a one-percentage point increase in failure probability, for example – the penalties for risk taking virtually vanish. To estimate the impact of FDICIA explicitly, we apply the post-FDICIA penalties for risk taking to the average pre-FDICIA bank. This approach controls for the sizable differences in bank capital levels across the two periods, differences resulting from imposition of the Basle Accords (Aggarwal & Jacques, 2001; Wall & Peterson, 1995). By this method, FDICIA would have reduced ROA through the jumbo-CD channel by one-tenth of a basis point.

ROBUSTNESS CHECKS

It is important to check our findings for robustness by using different lag structures for failure probability. In our baseline specification, failure probability enters with one lag because depositors usually learn about bank condition this quarter when call report data are released next quarter. Longer lags may be necessary to align failure probabilities more closely with average yields. For example, if a bank's CD portfolio has an average maturity of six months, the average yield paid will depend on at least two quarterly lags of failure probability. Additional lags may also be necessary because jumbo-CD holders face adjustment costs such as explicit penalties for early withdrawal or implicit costs of establishing new banking relationships.

We experiment with two different approaches to lagging failure probabilities. First, we enter the first three lags as separate regressors and sum the coefficients to determine their cumulative effect. Second, we enter the average of the first three lags as a single regressor. We use three lags to cover the period when most of the interest expense was incurred; average maturity in the sample varied from roughly six months at the beginning of the pre-FDICIA period to roughly nine months at the end of the post-FDICIA period. The results, displayed in Table 7, show that introducing lags does not alter our fundamental conclusions

Table 7. How Sensitive Are the Results to Different Lag Structures?

Because our average jumbo-CD yields are actually weighted averages of yields paid in previous quarters, our yields may reflect banks' past risk positions more than their present ones. To account for this possibility, we ran a distributed-lag model using three past quarters of failure probabilities. (The contemporaneous quarter is always omitted to avoid simultaneity issues and because information may not be immediately available to the market.) As shown in the table, the sums of the distributed-lag coefficients are not substantially different from the coefficients in our baseline model. We also tried a third specification, in which we used the mean failure probability at each bank over the previous three quarters. Again, these results differed little from those obtained with the baseline model.

	Yield Regression	
Lag Structure	Pre-FDICIA Coefficient(s)	Post-FDICIA Coefficient(s)
Lag 1 (Baseline)	0.0061**	0.0099***
Lags 1, 2, and 3	0.0059	0.0037
	–0.0035	0.0053
	0.0045	0.0016
	Sum 0.0069 **	Sum 0.0106 ***
Mean of lags 1, 2, and 3	0.0069 **	0.0105 ***
	Quantity Regression	
Lag 1 (Baseline)	–0.1506 ***	–0.1617 ***
Lags 1, 2, and 3	–0.1883 ***	–0.2157 *
	0.0834	–0.0184
	0.0432	0.0811
	Sum –0.1480 ***	Sum –0.1530 **
Mean of lags 1, 2, and 3	–0.1548 ***	–0.1395 **

– failure probability has a statistically significant but economically unimportant impact on jumbo-CD yields and run-off. In our baseline specification (one lag), the pre- and post-FDICIA coefficients are 0.0061 and 0.0099. The sum of the lagged coefficients for the pre-FDICIA sample is 0.0069 and for the post-FDICIA sample is 0.0106; the results for the average of the three lags, unsurprisingly, are virtually identical. In the quantity regression, the sum of the three lagged failure-probability coefficients is –0.1480 in the pre-FDICIA window, compared with –0.1506 in the baseline (one lag) specification. In the post-FDICIA window, the sum of the lagged coefficients is –0.1530, compared with –0.1617 in the baseline regression. Once again, the results for the average of three lags are virtually the same.

As another robustness check, we divide the sample banks into quartiles based on deposits-at-risk, dependence on jumbo-CD funding, and size; then we re-estimate the yield and runoff equations for each quartile. Breaking into quartiles may reveal patterns obscured by simply including these variables as independent regressors. For example, one possible reason for the economic insignificance of failure probability is that average uninsured balances barely exceed $100,000 for many of the sample banks. That is, ten holders of $101,000 jumbo CDs have less incentive to monitor and discipline the issuing bank than one holder of a $1,010,000 jumbo CD. Similarly, community banks that depend heavily on jumbo CDs might be more reliant on national markets where transaction terms are responsive to money market conditions and bank-specific risk. Finally, larger community banks may have more sophisticated jumbo-CD holders or may rely less on municipalities for jumbo CDs. Most municipal deposits are collateralized by blue-chip securities, so they are virtually free of default risk. We split the sample into quartiles based on each of these factors – deposits-at-risk, jumbo-CD balances as a percentage of total assets, and asset size – and estimate the yield and runoff equations for each quartile separately. With the exception of the yield equations for deposits-at-risk, no discernable pattern emerges from the data. The yield equations did show a slight rise in risk sensitivity for banks with larger average deposits-at-risk in the post-FDICIA equations. The estimated coefficients for the two highest quartiles, though statistically different from both zero and the coefficients for the lowest quartile, were still economically small.

DISCUSSION – DOES MEASUREMENT ERROR OR LIABILITY SUBSTITUTION ACCOUNT FOR THE RESULTS?

One possible non-economic explanation for our findings is measurement error. The chief source of this error is our use of *average* CD yields (i.e. total interest expense paid on CDs divided by total CDs outstanding) to proxy for *marginal* yields (i.e. the yields on newly issued CDs or CDs traded in an active secondary market). The extent of the error will be most pronounced when:

(1) a bank's CDs are of long maturity, so that yields adjust more slowly to current market conditions; and

(2) market yields are fluctuating rapidly, so that current market conditions are much different from past market conditions.

Measurement error is only a potential problem in the yield equation (Eq. (1)); the runoff variable in Eq. (2) is not subject to the average-vs.-marginal problem and thus is measured without error.

Measurement error inflates standard errors and biases coefficient estimates, so analyzing its potential effect on the yield equations is important. Inefficiency is of lesser concern for our purposes because the estimated risk coefficients are strongly significant in the yield equations for both periods. As for the potential bias, measurement error occurs chiefly in the dependent variable, so estimates of the risk coefficients are biased only if that error is correlated with failure probability. Moreover, as noted by Hoshi, Kashyap and Scharfstein (1991), even if an estimated coefficient is biased for a given sample, the difference in estimates of the same coefficient across two samples will not be biased if the degree of measurement error is the same in the two samples. In short, measurement error will affect our central result – the increase in discipline from the jumbo-CD market following FDICIA is economically trivial – if it is more highly correlated with failure probability in one period than in the other.

By definition, we cannot pinpoint the magnitude of the measurement error (or its correlation with failure probability) directly, but certain features of our data suggest that its effect is small. For example, the marginal-average measurement problem will be most pronounced among banks with long jumbo-CD maturities and in times when interest rates are changing rapidly. The correlation of failure probability with changes in average secondary-market CD rates is only 2% in the pre-FDICIA sample and just negative 1% in the post-FDICIA sample; the correlation with average CD maturity is only negative 3% in both periods.

By imposing assumptions on our data, we can get an even better impression of the magnitude of the measurement error problem. We cannot observe the marginal yield changes in each quarter, but they are likely to follow changes in money market interest rates closely. We therefore proxy changes in each bank's marginal yields with the change in the average secondary-market yield on six-month negotiable CDs, as reported in the Federal Reserve Economic Database. By further assuming that each bank's CD maturities are uniformly distributed, we can calculate the approximate measurement error resulting from the use of average rather than marginal yields. (Relevant summary statistics are reported in Table 8.) By these calculations, the correlation between estimated measurement error and failure probability in the pre-FDICIA sample is –0.02; in the post-FDICIA sample, it is 0.01. Although this difference is statistically

Table 8. How Big is the Measurement-error Problem?

This table presents evidence on the measurement-error bias introduced by our use of an accounting proxy for jumbo-CD yields. Because this proxy conflates the yield offered in any given quarter with yields offered in past quarters that have yet to mature, the error will be most severe when the actual market yields are changing rapidly and when banks have long average CD maturities. Because the yield proxy is a dependent variable, the measurement error will bias the coefficient on failure probability if the measurement error is correlated with failure probability. The low univariate correlations between (1) CD yields and SEER probabilities and (2) maturities and SEER probabilities suggest that the measurement error bias is low. Moreover, when we impose assumptions to construct an approximation of the measurement error (see text), we find that it is small and that adjusting for the error does not materially alter the results.

	Pre-FDICIA			Post-FDICIA		
	Mean	Standard Deviation	Correlation with Failure Probability	Mean	Standard Deviation	Correlation with Failure Probability
Average yield (%)	7.97	1.90	0.008	4.63	1.26	–0.002
Maturity (in years)	0.54	0.30	–0.041	0.85	0.45	–0.038
Change in secondary-market yield (%)	0.06	0.06	0.027	0.16	0.46	–0.004
Estimated measurement error (%)	0.02	0.49	–0.026	–0.09	0.48	0.010
Adjusted average yield (%)	7.94	1.88	0.015	4.72	1.15	–0.007

significant, the small magnitude suggests that coefficient bias differs little across the two periods.

We can also attempt to correct the bias in regression coefficients in both periods by subtracting the measurement-error estimates from our measured average yields and re-running the regressions on the corrected variables. The new estimates will still be subject to some measurement error, but this error will be second order. Following this procedure produces little change in the regression estimates. The coefficient on failure probability becomes 0.0062 in the pre-FDICIA period (rather than the 0.0061 estimated on the uncorrected yields) and 0.0098 (rather than 0.0099) in the post-FDICIA period. The coefficients on the control variables also do not change appreciably when the adjusted yield is used as the dependent variable. It thus appears that, although our yield variable is measured with error, the bias introduced by this error is negligible.

Another potential explanation for our findings is liability substitution. Billet, Garfinkel and O'Neal (1998) and Jordan (2000) document a tendency among risky institutions to substitute insured deposits for risk-priced funding to escape penalties for risk-taking. Although community banks had difficulty raising insured deposits in the post-FDICIA era, they were able to obtain easily another type of funding with no default-risk premium – Federal Home Loan Bank advances (Stojanovic, Vaughan & Yeager, 2001). Our estimated risk sensitivities may be low because risky banks funded most of their growth with FHLB funding rather than jumbo CDs.

To test this possibility we analyzed jumbo-CD usage in the post-FDICIA window for banks that joined and did not join the Federal Home Loan Bank System. For each bank that joined the FHLB System between 1993 and 1995, a peer was chosen based on asset size, geographic location, and initial overall risk level. We matched banks by initial risk level to determine whether FHLB joiners used less jumbo-CD funding, all other things equal, than non-joiners in the years following membership. The sample consisted of 1,743 banks that joined the FHLB between 1993 and 1995, each matched to a peer. A difference of means test, based on the two-year period following membership, shows that the jumbo-CD-to-total-asset ratio increased by 1.46% for joiners and 1.51% for non-joiners. This difference is not statistically significant at even the 10% level. In short, these tests provide no support for the notion that access to FHLB advances undermined the discipline of the jumbo-CD market in our post-FDICIA sample.

CONCLUSIONS

The Federal Deposit Insurance Corporation Improvement Act of 1991 directed the FDIC to resolve bank failures in the least-costly manner. This directive shifted more of the burden of failure-resolution costs to holders of jumbo certificates of deposits. Using call report data, we examined the sensitivity of community-bank jumbo-CD yields and runoffs to bank-specific risk before and after FDICIA. We also examined the economic significance of estimated risk sensitivities, looking at the implied impact of risk on funding costs and profits. The results indicate that yield and runoff measures were sensitive to bank-specific risk before and after FDICIA. But the estimated risk coefficients in the pre-act and post-act samples were small. Even more to the point, these coefficients were not statistically or economically different across the two sample periods. In short, the evidence suggests that the jumbo-CD market put little pressure on community banks to contain risk – even after uninsured depositors were exposed to more default risk.

Frictions in the jumbo-CD market could explain our results. As noted, it is possible that jumbo CDs issued by community banks are relatively free of default risk because balances belong mostly to municipalities and that our robustness check did not control adequately for this pledging. The call report notes the dollar value of investment securities that are pledged but does not indicate which liabilities are collateralized by the securities. Another possibility is that jumbo-CD rates posted by community banks "cluster" around integers and even fractions (Kahn, Pennacchi & Sopranzetti, 1999); such clustering would make rates less responsive to changes in bank risk. Similarly, jumbo-CD holders may also receive other services – commercial loans and checking services, for example – from their community bank and, thus, price the relationship comprehensively rather than CDs individually. A final possibility is that holders of community-bank jumbo CDs are simply noise traders, giving little thought to default-risk when deciding where to place their funds.

We are not persuaded, however, that market frictions account solely for our findings; the long business-cycle expansion of the 1990s, no doubt, also plays a role. Over this period, bank profitability ratios, capital ratios, and reserves-to-problem loan ratios soared to near record highs while failure rates plummeted to near record lows. In such an environment, jumbo-CD yields and runoff rates are unlikely to react strongly to bank risk because the benefits of monitoring are so low. Put another way, expected losses should failure occur rose with the implementation of least-cost resolution, but – at the same time – the probability of that failure plunged. (See Fig. 2). Thus, expected losses – the variable that motivates uninsured depositors to monitor and discipline risk – may actually have fallen. This explanation would account for the successful use of average yields in bank-risk studies a decade ago – a time when financial distress was fairly common and failures were sharply rising. In short, the peculiarity of the sample period may undermine attempts to assess the disciplinary potential of jumbo CDs. Assessing the potential of the jumbo-CD market as a third pillar in community-bank supervision may have to await data from all phases of the business cycle.

ACKNOWLEDGMENTS

Critical feedback from a number of sources greatly improved this work. Specifically, we would like to thank Nasser Arshadi, Rosalind Bennett, Lee Benham, Mark Carey, Mike Dueker, Doug Evanoff, Steve Fazzari, Mark Flannery, Alton Gilbert, Sylvia Hudgins, John Jordan, John Krainer, Bill Lang, Ed Lawrence, Jose Lopez, Evren Ors, Frank Schmid, Sherrill Shaffer, Scott Smart, Larry Wall, Dave Wheelock, and Tim Yeager for helpful comments and discussions. We also profited from exchanges with seminar participants at the Financial Management Association meetings, the Office of the Comptroller of the Currency, the Southern Finance Association meetings, and Washington University in St. Louis. Any remaining errors and omissions are ours alone. The views expressed in this paper do not represent official positions of the Federal Reserve Bank of St. Louis, the Board of Governors, or the Federal Reserve System.

REFERENCES

Aadland, D., Dahl, D., & Stephen, A. (2000). Deposit Rate Premiums and the Demand for Funds by Thrifts. In: G. Kaufman (Ed.), *Bank Fragility and Regulation: Evidence from Different Countries* (pp. 177–190). New York: Elsevier Science.

Aggarwal, R., & Jacques, K. T. (2001). The Impact of FDICIA and Prompt Corrective Action on Bank Capital and Risk: Estimates Using a Simultaneous Equations Model. *Journal of Banking and Finance, 25*, 1139–1160.

Baer, H., & Brewer, E., III (1986). Uninsured Deposits as a Source of Market Discipline: Some New Evidence. Federal Reserve Bank of Chicago. *Economic Perspectives*, (September/October), 23–31.

Bassett, W. F., & Brady, T. F. (2001). The Economic Performance of Small Banks, 1985–2000. *Federal Reserve Bulletin*, (November), 719–728.

Benston, G. J., & Kaufman, G. G. (1998). Deposit Insurance Reform in the FDIC Improvement Act: The Experience to Date. The Federal Reserve Bank of Chicago, *Economic Perspectives*, (2nd Quarter), 2–20.

Berger, A. N., & Davies, S. M. (1998). The Information Content of Bank Examinations. *Journal of Financial Services Research, 14*, 117–144.

Berger, A. N., & Hannan, T. H. (1989). The Price-Concentration Relationship in Banking. *Review of Economics and Statistics, 71*, 291–299.

Billet, M. T., Garfinkel, J. A., & O' Neal, E. S. (1998). The Cost of Market vs. Regulatory Discipline in Banking. *Journal of Financial Economics, 48*, 333–358.

Bliss, R. R., & Flannery, M. J. (2001). Market Discipline in the Governance of U.S. Bank Holding Companies: Monitoring vs. Influence. In: F. S. Mishkin (Ed.), *Prudential Supervision: What Works and What Doesn't* (pp. 107–143). Chicago: University of Chicago Press.

Brewer, E., III, & Mondschean, T. H. (1994). An Empirical Test of the Incentive Effects of Deposit Insurance. *Journal of Money, Credit, and Banking, 26*, 146–164.

Cannella, A. A., Jr, Fraser, D. R., & Lee, D. S. (1995). Firm Failure and Managerial Labor Markets: Evidence from Texas Banking. *Journal of Financial Economics, 38*, 185–210.

Cargill, T. F. (1989). CAMEL Ratings and the CD Market. *Journal of Financial Services Research, 3*, 347–358.

Cole, R. A., Cornyn, B. G., & Gunther, J. W. (1995). FIMS: A New Monitoring System for Banking Institutions. Federal Reserve. *Bulletin*, (January), 1–15.

Cook, D. O., & Spellman, L. J. (1994). Repudiation Risk and Restitution Costs: Toward Understanding Premiums on Insured Deposits. *Journal of Money, Credit, and Banking, 26*, 439–459.

Cooperman, E. S., Lee, W. B., & Wolfe, G. A. (1992). The 1985 Ohio Thrift Crises, the FSLIC's Solvency, and Rate Contagion for Retail CDs. *Journal of Finance, 47*, 919–941.

Crabbe, L., & Post, M. A. (1994). The Effect of a Rating Downgrade on Outstanding Commercial Paper. *Journal of Finance*, *49*, 39–56.

Crane, D. B. (1976). A Study of Interest Rate Spreads in the 1974 CD Market. *Journal of Bank Research*, (Autumn), 213–224.

DeYoung, R. (1999). Birth, Growth, and Life or Death of Newly Chartered Banks. Federal Reserve Bank of Chicago. *Economic Perspectives*, (3rd Quarter), 18–35.

Ellis, D., & Flannery, M. J. (1992). Does the Debt Market Assess Large Banks' Risk? *Journal of Monetary Economics*, *30*, 481–502.

Flannery, M. J. (1982). Retail Bank Deposits as Quasi-Fixed Factors of Production. *American Economic Review*, *72*, 527–536.

Flannery, M. J., & Houston, J. F. (1999). The Value of a Government Monitor for U.S. Banking Firms. *Journal of Money, Credit, and Banking*, *31*, 14–34.

Flannery, M. J., & Sorescu, S. M. (1996). Evidence of Bank Market Discipline in Subordinated Debenture Yields: 1983–1991. *Journal of Finance*, *51*, 1347–1377.

Gilbert, R. A. (1993). Implications of Annual Examinations for the Bank Insurance Fund. Federal Reserve Bank of St. Louis. *Review*, (January/February), 35–52.

Gilbert, R. A. (1992). The Effects of Legislating Prompt Corrective Action on the Bank Insurance Fund. The Federal Reserve Bank of St. Louis. *Review*, July/August, 3–22.

Gilbert, R. A., & Vaughan, M. D. (2001). Do Depositors Care about Enforcement Actions? *Journal of Economics and Business*, *53*, 283–311.

Gilbert, R. A., Meyer, A. P., & Vaughan, M. D. (2002). The Role of a CAMELS Downgrade Model in Bank Surveillance. Federal Reserve Bank of St. Louis. *Review*, (January/February), 47–63.

Goldberg, L. G., & Hudgins, S. C. (2002). Depositor Discipline and Changing Strategies for Regulating Thrift Institutions. *Journal of Financial Economics*, *63*, 263–274.

Goldberg, M. A., & Lloyd-Davies, P. R. (1985). Standby Letters of Credit: Are Banks Overextending Themselves? *Journal of Bank Research*, *16*, (Spring), 29–39.

Gunther, J. W., & Moore, R. R. (2000). Financial Statements and Reality: Do Troubled Banks Tell All? Federal Reserve Bank of Dallas. *Economic and Financial Review*, (3rd Quarter), 30–35.

Hannan, T. H., & Hanweck, G. (1988). Bank Insolvency Risk and the Market for Large CDs. *Journal of Money, Credit, and Banking*, (May), 438–446.

Hoshi, T., Kashyap, A., & Scharfstein, D. (1991). Corporate Structure, Liquidity, and Investment: Evidence from Japanese Industrial Groups. *Quarterly Journal of Economics*, *106*, 33–60.

James, C. (1991). The Losses Realized in Bank Failures. *Journal of Finance*, *46*, 1223–1242.

James, C. (1988). The Use of Loan Sales and Standby Letters of Credit by Commercial Banks. *Journal of Monetary Economics*, *22*, 395–422.

Jones, D. S., & King, K. K. (1995). The Implementation of Prompt Corrective Action. *Journal of Banking and Finance*, *19*, 491–510.

Jordan, J. S. (2000). Depositor Discipline at Failing Banks. Federal Reserve Bank of Boston. *New England Economic Review*, (March/April), 15–28.

Kahn, C., Pennacchi, G., & Sopranzetti, B. (1999). Bank Deposit Rate Clustering: Theory and Empirical Evidence. *Journal of Finance*, *56*, 2185–2214.

Keeley, M. C. (1990). Deposit Insurance, Risk and Market Power in Banking. *American Economic Review*, *80*, 1183–1200.

Martinez P., Soledad, M., & Schmukler, S. L. (2001). Do Depositors Punish Banks for Bad Behavior? Market Discipline, Deposit Insurance, and Banking Crises. *Journal of Finance*, *56*, 1029–1051.

Meyer, A. P., & Yeager, T. J. (2001). Are Small Rural Banks Vulnerable to Local Economic Downturns? Federal Reserve Bank of St. Louis. *Review*, (March/April), 25–39.

Morris, M. D., & Walter, J. R. (1993). Large Negotiable Certificates of Deposit. In: T. Q. Cook & R. K. LaRoche (Eds), *Instruments of the Money Market* (pp. 34–47). Richmond, VA: Federal Reserve Bank of Richmond.

Park, S. (1995). Market Discipline by Depositors: Evidence from Reduced-Form Equations. *Quarterly Review of Economics and Finance*, *35*, 497–514.

Park, S., & Peristiani, S. (1998). Market Discipline by Thrift Depositors. *Journal of Money, Credit, and Banking*, *30*, 346–364.

Peek, J., & Rosengren, E. S. (1995). Bank Regulation and the Credit Crunch. *Journal of Banking and Finance*, *19*, 679–692.

Peek, J., & Rosengren, E. S. (1997). Will Legislated Early Intervention Prevent the Next Banking Crisis? *Southern Economic Journal*, *64*, 268–280.

Stojanovic, D., Vaughan, M. D., & Yeager, T. J. (2001). Do Federal Home Loan Advances and Membership Lead to More Bank Risk? In: *The Financial Safety Net: Costs, Benefits, and Implications for Regulations – Proceedings of the 37th Annual Conference on Bank Structure and Competition* (pp. 165–196).

Wall, L. D., & Peterson, D. R. (1995). Bank Holding Company Capital Targets in the Early 1990s: the Regulators vs. the Markets. *Journal of Banking and Finance*, 563–574.

COMMENT

Benton E. Gup

IS MARKET DISCIPLINE WISHFUL THINKING?

The title of this session is *Market Discipline by Bank Creditors*. In order to put the papers presented at this meeting in perspective, I begin with a discussion of what is meant by market discipline, and then examine it as a tool for bank regulation. The three papers are considered within the broad context of their contribution to understanding market discipline.

WHAT IS MARKET DISCIPLINE?

Market discipline is not a new concept in banking, but its meaning has changed over time. Market discipline can be traced back to the free-banking era in Scotland (1695–1845) and it began in the U.S. in 1838. Then it was assumed that rational depositors with sufficient information would invest in safe banks, and banks that were not safe would fail. Leathers and Raines (2000), writing about the history of market discipline, say that in the extreme form, "market discipline means total reliance upon competitive market forces imposing losses and ultimately failure on suppliers that do not operate efficiently."[1]

While it is clear that market discipline in the Darwinian sense of the survival of the fittest does work, that is not the way it is defined by bank regulators. A 1999 Staff Study by the Federal Reserve defines direct and indirect market discipline.[2] Direct market discipline is the cost of borrowed funds which reflects the bank's risk profile. The study claims that cost provides an ex ante incentive for the bank to refrain from taking on more risk. Indirect market

Prompt Corrective Action in Banking: 10 Years Later, Volume 14, pages 95–102.

ISBN: 0-7623-0987-3

discipline is exerted by private parties, or government regulators, who monitor the secondary market prices of interest rate sensitive instruments to assess bank risk.

In January 2001, the Basel Committee on Banking Supervision issued a proposal for a New Basel Capital Accord that is based on three complementary Pillars:

(1) minimum capital requirements;
(2) supervisory review; and
(3) market discipline.[3]

The Basel Committee aims to encourage market discipline by developing a set of disclosure recommendations (and requirements) that will allow market participants to assess information on the scope of application, capital risk exposures, risk assessment and management processes, and therefore the capital adequacy of the bank.[4]

Andrew Crockett (2001), General Manager of the Bank of International Settlements and Chairman of the Stability Forum, said that "market discipline" denotes internal and external governance mechanisms in a free-market economy in the absence of direct government intervention. He goes on to say that for market discipline to be effective, participants require information, the ability to process it, incentives, and a mechanism to invoke the discipline.[5]

Benink and Wihlborg (2002) say that banks are given incentives by debt and equity market participants. Scott (1991) and Rose (1999) go further, and they claim that market discipline occurs when market participants "punish" banks for making bad decisions. The punishment may come in the form of having to pay higher rates on CDs and other borrowed funds, and lower stock prices.

The strongest definition presented here is from Bliss and Flannery (2000) who state that the concept of market discipline requires that investors *evaluate* the true condition of a firm, and that the managers *respond* to the investor feedback impounded in the security prices.

DIFFERENT INTEPRETATIONS OF INFORMATION

In general terms, market discipline means that good or bad information about a firm is reflected in the prices or interest rates of its' securities. What happens when inside and outside investors have adequate information, and they disagree about whether the information is good or bad?

Consider the Hewlett-Packard and Compaq merger. In September 2001, Hewlett-Packard's CEO, Carleton (Carly) Fiorina offered to buy Compaq Computer Corporation for about $21 billion – the largest high-tech merger to date. Both firms were earning less than their cost of capital.[6] Nevertheless, it was hoped that the merger would result in increased efficiencies. Was that good news or bad news? The answer is that it was good news for some and bad news for others. Several of Carly's own board members, including Walter B. Hewlett and David W. Packard, were against it, as were CalPERS, UBS Warburg, Wells Fargo & Co., and other institutional investors who considered it bad news. On the other hand, other institutional investors (e.g. Barclays Global Investors, Putnam Investment Management, and Alliance Capital management) supported the merger. In addition Institutional Shareholder Services (ISS, a proxy advisory firm) recommended that investors vote for the merger on March 19, 2002.[7] On March 6, 2002, the Federal Trade Commission approved the merger.

Hewlett-Packard Company won the proxy fight to buy Compaq Computer Corp by a small margin of 2.8% of the voting shareholders. This outcome can be interpreted to support market discipline, or to say that it is not effective because both insiders and outsiders disagreed on whether the merger is good or bad.

DEBT SPREADS

The study presented at this meeting by Evanoff and Wall (2002), *Subdebt and PCA* reveal that subordinated debt spreads over treasuries provide useful information to bank regulators. While that may be so, advocates of using subordinated debt to provide market discipline ignore the fact that both bank regulators and rating agencies treat the subordinated debt as though it were equity for purposes of capital regulation. They can call it whatever they want to, but debt by any other name is still debt, and it increases a firm's financial leverage and its financial risk.

In very general terms, large interest rate spreads over risk-free securities are associated with high risk. Frame and Wall (2002) laud Fannie Mae and Freddie Mac for their voluntary initiatives that are intended to improve their financial stability and make their risk positions more transparent by issuing subordinated debt. The spreads of their subordinated debt over risk-free securities are supposed to shed some light on how investors perceive the risk of those organizations. But spreads are not easy to interpret. Consider the Freddie Mac variable rate medium-term notes due February 28, 2012.[8] The note has a nominal interest rate of 10.125%, which is about 400 basis points above what Freddie Mac normally pays on a 10 year note. That rate is paid only when the London Interbank Offered Rate (LIBOR) is below 7%. If LIBOR goes above 7%, Freddie Mac pays no interest. The note is callable at par plus accrued interest. It is not clear what this subordinated debt's 400+ basis point spread over their usual rate signals about Freddie Mac, except that it has very sophisticated financing. This type of security is not unique. Finnerty and Emery (2002) describe a large number of innovative debt securities that could be used for subordinated debt.

Consider the case of Farmer Mac (the Federal Agricultural Mortgage Corporation), the largest issuer of unrated debt in the U.S. In June 2002, the bids on default swaps for Farmer Mac increased from 60 basis points to 200 basis points signaling credit markets concern over rising delinquencies in agricultural and rural mortgages.[9] The rising delinquencies were caused by a faltering economy, and there is little that Farmer Mac can do to change the state of the economy. And increasing their credit standards when the economy has bottomed out does not seem like a good strategy. Was the increase in the debt spread market discipline?

MONITORING INVESTMENTS

Now lets turn to the role of monitoring debt and equity investments. The California Public Employees' Retirement System (CalPERS) is widely known for pursuing corporate governance in companies in which it invests. CalPERS was a substantial investor in Enron as well as a partner in some of its Special Purpose Entities (SPEs). Enron was a leading energy, commodities and services company that had revenues of $101 billion in 2000, and it went bust in 2001. Some argue that a culture of greed combined with aggressive accounting practices and the use of SPEs to hide debts, overstate profits, and reduce taxes contributed to its failure. A *New York Times* article reporting on CalPERS relationships with Enron was titled "Even a Watchdog is Not Always Fully Awake."[9] If we can't depend on CalPERS to look out for the *public interest* and enforce market discipline – who can we count on?

CalPERS was not unique in investing in Enron SPEs. Other sophisticated included CSFB, Citigroup, JPM Chase, and Merrill Lynch. They had detailed information that was not available or disclosed to the shareholders. If these sophisticated investors/investment bankers invested in an Enron SPE, and three of them even underwrote Enron securities and they didn't foresee Enron's problems, how is the "average investor" supposed to invoke market discipline?

Federal Reserve Chairman Greenspan (2000) claimed that private market discipline works well for derivatives dealers. They must maintain strong credit ratings to participate in the credit markets. He said this before the Enron debacle. Enron was a very large energy trading company specializing in energy derivatives. He was wrong.

THE REGULATORS

Market discipline in the form of interest rates, interest rate spreads, and stock prices are supposed to provide red flags or triggers for bank regulators to take action. Lets examine their track record. An FDIC study found that "The record shows that 260 failed banks were not identified as requiring increased supervisory attention within 24 months of failure. Of these, 141 were not detected as troubled banks within 18 months of failure; 57 were not detected within 12 months of failure; and nine were not detected within six months of failure."[10]

In September 1999, the First National Bank of Keystone, West Virginia was closed amid allegations of fraud. A total of $515 million in loans were sold, yet they remained on the books. The bank had grown from $85 million in 1990 to $1.1 billion in 1999 by making high-risk subprime loans. The bank had only $15 million of uninsured deposits in about 500 accounts.[11] Market discipline didn't work here. Neither did the bank regulators who spotted internal control problems and audit deficiencies as many as eight years before the failure, but didn't act on them until it was too late.

When a bank is significantly undercapitalized, federal bank regulators must take Prompt Corrective Action (PCA) requiring the affected bank to correct the situation.[12] The banks are required to remedy their capital shortfall and take other actions to restore them to a sounder financial condition. Table 1 lists the

Table 1. PCA Enforcement Actions by the Office of the Comptroller of the Currency.

Year	Bank	Location
2001	NextBank N.A.	Phoenix, AZ
	Sinclair National Bank	Gravette, AR
2000	Metropolitan Bank	New York, NY
	Prairie National Bank	Belle Plaine, MN
1999	None	
1998	Monument National Bank	Ridgecrest, CA
	The Malta National Bank	Malta, OH
	Western American National Bank	Bedford, TX

Source: Office of the Comptroller of the Currency, www.occ.treas.gov (visited 6/11/02).

PCA Enforcement Actions by the OCC during the 1998–2001 period.[13] All of the banks listed had less than $1 billion in assets. NextBank, for example, had $700 million in assets, $554 million in deposits, of which $29.4 million was uninsured in about 2,000 accounts.[14] The noninsured depositors did not enforce market discipline on these small banks. This is consistent with Gilbert, Vaughan, and Myer (2002), *Value of Jumbo-CD Screens as Surveillance Tools* and Hall, Meyer, King and Vaughn (2002), *Did FDICIA Enhance Market Discipline of Community Banks*, who found that jumbo-CDs did little to improve off-site surveillance of community banks.

CONCLUSION

Federal Reserve Governor Susan Schmidt Bies (2002) said the following in connection with regulating large, complex firms. "... it has become clear in recent months that some companies have not been completely transparent in the application of accounting and disclosure standards to specific transactions. ... As a result, the market was not able to appropriately discipline the risk-taking activities of these firms on a timely basis because it lacked the information from either financial statements or other disclosures to do so."

Paul Volcker (2002), former Fed Chairman, and Chairman of the International Accounting Standards Committee, said "The issue we face is how far the newfound zeal for reforms will go, and whether it will persist for long as Enron, Global Crossing, Xerox, WorldCom and other accounting scandals fade from the front pages. The historical record affords no comfort on that score. In the face of earlier difficulties, the accounting firms and their trade associations firmly resisted meaningful reform. They have satisfied themselves with weak oversight bodies, usually dominated by the profession itself. That pattern is clearly reasserting itself in current lobbying efforts in the halls of Congress."

Until banks and other organizations become completely transparent, market discipline in the "signaling" sense of the word is wishful thinking. However, market discipline in the "Darwinian" sense of the word does work. By way of illustration, Enron failed, and its failure is having the effect of increasing the transparency of other firms and changing their accounting and corporate governance practices.

NOTES

1. Leathers and Raines (2000), 164.
2. Using Subordinated Debt as an Instrument of Market Discipline, 1999.
3. Basel Committee on Banking Supervision, Press Release, The New Basle Capital Accord, January 16, 2001. For additional details see: Basel Committee on Banking

Supervision, Consultive Document, *The New Basle Capital Accord*, Bank for International Settlements, Basel, Switzerland, January, 2001.

4. Tittonel (2001).

5. For additional comments on the requirements for market discipline and the results of prior studies, see Gup (2000).

6. Colvin (January, 2002).

7. For additional information about the merger battle, see Park and Kerstetter (December 24, 2001); Burrows and Park (March 18, 2002); Park and Burrows (March 25, 2002). Advertisements *against the merger* appeared in the *Wall Street Journal*, March 12, 2002 (C12 and C13); March 15, 2002 (C7 and C9); and advertisements *for the merger*, March 12, 2002, C22. This listing is for purposes of illustration and is not intended to be complete.

8. Freddie Mac, Variable Rate Medium-Term Notes Due February 28, 2012, issued January 28, 2002, (CUSIP Number 3129242Z5).

9. Henriques (February 5, 2002).

10. Bank Examination and Enforcement, 1997.

11. FDIC Press Release, PR-52-99 (9-03-99).

12. See 12 U.S.C. § 1831o and 12 C.F.R. Part 6. for details on the laws [editor – the footnote with the "o" is correct].

13. The OCC website states that this list may not be complete.

14. FDIC Press Release, PR-16-2002 (2-7-02).

REFERENCES

Bank Examination and Enforcement (1997). In: *History of the Eighties: Lessons for the Future* (vol. I, p. 433). Washington, D.C., Federal Deposit Insurance Corporation.

Basel Committee on Banking Supervision (2001). Consultive Document. *The New Basle Capital Accord*. Bank for International Settlements, Basel, Switzerland, January.

Basel Committee on Banking Supervision, Press Release (2001). The New Basle Capital Accord. Bank for International Settlements, Basel, Switzerland, January 16.

Benink, H., & Wihlborg, C. (2002). The New Basel Capital Accord: Making it Effective with Stronger Market Discipline. *European Financial Management*, *8*(1), 103–115.

Bies, S. S. (2002). Remarks by Governor Susan Schmidt Bies, Strengthening the Financial System of the 21st Century Through Sound Accounting and Disclosure, at the Symposium on Building the Financial System in the 21st Century, Rüschlikon, Switzerland (Board of Governors of the Federal Reserve System, Washington, D.C.), February 28.

Bliss, R. R., & Flannery, M. J. (2000). Market Discipline in Governance of U.S. Bank Holding Companies: Monitoring vs. Influencing, Federal Reserve Bank of Chicago, Working Paper WP 200–03.

Burrows, P., & Park, A. (2002). Compaq and HP: What's an Investor To Do? *BusinessWeek*, (March 18), 62–64.

Colvin, G. (2002). One Number That Won't Lie. *Fortune*, (January 21), 42.

Crockett, A. (2001). Market Discipline and Financial Stability. Speech before the Bank for International Settlements at the Banks and Systemic Risk Conference, Bank of England, London, May 23–25.

Evanoff, D. D., & Wall, L. D. (2002). Subdebt and PCA. Presented at the Western Economics Association, Seattle, WA, June 29–July 3.

FDIC Press Release (1999). FDIC Approves Assumption of Insured Local Deposits of First National Bank of Keystone. Keystone, West Virginia, PR–52–99, September 3.

FDIC Press Release (2002). FDIC Approves the Payout of Insured Deposits of NextBank National Association, Phoenix, Arizona, PR-16-2002, February 7.

Finnerty, J. D., & Emery, D. R. (2002) Corporate Securities Innovation: An Update. *Journal of Applied Finance*, (Spring/Summer), 21–47.

Frame, W. S., & Wall, L. D. (2002). Fannie Mae's and Freddie Mac's Voluntary Initiatives: Lessons from Banking. *Economic Review*, 1st Quarter, 45–59. Federal Reserve Bank of Atlanta.

Freddie Mac, Variable Rate Medium-Term Notes Due February 28, 2012, issued January 28, 2002, (CU.S.IP Number 3129242Z5), www.frediemac.com/debt/

Gilbert, A. R., Vaughan, M. D., & Meyer, A. P. (2002). Value of Jumbo-CD Screens as Surveillance Tools. Presented at the Western Economics Association, Seattle, WA, June 29–July 3.

Greenspan, A. (2000). Banking Evolution, appears in Federal Reserve Bank of Chicago. *The Changing Financial Industry Structure and Regulation: Bridging States, Countries, and Industries*, (May), 1–20.

Gup, B. E. (2000). Market Discipline and the Corporate Governance of Bank: Theory vs. Evidence. In: B. E. Gup (Ed.), *The New Financial Architecture: Banking Regulation in the 21st Century* (pp. 187–206). Westport, CT: Quorum Books.

Hall, J. R., Meyer, A. P., King, T. B., & Vaughn, M. D. (2002). Did FDICIA Enhance Market Discipline of Community Banks? Presented at the Western Economics Association, Seattle, WA, June 29–July 3.

Henriques, D. B. (2002). Even a Watchdog is Not Always Fully Awake. *New York Times*, (February 5), www.nytimes.com (visited 2/5/02).

Leathers, C. G., & Raines, J. P. (2000). Market Discipline for Banks: A Historical Review. In: B. E. Gup (Ed.), *The New Financial Architecture: Banking Regulation in the 21st Century* (pp. 163–185). Westport, CT: Quorum Books.

Park, A., & Burrows, P. (2002). The HP Fight is Still Too Close to Call. *BusinessWeek*, (March 25), 35.

Park, A., & Kerstetter, J. (2001). Carly's Last Stand. *BusinessWeek*, (December 24), 63–70.

Rose, P. S. (1999). *Commercial Bank Management* (4th ed.). Boston, MA: Irwin/McGraw-Hill.

Scott, W. L. (1991). *Contemporary Financial Markets and Services*. St. Paul, MN: West Publishing Co.

Tittonel, S. (2002). Member of the Secretariat, Basle Committee on Banking Supervision, e-mail message to Benton E. Gup concerning market discipline, March 18.

Using Subordinated Debt as an Instrument of Market Discipline (1999). Staff Study 172, Board of Governors of the Federal Reserve System, December.

Volcker, P. A. (2002). A Litmus Test for Accounting Reform. *Wall Street Journal*, (May 21), A18.

Wiggins, J. (2002). Farmer Mac Swap Rates Show Level of Concern. *Financial Times*, (June 4), 21.

COMMENT

Alan C. Hess

Markets may fail if either the good or service that would be traded is a public good, or if the good or service carries with it either positive or negative external effects. For some goods or services beset by market failure, collective action may be undertaken to facilitate supply. Systemic effects of runs on banks that have positive value but run-induced illiquidity may be an example of an action with negative external effects. To avoid potentially harmful macroeconomic effects of runs on banks by uninsured depositors, Congress established the Federal Deposit Insurance System to insure some deposits of banks.

Deposit insurance has both positive and negative external effects. One positive external effect is a potential reduction in runs on solvent banks. A possible negative external effect is increased risk taking by bank managers. Campbell and Kracaw's theory of financial intermediation argues that banks add value by signaling the true value of businesses. By dint of their economies of scale and specialization banks are able to produce valuation and monitoring services at lower costs than other potential suppliers. A bank's lending agreement signals to outside investors that the borrower has passed muster with the bank's credit analysts. Uninsured depositors and other outside investors can trust banks' valuation and monitoring skills because the banks have financially significant at-risk positions in their borrowers' cash flows.

Banks' capital ratios declined after the advent of deposit insurance as banks substituted insured deposits for equity capital. In the Campbell-Kracaw analysis, decreases in equity reduce the incentives of the bank's owners to be diligent in their valuation and monitoring activities. A possible consequence of this is increased bank failures due to poor underwriting. This appears to have happened in the U.S. in the 1980s when banks and thrifts suffered historically large decreases in cash flows and market values. Regulators, who were vested

Prompt Corrective Action in Banking: 10 Years Later, Volume 14, pages 103–106.

ISBN: 0-7623-0987-3

with authority to prevent these results, acquiesced by practicing forbearance. Government failure replaced market failure.

The Federal Deposit Insurance Corporation Improvement Act (1991) calls for regulators to take prompt corrective action to reduce the chances that poorly managed banks will fail and cause large losses of FDIC-insured deposits. Bank regulators conduct on-site examinations of banks and off-site surveillance to monitor bank risk. Regulators may enhance their off-site surveillance by using market data as a source of information about the financial conditions of banks. Investors may signal their perceptions of banks' failure probabilities by the premiums they charge banks on their uninsured debt instruments.

Evanoff and Wall (2002) used risk premiums on secondary market trades of subordinated debt issued by large banking organizations as market signals of banks' financial conditions. They found that the risk premiums are statistically significant in-sample predictors of banks' CAMEL-BOPEC ratings. Thus, for large banks regulators can use market data to enhance their off-site surveillance.

The studies by Gilbert, Meyer and Vaughan (2002), hereafter (GMV), and Hall, King, Meyer and Vaughan (2002), hereafter (HKMV), test whether book measures of rates paid by community banks on jumbo-CDs provide early warning signals on the banks' financial conditions. They found that their measure of the jumbo-CD yield was uninformative.

Table 1 summarizes salient features of each of the three studies. In conjunction with efficient market theory, the table suggests three possible ways that the differing results could be reconciled.

(1) Perhaps market yields on CDs are uninformative. To check this, repeat the Evanoff-Wall analysis using secondary market yields on CDs instead of yields on subordinated debt. If market-CD yield spreads for large banking organizations do not predict their CAMEL-BOPEC ratings, book-CD yields are likely to be even less informative. If market-CD yield spreads predict CAMEL-BOPEC ratings proceed to step 2.

(2) Perhaps book-CD yields are uninformative. Repeat the Evanoff-Wall analysis using book-CD yield spreads and compare the results with those obtained using market-CD yield spreads. Efficient markets theory suggests that the book-CD yield is likely to be uninformative. Prices and yields in an efficient market reflect investors' best assessments of the future cash flows from alternative investments. Figure 1 of HKMV shows that their measure of the book-CD yield lags market rates by six months. Whereas investors in efficient markets are forward-looking, the book-CD yield is

Table 1. Comparison of Findings of Evanoff and Wall (2002), Gilbert, Meyer and Vaughan (2002) and Hall, King, Meyer and Vaughan (2002) in Similar Tests.

	Evanoff and Wall	Gilbert, Meyer and Vaughan	Hall, King, Meyer and Vaughan
Null hypothesis	SND-RF does not predict CAMEL, Table 1	Jumbo CD yields and runoffs are unrelated to SEER risk-rank failure probabilities, Table 3	FDICIA did not change the effect of bank risk on jumbo CD yields and runoffs, Table 5
Sample	100 largest banking organizations. 1985–1999	Community banks. 1989–2000	Community banks. 1988–90 1993–95
Dependent variables	CAMEL	Book measure of jumbo CD rate: CD runoffs	Book measure of jumbo CD rate: CD runoffs
Regressors	SND-RF, Tier 1 leverage ratio	SEER failure probability, many control variables	SEER failure probability, many control variables
Results	Both regressors are significant in-sample predictors of CAMEL.	SEER regressor has statistically significant but economically small effects on CD rate and runoffs.	Coefficient of SEER regressor did not change after FDICIA.

backward looking. A bank's book-CD yield seems doomed to failure as a market signal of its forward-looking financial condition.

(3) Perhaps market yields are unrelated to SEER failure probabilities. Both the Evanoff and Wall paper and the GMV and HKMV papers studied the links between yields and measures of banks' financial performance. However, they use different yield measures and different performance measures. Evanoff and Wall studied the predictive power of subordinated debt yields for subsequent CAMEL-BOPEC ratings of banks. GMV and HKMV studied the links between SEER risk-rank failure probabilities and book CD-yields. Perhaps the failure of the GMV model is due to its use of SEER risk-rank failure probabilities instead of CAMEL ratings. To check this, estimate the GMV model using subordinated debt yields and SEER failure probabilities for large banking organizations. Repeat the analysis using

market CD yields for large banks. If market yields, especially CD yields are informative to SEER failure probabilities, and if SEER failure probabilities are accurate for both large banks and community banks, the findings of small links between book-CD yields and SEER failure probabilities are probably due to their use of book CD yields.

Let us assume that the results of these additional empirical tests reinforce the conclusion that there are no market price or yield data that are informative to regulators for the off-site surveillance of community banks. As a result, it may be more costly per dollar of a bank's assets or net income for regulators to monitor the financial performance of community banks than large banks. As a matter of public policy it seems worthwhile to estimate the incremental social costs and benefits of regulatory monitoring of banks. Among the questions to be addressed are: What is the optimal amount of regulatory monitoring? Does it differ between large and community banks? Is it possible that the costs of monitoring community banks exceed the social benefits of monitoring? Since community banks are small, will an ill-advised run on a community bank lead to runs on other banks? Would such runs, if they occurred, have significant social costs? If the expected social benefits of monitoring are small and the costs of monitoring are large, who should pay for the monitoring? Can community banks afford to bear the full cost of the current monitoring process? How might the conduct and pricing of regulatory monitoring be structured to ensure it is a value adding activity?

The three papers presented in this section of the conference give results consistent with efficient market theory. They lead to questions about whether the regulatory process is efficient. The study of regulatory efficiency is a useful line of future research.

REFERENCES

Campbell, T. S., & Kracaw, W. A. (1980). Information Production, Market Signalling, and the Theory of Financial Intermediation. *Journal of Finance*, *35*(4), 863–882.

Evanoff, D. D., & Wall, L. D. (2002). Subordinated Debt and Prompt Corrective Action. This volume.

Gilbert, R. A., Meyer, A. P., & Vaughan, M. D. (2002). Can Feedback from the Jumbo-CD Market Improve Off-Site Surveillance of Community Banks? This volume.

Hall, J. R., King, T. B., Meyer, A. P., & Vaughan, M. D. (2002). Did FDICIA Enhance Market Discipline of Community Banks? A Look at Evidence from the Jumbo-CD Market. This volume.

PART II:
PCA AND MARKET DISCIPLINE: THE U.S. EXPERIENCE

THE MAJOR SUPERVISORY INITIATIVES POST-FDICIA: ARE THEY BASED ON THE GOALS OF PCA? SHOULD THEY BE?

Robert A. Eisenbeis and Larry D. Wall

ABSTRACT

The prompt corrective action provisions in FDICIA 1991 provide the supervisors with an unambiguous goal: "to resolve the problems of insured depository institutions at the least possible long-term cost to the deposit insurance fund." Yet performance of the regulators in achieving this goal has been lacking in that substantial losses continue to be imposed on the insurance funds when banks fail. Is PCA misguided, or are there incentive defects in the law and how the requirements are being administered? This paper analyzes these issues in the context of recent proposals to reform the deposit insurance system.

I. INTRODUCTION

The post-FDICIA period has been marked by three major safety and soundness initiatives from the U.S. supervisory community: risk-based supervision, reform of the 1988 Basel Bank Supervisors Committee's risk-based capital regulations, and deposit insurance reform. Risk-based supervision, which followed from the 1988 Basel reforms, is intended to refocus bank examination

Prompt Corrective Action in Banking: 10 Years Later, Volume 14, pages 109–142.

ISBN: 0-7623-0987-3

away from verifying the past and present risks towards identifying future risks. The revisions to the risk-based capital regulations are intended to better align supervisory capital requirements with individual bank's risk exposure. Deposit insurance reform consists of a variety of measures that would reallocate the distribution of bank failure costs across time and interested parties including depositors, premium paying banks, the taxpayers and bank equity holders.

Are these reforms leading in the right direction? To answer this question, one must begin by asking what is the goal of bank supervision and regulation (S&R)? Over time, the goals of banking supervision have evolved, due to changes in law, to changes in regulatory and supervisory philosophy, and to changes in the financial market place. In the early years, following the establishment of Federal Deposit Insurance, the principal objective of banking supervision was to prevent systemic banking failures and panics, and it was thought that the best way to do this was to prevent banks from failing. The agencies were very effective in achieving this end. Few banks actually were declared failures from the 1940s through the mid 1970s. Most recently, Congress clearly spelled out the supervisors' primary goal in the prompt corrective action (PCA) provisions of the Federal Deposit Insurance Corporation Improvement Act of 1991 (FDICIA). PCA provides a structured procedure for addressing problem banks and gives the unambiguous goal of that process: "to resolve the problems of insured depository institutions at the least possible long-term cost to the deposit insurance fund."[1]

Superficially, the goals of failure prevention and loss minimization appear to be related. If a bank does not fail then it cannot impose losses on the deposit insurer. However, pursuit of these goals may have very different and potentially conflicting policy implications for the health of the banking system and for the deposit insurer. Each has different implications for the size of losses when they do occur and how they are distributed among the affected parties and the deposit insurance fund. They can also significantly affect risk-taking incentives by both healthy and distressed banks, and hence the size of future losses to the insurance fund.

Are the current supervisory initiatives consistent with the goal set by current law in FDICIA? Should these initiatives be consistent? This paper begins by reviewing the question of whether FDICIA's focus on minimizing deposit insurance losses is appropriate and concludes, for a number of reasons, that it is indeed correct. Sections II–IV evaluate each of the major S&R initiatives and their likely impact on the banking system. The evidence suggests that most of the supervisory efforts have continued to be directed toward minimizing the probability of failure rather than minimizing the expected losses due to failure. The fifth section evaluates deposit insurance reform issues. Section VI presents some ideas for an agenda focused on minimizing the expected costs of bank failure. The last section provides concluding remarks.

II. PREVENTING FAILURE VERSUS MINIMIZING INSURANCE LOSSES

The goals of preventing failure and minimizing deposit insurance losses make fundamentally different demands on bank supervisors and have different implications for loss sharing and incentives to management. The goal of preventing failure places a large share of the responsibility and accountability for a bank's failure with the bank supervisors. If a bank becomes financially distressed, then supervisors are expected to detect the problem and take appropriate remedial actions. When a bank fails, either the supervisor did not adequately evaluate the bank's risk or in some other way failed in its responsibilities.[2]

In contrast, minimizing deposit insurance losses means that when a bank fails, regulators attempt to limit losses to the deposit insurance fund. This involves ensuring that bank owners, managers, and uninsured creditors lose their equity or other liabilities before losses are born by the insurance fund. Because they are exposed to loss, risk taking and moral hazard behavior of managers and owners should be contained. Moreover, bank owners and managers have an incentive to protect their investment and to limit their loss exposure because they are explicitly responsible for the bank's performance. If a bank should fail, then either management took too much risk or the bank's future prospects were such that further investment by the bank's owners would not provide an adequate rate of return. Thus, the responsibility for the ultimate fate of a bank rests with its owners and managers, and not with its supervisors.

The next subsections present and evaluate the arguments for preventing failure and for limiting deposit insurance losses.

Preventing Failure

The public policy argument for the goal of preventing bank failure is based on the perception that failure poses costly externalities on other banks, on bank customers, or on financial markets more generally. To the extent that failure reduces confidence in other banks, self-fulfilling bank panics may become more likely. Failure may impair the ability of other economic participants to make payments or to obtain credit. Failure may result in the loss of valuable information about a bank's borrowers, and hence increase borrowing costs, ceteris paribus. Finally, the failure of large banks may pose extra problems because of their role as major players in many financial markets, both for their own accounts and as dealers to facilitate transactions by other parties.

The argument that bank failures cause irrational panics has been examined in a number of papers and found to have little support in the data.[3] Kaufman (1996) summarizes the evidence as "There is effectively no evidence of a depositor run driving an economically (market value) solvent bank into insolvency. Damaging runs were almost entirely on economically insolvent banks that were still open and operating." The evidence suggests that bank runs occur at banks where depositors have a reasonable basis for fearing loss and not at banks where there is no reason to doubt the bank's solvency.[4] Moreover, even if irrational deposit runs were a concern, the combination of deposit insurance and central bank operations would mitigate any problem. Deposit insurance stops runs by smaller depositors and may discourage runs by larger depositors. The central bank may offset any large increase in the demand for liquidity both through its open market operations and its lending to specific solvent institutions.

A related concern is that a bank failure may disrupt the payment system at either the wholesale or inter-bank level when banks become uncertain that other banks will honor their obligations. The events of September 11 illustrate this problem very clearly. When the World Trade Center collapsed, not only were securities trading firms, such as Cantor Fitzgerald, unable to make or complete transactions, but also disruptions to communications meant that some institutions were either only able to accept payments or were unable to route payments to their final recipients. Some institutions' balance sheets ballooned out of control while others found themselves in substantial deficit reserve positions as anticipated payments did not materialize by the end of the day. Again, the systemic nature of this disruption was essentially mitigated when the Federal Reserve stepped in and provided the necessary temporary liquidity so that institutions were able to close their books and avoid technical insolvency or default.[5]

Another concern is that failure may result in the temporary or permanent loss of lending ability of the failed bank. In part, this concern arises from a mistaken belief that resolving a failed bank necessarily implies liquidating the bank. In most cases the FDIC does not liquidate all of a failed bank's assets but rather seeks to sell the bank as an ongoing operation to other banks or to recapitalize it. Other banks are often willing to buy the entire failed bank or parts of it precisely because the expected revenue from operating the bank once stripped of its bad assets (and other claims) is greater than the costs. The acquirer has an incentive to continue operating the financially viable parts of the failed bank with minimal disruptions to customers. Some banks operate facilities where even very short-run disruptions, such as securities transfers, may be costly to the market. However, the magnitude of these costs depends critically on how the failure is resolved. An orderly, carefully thought through transfer may impose few if any costs.[6]

Minimizing Deposit Insurance Losses

The goal of minimizing deposit insurance losses should conceptually simplify the task of bank regulators in that their primary supervisory attention should be on dealing with problems and deteriorating institutions rather than focusing on both healthy and failing banks. In a world with deposit insurance, the value of the guarantee to healthy intuitions should be zero (or nearly so). Moral hazard associated with deposit insurance arises when unhealthy institutions are incented and able to take on more risk, so as to increase the value of insurance. Hence, the objective of supervisors should be to prevent banks from assigning a significant value to deposit insurance in determining their portfolio allocations. Since the value of insurance increases as an institution's net worth declines, supervisory attention is best concentrated on valuing assets and determining whether a bank's capital has deteriorated to the point where the market value of the bank's equity is near zero. The advantage in dealing with failing banks is that forbearance is generally not desirable.

In contrast, a supervisor that seeks to minimize bank failures wants the costs facing bankers to incorporate the supervisor's cost of failure. As such, the supervisor is not only seeking to undo the effect of deposit insurance but also to have the prices contain an added risk premium to reduce bank risk taking to levels consistent with supervisory goals. In setting a synthetic pricing schedule to reduce risk, the supervisor may use a combination of prohibiting certain portfolios, imposing risk-sensitive capital requirements and deposit insurance premiums, and by imposing higher supervisory costs on riskier banks.[7]

A variety of problems may emerge because of the supervisors' trying to impose a synthetic price schedule on bank portfolio choices. Even if supervisors were able to set the right relative prices of risk to accomplish their goal, the consequences may be less than optimal. If the supervisor's cost of bank failure is greater than society's cost of failure, then the bank internalizes the supervisors cost, and it will take less than the socially optimal amount of risk. Thus, even if market prices understate the total social cost of bank failure, giving banks a price schedule based on the cost of failure to supervisors may not improve social welfare.

Moreover, even if the supervisor and society assign the same cost to bank failure, information asymmetry poses potential problems. Bankers typically know more than supervisors about the distribution of returns associated with portfolios of various bank assets, liabilities and contingent claims. Thus, the supervisory agencies are unlikely to be able to avoid setting synthetic prices that are too high on some claims and too low on others. Supervisory errors are likely to result in banks making sub-optimal portfolio allocations even from the supervisor's perspective.

Further, the difference between the relative prices set by the supervisors and those set by financial markets creates an arbitrage opportunity. A bank may gain access to profitable opportunities by complying with the letter of the regulations while avoiding its intent, a process sometimes called regulatory arbitrage. This happened recently as banks restructured assets and liabilities and substituted off-balance sheet contingent liabilities for on-balance sheet liabilities to avoid Basel capital requirements. Supervisors may try to limit such arbitrage by adopting more detailed regulations, which creates incentives for banks to seek loopholes in the new regulation. Kane (1977) calls this process the regulatory dialectic and argues that it will continue unless and until the "budgetary cost, social inconvenience, economic waste and distributional inequity . . . become painfully obvious even to the ordinary citizen."

In contrast, if the goal is merely to minimize deposit insurance losses, supervisors' goal is simply to prevent market prices from incorporating expectations that the deposit insurer would absorb significant losses. This requires that the supervisors set relative prices so that a strategy of taking large gambles that could result in the rapid elimination of the bank's capital is shareholder wealth reducing. This also requires that the supervisors carefully monitor the value of the bank's portfolio so that they can intervene when capital falls below some minimal level at which moral hazard concerns become relevant and so that they can resolve the bank before it can impose large losses on the insurer. Indeed, if both of these goals are accomplished, the relative prices set in the financial market place will reinforce the supervisor's goal rather than providing an incentive to avoid the goal.

Another advantage of seeking to minimize losses to the deposit insurer is that doing so avoids creating any incentive for forbearance. Keeping the bank open creates a situation of asymmetric gains and losses in which the owners and managers retain the benefits if the bank returns to financial health but others – mostly uninsured creditors, the deposit insurer, and taxpayers – bear even larger losses if the bank fails. This asymmetry supplies the incentive for banks to engage in moral hazard behavior.

Regulatory Behavior Under FDICIA

One of the key intents behind the early intervention and prompt corrective action provisions in FDICIA was to refocus supervisory efforts on minimizing losses to the insurance funds by requiring the agencies to close institutions when insured institutions' book value of capital falls below 2%. The question arises as to how the regulators have performed since these provisions took effect in 1992, and whether this experience provides any clues as to whether regulatory agency behavior has changed?

Figure 1 shows the loss experience of the FDIC over the period 1986 through 2000. Looking at just the dollar amount of the losses, there is a clear decline shortly after the full effects of PCA began to take effect in 1993. However, looking at the loss percentages relative to assets, it is hard to notice any discernable trend pre and post the PCA provisions in FDICIA, except for the two years 1998 and 1999. If the agencies were truly following FDICIA's prompt corrective action and early intervention provisions, then these losses as a percentage of assets should be close to zero. It is clear that the losses are huge in both dollar amounts and as a percentage of assets. Losses over the entire 1986–2000 period averaged about 13%, and in the post PCA era averaged 26%. This latter period's average is driven up significantly by the experience in 1998 and 1999, when very large fraud-related losses were incurred on a single institution in each of those two years. However, PCA appears to have had no noticeable impact even if these two years are dropped from the analysis. Moreover, large losses continue with Blackwell (2002c) reporting that by early July 2002, the FDIC has closed three banks in that year, each of which had a loss-to-asset ratio of more than 50%.

As Table 1 indicates, there are some interesting differences in the patterns of losses when the experience is broken down by primary supervisor that have some interesting agency cost implications. One would theorize that the FDIC might be more sensitive to potential losses because it also has primary responsibility for the insurance funds. That is, the hypothesis would be that the losses and loss rates would be lowest on FDIC regulated institutions. However, the data do not seem to show such a pattern. All the regulators have dealt with institutions that failed, and that also imposed large, both in dollar amounts and in percentage of assets terms, losses on the insurance fund. Between 1986 and 2000 losses ranged from a low of 10.8% of assets for institutions supervised by the Federal Reserve to a high of 21.1% for institutions supervised by the FDIC. The experience for institutions supervised by the OCC and OTS were approximately the same at 11.3% and 11.7%, respectively. In some years,

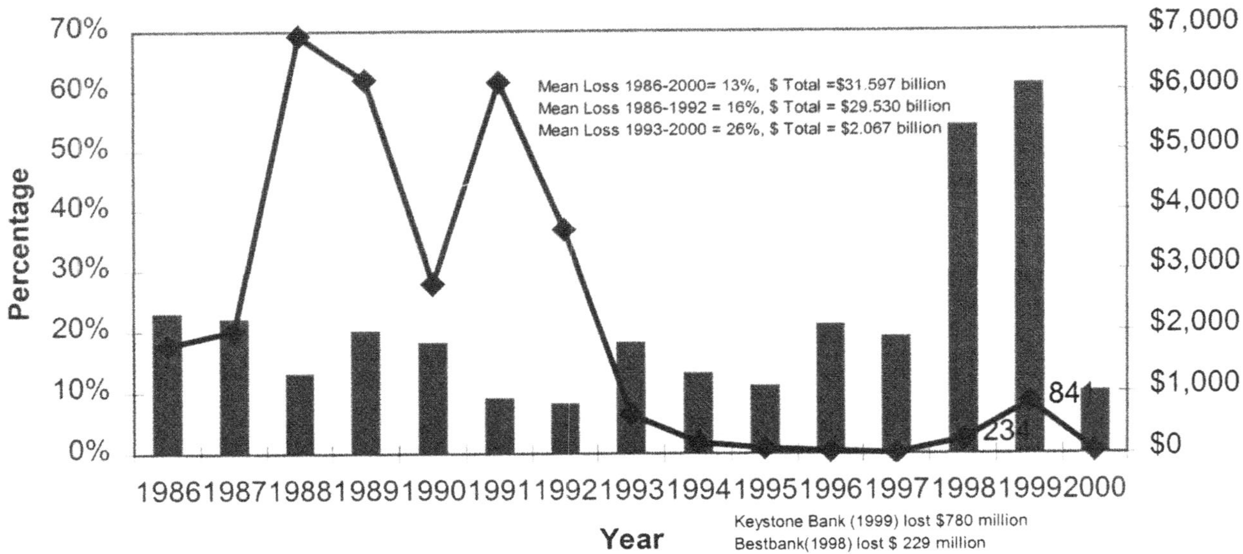

Fig. 1. Estimated Dollar Amount of Losses and Losses as a Percentage of Assets to the Deposit Insurance Funds.
Source: FDIC.

Table 1. Annual Losses due to Failure by Primary Supervisor.

	Estimated yearly loss FDIC	Ave. % of Assets Lost: FDIC	Estimated yearly loss OCC	Ave.% of Assets Lost: OCC	Estimated yearly loss OTS	Ave. % of Assets Lost: OTS	Estimated yearly loss FED	Ave. % of Assets Lost: FED
1986	$976,554,240	26.0%	$755,470,341	20.3%	$6,984,532	20.7%	$36,708,183	27.0%
1987	$1,106,501,283	20.5%	$740,903,476	25.4%	$63,567,730	12.7%	$112,047,662	26.9%
1988	$1,375,946,066	18.1%	$5,412,436,370	11.7%			$133,408,698	26.7%
1989	$1,077,926,300	19.0%	$4,698,994,148	19.1%	$288,209,804	33.0%	$134,168,454	25.7%
1990	$637,864,568	21.9%	$1,250,361,193	16.9%	$855,242,293	16.3%	$41,595,347	23.1%
1991	$1,457,784,779	21.2%	$1,767,011,143	3.9%	$2,907,336,882	15.6%	$16,639,598	12.3%
1992	$1,140,958,161	22.8%	$137,539,048	1.9%	$2,202,121,477	7.7%	$198,205,247	4.3%
1993	$233,001,142	21.1%	$257,928,650	18.3%	$117,863,581	12.5%	$38,558,415	50.9%
1994	$95,845,263	17.7%	$52,008,264	29.4%	$16,586,291	2.9%	$14,514,528	13.4%
1995	$61,474,953	13.5%	$2,593,302	27.7%	–		$20,988,865	7.6%
1996	$14,680,091	17.5%	$23,739,421	24.3%	$14,000	39.8%	–	
1997	–		–		–		$5,025,538	19.5%
1998	$234,049,254	54.2%	–		–		–	
1999	$47,223,873	27.8%	$791,726,586	66.3%	$1,343	2.1%	$2,221,575	16.4%
2000	$29,932,008	10.6%	$8,748,478	8.5%	$1,402	4.7%	–	
Average 1986–2000	$565,982,799	21.1%	$1,059,964,028	11.3%	$461,280,667	11.7%	$50,272,141	10.8%

Source: FDIC.

losses have been unexplainably large, especially given the agencies' mandate to minimize losses to the insurance funds.

There are several possible explanations for the large losses from 1993 onward. First, the agencies could still be pursuing forbearance and failure minimization policies rather than loss minimization. Second, the agencies may be closing institutions when book values reach the critical levels, but book values are such a poor indication of true underlying asset values that the trigger closure rules are badly miss-specified. Third, the institutions that were closed were largely engaged in hard-to-detect fraudulent activities, making effective implementation of PCA problematic. Fraud was a significant factor in the OCC-supervised Keystone Bank, WV, which resulted in a $780 million loss that amounted to nearly 75% of the institution's assets. Beyond a few spectacular cases, review of the specific case documents suggests that while fraudulent activities did play a role in some of the failures, it does appear that there were large delays in closing troubled institutions, suggesting that failure minimization may still be an important supervisory objective.

Summary

Our analysis suggests that the arguments for minimizing the probability of a bank failing are not very convincing and whereas the objective of minimizing deposit insurance losses is incentive compatible. The alleged harms of bank failure are overstated and those harms that do arise are best addressed through better resolution practices. A focus on preventing bank failure is mistaken in part because such a focus can unintentionally encourage forbearance at distressed banks. Moreover, the problems with a failure prevention focus go beyond those of forbearance. A focus on failure prevention results in supervisors trying to replace market signals with a synthetic set of signals that incorporate the supervisor's cost of bank failure. These synthetic signals may overstate the cost of failure, miss-price the relative riskiness of different assets, and encourage regulatory avoidance. In contrast, a focus on limiting losses to the deposit insurance fund seeks only to prevent banks from imposing part of the costs of bank failure on the safety net. To date, however, it does not appear that agencies have been very successful in limiting losses to the insurance fund.

III. RISK-BASED SUPERVISION

The U.S. bank regulators have adopted and implemented risk-based supervision during the 1990s. The *Commercial Bank Examination Manual* from the

Federal Reserve (2000) discusses the differences between risk-based supervision and the prior examination process.[8] On page 2, the *Manual* explains that "Historically, examinations relied significantly on transaction-testing procedures when assessing a bank's condition and verifying its adherence to internal policies, procedures, and controls." The *Manual* argues "Evolving financial instruments and markets have enabled banking organizations to rapidly reposition their portfolio risk exposures. Therefore, periodic assessments of the condition of a financial institution based on transaction testing alone cannot keep pace with the moment-to-moment changes occurring in financial risk profiles." The *Manual* then goes on to explain the change made by risk-based (or risk-focused) examination: "To ensure that institutions have in place the processes necessary to identify, measure, monitor, and control risk exposures, examinations have increasingly emphasized evaluating the appropriateness of these processes, evolving away from a high degree of transaction testing." The *Manual* does note that greater transactions testing may be necessary depending on the adequacy of the internal risk management and internal control processes.

A potentially important benefit of risk-based supervision is its reduction in the cost of examination. The increases in the size and complexity of many banking organizations have increased the cost of examining individual transactions to prohibitive levels. The cost of examination may be reduced under risk-based supervision because the change in approach allows the supervisors to focus on the major determinants of a bank's risk. Risk-based supervision may also contribute to the goals of minimizing the probability of bank failure and minimizing the losses to the deposit insurance fund. Banks that are not adequately managing their risk exposure are at higher risk of failure. If a bank's risk management process is sufficiently deficient, the bank may expose itself to losses so large that it poses the risk of significant lose to the deposit insurer.

The two different supervisory goals have important differences for the degree of emphasis supervisors should place on evaluating risk management systems. Given a goal of failure prevention, identifying and devising methods for penalizing risk concentrations is critical. The supervisors must identify ways in which banks are taking higher risk positions so that they can impose costs so as to reduce the expected rate of return on these activities, and thereby incent institutions to stop increasing and possibly even decrease these risky activities. The supervisors may impose these costs in a variety of ways. They may bring perceived deficiencies to the attention of the bank's management or board of directors. They may assign an unsatisfactory CAMELS rating to the bank, which increases its deposit insurance premiums. If these tactics appear insufficient, the supervisors may act directly by imposing constraints on the portfolio in the form of diversification requirements, limiting the investment in certain assets, or even demanding that the bank stop investing in certain types of assets.

In contrast, estimating the value of the bank's portfolio so as to come up with reliable measures of economic capital is less important if the goal is failure prevention. Lower levels of economic capital do raise the value of the deposit insurance subsidy to risk taking, inducing banks to take more risk. However, even at high levels of economic capital the value maximizing strategy for the bank may be to take more risk than is optimal for a supervisor seeking to prevent failure.

On the other hand, if the goal is deposit insurance loss minimization, obtaining a reliable estimate of the value of the bank's portfolio, and hence of its economic capital is critical. The supervisors must have a good estimate of a bank's economic capital if they are to intervene or close a bank before it becomes economically insolvent and poses a threat of substantial loss to the deposit insurance fund. Moreover, under loss minimization, the supervisors generally accept banks' choice of portfolio if the choice is not significantly influenced by the ability to shift losses to the deposit insurer. How a bank's portfolio is distributed among different assets and liabilities is less important, provided the portfolio can be valued, and reliable estimates of economic capital can be obtained. If a bank has sufficiently high levels of economic capital, supervisors need not intervene because the option value of deposit insurance is sufficiently far out of the money so that it is not important to the bank's risk taking decisions.

Evidence on the role of risk-based supervision in practice is mixed. In testimony to Congress, former Comptroller of the Currency Ludwig (1997) suggests that the goal of risk-based supervision is to prevent failure:

> And we also learned that supervision is much less effective if it is based on looking only at the current condition of an institution – in other words, what has already happened. What is needed is forward-looking supervision that identifies the problems that are emerging and how to manage them. Effective supervision cannot be limited to treating the disease. We also need to practice preventive medicine.

He later explains that, "we have developed a supervision-by-risk system that is forward looking and improves our ability to identify and address problems before they become crises." Ludwig's discussion suggests a belief that supervisors are ultimately responsible for limiting bank risk taking. Supervisors must identify problems and use their powers to change the relative returns to taking risks so that losses may be prevented.

Federal Reserve Chairman Greenspan (2001) provides a different perspective on risk-based supervision. His overall philosophy towards bank risk taking is that "while public policy needs to limit the financial and social costs of bank failures, we should not view every bank failure as a supervisory or regulatory failure." In the context of risk-based supervision he states:

> It is, of course, our belief that, for the larger banks, improving the measurement and management of risk will provide bank supervisors with more reliable and efficient ways to evaluate a bank's financial health. That thought underlies the concept of risk-based supervision and our increased focus on internal processes and controls. If we can gain greater confidence in a bank's operating procedures and in its own evaluation of risk, we should be able to reduce our oversight role – certainly when compared with what would otherwise be required.

Greenspan's arguments suggest the potential for risk-based supervision to support the goal of minimizing deposit insurance losses by helping supervisors identify threats to the deposit insurance fund before the losses are unavoidable.

IV. REVISED RISK-BASED CAPITAL UNDER BASEL II

The modern history of U.S. capital regulation begins with the announcement of numerical capital guidelines in 1981. When first announced, these guidelines focused exclusively on the asset side of the balance sheet and excluded contingent claims such as derivatives and loan commitments. Moreover, these guidelines assigned an equal weight to all of the assets on the balance sheet. The announcement of these regulations included explicit statements that the supervisors believed the largest banks, the multinational category, needed to raise their capital ratios. U.S. banks moved to increase their equity capital as intended by the supervisors, but they also raised their regulatory capital adequacy ratios by reducing their holdings of highly liquid, low risk assets that had a low return while boosting their involvement in contingent claims. As a response, the U.S. supervisors together with their counterparts in other developed countries met as the Basel Bank Supervisors Committee and announced a new set of risk-based capital regulations for internationally active banks in 1988. These guidelines provided for a form of crude credit risk weighting and brought in the credit risk of contingent claims. However, banks responded to the 1988 guidelines in a similar manner to the 1981 guidelines: new capital was issued but banks have also sought ways to reduce measured risk without decreasing actual risk.

The effort to reform the 1988 guidelines has gathered considerable momentum in recent years. The proposal contains three parts or "pillars." The first pillar establishes a minimum capital adequacy ratio and provides procedures for calculating that ratio. These rules specify three different ways to measure a bank's risk exposure, each of which is intended to be more accurate than the 1988 standards. An innovative feature of the more sophisticated risk measurement proposals, the internal ratings based and advanced internal ratings based approaches, is that they provide for the use of banks internal credit ratings to set capital requirements. The regulations seek to raise the overall cost of risk taking to banks but to leave the relative costs of different types of risk taking unchanged (at least with respect to credit risk). The intent in doing so is to reduce the distortion on bank portfolio allocations introduced by regulation.[9]

The second pillar of the new regulations is supervisory evaluations of bank's capital adequacy. Most of the provisions of this pillar will have more of an effect on some foreign supervisors than on U.S. bank supervisors.

The final pillar is market discipline, which focuses exclusively on providing additional information to financial markets, it does not call for market participants to be exposed to greater losses in the event of bank failure or call on supervisors to use market signals. The idea behind the third pillar is that market participants would exert more effective discipline over banks if they had better information. The extent to which market participants will exert discipline, however, also depends on the extent to which they are at risk. If the supervisor's goal is to prevent bank failure, market participants may perceive their risk of loss to be small, and this seems to be consistent with recent experience. Whereas, if the goal is to minimize losses to the deposit insurer, then uninsured participants may perceive a great deal of risk.

Most of the attention on Basel II seems to be focused on the first pillar, revised capital adequacy measures, suggesting that it is perceived to have the greatest impact on banks. Regulation specifying minimum capital adequacy ratios plays an important role under both the goals of minimizing the probability of bank failure and minimizing expected deposit insurance losses, however, its role and implementation are very different under the two goals. If the goal is to minimize the probability of failure, capital regulations should generally exercise a binding influence on bank equity capital. That is, one way of taking implicit risk-based supervision and making it explicit is by putting regulatory (as distinct from market) prices on risk. The actual level of bank capital ratios may be greater than the minimum supervisory requirements, but the excess is a deliberate cushion held by the bank both to reduce the risk that unexpected losses will force the ratio below the requirements and to allow the bank to exploit unanticipated profitable growth opportunities. To the extent that required equity capital allocations are greater than would be imposed by the market, or are relatively different from what the market might charge on different asset classes, they will either reduce profits and/or induce innovations to avoid the capital constraints, such as increased reliance upon off-balance sheet activities or on derivatives. Note that risk-based capital is not the same thing as economic capital. Moreover the risk-based capital ratio is calculated using book values instead of market values.

In contrast, if the goal is to minimize expected losses to the deposit insurer, regulatory equity capital tranches will be set to trigger supervisory action only at distressed or failing banks, and should not affect asset allocations or the portfolio choices of healthy institutions. The equity capital trigger would require supervisory intervention before a bank becomes insolvent, partly to alert the bank to the supervisor's view of its portfolio value and partly to limit moral hazard as the value of deposit insurance increases. These requirements would force supervisory action if a bank's capital deteriorated to the point where the bank faced a substantial moral hazard problem or if the bank posed a threat to the deposit insurance fund. Given these goals, the equity capital trigger ratios set by the supervisors would generally be well below the capital ratios relevant to a well-run institution or that would maximize bank shareholders' wealth.

Capital regulation designed to protect the deposit insurance may also differ from regulation to prevent failure in two other ways. First, the measurement of capital should be done in economic values rather than historical cost accounting values. Historical cost accounting values are irrelevant to the deposit insurer if a bank must be resolved. Losses will only be controlled if assets can be sold at market prices sufficiently high as to cover liquidity needs and meet creditor demands for funds.[10] However, if the goal is failure prevention then book value capital is the best measure of capital. Book value is superior to market value because supervisors may exert more control over book capital, allowing them to defer recognition of losses and the associated pressure to resolve failing banks.

Second, uninsured liabilities may serve as a form of contingent capital, ready to absorb losses to the extent that a bank's reported economic value exceeds its value in resolution. However, equity capital is preferred by supervisors if the goal is failure prevention because equity can absorb losses without the bank failing, whereas contingent capital absorbs losses only if the contingency of failure arises.

The 1981 and 1988 regulatory capital regulations were intended to be binding upon bank portfolio choice, and as such clearly fall under the goal of minimizing the probability of failure. The intent of Basel II also appears to be failure prevention. Supervisors have indicated on several occasions that they view the overall level of capital in the banking system to approximately the right amount but they have concerns about its distribution. This implies that while Basel II will lower requirements for some banks, it will bind at even higher levels for other banks. Basel II leaves largely unchanged the 1988 definitions and measurement of bank capital, which are book value equity capital with a minimal role for contingent capital. These are the sorts of issues that are important considerations for regulations that bind most banks but which would be relatively unimportant for regulations that bind few banks.

The new proposal seeks to minimize the distortions arising from the 1988 standards in two ways. First, for banks with less sophisticated risk measurement systems, Basel II proposes a "Standard Model" that would use bank borrower credit ratings from agencies such as Moody's to set more requirements. While the new weights attempt to be reflective of relative credit risk, any such simple risk weighting scheme that imposes uniform weights by categories will inevitably overweight some assets and underweight others. Even given this unavoidable problem, the proposal makes unnecessary errors. Altman, Bharath and Saunders (2002) demonstrate that the risk weightings on rated loans still underweight risky assets. Moreover, they argue that the proposed weighting of unrated loans is too low and would discourage weaker firms from obtaining ratings.

Second, more sophisticated banks would be allowed to use their internal risk weightings to set the capital charges for each asset. However, the relative weights assigned by internal ratings depend upon the model of credit risk and the data used to parameterize the model. Banks will have opportunities to engage in old-style arbitrage of the risk weightings if the bank learns of flaws in the model or obtains new information suggesting that historic parameters are wrong. To be sure, these arbitrage opportunities may be more limited than under the 1981 and 1988 standards, but that in large part reflects the very crude nature of the risk measurements under those standards. Moreover, by relying on banks' internal ratings the supervisors have raised the cost of producing an unbiased estimate of the credit risk of any given obligation. Given a choice of how to rate the credit risk of a particular obligation, the existence of binding capital requirements raises the cost to institutions of using a procedure that generates the higher estimate of credit risk, creating an incentive to employ systematically biased models to measure credit risk. Supervisors will review bank's rating systems to assure compliance with minimum standards and will have an advantage in being able to see how different banks evaluate similar loans. However, banks will still have advantages in having better paid and likely more people working on the models, and in being able to observe market conditions that are not yet observable in historical loan loss data.

While bank capital regulation would be structured differently if the goal was to minimize expected deposit insurance losses, supervisors would still be interested in a bank's internal risk measurement models. Such models would be helpful in evaluating the riskiness of a bank's portfolio and the value of deposit insurance to a bank. Moreover, all banks would benefit from the use of such models to the extent they help their pricing and portfolio management. However, the use of internal models to set capital requirements imposes higher costs on supervisors and creates an incentive for banks to favor models that underestimate their risk exposure. These adverse incentives only increase the distortions resulting from binding capital regulation.

V. DEPOSIT INSURANCE REFORM[11]

The FDIC (2001) recently made a number of proposals to reform the existing deposit insurance system. Among the more important of these are proposals to:

(1) levy insurance premiums on all banks regardless of their condition and the size of the fund;
(2) allow the FDIC to issue credits against future premiums so that it can charge premiums to all banks without the fund becoming excessively large;
(3) merge the Bank Insurance Fund (BIF) and the Savings Associations Insurance Fund (SAIF);
(4) give the FDIC greater flexibility in setting the size of the fund; and
(5) index the current $100,000 limit on deposit coverage to a price index with the first adjustment in 2005.

All of these reforms focus on the distribution of losses across depositors, banks, taxpayers and time. The first four of these reforms relate to the size of the net premiums (premiums minus rebates) paid by different groups of insured institutions; the timing of premium collections, now or in the future; and the risk that taxpayers will be asked to cover losses. The last relates to the distribution of risk between depositors and those paying for losses to the insurance fund.

The structure and role of deposit insurance depends to a very large extent on the goal of the bank supervisors. To the extent that the goal is to minimize failure, deposit insurance plays a central role and its funding structure is potentially important. Deposit insurance reduces the cost of bank failure to depositors and, thereby, reduces the probability of an adverse externality in the form of a bank run that forces the closure of a bank. The reduced probability of a run, gives supervisors more time to help distressed banks recover. In those cases where the bank does not recover, the bank is likely to have incurred further losses necessitating payments by the insurance fund to protect insured depositors, and possibly protect uninsured depositors and even non-deposit liabilities.

The existence of deposit insurance, implicit and/or explicit, plays a central role in the need for regulation under loss minimization. However, far from seeking to prevent market discipline in the form of bank runs, a loss minimization goal would welcome occasional runs. If the supervisors have confidential information that suggests the bank is not in danger of becoming insolvent, the bank may be kept liquid by short-term loans from the discount window. Such a short-term supply of liquidity would give the bank time to convince the market that it was indeed solvent.[12]

The following three sections consider the major changes proposed by the FDIC. The first subsection takes the first two proposals, the next one takes the third and fourth proposals, and the fifth discusses the last proposal.

Premiums and Rebates

The proposals to charge all banks a premium and rebate collections if the fund exceeds some target are related proposals intended to allow the FDIC to charge a premium to all banks. FDIC Chairman Donald Powell (2001) says that the "FDIC wants to be able to fulfill the original mandate Congress gave it in 1991 to design and establish a truly risk-based system." The current restrictions on the size of the deposit insurance fund limit the FDIC's ability to charge such premiums. Indeed, the FDIC is prevented by law from charging premiums to well capitalized banks with satisfactory ratings if the fund exceeds 1.25% of insured deposits. As a result, the overwhelming majority of banks have paid no premiums in recent years. Powell further argues that if the appropriate premiums to discourage risk taking turn out to be too high ex post, then the FDIC should have the authority to rebate the excess. Relaxing this constraint would give the FDIC more freedom to charge premiums to all banks while keeping the fund within some desired range.

If the goal is to minimize the probability of bank failure, the pricing of deposit insurance is a potentially valuable tool. The premium payments may be scaled to the bank's riskiness in order to reduce the returns to holding a risky portfolio. As such, premium payments provide a relatively direct mechanism for influencing relative prices. The main constraint on scaling the premiums to risk is that they must not fully reflect the risk to the fund of distressed banks, as collecting higher premiums from these banks will reduce their probability of survival.

However, if the goal is to minimize losses, then setting premiums on the volatility of bank portfolio values misses the primary risk to the deposit insurance fund, which is that the supervisor will not close the bank in a timely manner. There is still an argument for trying to limit losses by charging premiums for risk, but it rests on a completely different foundation than is the case for premiums to minimize the risk of failure. Regulatory agencies charged with monitoring the solvency of depository institutions are faced with a number of alternatives. At one extreme, they could engage in continuous supervision and monitoring of all material aspects of a bank's portfolio. Doing so would not only be costly but also would probably be wasteful of resources. At the other extreme, agencies might not monitor at all and would simply pay off losses as they occur. This alternative too might be wasteful and clearly would lead banks to moral hazard behavior and risk taking. Regulators need, therefore, to balance the expected costs of supervision and monitoring and the risks that institutions may become economically insolvent between examinations. This risk is a function of the ease and costs of monitoring, the transparency of the accounting system, and the short-run, risk-taking propensities of insured institutions between examinations. It should also be recognized that because experience is proving that not all realized risks can be readily detected, some portion of the FDIC's price should reflect the realization that not all the actuarial risk is solely related to the time between examinations.

From the perspective of ensuring transparency, the rationale for premiums that vary across banks is transformed from pricing exclusively for risk to pricing based primarily on transparency. As mentioned previously, a portion of the FDIC's premium levy may still reflect multi-period risk because the fund may incur some losses when a bank fails with losses that were not detected at the time of examination. However, the primary factor would be banks' transparency. Banks that are relatively easy to value would pay lower insurance premiums; at the limit would be banks that invest solely in marketable assets (such as money market mutual funds), where the potential loss could be trivial. Conversely, banks that are harder to value would pay higher fees reflecting their potential to incur greater losses before their problems are recognized. Moreover, the incentive created by deposit insurance premiums could be augmented by examination charges that reflect the frequency and difficulty of the examination process (see Flannery, 1991). Continuous monitoring of the net worth of all depository institutions is extremely costly, so risk-related premiums serve the function of balancing the costs of monitoring vs. the chance that losses will materialize between examination periods.[13] Presumably, the less risky and complex an institution's portfolio is, the lower the costs of monitoring.

The Size of the Fund

Powell (2001) points out a number of problems caused by the current restrictions on the FDIC's discretion when the fund is too high or too low. He argues that premium limits imposed by the restrictions on the fund's size not only make risk-based premiums less effective but also allow new deposits to enter without paying any premiums. He also notes that if the fund ratio falls below the target then deposit insurance premiums must be increased to 23 basis points. Such an increase would most likely happen at a point in the business cycle when it would be a significant drain on banks' earnings. Powell argues that the consequence of this drain could be "impeding credit availability and economic recovery" (2001).

The starting point for evaluating Powell's comments on the size of the FDIC's insurance fund is to recognize that it is not an insurance fund like that held by a private insurer. Indeed, as William Isaac, former chairman of the FDIC, notes, "It's important to understand that there is no deposit insurance 'fund' " (2000). Premiums paid to the FDIC are remitted to the Treasury and go into the General Fund of the United States.[14] Outlays by the FDIC increase the federal deficit. Further, he asserts, "The object in collecting premiums from banks and thrifts is not to build a 'fund,' but to ensure that over time the deposit insurance program pays for itself. The so-called 'fund' is simply a running scorecard to determine whether banks and thrifts have paid in more than they have taken out" (p. 36).[15]

Current law places limits on the size of the fund relative to insured deposits. These limits affect:

(1) the resources available to the FDIC to resolve failed banks without having to rely on congressional appropriation;
(2) the way losses are shared between taxpayers and insured institutions; and
(3) the incentives of institutions, taxpayers, and Congress to monitor supervisory agencies' compliance with the goal of FDICIA to ensure that losses are minimized.

Each of these issues is considered below.

Resources Available to the FDIC

The FDIC has historically had the authority to buy assets and absorb losses up to at least the current value of the fund without seeking congressional authorization. It also may use these resources to provide temporary loans to receiverships to aid in resolving failed institutions. In effect, the fund serves as working capital for the agency, and efficiency considerations may argue for maintaining a minimal-sized account with the Treasury simply to facilitate the handling and finance of routine disposals of failed institutions. The minimum amount of resources readily available to handle failures should be sufficient to resolve problem banks as appropriate under both the goals of minimizing the probability of failure and minimizing expected deposit insurance.

The size of the fund is somewhat less important under the goal of minimizing the probability of failure. Under this goal, the fund must have access to sufficient resources so that depositors will not run problem banks due to a fear that the insurance fund will be unable to cover their losses. Depositors may be reassured either by the fund holding sufficient resources to deal with existing problem banks or by a sufficiently strong political commitment to recapitalize the FDIC at some point in the future.

The size of the fund is more important under the goal of minimizing losses because the FDIC cannot resolve a failing bank if it lacks loss bearing ability. For example, a shortfall in the Federal Savings and Loan Insurance Corporation fund inhibited thrift regulators in the late 1980s, resulting in large losses to taxpayers.[16] In this regard, having an account with the Treasury affects funds available to the FDIC and potentially its incentives. The FDIC may request additional resources from Congress if it lacks immediate access to sufficient funds, but the Congressional legislative schedule may not provide the needed funds to the FDIC on a timely basis as happened during the thrift debacle.

Loss Sharing

Under the DIF Act, any deficiency in the fund, should it be totally or partially depleted, is to be made up through an ex post levying of a tax in the form of higher premiums on surviving institutions. When the coverage ratio is restored, payments stop. Thus, the coverage ratio serves solely as a means for banks to stop taxing themselves ex ante for future claims on taxpayer funds. Under this system, institutions are providing a de facto loan to taxpayers over and above the income taxes they pay each year. The principal reason for a larger fund coverage ratio is that it reduces the costs of failure to surviving banks by lowering the ex post tax on healthy institutions who were not responsible for either failed institutions' risk taking nor for regulatory policies, a point that will be explored in more detail later.

This current situation can be described more formally to aid subsequent analysis. The Deposit Insurance Funds Act provides that as long as the ratio

$\alpha = F/D$, or the actual size of the fund (F) to insured deposits (D) is less than the statutory required or target ratio, $\underline{a} = 1.25\%$ (that is, $\alpha \leq \underline{a}$), premiums will be collected from all institutions. Although called a premium, the charges are better regarded as a tax or user fee because the size of the charge is not related to the perceived or actual actuarial risk of loss to the insurance fund, which is determined primarily by regulatory behavior rather than institution risk.

Should an institution fail and its resolution result in a loss to the fund, then healthy institutions bear the ultimate cost of the loss in the form of either a larger tax or paying the existing tax for a longer period of time until the fund returns to the required coverage ratio, a. Now consider the case when the actual fund coverage ratio is greater than the statutory required ratio, $\alpha \geq \underline{a}$. Then, according to the provisions of the 1996 DIF Act, premium or user fee collections cease for all but the riskiest institutions.

The actual coverage ratio may be greater than or equal to a, even if failures occasionally occur, because interest on Treasury debt allocated to the insurance fund (via accounting transactions) accumulates and premiums/taxes are still collected from the riskiest institutions.[17] Should the loss to the fund as a proportion of insured deposits, L, occur at any time, t, but not be sufficiently large to force the actual coverage ratio, α_{t+1}, to fall below its statutory target, $\underline{a}$ (that is, after the loss, α_{t+1} is still greater than $\underline{a}$), then taxpayer monies from the General Fund must be allocated to cover the losses.

If losses, L, are sufficiently large so that after the resolution the actual coverage ratio falls below its statutory target ($\underline{a} \geq \alpha_{t+1}$), then losses are shared between taxpayers and surviving depository institutions as follows. The proportion of the loss, s, represented by the extent to which the existing coverage ratio exceeds the target or statutory ratio, $s = \underline{a} - \alpha$, is borne by taxpayers. The additional or remaining proportion of the loss, $L - s$, is paid for over time by surviving depository institutions until the fund is restored to its statutory target coverage ratio.[18]

In order to continue collecting risk-related premiums, supposedly to control its risk exposure, the FDIC has proposed rebating excess premiums whenever the fund exceeds the statutory target by some fraction. Such a proposal, again, has important loss-sharing implications. For example, if there is a cap on the coverage ratio, $\bar{a}$, such that once the ratio exceeds the critical value $\underline{a} \geq \bar{a} \geq \alpha$, premiums are rebated to insured institutions. Instituting a cap on the coverage ratio puts a ceiling on the amount of losses that are borne by taxpayers and shifts more risk in any given year to surviving insured institutions. The lower the value of the cap relative to the statutory target level, the smaller are the losses borne by taxpayers and the larger the losses borne by surviving insured institutions.

Loss Bearing and Incentives

Bank supervisors are acting as agents for society in the performance of its mission. Ex ante alignment of agents' incentives with that of their principle is generally difficult, and outcomes are often improved by ex post monitoring. The two obvious candidates for monitoring the supervisors are the banks and Congress.

Banks' concern about supervisory performance comes about both because of the direct impact of supervisory activities on individual banks and because banks bear most of the expected losses to the deposit insurer through their deposit insurance payments. Congress may care about the failure of individual banks; many failures have a clear set of losers that exert political pressure on Congress to recover their losses or at least punish those perceived responsible for the losses. Congress may also care about deposit insurance losses to the extent it impacts the measure of the federal government's fiscal surplus or deficit used by Congress. As noted above, the FDIC's insurance funds are merely memo entries in the federal government's accounting. The difference between the agency's receipts and expenditures flows through to the government's fiscal position in the current year. Thus, the marginal cost of failure is reflected in the reported surplus or deficit. If unexpected failure resolution costs occur, Congress must either accept a higher fiscal deficit, or offset the impact on the deficit with higher taxes or lower expenditures for other on-budget activities. Conversely, to the extent that the cost of failure is lower than expected, that will result in some combination of a lower fiscal deficit, lower taxes and higher spending. As a result, Congress also has an incentive to monitor the performance of the agencies in minimizing losses.

If the goal of the supervisors should be to minimize the failure rate, monitoring should be triggered by bank failures but its intensity should not depend on the costs of resolution. Bank payments to the deposit insurance fund should be insensitive to contemporaneous losses, as may be the case if premiums exceed expected losses to reflect the social costs of bank failure. On the Congressional side, the current budget system is less than optimal from the perspective of the goal of minimizing failures because it gives Congress an incentive to increase monitoring when the net costs of failure increase within the year.[19] A better system would reduce Congress's incentives to monitor the costs of resolution, a goal which may be met by changing the measured fiscal deficit to exclude resolution costs.

However, if the goal is to minimize deposit insurance losses, monitoring intensity should depend on resolutions costs but not failure per se. Conceptually, the incentives of Congress and taxpayers should be clearly aligned since any loss to taxpayers will be reflected in the current year's fiscal budget. If a target exists for the fiscal balance (surplus or deficit), Congress will have a strong incentive to be concerned about, and to monitor, regulatory agency behavior, because failure to close insolvent institutions could impinge upon tax or spending programs. Furthermore, a statutory mechanism exists for holding the regulatory agencies accountable to Congress.

It is less clear how regulatory agencies' incentives align with those of surviving depository institutions when regulatory failure to close institutions imposes potentially large losses on those institutions. One could argue that these incentives are not necessarily well aligned and may also have undesirable effects on systemic risk. Congress, for example, clearly has little incentive to discipline regulatory agencies when they impose costs on depository institutions. Institutions do not vote, and, moreover, they are perceived to be better able to bear the costs than taxpayers are.[20] On the other hand, adjusting premiums to impose the current year's losses on the surviving banks will clearly affect earnings and returns to shareholders. Thus, banks may be motivated to use their political power to support timely resolution of the failed banks, thereby minimizing surviving banks' cost of deposit insurance.

The downside of imposing losses on banks is, as Powell (2001) points out, that the demand for funds to resolve failed banks is likely to occur at times when the entire banking system is under financial distress, such as during recessions. Imposing additional costs on already weakened institutions would act to tie the health of financial institutions together and make their returns and likely failures more correlated. Sound financial institution policies would argue that regulatory agencies should seek to make failures isolated and independent events, both in actuality and in the minds of the public, so as to reduce the chances that systemic events and runs occur.

In the end, the choice of imposing costs on institutions or the taxpayers hinges on a judgment about the relative strengths of the incentives of taxpayers or banks to bring and exert pressure on Congress to monitor and discipline the regulatory agencies. Given that Congress is more likely to respond to budget pressure, a case can be made for a lower, rather than a larger, fund, and, if pushed to the extreme, an argument may be made for no fund at all.

Given Isaac's (2001) observation that the fund is really just a scorecard, the existence of the fund could mislead some into believing that the resources available to deal with failed banks are limited to the size of the fund. However, given that the losses are first covered out of the General Fund and that deposit insurance ultimately rests on the full faith and credit of the government, there is little case to be made for earmarking a contingent set of claims on the fund keyed to bank tax or premium payments.[21] Thus, the case for maintaining a deposit insurance "fund" in an accounting sense rests on the need for the FDIC to have access to sufficient loss-bearing ability to resolve failed banks without requiring a special appropriation by Congress for every resolution. However, the requirements for a working capital fund would not necessarily result in the same optimal level as that which would result from viewing the fund as banks' paid-in capital to cover future losses.

VI. WHAT ARE THE REAL ISSUES?

This discussion has argued that the thrust of supervisory efforts post-FDICIA have been fundamentally misplaced.[22] Under careful examination, a large fraction of supervisory efforts is directed towards the goal of minimizing the probability of bank failure rather than that of minimizing the losses to the deposit insurer. Such efforts reflect a misunderstanding of the real source of losses to society, which are better measured by the losses to the insurer than by the number and size of failed banks. What then should the agenda look like if the goal is minimizing deposit insurance losses? This study contends that the primary issue is strengthening the incentives to resolve failures at the lowest cost to the FDIC. After FDICIA went into effect, FDIC records indicate that losses from 1992 through the second quarter of 2001 on bank failures to the BIF were 10.8% of assets in the aggregate, and that thrift institution losses to the SAIF (excluding Superior) were 4% of assets. On a yearly basis, losses on BIF-insured failures during this period ranged from 8% to 61%, and for SAIF-insured failures, from 2% to 63%.

Admittedly, while some of the risks may be difficult to detect, the large losses the FDIC has borne with some failures, including Superior Bank, suggest that in at least some cases the rewards to supervisors of engaging in forbearance exceed the costs. FDICIA sought to realign the incentive structure, for example, by requiring in Section 131 of the act that material losses be investigated by the agencies' inspector generals with public disclosure.[23] However, this incentive is apparently insufficient. Thus, further consideration of the supervisory incentive system appears desirable.

The first principle may be to do no harm in the sense of making changes that further misalign incentives. Because there is no insurance fund, any net losses borne by the FDIC flow through to the federal government's fiscal budget for the current year. The risk of changes in the deficit due to bank failures provides an incentive for Congress to monitor bank supervisors even if banks are likely to pay the entire cost of deposit insurance over some longer horizon.[24] Thus, bank premiums should not be tightly linked to the cost of bank failures in the current year in order to give Congress an incentive to monitor the supervisors.

A useful step forward would be to implement FDICIA's mandate in Section 121 to develop and implement supplemental disclosure of the economic value of banks' assets and liabilities. Academics have long argued that increasing the transparency of bank risk taking is one way to improve regulators' ability to monitor bank risk exposure. Immediate action to provide for market value disclosure could improve transparency, allowing outside parties to better monitor the regulators' performance. Further, the disclosure of economic values would help concentrate supervisory and bank attention on changes in the economic value of banks rather than on the manipulation of historic cost-accounting figures to produce desired levels of book capital. Moreover, the intent should be to move market value accounting for the purposes of prompt corrective action as supervisors and banks become more familiar with the concepts.[25]

While a focus on economic values could be a significant improvement, the adoption of market value accounting will not be sufficient by itself to implement the intent of prompt corrective action. For example, a significant part of the losses at Superior Bank occurred in assets that were required to be accounted for at market value but for which market value was substantially overestimated. Even with market value accounting, supervisors must be willing to demand accurate valuations and insist on timely revaluations when material errors are discovered. Thus, an insistence on accurate valuations is an important part of any reform. Moreover, the nature of these valuations, and in particular, reliance upon accruals vs. actual cash flows may reflect the going concern value of a banking organization, but may not reflect the value of assets available upon liquidation or closure.

A full solution to the incentive problem requires further consideration and likely will require a package of steps. This package should contain measures to increase both the political and financial costs of engaging in forbearance. FDICIA's provisions to require special assessments of banks in certain cases of large bank failure are designed to encourage banks to put pressure on supervisors to avoid costly failures.[26] However, these provisions have an offsetting effect of reducing Congress's incentive to monitor the supervisors. This effect may be small for the failure of a very large bank because such a failure is likely to involve other externalities that could affect large numbers of voters. In more general cases, however, there may be an unavoidable trade-off between trying to create incentives for banks to provide political pressure and maintaining incentives for Congress to monitor on its own.

Kane (1997) and Wall (1997) have recently made proposals to make supervisors' compensation depend in part on deposit insurance losses.[27] Such proposals may not be the most efficient way of providing incentives to supervisors, given that the conditions that lead to bank failure may vary substantially through time. Nevertheless, these or related proposals deserve some consideration as part of a package to increase the costs to supervisors of forbearance. As a backstop to supervisory action, market mechanisms may apply pressure on banks and supervisors when supervisors choose not to act on their own. The provisions of FDICIA Section 141 create such an incentive by mandating that the FDIC should resolve banks at the least possible cost to the deposit insurance fund. Prior to FDICIA, most uninsured bank creditors could expect that the FDIC would resolve a failed bank in a way that protected all creditors. The least cost provisions of FDICIA and the FDIC's procedures in the wake of FDICIA appear to have substantially reduced expectations of such a bailout.

The least cost provisions appear to have had some effect in the case of Superior Bank. While some depositors were surprised by the failure of Superior, the record suggests that many uninsured depositors bailed out long before the failure. The Thrift Financial Report submitted by Superior Bank to the Office of Thrift Supervision (and available on the FDIC's Web site at http://www2.fdic.gov/call_tfr_rpts/?catNumber=74) indicates that Superior had uninsured deposits of $572.4 million at its peak in March 2000. This figure dropped to $492.0 million in September, to $253.6 million in December, and to $52.6 million by March 2001. The discipline exerted by uninsured depositors did not prevent the bank from costly failure, likely in large part because of the presence of risk-insensitive funding that Superior was able to attract as uninsured depositors withdrew their funds. Insured deposits rose by $220 million (from $1.052 billion to $1.272 billion) between March 2000 and March 2001. Similarly, short-term federal funds and repurchase agreements, which are typically protected by perfected collateral in the event of a failure, grew by $73 million (from $179.1 million to $252.9 million).[28]

Smaller banks may be able to rely entirely on insured deposits for funding, but the backstop provided by market pressure could be strengthened both for medium-sized and larger banks, which are typically more reliant on uninsured funding. One way of enhancing the role of market discipline would be to limit the ongoing growth of Federal Home Loan Bank (FHLB) advances, which provide a safety valve for banks.[29] The FHLB may advance money to even the most distressed bank without significant fear of loss because the advances are overcollateralized and backed by a super-priority lien on all of the bank's assets. These collateral agreements allow a bank to withstand a greater volume of withdrawals before becoming illiquid and to shift losses to the FDIC if the bank does fail.

Market discipline may also be enhanced by addressing market perceptions that the largest banks are "too big to fail" – that is, too large to be resolved in a way that imposes significant losses on most creditors, including all depositors.[30] One method of enhancing market discipline is to accept that perceptions that some banks are too big too fail are unavoidable in the near future and to seek to substitute market signals that are less subject to too-big-to-fail views. Evanoff and Wall (2000) have suggested that subordinated debt is viewed as highly unlikely to benefit from too-big-to-fail perceptions and, accordingly, its pricing could be used as a signal for prompt corrective action. A more direct, albeit longer-term project, would be to directly attack the perception that some banks are too big to fail by developing and publicizing plans to close very large banks without protecting uninsured creditors.

VII. SUMMARY AND CONCLUSIONS

Recent supervisory efforts appear to be directed towards the long-standing goal of minimizing the probability of bank failure, despite the fact that FDICIA was explicitly designed to minimize losses to the deposit insurance fun. In this respect, Basle II and related efforts represents a significant step back from the PCA provisions of FDICIA. Minimizing the insurance losses from failed banks is critical to minimizing the social costs of bank failure and eliminating moral hazard behavior. Moreover, attempts to minimize the probability of failure require supervisors to try to supplant the pricing schedule set by financial markets with one set by the supervisors. Such efforts to impose artificial price schedules inevitability lead to resource misallocation and avoidance efforts by banks.

On the other hand, minimizing losses to the deposit insurer requires relatively less intervention in the relative price schedule. The supervisors need only make sure that banks do not price in a deposit insurance subsidy to risk-taking because the deposit insurer is not going to bear significant risk. As such, the agenda for reform to accomplish the goals of PCA is shorter and focuses on the steps needed to change supervisory priorities to that of limiting deposit insurance losses. Implementing such an agenda may not be easy, but it will be more valuable in the long run.

NOTES

1. Section 131 of FDICIA, titled "Prompt Regulatory Action," creates a new Section 38 of the Federal Deposit Insurance Act. PCA is a modified version of Benston's and Kaufman's (1988) structured early intervention and resolution (SEIR).

2. Historically, this was clearly the FDIC's objective in the 1950s.

3. For a summary of the evidence, see Kaufman (1994).

4. A recent example of runs limited to failing institutions, see Kane (1987).

5. The classic case of systemic externalities occurred during the late 1800s under the fractional reserve system of the National Banking Act. Because banks were allowed to keep required reserves in the form of deposits at Reserve City and Central Reserve banks, a withdrawal of funds from weak institutions would sometimes pyramid into withdrawals of reserve funds from healthy institutions. The Federal Reserve Act eliminated this problem. See Eisenbeis (1997) for a further discussion of the sources of systemic risk.

6. Indeed, these costs should not be overestimated given the recent experience with market disruption on a scale far in excess of that which would result from the failure of any individual firm.

7. See Merton and Perold (1993) for a discussion on the problems in holding company organizations for relying strictly upon capital, as reported, to capture the nature of the risk relationships in complex organizations.

8. *Commercial Bank Examination Manual*, "Examination Strategy and Risk-Focused Examinations," Section 1000.1.

9. One way of thinking about the impact of capital regulations on portfolio allocations is in a CAPM type model. A bank locates itself on something like the securities market line which is a line with one point determined by the risk-free rate and another by a tangency portfolio on the set of efficient portfolios. If capital regulation could move banks along this line, it would induce banks to hold more capital but would not change portfolio allocations. However, capital regulation may change bank portfolios if it changes the optimal scale of the bank. In particular, the elasticity of prices is unlikely to be constant across all bank asset categories. Thus a change in the scale of a bank is likely to change its portfolio allocations. Moreover, if the risk weights do not exactly correspond with the market's assessment then capital regulation will change the shape of the efficient frontier and banks' portfolio allocations. Such distortions appear unavoidable given that Basel II evaluates the riskiness of assets on a stand-alone basis rather than in a portfolio context.

10. The economic value of some information-intensive bank assets depends on who owns the assets. The assets may have greater value in the hands of the bank than if the bank is sold or liquidated.

11. This section is derived from Eisenbeis and Wall (2002).

12. See Smith and Wall (1992).

13. See Flannery (1991) for a discussion of these trade-offs. See Shadow Financial Regulatory Committee (2000a) for a slightly different view.

14. An Electronic version of Isaac's comments may be found at http://woodrow.mpls.frb.fed.us/pubs/region/00-03/isaac.html

15. The FDIC annual report indicates the nature of the fund's investments and income, but these are only bookkeeping entries, similar to the Social Security Trust Fund.

16. White (1991), for example, documents the ways that the Federal Home Loan Bank System adopted policies of forbearance that ultimately resulted in large losses to the Federal Savings and Loan Insurance Corporation and taxpayers.

17. Presently, the FDIC is collecting premiums from only about 8% of insured institutions, according to Murton (2001).

18. How quickly the fund is rebuilt, from premiums paid by surviving institutions, may have solvency and systemic risk implications for the survivors.

19. The net cost of failure within the year is the losses recognized by the fund less any increase in deposit insurance premiums directly attributable to the costs of the failure. For example, if a bank failure resulting in losses of $500 million and the FDIC collected no premiums then the net failure cost would be $500 million. The failure cost would also be $500 million if the FDIC charged premiums but the premiums were already at their maximum and did not increase as a result of the failure. However, if as a result of the failure, the FDIC collected an extra $300 million in premiums then the net cost of failure would be $200 million.

20. Institutions and their principles do make campaign contributions, but these have become relatively limited as a result of campaign financing reforms.

21. Some would argue that under FDICIA, taxpayers incur an insurance liability or loss only when the equity of the banking system is exhausted. The previous analysis suggests that this idea is not quite correct. Moreover, it is both unrealistic and unlikely that the government would let the banking system be destroyed before stepping in. Clearly, government has recently intervened on behalf of the airline Industry in the aftermath of September, and there is clearly less of a statutory mandate and history to bail out that industry than there is for banking.

22. Blackwell (2002a, b) reports on an FCIE-commissioned study of private reinsurance for the FDIC. The benefits of obtaining reinsurance would be twofold: to spread the risk of loss and (as a "senior FDIC official" said in an interview that the pricing of the reinsurance "may yield a valuable free-market perspective on the risk of loss banks and thrifts pose" (2002a, p. 1). However, the analysis in this article suggests that neither of these benefits would be significant. The risk of loss is already spread throughout the banking system, which is effectively providing its own reinsurance. It is not clear how that capacity would be significantly increased by reinsurance, not is it clear how reinsurance would affect regulatory incentives to close economically insolvent institutions or to engage in least cost resolution since any premiums would be passed on to the industry by the FDIC, either directly or indirectly. Finally, the primary risk that would be priced by a private reinsurer is regulatory risk and not market risk. Blackwell (2002b) quotes George Kaufman as saying, "Reinsurers have to guess how well the FDIC will act. This is a problem you don't have in other types of reinsurance. In terrorism insurance, victims are not in control of the terrorists (2002b, p. 4).

23. FDICIA defines a material loss as the greater of $25 million or 2% of the institution's total assets at the time the FDIC was appointed receiver or initiated open bank assistance.

24. This condition should hold if the scorecard (insurance fund) has sufficient funds to pay the loss without increasing premiums. The condition will also hold even if the scorecard has insufficient funds so that banks will have to pay in the future, provided that the congressional discount rate on future payments is greater than the interest rate at which bank obligations are cumulating.

25. The Financial Accounting Standards Board (FASB) has been working on revisions to generally accepted accounting principles (GAAP) that would mandate the use of fair-value accounting for all financial instruments. Its preliminary views were published in FASB (1999).

26. The provisions for rebuilding the fund in the event that least cost resolution is suspended are in Section 141 of FDICIA.

27. Wall (1997) provides the incentive through a system in which the repayment of bonds issued by the FDIC to investors is contingent on the state of the deposit insurance fund. That proposal could easily be modified so that repayment of the bonds is contingent on the losses to the deposit insurance fund, possibly averaged over some period of time.

28. Superior's ability to attract such funds provides further evidence of the desirability of increasing the limits on insured deposits.

29. See Stojanovic, Yeager and Vaughan (2000) for a discussion of the implications of FHLB advances for deposit insurance.

30. The term "too big to fail" should not be taken too literally. While depositors may not suffer losses, equity holders may lose their investments and senior management may lose their jobs.

ACKNOWLEDGMENTS

The authors would like to thank William Estes, Alton Gilbert, Lynn Shibut Myron Kwast and Allen Berger for helpful comments and suggestions on an earlier version and Lisle Cormier for research assistance. The views expressed here are those of the authors' and do not reflect those of the Federal Reserve Bank of Atlanta, the Board of Governors, or the Federal Reserve System. Any remaining errors are the authors' responsibility.

REFERENCES

Altman, E. I., Bharath, S. T., & Saunders, A. (2002). Credit ratings and the BIS capital adequacy reform agenda. *Journal of Banking and Finance*, *5*, (May), 909–921.

Benston, G. J., & Kaufman, G. G. (1998). Risk and Solvency Regulation of Depository Institutions: Past Policies and Current Options. Salomon Brothers Center for the Study of Financial Institutions Monograph 1988–1, New York: New York University Press.

Benston, G. J., & Kaufman, G. G. (1994). The intellectual history of the Federal Deposit Insurance Corporation Improvement Act of 1991. In: G. G. Kaufman (Ed.), *Reforming Financial Institutions and Markets in the U.S.* Boston: Kluwer Academic Publishers.

Benston, G. J., & Kaufman, G. G. (1995). Is the banking and payments system fragile? *Journal of Financial Services Research*, *9*, (September), 209–240.

Blackwell, R. (2002a). FDIC study backs reinsuring funds. *American Banker*, (January 7).

Blackwell, R. (2002b). Reinsurance for FDIC raises eyebrows. *American Banker*, (January 8).

Blackwell, R. (2002c). Latest Crop of Failures Brings Steeper Costs, July 8.

Bovenzi, J. F., & Murton, A. J. (1988). Resolution costs of bank failures. *FDIC Banking Review*, *3* (Fall), 1–13.

Brown, R. A., & Epstein, S. (1992). Resolution costs of bank failures: An update of the FDIC historical loss model. *FDIC Banking Review*, *5*, (Spring/Summer), 1–16.

Brumbaugh, R. D., Jr. (1993). *The collapse of federally insured depositories: The savings and loan as precursor.* New York: Garland Publishing.

Carnell, R. S. (1997a). FDICIA after five years: What has worked and what has not? FDICIA: Bank reform five years later and five years ahead. In: G. G. Kaufman (Ed.), *Research in Financial Services: Private and Public Policy* (vol. 9, pp. 11–16). Greenwich, Conn.: JAI Press.

Carnell, R. S. (1997b). A partial antidote to perverse incentives: The FDICIA Improvement Act of 1991. FDICIA: Bank reform five years later and five years ahead. In: G. G. Kaufman (Ed.), *Research in Financial Services: Private and Public Policy* (vol. 9, pp. 199–233). Greenwich, Conn.: JAI Press.

Eisenbeis, R. A. (1997). Bank deposits and credit as sources of systemic risk. Federal Reserve Bank of Atlanta. *Economic Review, 82*, (3rd Quarter), 4–19.

Eisenbeis, R. A., & Horvitz, P. M. (1994). The role of forbearance and its costs in handling troubled and failed depository institutions. In: G. G. Kaufman (Ed.), *Reforming Financial Institutions and Markets in the U.S.* Boston: Kluwer Academic Publishers.

Eisenbeis, R. A., & Wall, L. D. (2002). Reforming Deposit Insurance and FDICIA. Federal Reserve Bank of Atlanta. *Economic Review, 87*, (1st Quarter), pp. 1–16.

Evanoff, D. D., & Wall, L. D. (2000). Subordinated debt as bank capital: A proposal for regulatory reform. Federal Reserve Bank of Chicago. *Economic Perspectives, 14*, (2nd Quarter), 40–53.

Federal Deposit Insurance Corporation (FDIC) (2000). *Options paper.* Washington, D. C.: FDIC, August.

Federal Deposit Insurance Corporation (FDIC) (2000). *Keeping the promise: Recommendations for deposit insurance reform.* Washington, D.C.: FDIC, April.

Financial Accounting Standards Board (FASB) (1999). Reporting financial instruments and certain related assets and liabilities at fair value. *Preliminary Views*, (December 14).

Flannery, M. J. (1991). Pricing deposit insurance when the insurer measures bank risk with error. *Journal of Banking and Finance, 15*, (September), 975–998.

Fuerbringer, J., & Kilborn, P. T. (2002). Bank Trader's Losses Total $750 Million: Allied Irish Discloses Currency Unit Trouble. *New York Times*, (February 7), C1, C14.

Greenspan, A. (2001). The financial safety net. Speech delivered at 37th Annual Conference on Bank Structure and Competition of the Federal Reserve Bank of Chicago, May 10, Chicago, Illinois.

Isaac, W. M. (2000). Financial reform's unfinished agenda: A look at deposit insurance funds. Federal Reserve Bank of Minneapolis. *Special Issue of The Region, 14*, (March), 34–37.

James, C. (1991). The losses realized in bank failures. *Journal of Finance, 46*, (September), 1223–1242.

Jensen, M. C., & Meckling, W. H. (1976). Theory of the firm: managerial behavior, agency costs, and ownership structure. *Journal of Financial Economics, 3* (October), 305–360.

Kane, E. J. (1977). Good Intentions and Unintended Evil: The Case against Selective Credit Allocation. *Journal of Money, Credit and Banking, 9* (February), 55–69.

Kane, E. J. (1983). The role of government in the thrift-industry's net-worth crisis. In: G. J. Benston (Ed.), *Financial Services: The Changing Institutions and Government Policy.* Englwood Cliffs, N.J.: Prentice-Hall.

Kane, E. J. (1987). Who should learn what from the failure and delayed bailout of the ODGF. National Bureau of Economic Research Working Paper 2260, March.

Kane, E. J. (1989). Changing incentives facing financial-services regulators. *Journal of Financial Services Research, 2* (September), 263–272.

Kane, E. J. (1997). Ethical foundations of financial regulation. *Journal of Financial Services Research, 12* (August), 51–74.

Kane, E. J. (2002). What lessons might crisis countries in Asia and Latin America have learned from the S&L mess? Paper presented at the conference What Can an Examination of S&Ls Reveal About Financial Institutions, Markets, and Regulations? sponsored by the UCLA Anderson School of Management and the Milken Institute, Los Angeles, Calif., January 25.

Kaufman, G. G. (1994). Bank contagion: A review of the theory and evidence. *Journal of Financial Services Research, 8* (April), 123–150.

Kaufman, G. G. (1996). Bank failures, systemic risk, and bank regulation. *The Cato Journal, 16* (Spring/Summer), 17–45.

Kaufman, G. G. (2001a). Prepared testimony of George G. Kaufman for the hearing on the failure of Superior Bank, FSB, Hinsdale, Illinois, before the U.S. Senate Committee on Banking, Housing, and Urban Affairs, September 11. <www.senate.gov/~banking/01_09hrg/091101/kaufman.htm>

Kaufman, G. G. (2001b). The current status of deposit insurance in the United States and proposals for reform. Loyola University, Chicago. Unpublished working paper, December.

Koehn, M., & Santomero, A. M. (1980). Regulation of bank capital and portfolio risk. *Journal of Finance, 35* (December), 1235–1244.

Litan, R. E. (1987). *What should banks do?* Washington, D.C., Brookings Institution.

Maremont, M. (2001). Pritzkers to pay $460 million over bank failure. *Wall Street Journal,* (December 11).

Merton, R. C., & Perold, A. F. (1993). The management of risk capital in financial firms. In: S. L. Hayes III (Ed.), *Financial Services: Perspectives and Challenges.* Boston, MA: Harvard Business School Press.

Murton, A. J. (2001). BIF assessment rates for first semiannual assessment period of 2002. Memorandum to Board of Directors, Division of Insurance, FDIC. <www.fdic.gov/deposit/insurance/risk/Bif2002_01.html>

Powell, D. E. (2001). Statement of Donald E. Powell, chairman, Federal Deposit Insurance Corporation, on deposit insurance reform before the Subcommittee on Financial Institutions and Consumer Credit, Committee on Financial Services, U.S. House of Representatives, October 17. www.fdic.gov/news/news/speeches/chairman/sp17oct01.html>

Shadow Financial Regulatory Committee (1999). The failures of BestBank and First National Bank of Keystone. Statement No. 157 of the Shadow Financial Regulatory Committee, September 27.

Shadow Financial Regulatory Committee (2000a). Proposal on full cost pricing of supervisory and examination services by the federal banking agencies. Statement No. 161 of the Shadow Financial Regulatory Committee, May 8.

Shadow Financial Regulatory Committee (2000b). Deposit insurance reform options. Statement No. 165 of the Shadow Financial Regulatory Committee, December 4.

Smith, S. D., & Wall, L. D. (1992). Financial Panics, Bank Failures and the Role of Regulatory Policy. Federal Reserve Bank of Atlanta. *Economic Review,* (January/February), 1–11.

Sprague, I. H. (1986). Bailout: An insider's account of bank failures and rescues. New York: Basic Books.

Stojanovic, D., Yeager, T. J., & Vaughan, M. D. (2000). Is Federal Home Loan Bank funding a risky business for the FDIC? Federal Reserve Bank of St. Louis. *The Regional Economist,* (October), 5–9.

Wall, L. D. (1997). Taking note of the deposit insurance fund: A plan for the FDIC to issue capital notes. Federal Reserve Bank of Atlanta. *Economic Review, 82,* (1st Quarter), 14–30.

Wall, L., & Peterson, D. R. (1990). The effect of Continental Illinois's failure on the performance of other banks. *Journal of Monetary Economics, 26* (August), 77–99.

White, L. J. (1991). *The S&L debacle: Public policy lessons for bank and thrift regulation*. New York: Oxford University Press.

DIFFERENTIATING AMONG CRITICALLY UNDERCAPITALIZED BANKS AND THRIFTS

Lynn Shibut, Tim Critchfield and Sarah Bohn*

ABSTRACT

Seeking improvements to prompt corrective action (PCA) or the supervisory process, we studied FDIC-insured institutions that became critically undercapitalized from 1994 through 2000. We grouped the institutions by outcome and analyzed differences between groups. Most of the critically undercapitalized institutions avoided failure, while those that failed imposed substantial costs on the insurance funds. While we did not find many significant differences, a few key differences in reserve levels and nonperforming assets did materialize in the last year of operation. These difference help characterize troubled institutions, and further research may prove useful for the supervisory process.

1. INTRODUCTION

The Prompt Corrective Action (PCA) provisions in FDICIA require that regulators set a threshold for critically undercapitalized institutions, and that regulators promptly close institutions that breach the threshold unless they quickly recapitalize or merge with a healthier institution. Many economists

* Lynn Shibut and Tim Critchfield work in the Division of Insurance and Research at the FDIC. Sarah Bohn is currently a graduate student at the University of Maryland..

Prompt Corrective Action in Banking: 10 Years Later, Volume 14, pages 143–202.

ISBN: 0-7623-0987-3

expected that these provisions would result in dramatically reduced loss rates, or even zero loss rates, for bank failures.

Bank regulators set the threshold for critically undercapitalized institutions to 2% tangible capital. There are a number of reasons why a threshold above 0% is appropriate. Since the value of many types of bank assets is opaque and difficult to estimate, and since troubled banks have an incentive to overstate asset values, it is not unusual for the capital levels of troubled banks to be overstated.[1] Thus a threshold slightly above 0% may better approximate insolvency on a market value basis. In addition, a higher threshold may increase the likelihood that a private-sector solution can be found for a failing institution.

Critics have complained that the 2% capital threshold set by regulators is too low. For example, Benston and Kaufman (1997) argue that it appears to be "much too low" and should be increased, citing as evidence the likelihood that most banks with 2% tangible capital already have negative market-value capital, the ability of troubled banks to change risk exposure quickly by using derivatives, and the loss rates of post-FDICIA failures.[2]

Setting the thresholds involves tradeoffs. Peek and Rosengren (1996) summarized them as follows:

> It is easy to identify a problem bank at the time of its failure. The challenge is to identify a problem bank in time to prevent its failure or at least in time to alter its behavior in order to limit the losses to the deposit insurance fund. Thus an appropriate slogan for early intervention might be "the earlier the better." However, such an approach must be tempered by giving appropriate weight to the costs associated with supervisory intervention in banks that are incorrectly identified as "troubled."

In this paper, we studied FDIC-insured institutions that have crossed the 2% tangible capital threshold or failed between 1994 and 2000. We separated these banks[3] into four groups (low-cost failures, high-cost failures, near-failures that survived, and near-failures that were purchased), and we analyzed differences between the groups. If there are consistent differences that separate failed banks (and particularly high-cost failed banks) from other seriously troubled banks, there may be opportunities to improve the regulatory treatment of troubled banks – either through a change in the PCA threshold for a critically undercapitalized bank or by other means.

Section 2 provides background information, including a discussion of related literature and the tradeoffs associated with setting the threshold for critically undercapitalized banks. Section 3 discusses the data and methodology, and Section 4 reports the results of various comparisons across groups. Section 5 concludes and Section 6 makes recommendations.

2. BACKGROUND AND LITERATURE REVIEW

The PCA provisions in FDICIA were motivated by a desire to reduce supervisory forbearance and failure costs in the banking industry. Many people, including members of Congress, believed that regulators should have supervised banks and thrifts differently in the 1980s. Appendix 1 provides a summary of these provisions.

Carnell (1997b) concisely described the overarching goal of PCA: "to resolve the problems of insured depository institutions at the least-possible long-term loss to the deposit insurance fund (i.e. to avoid or minimize loss to the fund)." The means for achieving the goal center on incentives. For banks, PCA was designed to reduce the "moral hazard" inherent in federal deposit insurance by giving the owners and managers of troubled banks an incentive to avoid taking excessive risks by encouraging them to maintain enough capital and by limiting their discretion if capital is impaired. For regulators, PCA was designed to encourage aggressive action against troubled banks by limiting their ability to practice forbearance and by requiring audits after failures. PCA also clarified the rules of the game for both bankers and regulators.

Technically, the goal of PCA can be accomplished by reducing either the loss rate of failed banks or the failure rate of banks (or both). The limits triggered by the thresholds for an undercapitalized bank focus largely on avoiding failure and thus reducing the failure rate. In contrast, the closure rules triggered by the threshold for a critically undercapitalized bank focus more heavily on reducing the loss rate by ensuring prompt closure of nonviable banks. But the closure rules could also reduce the failure rate by encouraging banks to seek capital earlier than they would if closure occurred when banks become insolvent on a book value basis.[4]

We found no empirical studies that concentrated specifically on the 2% PCA threshold. However, several studies have focused on early intervention and the likelihood that the new thresholds reduced regulatory forbearance. Peek and Rosengren (1996) studied banks and savings banks in New England from 1988 through 1994, and they found that more than two-thirds of banks downgraded to a CAMEL rating of 4 had a tangible capital ratio that indicated that they were adequately capitalized under PCA. They concluded that "examiners usually identify problems before PCA guidelines are triggered."[5] The GAO (1996) came to a similar conclusion in their review of activities from 1992 through 1995. Peek and Rosengren (1997) also studied the pattern of formal and informal enforcement actions imposed on commercial banks and savings banks in New England from 1989 through 1992. They found that "formal regulatory actions tend to occur well before most banks become undercapitalized according to PCA capital thresholds, and they include restrictions on bank behavior that tend to be more comprehensive than those in the PCA provisions." Jones and King (1995) studied commercial banks operating from 1984 through 1989, and they concluded that the risk-based capital (RBC) thresholds for undercapitalized banks do little to limit supervisory forbearance.[6] Thus several authors suggest that the PCA capital thresholds do little to force earlier or stronger intervention by regulators at the stage when the probability of failure is most likely to be reduced.[7]

Two studies investigated changes to the RBC threshold for undercapitalized institutions. Berger et al. (1991) examined RBC thresholds as part of an analysis of the problems associated with market value accounting proposals. Noting that the GAO (1990) had found that some banks in poor condition underreport their loan loss reserves, they explored several alternative RBC standards that incorporated adjustments to the loan loss reserve based on nonperforming loan data. They used Call Report data for all banks from 1982–1989 to develop statistical methods for estimating alternative loan loss reserves. Using the revised loan loss reserve figures, they adjusted the RBC ratios for all banks as of year-end 1989 and compared the adjusted results to the actual RBC ratios. All of their alternative measures resulted in substantial increases in the number of banks that would have been classified as undercapitalized.[8] They concluded that the revision would expand and probably improve the distribution of regulatory scrutiny.

Jones and King (1995) developed an alternative RBC threshold by using data on classified assets and noncurrent loans to enhance the current threshold. To measure the effectiveness of their alternative, they estimated the prediction error of the actual and revised RBC standard, assuming that all troubled institutions should be classified as undercapitalized under the RBC standard.[9] Their revised RBC standard resulted in a significant reduction in the prediction error.

These studies suggest that an investigation of the tradeoffs associated with the 2% threshold might bear fruit. If one can identify the tradeoffs related to the threshold, consider the costs inherent in each, and consider the effects of changing the threshold, one can make a well-informed judgement about the threshold that provides the highest net benefit to society.[10] In this paper, we are most interested in the potential costs and benefits associated with a marginal change in the 2% threshold for critically undercapitalized institutions.[11] We examine the consequences of thresholds that identify failure candidates either before or after the optimum point in time.

We first review the costs associated with the delay of closure. Theoretically, this includes the operating costs of running an insolvent institution, plus any additional costs associated with risks taken by the banks in hope of surviving. Gilbert (1992) analyzed commercial banks and concluded that these costs may not be very high. Based on a review of commercial bank failures from 1985 through 1990, he found no statistically significant differences in the loss rates of BIF-member banks that were undercapitalized for different lengths of time. Thus, whether PCA encourages regulators to close undercapitalized banks earlier (or later), Gilbert predicts that the loss rates do not change significantly. However, the savings and loan crisis and the Japanese banking crisis provide ample evidence that these costs can be extremely high – particularly if regulators do not carefully monitor undercapitalized banks and limit their activities, or if the delay lasts a long time.

One might argue that the cost of delay can be calculated as the cost of failure (for both the FDIC and other creditors of the receivership), since regulators have the authority to close banks when their market value is zero.[12] However, a large part of these costs is probably attributable to the difficulties of measuring the market value of a troubled bank, large shifts in market value, or fraud, rather than the capital threshold used for PCA.[13] It is very difficult to separate losses attributable to measurement errors inherent in certain assets or market shifts from losses attributable to a delay in closure caused by a sub-optimal PCA threshold – especially since regulators have the authority to define capital (effectively changing accounting standards) as well as choose the capital threshold.[14] The cost associated with fraud may be somewhat easier to ascertain, but one should not automatically assume that there were no delays in closure for bank failures that involved fraud.

Next, we look at the consequences of a PCA threshold that flags failure candidates too soon. The associated costs differ depending on the outcome of the PCA action. Possible outcomes include:

- The bank is closed.
- The bank survives, either with or without a capital infusion.
- The bank is quickly sold to another institution.

If the bank is closed, the costs are relatively high. The owners suffer a loss of the freedom to control their assets and the stigma of failure on their reputation. They also bear costs that would have been avoided if the bank had stayed open.[15] In some circumstances, the bank's customers or the local community could suffer.[16]

If the bank survives intact, then the costs to the owners may be very low.[17] If the bank reaches the 2% threshold and the owners sell the bank to another institution, then the costs are probably somewhere in between those of the other outcomes.[18]

The dynamic effects of the PCA threshold should also be considered. For some banks, the PCA threshold for critically undercapitalized institutions increases the bank's resolve to act decisively or accelerates a search for new capital or potential acquirers. If the PCA threshold triggers a more effective response by the bank, and the improvement in the bank's response causes the bank to avoid failure, then the PCA threshold would yield a net benefit to the bank (and, most likely, to the FDIC).

Under the current PCA threshold, we see little evidence that viable banks have been closed, and thus the costs of unnecessary closure to date have probably been negligible or zero.[19] It is more difficult to gauge the net cost for the other two outcomes because they involve predicting the relationship between the threshold level and outcomes of troubled banks, estimating the associated economic effects, and balancing the economic effects against the lost freedom experienced by the bank owners.

The optimum threshold for critically undercapitalized banks may well vary across the business cycle. Because banks that breach the PCA threshold have such a short time to recapitalize, it appears likely that the costs imposed by a threshold that was set too high would be heavier during times when the market for bank franchises is weak, and lower during times when markets are strong.[20] The cost of lengthy delays can be extremely high, although the cost of brief delays (if accompanied by close supervision) may be low. In some unusual circumstances, the cost of identifying banks too early could be substantial. For example, the application of PCA thresholds on money center banks during the less-developed-country (LDC) crisis in the early 1980s might have caused serious damage to the economy.[21] Thus the GAO (1996) states that "we see the issue as one of striking a proper balance between the need for sufficient regulatory discretion to respond to circumstances at a particular institution and the need for certainty for the banking industry about what constitutes an unsafe and unsound condition and what supervisory actions would be expected to result from those conditions." Mishkin (1997) specifically raises the need for discretion in unexpected situations that involve systemic risk.[22] In more normal circumstances, the cost of identifying banks too early would be much lower.

Few studies have attempted to quantify the net cost or benefit of changing the capital thresholds for closure. The FDIC (1997) made an admittedly very rough estimate of the benefits if PCA had been in effect from 1980 through 1992 by assuming that a failing bank's operating losses (excluding loan loss provisions) would have been avoided if closure had occurred according to the PCA rules. They found that 343 failed banks would have been closed earlier, yielding a cost savings of about $825 million. They identified 143 banks that breached the 2% PCA threshold but did not fail, but made no attempt to estimate the associated costs.

Barakova and Carey (2001) shed some light on these tradeoffs in their analysis of the pace and characteristics of banks that recover from distress.[23] Using data from FDIC-insured commercial banks from 1984 through 1999, they identified 345 banks whose equity ratios fell below 2% but did not fail. Only 51% of those banks recovered in one year; 71% recovered in two years; and 91% in four years.[24] They found that the typical sources of bank recapitalization differed with the recovery time frame. Equity infusions played a substantial role regardless of the recovery time frame, but the role of equity infusions was smaller, and the role of income larger, for banks that recovered more slowly. They concluded that regulators should insist on the rapid issuance of sufficiently large amounts of capital if they want a rapid recovery of a seriously undercapitalized bank. This analysis indicates that an increase in the PCA threshold may well force some banks to merge (or possibly even fail) that would otherwise survive intact if it causes viable banks to be classified as critically undercapitalized.

Barakova and Carey also found that most distressed banks did not issue new equity until *after* loan losses began to decline – both before and after FDICIA, perhaps because the cost of equity is prohibitive when significant loan losses are being reported. This indicates that viable banks that breach the threshold while their loan losses have not clearly declined may be most likely to suffer from the costs associated with a PCA threshold above the optimum level.

By analyzing groups of critically undercapitalized banks since FDICIA, we provide insight into the effects of the 2% threshold to date, and we highlight areas where changes in the threshold could provide a net benefit to society. Note, however, that the best regulatory change may be something other than a change in the PCA threshold – particularly if the differences between the outcome groups are unrelated to capital.

3. DATA AND METHODOLOGY

This section discusses the data and methods used for analysis.

3.1. Sample Selection

For 1994 to 2000, we analyzed the bank failures plus any bank that fell below the 2% capital requirement from the PCA rules established in FDICIA. We began in 1994 because the FDICIA provisions made to reduce the FDIC's losses would have been fully implemented by then. For each failed institution we segregated the institutions with relatively low resolution costs from other failures. For each institution that fell below 2% tangible capital without failing, we looked to see what happened to the institution after getting into capital trouble. We found that about one-half of this group was absorbed by other organizations and one-half survived independently.

There were 48 failures from 1994 to the end of 2000. Three notable failures were eliminated from our analysis because of massive fraud or other extraordinary circumstances.[25] We labeled 16 failed institutions with an estimated resolution cost of less than 12% of assets as low-cost failures. This left 29 institutions with an estimated resolution cost of over 12% of assets. We selected 12% as the cut-off for low-cost failures because it was well below the average loss rate experienced by the FDIC and also provided a reasonable sample size. We used two different reference periods to analyze the data: for the 32 failures that became critically undercapitalized prior to failure, we used the date that they breached the threshold; for the remaining 13 institutions, we used the final Call Report date.[26] We will loosely refer to the analysis date as the date an institution fell below the PCA limit for the remainder of the paper, despite the fact that a few of these dates were failure dates.[27]

We found 44 institutions that fell below 2% tangible capital from 1994 to 2000 and that did not fail as of the fourth quarter of 2001. There were five institutions in this group that were eliminated because of special circumstances.[28] The remaining 39 institutions were segregated into 21 institutions that were absorbed into another organization within one year of breaching the threshold and 18 institutions that survived intact for at least one year.[29] We refer to the total group as near-failures.

3.2. Pre-PCA Condition Data

We collected a large volume of data from Call Reports and Thrift Financial Reports on all the institutions selected. We constructed variables from both reports that correspond to consistent measures of financial performance for the two-year period before an institution failed or fell below 2% tangible capital; for institutions that survived after reaching the threshold, we also collected data for the year after they fell below 2% tangible capital. We developed annualized performance ratios from a rolling set of the past four quarters. This calculation allowed us to create aggregate data from any ending quarter that would contain annual ratios that covered all four seasons, and this tended to smooth the effects of sudden changes in accounting or performance.

Examination data were collected for each institution from any full examination over the last three years before failure or the three years before an institution fell below 2% tangible capital. Classified loans were taken from the last full examination before the institution fell below the PCA capital limit. These loans were measured against assets reported in the quarter after the examination was completed or the previous quarter if a failed institution did not file its last report.[30]

To measure local bank distress, we created a problem bank index based on CAMELS 4- and 5-rated banks in each metropolitan statistical area (MSA) or county. The index represents the percentage of deposits in each bank's location (or locations) that were held by problem banks.[31]

We also used branch-level data to create a geographic distribution index, similar to the Herfindahl-Hirschman Index (HHI). Instead of measuring market concentration, our geographic index measures an institution's exposure to each market that it operates in (from 0, complete diversification, to 1, no diversification).[32]

To test for understated reserve levels, we followed the technique adopted by Jones and King (1995). Jones and King calculated an adjusted reserve level based on a pooled time-series regression, where charge-offs over a two-year period were regressed against the amount of classified loans as of the beginning of the two-year period. The resulting equation is shown below.[33]

$$\text{Two-year Chargeoffs} = 0.006 + 0.95{*}\text{Loss} + 0.57{*}\text{Doubtful} + 0.15{*}\text{Substandard} + 0.04{*}\text{Special Mention}$$

They estimated the appropriate reserves by applying these parameter estimates to the classified assets held by each bank in the sample (implicitly assuming that reserves should cover about two years of chargeoffs).[34] We compared the total from this calculation to the reserves reported in the financial reports filed in the closest quarter around the examination date.

3.3. Resolution and Receivership Data

We collected data about the resolution and the receivership for each failed institution. The resolution data came from FDIC board cases and associated working papers; it included the number of bidders, the premiums for the top two bids, and the FDIC's estimated loss at the time of failure. The receivership data came primarily from the FDIC's general ledger, the FDIC Failed Bank Cost Analysis, and from "pro-forma" financial statements prepared at bank closing. For the most part, we reported results over the life of the receivership; for receiverships that had not terminated as of year-end 2000, results through year-end 2000 were used.[35] To improve comparability across banks, we reported many items as a percentage of total assets at failure. The FDIC general ledger was the source for asset loss rates, assets sold to acquirers, balance sheet composition (including adjustments to the balance sheet made during the receivership), and receivership income and expense items. The primary source for the FDIC loss rates used in this study was the Failed Bank Cost Analysis, which relies on FDIC general ledger data. Appendix 2 includes a discussion of our method used to calculate FDIC loss rates.

We also collected receivership data from the "pro-forma" statements prepared during the institution closings. These provided the banks' balance sheets as of the date of failure, adjustments made to the balance sheet to switch from Generally Accepted Accounting Principles (GAAP) accounting to the cash basis accounting used by the FDIC's receiverships, and the initial balance sheet recorded on the FDIC's general ledger.

The accounting differences between ongoing institutions and receiverships are substantial, and thus any comparison of pre-failure and post-failure results must be done carefully. Appendix 2 discusses the major accounting differences, as well as certain adjustments that we made to improve the comparability of the data across institutions and across time.

3.4. Statistical Analysis Methods

With a wealth of data collected for the institutions selected for this study, we required a statistical test for finding significant differences in measures of central tendency for any two of the institution groupings. We were limited by a relatively low number of institutions in each group, since the study period was only 1994–2000. The groups ranged in size from 16 to 45. In addition, many of the financial ratios in this study tended not to be distributed normally. Although a two-sample t-test (difference of means test or analysis of variance) is robust against minor normality departures, this study's data contain extreme outliers and are highly skewed. Thus, the reliability of a simple parametric test is suspect.[36] In this study, a nonparametric analysis appears more appropriate since it does not involve assumptions of normality, and is not sensitive to the presence of outliers.

We used the Wilcoxon rank sum test to compare the location of two given distributions with the same general shape, which is essentially a difference of medians test. Given a financial or other ratio and two institution groups, the Wilcoxon statistic tests the null hypothesis that the two groups have the same probability distribution vs. the alternative hypothesis of a location shift (that is, a difference in medians). The test provides a p-value for use in determining the conclusion of the test, given a level of significance. We are particularly interested in financial ratios for the compared groups that are statistically different at the 1%, 5%, and 10% significance levels.

In addition to the Wilcoxon test, we employed the Kendall's tau test to analyze failure data. As explained in Section 3.1 above, failures were split into two groups – high-cost and low-cost – for the purpose of refining differentiation between undercapitalized institutions. This involved an educated but somewhat arbitrary selection of a loss rate to divide the failures into the two groups. Although the group by group analysis is valuable especially for comparing failures to near-failures and low-cost failures to near-failures, we also chose to study the correlation of failure loss rate to other variables without making a loss rate a simple binary variable. The Kendall's tau test allows us to make full use of the failure data since it computes a correlation statistic based on the rank-level of the loss rate compared to that of another variable. This non-parametric test is robust to outliers and tests the whole distribution rather than only the median. For this reason, the Kendall's tau test provides a slightly more powerful analysis of the failure data. The test provides a statistic measuring the strength of the correlation (ranging from –1 to 1) and a *p*-value for the significance of the correlation.

4. RESULTS

We begin with a comparison of failures and near-failures. This is followed by comparisons of low-cost and high-cost failures, low-cost failures and near-failures, near-failures by outcome (survived vs. purchased), and surviving near-failures over time (PCA date vs. one year later). Most of the comparisons were based on the PCA date, defined as the quarter-end date when the institution breached the 2% threshold; for failed institutions that never breached the threshold, the final Call Report date was treated as the PCA date.

4.1. Failures Versus Near-failures

This section discusses failures compared to near-failures that breached the PCA threshold. Table 1 provides the comparison of failures and near-failures as of the quarter of PCA failure; Table 2 provides the same comparison one year earlier. The 45 failures in our study held \$4.1 billion in assets as of the PCA date, and the near-failures held \$9.0 billion in assets as of the PCA date. The average size for the failures was just \$92 million while the average size for the

Table 1. Comparison of Failures and Near-Failures as of the PCA Date.

	Failures	Near-Failures	Difference
Number of Institutions	45	39	(6)
Median Total Assets ($MM)	64	57	(7)
Median Asset Growth	(12.61)	(8.52)	4.09*
Institutions with CAMELS Rating of 4 or 5 (%)	93.30	84.60	(8.70)
Median Balance Sheet Percentages			
Investment Securities	9.40	11.51	2.11
1–4 Family Mortgages	11.08	16.38	5.30
Commercial Real Estate	16.27	11.03	(5.24)
Multifamily Real Estate	1.40	1.04	(0.36)
Commercial & Industrial Loans	10.91	11.84	0.93
Deposits	97.00	98.00	1.00
Median Rolling 4 Quarter Performance Ratios			
Return on assets	(5.62)	(5.76)	(0.14)
Return on equity	(124.93)	(124.24)	0.69
Yield on earning assets	8.40	8.77	0.37
Cost of funding earning assets	3.85	4.37	0.52
Net interest margin	4.62	4.69	0.07
Nonint. inc. to earning assets	1.58	1.12	(0.46)
Nonint. exp. to earning assets	8.19	6.66	(1.53)*
Net operating income to assets	(5.60)	(6.04)	(0.44)
Net chargeoffs to loans	3.44	3.98	0.54
Loss provision to avg. assets	3.37	3.58	0.21
Loss provision to net charge-offs	120.18	122.95	2.77
Efficiency ratio	135.07	123.03	(12.04)
Median Condition Ratios			
Loss allowance to loans	4.37	4.50	0.13
Loss allowance to noncurrent (Coverage Ratio)	43.00	63.98	20.98**
Noncurrent & OREO to assets	9.93	6.69	(3.24)*
OREO to assets	2.47	0.80	(1.67)*
Noncurrent RE loans to RE loans	7.97	3.54	(4.43)**
Noncurrent total loans and leases	9.54	7.24	(2.30)
Noncurrent loan growth	31.20	29.44	(1.76)
Equity capital ratio	1.39	0.97	(0.42)
Core capital (leverage) ratio	1.28	0.87	(0.41)**
Equity capital plus reserves	4.22	4.03	(0.19)
As of Mid-Year Before PCA Date, or Most Recent Exam			
Median Economic Condition Measures			
Problem Bank Index	0.08	0.02	(0.06)
Geographic Diversification Index	1.00	1.00	0.00
Median Examiner Classification Ratios			
Reserves to Estimated Reserves	101.34	94.81	(6.52)
Classified Assets to Assets	13.00	10.47	(2.52)

* Significant at the 10% level.
** Significant at the 5% level.
Note: For failed institutions that did not file a Call Report or TFR showing that they were critically undercapitalized, the Final Call Report or TFR was used.

Table 2. Comparison of Failures and Near-Failures as of One Year Before the PCA Date.

	Failures	Near-Failures	Difference
Number of Institutions	45	39	(6)
Median Total Assets ($MM)	71	59	(12)
Median Asset Growth	(4.21)	0.34	4.55
Institutions with CAMELS Rating of 4 or 5 (%)	77.80	64.10	(13.70)
Median Balance Sheet Percentages			
Investment Securities	8.93	10.35	1.42
1–4 Family Mortgages	12.20	15.28	3.08
Commercial Real Estate	14.38	10.76	(3.62)
Multifamily Real Estate	1.60	1.00	(0.60)
Commercial & Industrial Loans	10.07	8.85	(1.22)
Deposits	92.00	92.00	0.00
Median Rolling 4 Quarter Performance Ratios			
Return on assets	(1.20)	(0.72)	0.48
Return on equity	(18.01)	(12.89)	5.12
Yield on earning assets	8.76	8.46	(0.30)
Cost of funding earning assets	3.94	4.04	0.10
Net interest margin	4.93	4.68	(0.25)*
Nonint. inc. to earning assets	1.22	1.54	0.32
Nonint. exp. to earning assets	6.10	6.21	0.11
Net operating income to assets	(1.27)	(0.75)	0.52
Net chargeoffs to loans	1.40	1.48	0.08
Loss provision to avg. assets	1.46	1.21	(0.25)
Loss provision to net charge-offs	123.47	129.06	5.59
Efficiency ratio	97.83	90.36	(7.47)
Median Condition Ratios			
Loss allowance to loans	2.62	2.07	(0.55)
Loss allowance to noncurrent (Coverage Ratio)	44.74	43.47	(1.27)
Noncurrent & OREO to assets	8.56	4.62	(3.94)
OREO to assets	2.66	1.08	(1.58)
Noncurrent RE loans to RE loans	4.10	3.14	(0.96)
Noncurrent total loans and leases	5.62	4.33	(1.29)
Noncurrent loan growth	10.64	3.92	(6.72)
Equity capital ratio	5.85	6.28	0.43
Core capital (leverage) ratio	5.71	5.94	0.23
Equity capital plus reserves	8.14	7.77	(0.37)

* Significant at the 10% level.

Note: For failed institutions that did not file a Call Report or TFR showing that they were critically undercapitalized, the Call Report or TFR one year before the Final Report was used.

near-failures was more than twice as large, at $230 million. However, the difference in the median size was much smaller and statistically insignificant.

As of the last examination before failure, 93% of the failures and 85% of the near-failures had a CAMELS rating of 4 or 5. None of the institutions had a CAMELS rating of 1, but six institutions were rated 2; only one of the six failed.

The median ratios calculated for condition and performance of each group revealed a few differences but for many items there was no meaningful difference. At the quarter that the failures fell below the PCA threshold, their condition was predictably worse than the near-failures in most aspects except capital. The failures had higher median equity capital ratios than the near-failures (1.39 compared to 0.97%), and statistically significant higher core capital (leverage) ratios (1.28 vs. 0.87%). The 13 failures that had capital above the PCA threshold appear to have lifted the core capital ratio for the entire group of failed institutions, explaining the significant differences in capital ratios.[37]

For both groups, median capital declined precipitously – over 400 basis points – during the year before they breached the PCA threshold or failed. This provides evidence that a modest increase in the PCA threshold may not result in a substantial change in the timing of the associated regulatory actions for institutions that currently breach the threshold.

The portfolio composition measures showed median values that were generally worse for the institutions that eventually failed, but the differences in medians were statistically insignificant. On the balance sheet, the failed institutions held a median of just 9% of assets in securities while the near-failures held 12%. For the failed institutions this ratio held at 9% for the year before they fell below the PCA threshold, but the near-failures actually increased their median value for the percentage of assets held in securities from 10% in the year before falling below the threshold. The composition of the loan portfolios for the failed institutions appeared slightly more risky than the near-failures, but again none of these differences were significant. The median value for the percentage of assets held in 1–4 family mortgages was 11% for the failed institutions while the near-failures held 16% of this typically less risky loan. For commercial real estate (excluding multifamily residential property), a generally riskier loan type that caused many failures in the 1980s, the median value was 16% for the failures while the near-failures held just 11%. The failed institutions actually showed an increase, up from 14%, in the median value for commercial real estate during the year before falling below the PCA threshold. This may relate to the higher shrinkage in total assets experienced by the failures (12.61% vs. 8.52% median shrinkage in the year preceding the PCA date), as they sold off more marketable assets to improve their capital ratios.

The patterns in troubled loans showed more pronounced differences between the two groups. The level of nonperforming assets in failed institutions was significantly higher than in near-failures. For failed institutions, the median value for the noncurrent assets plus other real estate owned (OREO) as a percentage of assets was 9.93% at the PCA date. The near-failures reported a median level of 6.69% of assets, which was 3.24% less than the failed institutions. One year earlier the failures registered a median of 8.56% while the near-failures were at 4.62%, but the difference was not statistically significant. The source of higher nonperforming assets was real estate loans: the median ratio of noncurrent real estate loans was 7.97% for failures – significantly higher than the 3.54% median value for near-failures. Moreover, the failures held significantly more OREO (2.47% of assets for the failures; 0.80% for the near-failures as of the PCA date). For commercial and industrial loans the differences were not as dramatic nor were they significant, but the problems in these loans arose earlier for the failures. The failed institutions increased to a median noncurrent rate of 8.73% for commercial and industrial (C&I) loans when they hit the PCA threshold from 5.46% one year earlier. The near-failures experienced a sharper change, from 1.70% one year before hitting the PCA threshold to a median noncurrent rate of 7.23% at the PCA date. However, the median growth in noncurrent loans was not significantly different between the groups in either time period.

The differences in nonperforming assets across the groups were not accompanied by significant differences in loan provisions and charge-offs. The charge-off rates were very similar for the two groups, with the near-failures recording slightly higher rates than the failures in both years. In the last four quarters the median net charge-off rate on loans more than doubled from one year earlier for both groups. Loan loss provisions (as a percentage of average assets) showed a similar increase over time. In both time periods, the ratio of loss provisions to average loans was also comparable across groups. The ratio of the loss allowance to total loans was higher for the failures one year before the PCA date (2.62% vs. 2.07%). As of the PCA date, the ratio had increased substantially for both groups, but the increase was larger for near-failures. Thus at the PCA date, the ratio of loss allowance to total loans was 4.37% for failures and 4.50% for near-failures.

At the PCA date, the relationship between reserves and noncurrent loans was significantly weaker for the failed institutions than for the near-failures. The coverage ratio, by measuring the dollar amount of reserves set aside for each dollar of noncurrent loans, gives a relative measure of the protection available for charge-offs before earnings and capital must suffer. The median coverage ratio was slightly higher for the failures than the near-failures one year before the PCA date (44.74% vs. 43.47%). While the near-failures improved their ratios in the following year (to 63.98%), the coverage ratio for the median failure deteriorated to 43.00% as of the PCA date. While their capital levels were slightly lower, the near-failures' reserve levels were much better than the institutions that eventually failed. Figure 1 shows the distribution of coverage ratios across the groups as of the PCA date. It shows that more than one-half of the high-cost failures had coverage ratios below 40%, but less than 30% of the low-cost failures and near-failures had coverage ratios below 40%.

The failures had a higher level of classified assets (13.00% vs. 10.47%), but the difference was smaller than that of the nonperforming assets and insignificant. Surprisingly, the Jones and King estimate of reserves was lower than actual reserve for the failures, but higher than actual reserves for the near-failures; however, the difference between the groups was insignificant. There are two phenomena that might explain this result. First, when examiners find that a bank is insolvent, they stop identifying losses and instead shift to failure preparation. Therefore the classified asset figures are probably incomplete (and thus understated) for some, perhaps most, of the failures. Second, the formula relied on examination data from the last full exam before an institution fell below the PCA threshold. Because we had to reach back in time to get the data for this approach, the formula would not have captured changes to the balance sheet during the intervening period. Since many of the institutions experienced increases in noncurrent loans during the year prior to breaching the PCA threshold, and the institutions may also have experienced deterioration in classification levels,[38] we feel that the classified loan data were too distant from the date these institutions fell below the PCA threshold.

Comparing capital plus reserves as a percentage of assets when these institutions fell below the PCA limit, the differences between the failed institutions and the near-failures virtually disappear. The median ratio of equity capital plus reserves to assets was 4.22% for the failed institutions while the near-failures were not significantly different at 4.03%. Even one year before, the failures had a median ratio of 8.14% while the near-failures had a median ratio of 7.77%. Thus, when noncurrent loan levels are not considered, the difference between the groups was insignificant.

The performance up to the quarter when all these institutions fell below the PCA threshold was remarkably similar. The return on assets (ROA) for the four quarters leading up to the violations of the PCA threshold were poor for both groups. The failures had a median ROA of –5.62%, which was slightly lower than the median loss for the near-failures, at –5.76%. Compared to the near-

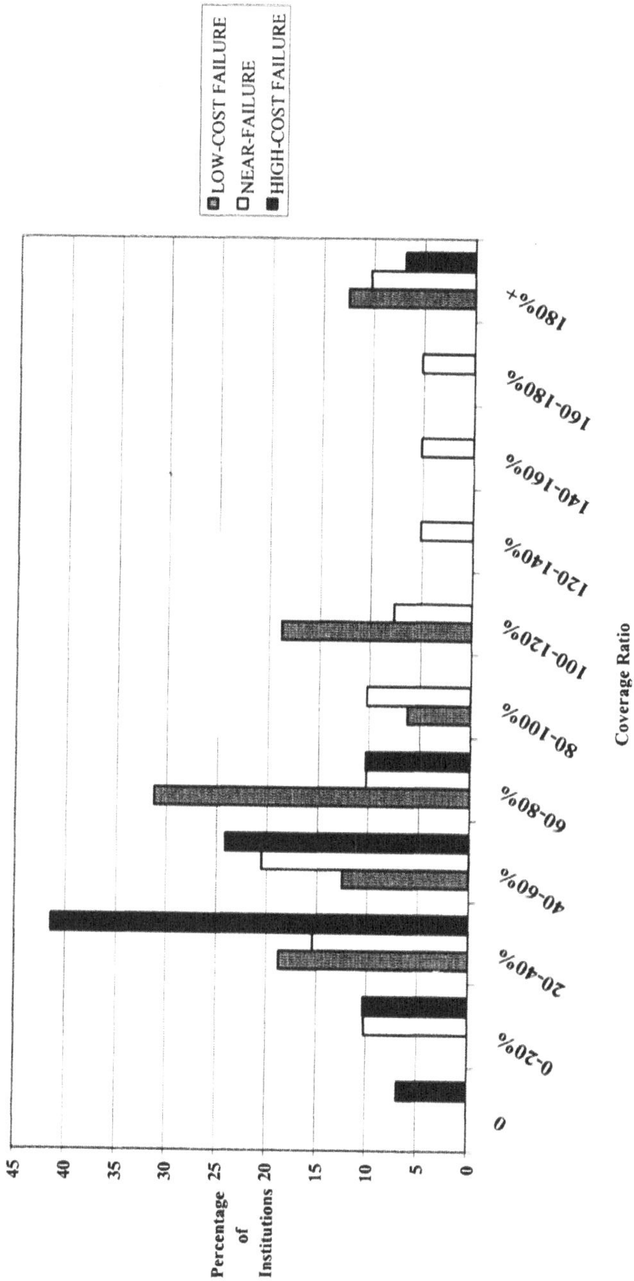

Fig. 1. Distribution of Coverage Ratio as of PCA Date.

failures, the failures had somewhat lower earnings the year before (–1.20% ROA for failures; –0.72% ROA for near-failures). The failures began reporting quarterly losses in their last 7 quarters before falling below the PCA threshold. The near-failures showed median quarterly losses for their last 5 quarters before falling below the PCA threshold.[39]

Some performance ratios showed significant differences. The failed institutions generated a median ratio of noninterest expenses to earning assets of 8.19% in their last four quarters, up from 6.10% one year earlier. The near-failures generated a noninterest expense ratio of just 6.66%, up from 6.21% one year earlier. While the two groups started at nearly the same level of noninterest expenses, the failing institutions generated more losses from noninterest expenses than the near-failures. This may relate to the higher levels of troubled assets, since asset workouts are resource intensive.

The only statistically significant difference in performance between the groups in the year before these institutions fell below the PCA threshold was net interest margin. The failing institutions reported a net interest margin of 4.93%, while the near-failures reported 4.68%, a statistically significant 25 basis point difference. The yield on assets was a statistically insignificant 30 basis points higher for the failures and the cost of funding earning assets was a statistically insignificant 10 basis points lower for the failures. While it is difficult to discern from the financial reports, the net-interest-margin advantage enjoyed by the failures may have been from interest accruals on loans that became past due as these institutions came closer to failing.

In summary, the most important differences between failures and near-failures related to reserve levels and nonperforming assets. On balance sheet composition, capital, and performance, these two groups were not very different.

4.2. Low-cost Failures Versus High-cost Failures

A comparison of low-cost and high-cost failures provides insight into whether the capital measure provides the optimal intervention timing for banks and regulators, and whether additional considerations might reduce losses to the insurance funds.

4.2.1. Comparisons of Pre-failure Financial Condition and Performance

Table 3 provides the comparison of low-cost and high-cost failures as of the PCA date, and Table 4 provides the same comparison one year earlier. Table 5 provides Kendall's tau correlations with the FDIC loss rate for both periods.[40] There were 16 low-cost failures, holding $1.4 billion in assets as of the PCA

Table 3. Comparison of Low-Cost and High-Cost Failures as of the PCA Date.

	Low-Cost	High-Cost	Difference
Number of Institutions	16	29	13
Median Total Assets ($MM)	66	64	(2)
Median Asset Growth	(18.04)	(11.92)	6.12
Insitutions with CAMELS Rating of 4 or 5 (%)	93.80	93.10	(0.70)
Median Balance Sheet Percentages			
Investment Securities	10.14	8.74	(1.40)
1–4 Family Mortgages	15.61	9.42	(6.19)*
Commercial Real Estate	15.93	17.57	1.64
Multifamily Real Estate	1.55	1.01	(0.54)
Commercial & Industrial Loans	10.51	11.00	0.49
Deposits	95.13	97.30	2.17*
Median Rolling 4 Quarter Performance Ratios			
Return on assets	(5.23)	(5.92)	(0.69)*
Return on equity	(106.23)	(134.99)	(28.76)*
Yield on earning assets	8.11	8.42	0.31
Cost of funding earning assets	3.69	4.16	0.47*
Net interest margin	4.41	4.80	0.39
Nonint. inc. to earning assets	1.36	2.02	0.66
Nonint. exp. to earning assets	7.87	9.23	1.36
Net operating income to assets	(4.85)	(5.73)	(0.88)*
Net chargeoffs to loans	3.85	3.09	(0.76)
Loss provision to avg. assets	2.44	3.71	1.27
Loss provision to net charge-offs	129.41	119.57	(9.84)
Efficiency ratio	117.61	138.75	21.14
Median Condition Ratios			
Loss allowance to loans	4.50	4.37	(0.13)
Loss allowance to noncurrent (Coverage Ratio)	69.03	37.85	(31.18)***
Noncurrent & OREO to assets	6.44	12.92	6.48***
OREO to assets	0.46	4.17	3.71**
Noncurrent RE loans to RE loans	4.35	9.20	4.85**
Noncurrent total loans and leases	5.67	11.37	5.70**
Noncurrent loan growth	14.21	31.86	17.65
Equity capital ratio	2.09	0.78	(1.31)*
Core capital (leverage) ratio	2.03	0.98	(1.05)**
Equity capital plus reserves	5.79	3.95	(1.84)
As of Mid-Year Before PCA Date, or Most Recent Exam			
Median Economic Condition Measures			
Problem Bank Index	0.01	0.11	0.10*
Geographic Diversification Index	1.00	1.00	0.00
Median Examiner Classification Ratios			
Reserves to Estimated Reserves	114.13	97.02	(17.12)
Classified Assets to Assets	12.20	13.77	1.57

* Significant at the 10% level.
** Significant at the 5% level.
*** Significant at the 1% level.

Note: For failed institutions that did not file a Call Report or TFR showing that they were critically undercapitalized, the Final Call Report or TFR was used.

Table 4. Comparison of Low-Cost and High-Cost Failures as of One Year Before the PCA Date.

	Low-Cost	High-Cost	Difference
Number of Institutions	16	29	13
Median Total Assets ($MM)	72	71	(1)
Median Asset Growth	5.06	(5.94)	(11.00)
Institutions with CAMELS Rating of 4 or 5 (%)	75.00	79.30	4.30
Median Balance Sheet Percentages			
Investment Securities	15.00	8.39	(6.61)*
1–4 Family Mortgages	16.95	10.20	(6.75)*
Commercial Real Estate	14.35	15.85	1.50
Multifamily Real Estate	1.42	1.66	0.24
Commercial & Industrial Loans	7.43	12.93	5.50
Deposits	90.66	92.23	1.57
Median Rolling 4 Quarter Performance Ratios			
Return on assets	(0.09)	(1.56)	(1.47)
Return on equity	(4.43)	(23.27)	(18.84)
Yield on earning assets	8.66	8.86	0.20*
Cost of funding earning assets	3.90	4.05	0.15
Net interest margin	4.70	5.32	0.62**
Nonint. inc. to earning assets	1.16	1.42	0.26
Nonint. exp. to earning assets	5.57	6.96	1.39
Net operating income to assets	(0.81)	(1.73)	(0.92)
Net chargeoffs to loans	0.56	1.81	1.25
Loss provision to avg. assets	0.99	1.73	0.74
Loss provision to net charge-offs	149.17	103.65	(45.52)
Efficiency ratio	97.91	97.91	0.00
Median Condition Ratios			
Loss allowance to loans	2.00	2.91	0.91
Loss allowance to noncurrent (Coverage Ratio)	58.67	37.83	(20.84)
Noncurrent & OREO to assets	4.32	9.79	5.47***
OREO to assets	0.97	3.15	2.18**
Noncurrent RE loans to RE loans	2.22	6.53	4.31*
Noncurrent total loans and leases	3.63	6.93	3.30
Noncurrent loan growth	43.67	1.90	(41.77)*
Equity capital ratio	6.68	5.65	(1.03)
Core capital (leverage) ratio	6.56	5.59	(0.97)
Equity capital plus reserves	8.19	8.14	(0.05)

* Significant at the 10% level.
** Significant at the 5% level.
*** Significant at the 1% level.
Note: For failed institutions that did not file a Call Report or TFR showing that they were critically undercapitalized, the Call Report or TFR one year before the Final Report was used.

Table 5. Kendall Tau Correlation Coefficients: Pre-failure Items Versus Total Loss Rate.

	One Year Before	At PCA Date
Number of Institutions	45	45
Median Total Assets ($MM)	(0.07)	(0.06)
Median Asset Growth	(0.08)	0.01
Median Balance Sheet Percentages		
Investment Securities	(0.28)***	(0.27)***
1–4 Family Mortgages	(0.24)**	(0.26)**
Commercial Real Estate	(0.07)	(0.09)
Multifamily Real Estate	0.00	(0.07)
Commercial & Industrial Loans	(0.02)	(0.02)
Deposits	0.12	0.22**
Median Rolling 4 Quarter Performance Ratios		
Return on assets	(0.10)	(0.26)**
Return on equity	(0.11)	(0.18)*
Yield on earning assets	0.24**	0.18*
Cost of funding earning assets	0.06	0.20*
Net interest margin	0.23**	0.07
Nonint. inc. to earning assets	0.09	0.15
Nonint. exp. to earning assets	0.14	0.21**
Net operating income to assets	(0.04)	(0.27)***
Net chargeoffs to loans	0.23**	0.09
Loss provision to avg. assets	0.14	0.15
Loss provision to net charge-offs	(0.07)	0.07
Efficiency ratio	0.00	0.12
Median Condition Ratios		
Loss allowance to loans	0.10	0.01
Loss allowance to noncurrent (Coverage Ratio)	(0.19)*	(0.12)
Noncurrent & OREO to assets	0.26**	0.33***
OREO to assets	0.26**	0.28***
Noncurrent RE loans to RE loans	0.09	0.20*
Noncurrent total loans and leases	0.07	0.16
Noncurrent loan growth	(0.21)*	0.08
Equity capital ratio	0.01	(0.15)
Core capital (leverage) ratio	(0.01)	(0.15)
Equity capital plus reserves	(0.01)	(0.14)

* Significant at the 10% level.
** Significant at the 5% level.
*** Significant at the 1% level.

date.[41] There were 29 high-cost failures, holding $2.7 billion in assets, as of the PCA date. There were no significant differences related to asset size.

As expected, most of the median condition ratios for the high-cost failures were worse than for the low-cost-failures. The median capital ratio of the low-cost failures was 2.09%, down from 6.68% one year before falling below the PCA threshold. The median for the high-cost failures was 0.78%, down from 5.65% one year earlier. The median capital held by low-cost failures was significantly higher than the high-cost failures when they fell below the PCA threshold, but the difference one year earlier was insignificant. Similarly, the median for the core capital (leverage) ratio was 2.03% for the low-cost failures and 0.98% for the high-cost failures (significantly different). However, the correlations between the capital measures and the FDIC loss rate were insignificant.

A related difference appeared in the level of deposits funding assets. The low-cost failures ended up with deposits that were 95% of assets, while the high-cost failures ended up with deposits as 97% of assets. This significant difference may have been caused simply by the lower capital backing the assets of the high-cost failures.

The low-cost failures had a higher proportion of low risk assets than the high-cost failures. The low-cost failures had a median ratio of securities to assets of 10%, while the high-cost failures had 9%. The low-cost failures had a median 15% in securities one year earlier, while the high-cost failures had even less, 8%. In both periods, there was a statistically significant correlation between securities holdings and FDIC losses (–0.27 as of the PCA date; –0.28 one year earlier). The median for single-family residential mortgages of the low-cost failures was 16%, while the high-cost failures showed a median of 9% of their assets in these loans. The year before falling below the PCA threshold both groups held just slightly more, 17% and 10%, respectively. In both time periods the difference in medians and the correlations with the FDIC loss rate were significant. The two groups showed a slight insignificant difference in commercial real estate (excluding multifamily residential properties) as a percentage of assets. The low-cost failures had a median 16% of assets in commercial real estate, while the high-cost failures had 18%; both medians had increased by 2% from the year before. These mortgages are much more difficult to dispose of when an institution tries to shrink as capital becomes scarce.

Nonperforming assets, including noncurrent loans and OREO, were dramatically different for the two groups of failures. The median percentage of nonperforming assets to total assets for the low-cost failures was 6.44%, up from 4.32% one year earlier. The median percentage of nonperforming assets was 12.92% for the high-cost failures, up from 9.79% one year earlier. The high-cost failures started at a higher level and rose to almost double the median rate of the low-cost failures. There was a 0.33 correlation between nonperforming assets and the FDIC loss rate as of the PCA date, and a 0.26 correlation one year earlier. The differences in medians and the correlations were statistically significant in both time periods.

A primary cause of this difference was the level of noncurrent commercial real estate, which was significantly higher for the high-cost failures one year before they fell below the PCA limit. The median low-cost failure had no noncurrent commercial real estate, while the high-cost failures had a median noncurrent rate for commercial real estate of 3.93%. Commercial real estate probably influenced the OREO levels, which were significantly higher for the high-cost failures in both time periods. As of the PCA date, the high-cost failures had a median 4.17% of assets in OREO, whereas the low-cost failures only had 0.46%. Total noncurrent loans exhibited a pattern similar to all nonperforming assets, except that in the year before falling below the PCA threshold the difference was insignificant. The median level of noncurrent loans as a percentage of total loans was 5.67% for the low-cost failures when they fell below the PCA limit, while the high-cost failures had a median of 11.37%. The median net charge-off rate on loans during the last four quarters of operations was 3.85% for the low-cost failures, while the high-cost failures had a median of 3.09%, which was not significantly different. Despite similar net charge-offs, the levels of noncurrent loans left behind by the high-cost failures was still higher for this group.

At failure, reserves and capital serve to cover losses in the loan portfolio. In this respect, the groups looked similar. The median ratio of equity capital plus reserves to assets was 5.79% for the low-cost failures, while the high-cost failures had a slightly lower ratio of 3.95%, but this difference was not significant. One year earlier these ratios were within 5 basis points, at 8.19% and 8.14% respectively. However, the high-cost failures needed more reserves to cover their higher level of noncurrent loans. The coverage ratio, reserves to noncurrent loans, was much lower for the high-cost failures. The median coverage ratio for the low-cost failures was 69.03%, while the high-cost failures had just 37.85% – a statistically significant difference of 31.18%. One year earlier, the low-cost failures had a less favorable median of 58.67%, while the high-cost failures were stuck at virtually the same level with a median coverage ratio of 37.83%; the difference between groups was insignificant. Surprisingly, the correlation between the coverage ratio and the FDIC loss rate was insignificant as of the PCA date. One year earlier, it was –0.19 and significant at the 10% level.

During the year leading up to the PCA date, the correlation between ROA and the FDIC loss rate was –0.26 (negative as expected) and significant; it was insignificant one year earlier. The low-cost failures had a median loss of 5.23% of assets in the year leading up to the PCA date, while the high-cost failures had a loss of 5.92% of assets. The difference in medians was relatively small (0.69) but significant at the 10% level. The net interest margin and the yield on earning assets favored the high-cost failures in both time periods, and some of the differences were significant. One possible explanation for this result is that the high-cost institutions might have accrued more interest that was never subsequently collected, but this is hard to determine from the data we collected. The low-cost failures had a lower cost of funds in both periods: the difference in medians was 47 basis points (3.69% vs. 4.16%) and significant in their last year of operations before falling below the PCA limit. During that period, the median ratio of non-interest income to earning assets favored the high-cost failures by 66 basis points, but was statistically insignificant. The median ratio of non-interest expenses to earning assets favored the low-cost failures by 136 basis points. While the difference in medians was insignificant, the correlation was 0.21 and significant.

The low-cost failures operated in markets with much lower levels of problem banks than the high-cost failures. We measured the level of deposits held by problem banks from each market that the failing institutions operated in during the June before they fell below the PCA limit. The low-cost failures registered a median index of just 0.01, while the high-cost failures showed an index of 0.11 for their markets. This difference was significant and shows that the markets in which they operated were troubled enough to stress other institutions as well as their own resources.[42] This relates to an important characteristic of the sample. While the near-failures and low-cost failures were more-or-less evenly distributed over the sample period, most of the high-cost failures occurred in 1994 and 1995. Figure 2 demonstrates this phenomenon.

Therefore, some of the differences between the high-cost failures and the other institutions were probably related to the economy, industry conditions, and/or regime changes instead of the characteristics of the banks. As confirmed by the problem bank index, many of the high-cost failures occurred when a substantive number of nearby banks were experiencing difficulties and some markets (notably real estate in New England) were still suffering from excess supply – particularly the markets for troubled assets. At the beginning of our sample period (January 1994), over 10% of BIF member banks had CAMEL ratings of 3, 4 or 5 (indicating that the banks had significant problems); by year-end 1995, only 5% of BIF members had CAMEL ratings of 3, 4 or 5.

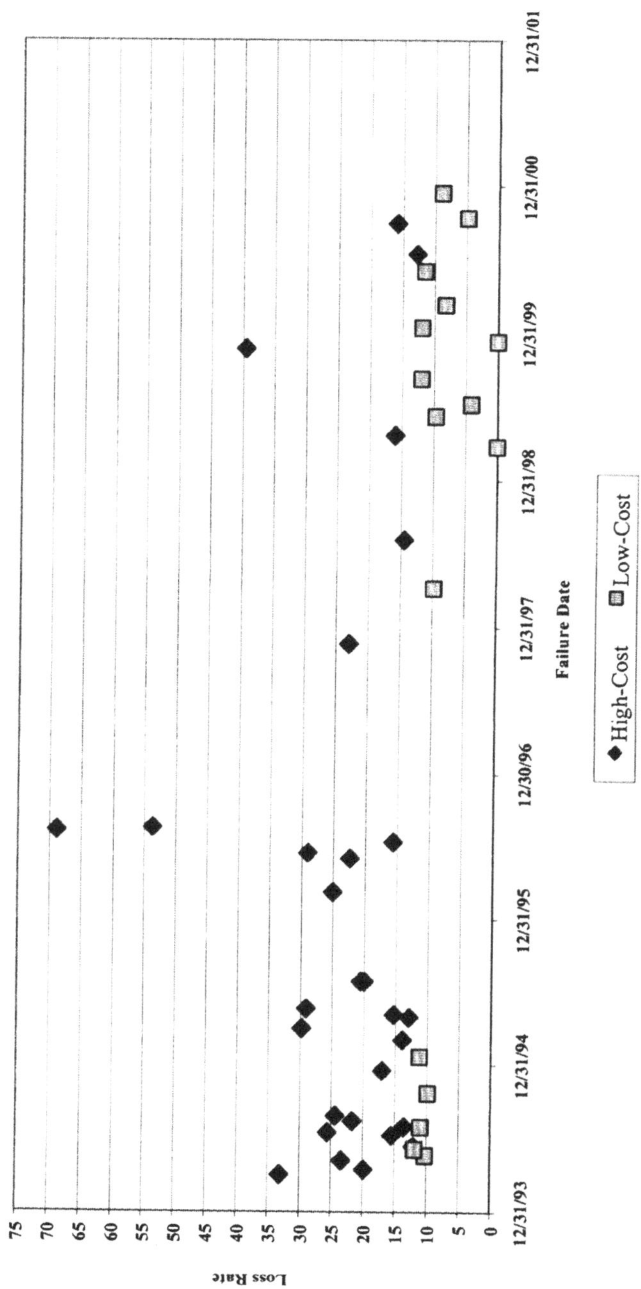

Fig. 2. Loss Rates Over Time: Low-Cost and High-Cost Failures.

These results indicate that failures may well be more expensive during periods of stress – regardless of PCA.[43] Periods of stress are often characterized by large, and sometimes sudden, shifts in market values. For example, fixed-rate mortgage loan values plummeted in the late 1970s and early 1980s, farm prices fell sharply during the agricultural crisis in the mid-1980s, and commercial real estate prices plunged in Texas and New England during regional recessions. Some of the high-cost failures may have become market value insolvent before the markets bottomed out.[44] Because markets are often thin during periods of stress, asset valuation becomes more difficult as well. Therefore, it may not be feasible or desirable to create a regulatory regime that results in near-zero losses to the insurance funds during periods of stress.[45]

We briefly looked at the relationship between coverage ratios and industry stress. Coverage ratios were not correlated with the problem bank index. As shown in Fig. 3, coverage ratios varied widely over the sample (both for failed banks and near-failures) throughout the sample period.

In addition, some of the costs experienced by the high-cost failures might be attributable to regulatory regime changes. Most banks that crossed the 2% PCA threshold after 1995 would have experienced their entire period of decline after FDICIA was passed and the enabling regulations were in place. Those that crossed the threshold in 1994 (and perhaps also in 1995) may have had a less rigorous incentive structure in place during the early phases of their decline.

We also investigated the level of classified loans in each group based on the last full examination before falling below the PCA limit, but none of our measures showed a significant difference. The median low-cost failure had 12.20% of its loans classified by examiners during their last full examination, while the median high-cost failure had 13.77%. Based on classified loans, we estimated appropriate levels of reserves and compared these to the actual reserves reported. The median low-cost failure reported reserves that were 114% of the estimated level, while the median high-cost failure reported reserves of 97% of the estimated level. This difference was not significant, but this does support the higher level of reserves to noncurrent loans held by the low-cost failures.

Like the comparison between failures and near-failures, the coverage ratio and the level of nonperforming assets were important characteristics that distinguished between low-cost and high-cost failures. These items appear to be the most fruitful for considering any policy changes that might reduce loss rates for failed banks. There were also important differences related to industry stress and the timing of the failures. We found evidence that failure costs were influenced by industry conditions. Changes in the regulatory treatment of seriously troubled banks may not influence the level of industry stress. Some

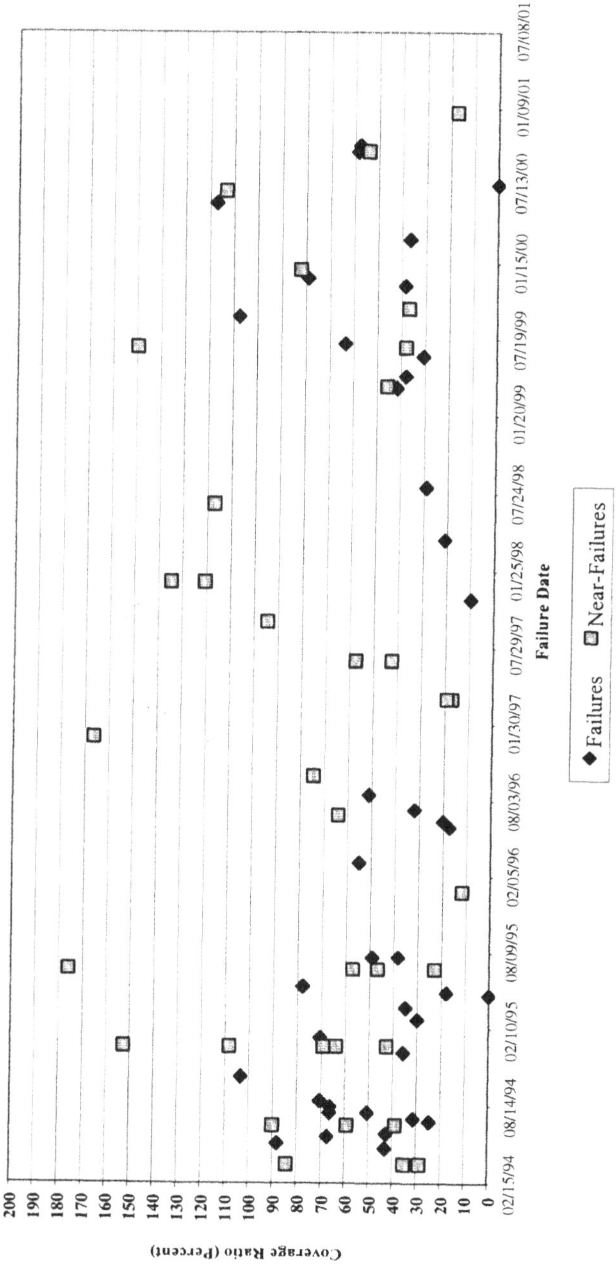

Fig. 3. Coverage Ratio Over Time: Failures and Near-Failures.

Note: 8 outlying observations have been omitted from this graph.

differences in asset composition and performance were also statistically significant and may also prove useful.

4.2.2. Comparisons at Resolution

We examined the number of institutions that submitted bids at failure. The median number of bidders was four for both the low-cost and high-cost failures, and the distribution around the median was similar. Thus, it appears that the market exposure was sufficient for both groups.[46] The bid results (shown in Tables 6 and 7) were somewhat different. As anticipated, low-cost failures generally had deposit franchises that were worth more than those held by high-cost failures. At 3.01%, the median bid-to-deposit ratio for low-cost failures was 26% higher than the median for high-cost failures. While the differences in medians were insignificant, we found a relative strong (–0.22) and significant correlation between this ratio and the FDIC loss rate. Even so, the differences explain a relatively small portion of the overall cost differences.

4.2.3. Comparisons of Receivership Performance

Table 6 provides comparisons of receivership performance and Table 7 provides correlation statistics to loss rates. As anticipated, there was a strong relationship between asset loss rates and the FDIC loss rate. The asset type with the largest losses was OREO, where even the low-cost failures suffered a 21% median loss rate on their asset sales. The asset types with the largest differences between the two groups were OREO (21.03 percentage points), C&I loans (13.11 percentage points), and other assets (10.14 percentage points). The asset type with the strongest correlation with the FDIC loss rate was C&I loans (0.44). The correlations were significant for most asset types. Thus it appears that asset quality at the high-cost institutions was worse across the board.

The median loss rate on total assets for high-cost institutions was more than $2\frac{1}{2}$ times the loss rate for low-cost institutions. The difference exceeded the differences for most asset types, indicating that the high-cost failures held more of their portfolio in the types of assets that experienced significant losses.[47] This comports with our comparisons of low-cost and high-cost failures prior to failure (Section 4.2.1).[48]

The receivership data showed that reserve levels were about the same for the two groups (3% of total assets). While the reserve ratios were much higher than industry averages (as a percentage of loans), reserves were much lower than the asset losses experienced by the receiverships. Reserves covered only 29% of the losses for the low-cost failures and a mere 14% for the high-cost failures.[49] Just as the coverage ratio was significantly higher for the low-cost failures, here

Table 6. Comparison of Low-Cost and High-Cost Failures at Resolution and in Receivership.

	Low-Cost	High-Cost	Difference
Number of Institutions	16	29	13
Median Total Assets ($MM)	66	64	(2)
Median Resolution Data			
Total bid/Total deposits	3.01	2.38	(0.63)
Deposit bid/Total deposits	2.88	1.42	(1.46)
Median Loss Rates over life of the Receivership			
(as % Total Asset at Failure)			
Investment Securities Loss+	0.00	0.00	0.00
C&I Loan Loss	15.00	28.11	13.11***
Mortgage Loan Loss++	14.99	16.22	1.23
Consumer Loan Loss	9.26	13.37	4.11
Owned Real Estate (OREO) Loss	21.27	42.30	21.03**
Investment in Subsidiaries Loss	3.03	0.00	(3.03)
Other Asset Loss	5.97	16.11	10.14
Total Asset Loss	7.99	21.96	13.97***
Median Receivership Memorandum			
Reserves/Total Assets	2.84	3.04	0.20
Reserves/Total Asset Losses	28.67	14.27	(14.40)**
Median Performance over life of the Receivership			
Pct Point Change in Cost Estimate (original to 12/2000)	2.88	8.03	5.15***
(as % Total Asset at Failure)			
Receivership Income	0.51	4.58	4.07***
Receivership Expenses (excl. holding costs)	2.97	11.24	8.27***
Holding Costs	0.58	3.34	2.76***
Assets Passed to Acquirer	62.99	24.84	(38.15)**
(as % Total Expenses)			
Legal expenses	1.47	1.61	0.14
OREO expenses (net of OREO income)	0.72	3.03	2.31*
Indirect expenses	59.74	62.57	2.83

* Significant at the 10% level.
**Significant at the 5% level.
***Significant at the 1% level.

Note: The total bid includes all items that reduce the FDIC's cost; the deposit bid includes only the amount that is directly tied to deposits.

Note: Receivership income and expenses exclude gains and losses from asset sales and adjustments made directly to equity.

+ For failures that occurred in 2000, gains/losses on investment securities that were sold to the acquirer are excluded from these figures. Also note that some acquirers may bid for investment securities at par and adjust their bid for deposits accordingly, particularly if the deposit bid is contingent on receiving the securities as well.

++ Note that mortgage loss rates (and possibly the difference between low-cost and high-cost failures) may be understated because of foreclosure activity. If the FDIC forecloses on a property, the receivership reclassifies the asset to an OREO asset prior to sale. Thus the losses from selling the underlying real estate are recorded under OREO instead of mortgages. We calculated the change in the percentage of the banks' assets held in OREO over the course of the receivership, and we found that the median increase (in percentage points) was 2 percent for the both groups of banks.

Table 7. Kendall Tau Correlation Coefficients: Resolution and Receivership Items Versus Total Loss Rate.

	All Failures
Number of Institutions	45
Median Total Assets ($MM)	(0.06)
Median Resolution Data	
Total bid/Total deposits	(0.15)
Deposit bid/Total deposits	(0.22)**
Median Loss Rates over life of the Receivership	
(as % Total Asset at Failure)	
Investment Securities Loss	(0.03)
C&I Loan Loss	0.44***
Mortgage Loan Loss	0.19*
Consumer Loan Loss	0.25**
Owned Real Estate (OREO) Loss	0.28***
Investment in Subsidiaries Loss	0.09
Other Asset Loss	0.09
Total Asset Loss	0.48***
Median Receivership Memorandum	
Reserves/Total Assets	(0.03)
Reserves/Total Asset Losses	(0.27)**
Median Performance over life of the Receivership	
Pct Point Change in Cost Estimate (original to 12/2000)	0.44***
(as % Total Asset at Failure)	
Receivership Income	0.27***
Receivership Expenses (excl. holding costs)	0.48***
Holding Costs	0.24**
Assets Passed to Acquirer	0.30***
(as% Total Expenses)	
Legal expenses	0.09
OREO expenses (net of OREO income)	(0.18)*
Indirect expenses	0.21**

* Significant at the 10% level.
** Significant at the 5% level.
*** Significant at the 1% level.

the reserves relative to actual losses were higher for the low-cost failures. Many of these banks, and particularly the high-cost banks, may have had inadequate reserves; however, we do not have enough information to determine this with certainty.[50]

Receivership income, receivership expenses, and holding costs were all much higher for the high-cost institutions, and both the correlations and the differences in medians were highly significant.[51] There were almost no receivership income or holding costs for the low-cost institutions. For the high-cost institutions, median receivership income over the life of the receivership was 4.58% of total assets at failure, and median holding costs over the life of the receivership were 3.34% of total assets at failure.[52] The difference in median receivership expenses was even larger: 2.97% vs. 11.24% of total assets at failure. At 0.48, the correlation between receivership expenses and the FDIC loss rate was quite strong. Even with the extra income as an offset, it is clear that the net effect of these items made up a large portion of the cost differential between these groups of institutions.[53]

These differences were closely tied to the enormous divergence in the portion of assets passed (that is, sold) to the acquirer.[54] The FDIC passed 62.99% of assets to acquirers for the median low-cost institution, but only 24.84% for the median high-cost institution (Fig. 4).[55] For 75% of the high-cost institutions, the FDIC retained over one-half of the assets in the receivership. On the surface, the cause of these immense differences appears to be the FDIC's sales methods. The true cause is not as simple.

One likely reason for the difference in assets sold to the acquirer is the quality of the assets held by the banks: assets of the high-cost banks were generally riskier and of lower quality. The markets for the riskier assets are typically thinner, and it may be harder to estimate the market price. The due diligence effort required for lower quality assets is more extensive as well. Thus there might have been fewer interested buyers, and the odds of finding a buyer to purchase the deposits and the riskier assets simultaneously – and on a relatively tight time line – would probably have been much smaller.

The marketplace differences discussed in Section 4.2.1 would almost certainly have affected the asset pass rates and the loss rates for some types of assets. As noted earlier, a relatively large proportion of the high-cost failures occurred when the industry was experiencing distress and when the markets were still absorbing large amounts of troubled assets. Based on our analysis, real estate loans were a large problem for the high-cost failures. Vacancy rates for office space dropped precipitously during the early years of our sample period, and the volume of sales transactions for office space increased dramatically in 1998.[56] Therefore, some of the variance in receivership performance across the groups almost certainly related to differences in market conditions. The marketing process works best when the economy and the industry are performing well.[57]

Policy changes made at the FDIC may also have contributed to this result. The FDIC combined its Division of Resolutions and Division of Depositor and Asset Services in 1996. The merger facilitated a more cohesive sales approach

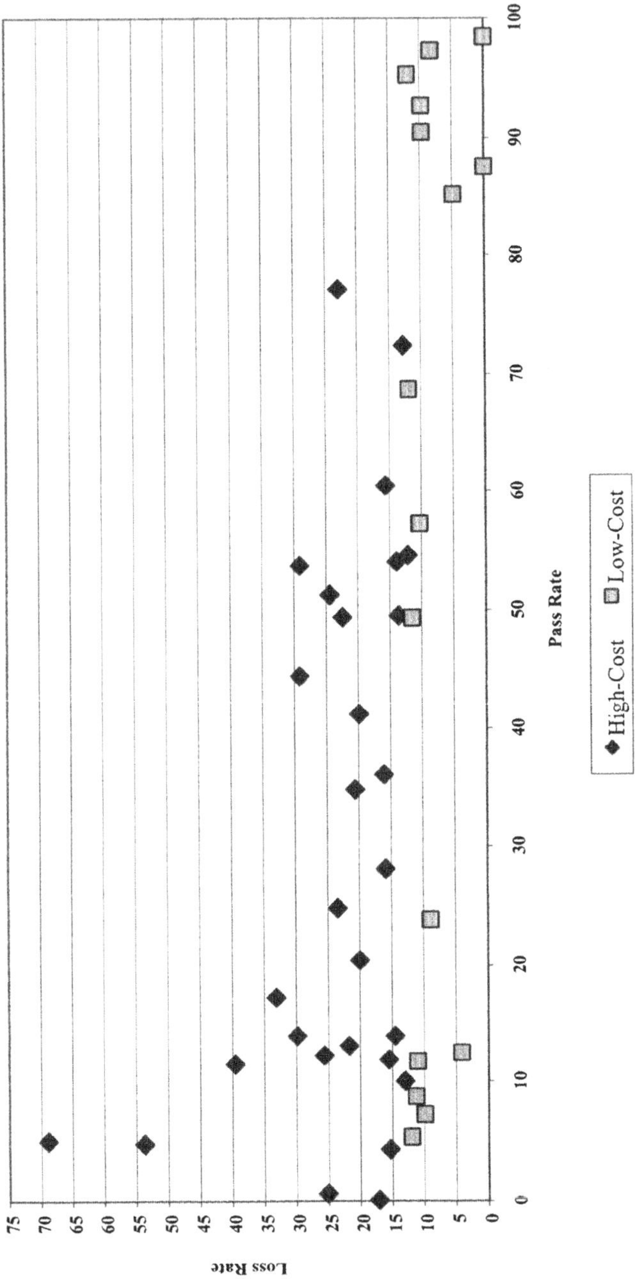

Fig. 4. Loss Rate Versus Pass Rate: Low-Cost and High-Cost Failures.

that starts before failure and continues past resolution with few disruptions from changes in staff or strategy at resolution. In 1997, the FDIC adopted a new asset sales procedure called "joint asset marketing." It emphasizes marketing homogeneous pools of assets to a large number of potential buyers quickly (preferably at resolution). The new procedures, combined with the strong economy, have shortened the pace of asset sales from FDIC receiverships considerably since the mid-1990s.

In summary, the comparison of resolution and receivership results is consistent with the earlier findings. For the most part, these results merely demonstrate the way that losses are realized when banks fail. However, the differences in asset pass rates and receivership performance may provide some evidence that FDIC losses are influenced by market conditions. To the extent that this is the case, it may be difficult or impossible to develop changes in regulatory treatment that yield near-zero losses to the insurance funds during times of industry stress.

4.3. Low-cost Failures Versus Near-failures

A comparison of low-cost failures to near-failures allows us to search, at the margin, for differences that distinguish failing banks from banks that can survive serious problems. This comparison investigates the robustness of the earlier comparison of all failures to near-failures. Any marginal distinctions may provide useful insights when considering marginal changes in the PCA threshold, or they could be helpful to examiners of similar banks. Our comparisons, shown in Tables 8 and 9, reveal only a few significant differences between the low-cost failures and the near-failures. Some of these differences – such as capital levels – may relate to the fact that some failures never fell below the PCA limit, but all near-failures fell below the limit by definition.

The low-cost failures' median capital levels were significantly higher than those of the near-failures. The median equity capital ratio for the low-cost failures was 2.09% at our analysis date, while the near-failures reported 0.97% when they fell below the PCA limit. The core capital (leverage) ratio also was significantly higher for the low-cost failures, at 2.03% compared to 0.87% for the near-failures. Also, deposits were significantly different between these two groups; deposits as a percentage of assets were a median 95% for low-cost failures compared to 98% for the near-failures. This difference was probably caused by the difference in capital.

For the performance of the two groups, the overall ROA was not significantly different, but the operating ROA exhibited a significant difference. The difference in overall ROA and operating ROA by our measures was the gains

Table 8. Comparison of Low-Cost and Near-Failures as of the PCA Date.

	Low-Cost	Near-Failures	Difference
Number of Institutions	16	39	23
Median Total Assets ($MM)	66	57	(9)
Median Asset Growth	(18.04)	(8.52)	9.52
Institutions with CAMELS Rating of 4 or 5 (%)	93.80	84.60	(9.20)
Median Balance Sheet Percentages			
Investment Securities	10.14	11.51	1.37
1–4 Family Mortgages	15.61	16.38	0.77
Commercial Real Estate	15.93	11.03	(4.90)
Multifamily Real Estate	1.55	1.04	(0.51)
Commercial & Industrial Loans	10.51	11.84	1.33
Deposits	95.13	98.00	2.87**
Median Rolling 4 Quarter Performance Ratios			
Return on assets	(5.23)	(5.76)	(0.53)
Return on equity	(106.23)	(124.24)	(18.01)
Yield on earning assets	8.11	8.77	0.66
Cost of funding earning assets	3.69	4.37	0.68**
Net interest margin	4.41	4.69	0.28
Nonint. inc. to earning assets	1.36	1.12	(0.24)
Nonint. exp. to earning assets	7.87	6.66	(1.21)
Net operating income to assets	(4.85)	(6.04)	(1.19)*
Net chargeoffs to loans	3.85	3.98	0.13
Loss provision to avg. assets	2.44	3.58	1.14
Loss provision to net charge-offs	129.41	122.95	(6.46)
Efficiency ratio	117.61	123.03	5.42
Median Condition Ratios			
Loss allowance to loans	4.50	4.50	0.00
Loss allowance to noncurrent (Coverage Ratio)	69.03	63.98	(5.05)
Noncurrent & OREO to assets	6.44	6.69	0.25
OREO to assets	0.46	0.80	0.34
Noncurrent RE loans to RE loans	4.35	3.54	(0.81)
Noncurrent total loans and leases	5.67	7.24	1.57
Noncurrent loan growth	14.21	29.44	15.23
Equity capital ratio	2.09	0.97	(1.12)**
Core capital (leverage) ratio	2.03	0.87	(1.16)***
Equity capital plus reserves	5.79	4.03	(1.76)
As of Mid-Year Before PCA Date, or Most Recent Exam			
Median Economic Condition Measures			
Problem Bank Index	0.01	0.02	0.01 n/a
Geographic Diversification Index	1.00	1.00	0.00 n/a
Median Examiner Classification Ratios			
Reserves to Estimated Reserves	114.13	94.81	(19.32) n/a
Classified Assets to Assets	12.20	10.47	(1.73) n/a

* Significant at the 10% level.
** Significant at the 5% level.
***Significant at the 1% level.

Table 9. Comparison of Low-Cost and Near-Failures as of One Year Before the PCA Date.

	Low-Cost	Near-Failures	Difference*
Number of Institutions	16	39	23
Median Total Assets ($MM)	72	59	(13)
Median Asset Growth	5.06	0.34	(4.72)
Institutions with CAMELS Rating of 4 or 5 (%)	75.00	64.10	(10.90)
Median Balance Sheet Percentages			
Investment Securities	15.00	10.35	(4.65)
1–4 Family Mortgages	16.95	15.28	(1.67)
Commercial Real Estate	14.35	10.76	(3.59)
Multifamily Real Estate	1.42	1.00	(0.42)
Commercial & Industrial Loans	7.43	8.85	1.42
Deposits	90.66	92.00	1.34
Median Rolling 4 Quarter Performance Ratios			
Return on assets	(0.09)	(0.72)	(0.63)
Return on equity	(4.43)	(12.89)	(8.46)
Yield on earning assets	8.66	8.46	(0.20)
Cost of funding earning assets	3.90	4.04	0.14
Net interest margin	4.70	4.68	(0.02)
Nonint. inc. to earning assets	1.16	1.54	0.38
Nonint. exp. to earning assets	5.57	6.21	0.64
Net operating income to assets	(0.81)	(0.75)	0.06
Net chargeoffs to loans	0.56	1.48	0.92
Loss provision to avg. assets	0.99	1.21	0.22
Loss provision to net charge-offs	149.17	129.06	(20.11)
Efficiency ratio	97.91	90.36	(7.55)
Median Condition Ratios			
Loss allowance to loans	2.00	2.07	0.07
Loss allowance to noncurrent (Coverage Ratio)	58.67	43.47	(15.20)
Noncurrent & OREO to assets	4.32	4.62	0.30
OREO to assets	0.97	1.08	0.11
Noncurrent RE loans to RE loans	2.22	3.14	0.92
Noncurrent total loans and leases	3.63	4.33	0.70
Noncurrent loan growth	43.67	3.92	(39.75)
Equity capital ratio	6.68	6.28	(0.40)
Core capital (leverage) ratio	6.56	5.94	(0.62)
Equity capital plus reserves	8.19	7.77	(0.42)

* None of these differences were found to be statistically significant at the 10% level.

on the sales of securities and extraordinary items. The low-cost failures reported a loss on assets of 5.23%, but this loss was less for operating earnings, at 4.85% of assets. The near-failures reported a median loss of 5.76% of assets, but the median operating loss was higher at 6.04% of assets. Although we did not collect a ratio for the level of gains on the sales of securities or extraordinary items, the result on loss implies that the low-cost failures reported non-operating gains that reduced their loss, while the near-failures reported non-operating losses that increased their loss. The low-cost failures also reported significantly lower median costs of funding earning assets, at 3.69%, while the near-failures reported 4.37%.

The level of nonperforming assets reported by these groups was not very different, but the low-cost failures reported significantly lower net charge-offs on real estate loans. Their net charge-offs were just 0.05% of real estate loans, while the near-failures had net charge-offs that were 1.26% of real estate loans over the last four quarters before falling below the PCA limit. Both at the PCA date and one year earlier, the median coverage ratio was higher for the low-cost failures than for the near-failures. The differences were relatively large (69.03% vs. 63.98% at the PCA date; 58.67% vs. 43.47% one year earlier) but not statistically significant.

Because the results for low-cost failures were remarkably similar to – and in many ways superior to – the near-failures, one might conclude that the failed institutions could have survived, given the chance. However, only two of these failures resulted in no costs to the FDIC; our review of these two extraordinary cases indicates that failure was appropriate.[58] The remaining low-cost failures had loss rates that ranged from 3% to 12% of assets. On the other hand, some of the near-failures could easily have joined our list of failures without the sale to another organization or the infusion of capital. All in all, this comparison highlights the difficulty of predicting failure. Given the lack of quantitative differences between these two groups, it is hard to identify changes in the PCA threshold that would consistently improve the cost tradeoffs.

4.4. Near-failures Purchased Versus Near-failures That Survived

We split the near-failures into groups based on the way they survived. There were 21 institutions that were absorbed into other organizations within one year after they fell below the PCA limit. There were 18 near-failures that survived their problems and remained independent for at least one year. We expected that the institutions that survived might have been in slightly better condition than the institutions absorbed by other organizations, but very few differences were significant (see Tables 10 and 11).

Both the median and average size of the survivors was much greater than the institutions purchased, but there were no statistically significant differences in

Table 10. Comparison of Near-Failures by Outcome as of the PCA Date.

	Survivors	Purchased	Difference
Number of Institutions	18	21	3
Median Total Assets ($MM)	91	38	(53)
Median Asset Growth	(7.24)	(12.57)	(5.33)
Institutions with CAMELS Rating of 4 or 5 (%)	77.80	90.50	12.70
Median Balance Sheet Percentages			
Investment Securities	12.46	8.83	(3.63)
1–4 Family Mortgages	18.01	16.38	(1.63)
Commercial Real Estate	6.42	12.39	5.97
Multifamily Real Estate	1.42	0.53	(0.89)
Commercial & Industrial Loans	6.44	12.60	6.16
Deposits	97.44	97.89	0.45
Median Rolling 4 Quarter Performance Ratios			
Return on assets	(4.20)	(6.04)	(1.84)
Return on equity	(116.31)	(125.72)	(9.41)
Yield on earning assets	8.55	9.12	0.57
Cost of funding earning assets	4.15	4.46	0.31
Net interest margin	4.75	4.69	(0.06)
Nonint. inc. to earning assets	1.49	0.83	(0.66)*
Nonint. exp. to earning assets	8.11	6.14	(1.97)
Net operating income to assets	(4.33)	(6.07)	(1.74)
Net chargeoffs to loans	3.17	4.56	1.39
Loss provision to avg. assets	1.96	4.08	2.12**
Loss provision to net charge-offs	118.54	124.65	6.11
Efficiency ratio	133.11	115.98	(17.13)
Median Condition Ratios			
Loss allowance to loans	2.73	5.05	2.32
Loss allowance to noncurrent (Coverage Ratio)	61.40	74.66	13.26
Noncurrent & OREO to assets	7.89	6.02	(1.87)
OREO to assets	1.10	0.57	(0.53)
Noncurrent RE loans to RE loans	2.98	3.54	0.56
Noncurrent total loans and leases	8.53	6.36	(2.17)
Noncurrent loan growth	22.71	29.44	6.73
Equity capital ratio	1.00	0.88	(0.12)
Core capital (leverage) ratio	0.77	1.26	0.49
Equity capital plus reserves	3.80	4.11	0.31
As of Mid-Year Before PCA Date, or Most Recent Exam			
Median Economic Condition Meaures			
Problem Bank Index	0.05	0.01	(0.03)
Geographic Diversification Index	1.00	1.00	0.00
Median Examiner Classification Ratios			
Reserves to Estimated Reserves	104.05	91.97	(12.08)
Classified Assets to Assets	5.93	12.97	7.04

* Significant at the 10% level.
** Significant at the 5% level.

Table 11. Comparison of Near-Failures by Outcome as of One Year Before the PCA Date.

	Survivors	Purchased	Difference
Number of Institutions	18	21	3
Median Total Assets ($MM)	82	44	(38)
Median Asset Growth	(1.08)	0.34	1.42
Institutions with CAMELS Rating of 4 or 5 (%)	66.70	61.90	(4.80)
Median Balance Sheet Percentages			
Investment Securities	8.51	10.55	2.04
1–4 Family Mortgages	16.65	14.99	(1.66)
Commercial Real Estate	7.41	13.95	6.54
Multifamily Real Estate	1.91	0.69	(1.22)
Commercial & Industrial Loans	4.41	10.41	6.00
Deposits	90.64	92.09	1.45
Median Rolling 4 Quarter Performance Ratios			
Return on assets	(0.75)	(0.72)	0.03
Return on equity	(12.91)	(12.37)	0.54
Yield on earning assets	8.21	8.70	0.49
Cost of funding earning assets	3.65	4.12	0.47
Net interest margin	4.59	4.68	0.09
Nonint. inc. to earning assets	2.19	0.83	(1.36)**
Nonint. exp. to earning assets	7.30	4.52	(2.78)*
Net operating income to assets	(0.78)	(0.75)	0.03
Net chargeoffs to loans	1.74	1.46	(0.28)
Loss provision to avg. assets	1.14	1.25	0.11
Loss provision to net charge-offs	101.73	129.64	27.91
Efficiency ratio	94.12	86.45	(7.67)
Median Condition Ratios			
Loss allowance to loans	1.82	2.09	0.27
Loss allowance to noncurrent (Coverage Ratio)	51.35	35.08	(16.27)
Noncurrent & OREO to assets	5.96	4.50	(1.46)
OREO to assets	1.80	0.71	(1.09)
Noncurrent RE loans to RE loans	7.02	2.25	(4.77)
Noncurrent total loans and leases	5.24	3.61	(1.63)
Noncurrent loan growth	(2.63)	20.08	22.71
Equity capital ratio	5.71	6.47	0.76
Core capital (leverage) ratio	5.32	6.02	0.70
Equity capital plus reserves	7.28	8.03	0.75

* Significant at the 10% level.
** Significant at the 5% level.

asset size. As of the PCA date, the 18 institutions had a median asset size of $91 million; the 21 institutions purchased had a median asset size of $38 million.

The survivors had significantly higher noninterest income (which is common for larger institutions) in the year before they fell below the PCA limit. They reported a median 2.19% of earning assets in noninterest income, while the institutions purchased reported 0.83%. This difference dwindled as the survivors approached the PCA threshold and was not significant by the time they fell below the PCA limit. At that time they reported 1.49%, while the purchased institutions reported 0.83%.

The near-failures that were purchased held a higher median percentage of commercial real estate and C&I loans, but this difference was not significant. Capital and reserves were higher for the purchased institutions, but again the difference was not significant. The level of nonperforming assets was lower for the purchased institutions, but not significantly. The performance of the purchased institutions seemed worse due to higher losses, higher net charge-offs and higher provisions for loan losses, but none of these differences were significant. As targets for acquisition, higher levels of capital and reserves and lower nonperforming assets would seem attractive to a buyer, but the lower performance might make a buyer take pause.

4.5. Tracking Near-failures That Survived One Year Later

We analyzed the 18 near-failures that survived one year after they fell below the PCA limit, and the results are in Table 12. There were many significant differences in this group across the two time periods, mainly related to capital and performance.

All measures of capital were significantly higher which was due largely to capital infusions. Equity capital increased from a median of 1.00% as of the PCA date to 5.28% one year later. These results provide some evidence of the importance of capital infusions that are large enough to ensure survival. Barakova and Carey (2001) found that both failed banks and near-failures had capital infusions, but the infusions were larger for the near-failures. We found that some of the failed institutions in our sample also had capital infusions, but the amounts were insufficient. Regulators might be able to use this evidence to encourage troubled banks to seek enough capital to materially improve their survival chances.

The capital position of these institutions improved much faster than nonperforming assets. Nonperforming assets as a percent of total assets improved from a median level of 7.89% to 4.80%, but this was insignificant.

Table 12. Comparison of Survivors at the PCA Date and One Year Later.

	At PCA Date	One Year Later	Difference
Number of Institutions	18	18	0
Median Total Assets ($MM)	91	104	13
Median Asset Growth	(7.24)	(4.74)	2.50
Median Balance Sheet Percentages			
Investment Securities	12.46	10.26	(2.20)
1–4 Family Mortgages	18.01	20.39	2.38
Commercial Real Estate	6.42	7.59	1.17
Multifamily Real Estate	1.42	1.25	(0.17)
Commercial & Industrial Loans	6.44	10.83	4.39
Deposits	97.44	92.23	(5.21)***
Median Rolling 4 Quarter Performance Ratios			
Return on assets	(4.20)	(0.73)	3.47***
Return on equity	(116.31)	(19.16)	97.15***
Yield on earning assets	8.55	8.48	(0.07)
Cost of funding earning assets	4.15	4.11	(0.04)
Net interest margin	4.75	4.54	(0.21)
Nonint. inc. to earning assets	1.49	1.01	(0.48)
Nonint. exp. to earning assets	8.11	6.81	(1.30)
Net operating income to assets	(4.33)	(0.77)	3.56***
Net chargeoffs to loans	3.17	1.37	(1.80)
Loss provision to avg. assets	1.96	0.60	(1.36)***
Loss provision to net charge-offs	118.54	54.30	(64.24)**
Efficiency ratio	133.11	98.59	(34.52)
Median Condition Ratios			
Loss allowance to loans	2.73	2.23	(0.50)
Loss allowance to noncurrent (Coverage Ratio)	61.40	51.27	(10.13)
Noncurrent & OREO to assets	7.89	4.80	(3.09)
OREO to assets	1.10	1.06	(0.04)
Noncurrent RE loans to RE loans	2.98	3.08	0.10
Noncurrent total loans and leases	8.53	5.73	(2.80)
Noncurrent loan growth	22.71	(29.97)	(52.68)*
Equity capital ratio	1.00	5.28	4.28***
Core capital (leverage) ratio	0.77	5.28	4.51***
Equity capital plus reserves	3.80	7.58	3.78***

* Significant at the 10% level.
** Significant at the 5% level.
*** Significant at the 1% level.

Behind these numbers was a significant improvement in noncurrent C&I loans, down from 7.62% to 3.56%.

Over this one-year time span the performance improved significantly, but these institutions still reported a median loss on assets of 0.73%, down from a loss of 4.20% one year earlier. The lower provision expense was a driving force in reducing losses. Provision expenses fell significantly from a median of 1.96% of average assets to 0.60%. Net charge-offs declined, but not significantly. Provisions declined significantly from a median of 119% of net charge-offs to 54% one year later.

5. CONCLUDING REMARKS

Contrary to the expectations of many economists, PCA has not resulted in the FDIC experiencing little or no loss when a depository institution fails. From 1994 to 2000, most failures imposed significant costs (as a percentage of assets) on the insurance funds. However, 55% of the FDIC-insured institutions that fell below the PCA threshold for critically undercapitalized institutions avoided failure, and almost 30% of the failed institutions never breached the PCA threshold.

We explored the tradeoffs associated with the PCA threshold for critically undercapitalized institutions. When market-value solvent institutions breach the threshold, both financial costs and non-financial costs (loss of freedom) are imposed on many of the bank owners and, to a lesser extent, supervisors. These costs are probably offset by savings associated with prompt closure (for failed institutions) and with higher survival rates for troubled institutions (if the threshold successfully aids in recapitalizing some institutions that would otherwise fail). Ideally, the PCA threshold would be set at the level that balances these tradeoffs to yield the highest net benefit to society. Because the tradeoffs are difficult to measure, we do not know the optimum level. However, the decidedly mixed outcomes of the institutions that have breached the threshold to date provide us with some comfort that the current threshold is not too wide off the mark. If almost all of the institutions that breached the threshold had survived, or if almost all of them had failed, then it would be more likely that an adjustment to the threshold level would yield substantial benefits.

We investigated the differences between the critically undercapitalized institutions that did and did not fail, in hopes of finding information that could be used to improve the regulatory treatment of seriously troubled banks. The most meaningful differences across outcomes related to nonperforming assets, coverage ratios (calculated as reserves divided by noncurrent loans), and the local economy. The failed institutions had median nonperforming ratios that were significantly higher than those of the near-failures, particularly for real estate loans. The high-cost failures had nonperforming levels that were roughly double those of the low-cost failures. The nonperforming levels of the low-cost failures and the near-failures were roughly the same.

Of all the measures we tested, the coverage ratio appears to be the most useful indicator that serious losses may await the FDIC. At the PCA date, the median coverage ratio was 43% for the failures and 64% for the near-failures. However, the median coverage ratio was higher for the low-cost failures than for the near-failures (69% vs. 64%). The median coverage ratio for high-cost failures was only 38%.

The high-cost failures were much more likely to be located in areas where a relatively large number of banks were experiencing problems. Unlike the low-cost failures and near-failures, they were also more likely to have occurred in 1994 and 1995 – a period at the end of the banking crisis when some markets for troubled assets (particularly commercial real estate markets) were sluggish. Thus some of the differences in outcome are probably related to the marketplace rather than individual bank characteristics. During periods of stress, asset values sometimes experience steep declines, and slow-moving markets increase the difficulty of measuring asset values. Because of these phenomena, the FDIC may experience higher loss rates during periods of stress than during good times, even with PCA.

The differences in other items were smaller. The failed banks had somewhat riskier asset portfolios than the near-failures; likewise, the high-cost failures had riskier asset portfolios than the low-cost failures. The performance measures were similar across groups. There were few differences between the low-cost failures and near-failures, and surprisingly the differences tended to favor the low-cost failures. The near-failures that were purchased were also similar to those that survived, except that the surviving institutions were larger.

There are several reasons why these results may not be robust in the future. Our sample period did not include a full business cycle, and we have found limited evidence that the results vary across the business cycle. A disproportionate number of the high-cost failures occurred in 1994–1995, and thus regime changes (that we were unable to isolate) may have influenced the results. We did not test for intangible items such as the quality of bank management, which could be important. And of course, historical results do not always provide a good indicator of future performance.

6. RECOMMENDATIONS

The PCA regulations emphasize capital and not reserves. Because we found that loan loss reserves differentiate relatively strong and weak institutions that have already fallen below the PCA threshold, we feel that the level of reserves should be studied more closely. Regulators may want to refine the rules governing reserves or limit the discretion of seriously troubled banks to set their own reserve levels instead of trying to find a better threshold capital level for critically undercapitalized institutions.[59] If troubled banks consistently adjust their reserves so they are always adequate to absorb the estimated credit losses associated with their loan portfolios, then capital would become a better measure of condition.

We recommend that regulators attempt to develop a formula for minimum reserve levels that could potentially be used to improve the supervision of seriously troubled institutions.[60] Our results give us hope that such a formula would be feasible.[61] Once such a formula were developed, regulators could require that seriously troubled banks set reserve levels by using the higher of their normal reserving procedures or the formulaic approach – at least for calculating regulatory capital.[62] Alternately, seriously troubled banks could be allowed to record reserve levels that fell below the formula only if approved by an examiner or the FDIC.[63] Because many troubled institutions are slow to adjust reserve levels for deteriorating conditions, this approach could potentially reduce insurance fund costs by hastening the closure of non-viable banks. It might also improve the tradeoffs associated with the 2% PCA threshold, since it appears that the high-cost failures would be more seriously impacted by such a change than the low-cost failures or the near-failures. Alternately, regulators could adopt other, less prescriptive, ways to use this information in the supervisory process.

NOTES

1. If troubled banks overstate asset values, their capital is artificially increased: this may allow them to avoid or delay adverse consequences. GAO (1992) documented the problem. There is also ample evidence that examinations of troubled banks often result in increased reserve levels (which causes capital to fall). See for example Dahl et al. (1998) and Gunther and Moore (2000).

2. Throughout the paper, loss rates are defined as the FDIC loss divided by total assets of the failed bank.

3. Throughout the paper, we use the term banks to mean all FDIC-insured depository institutions.

4. Since the 2% threshold allows the bank only 90 days to improve its condition prior to closure, the bank's viability at this point is almost entirely determined by events that

occurred prior to reaching the threshold. If banks have not begun seeking capital well before reaching the 2% threshold, the 90-day time limit is tantamount to closure. However, regulators are allowed to delay this action for up to 270 days (inclusive of the first 90 day period) if the primary supervisor determines, and the FDIC concurs, that the delay would better achieve the purpose of FDICIA. The act also prescribes extremely narrow and explicit conditions for a delay beyond 270 days.

5. They tested only for the 4% leverage ratio threshold. There are two other capital thresholds that define undercapitalized banks, and some of the banks with leverage ratios above 4% may have breached one of the other thresholds.

6. They found that regulators have already downgraded the institutions to a CAMEL 4/5 rating before they meet the RBC threshold for an undercapitalized institution.

7. PCA may have had significant indirect effects on the behavior of both banks and regulators that were not addressed in these studies. For example, banks might protect themselves from the PCA restrictions by holding more capital than they would have held absent PCA.

8. Depending on the method employed, from 214 to 314 banks would have been adequately capitalized under the RBC standards in place but would have been undercapitalized under the revised RBC standards. Very few banks that were undercapitalized under the RBC standard in place at that time would have become adequately capitalized under the revised method. The authors normalized the RBC levels across banks so that they captured only differences in the distribution of RBC across banks, instead of a combination of an increased standard and changes in the distribution across banks.

9. They used three definitions for troubled institutions: (1) all institutions with a CAMEL rating of 4 or 5; (2) all institutions with tangible capital below 2%; and (3) all institutions that met either of the first two standards. Their estimates of prediction error assumed that all such institutions should be classified as undercapitalized and that all other institutions should not be classified as undercapitalized.

10. The literature on public finance supports the assumption that government intervention should strive to maximize the net benefit to society. Therefore, banking regulators should not focus solely on minimizing losses to the insurance funds when selecting PCA thresholds.

11. More general discussions of the benefits of PCA can be found in Carnell (1997a) and Mishkin (1997).

12. Regulators have the authority to close banks when they are operating in an unsafe or unsound manner, regardless of capital levels. Presumably any bank with no market value would meet this criterion.

13. Several authors have noted the difficulties in measuring capital at banks. See, for example, GAO (1992).

14. Regulators are not allowed to set standards that are less stringent than GAAP. Under Section 37 of the FDI Act, regulators have the authority to set standards that are more stringent than GAAP. Note, however, that taking such an action introduces new costs into the equation (including introducing new regulatory burden to banks and reducing the comparability of bank financial reports and information from other related industries) and thus should not be undertaken lightly – particularly if alternative means of meeting the objective are available.

15. Benston and Kaufman (1997) argue that the closure of an institution that is solvent on a market-value basis "would not be a 'taking' by the government as any

remaining capital would be returned to the shareholders." From a legal standpoint, they are probably correct. However, there are real costs, including the overhead expenses associated with administering a receivership, prepaid expenses that are rendered worthless at failure, transaction costs associated with transferring information from the seller to a buyer, and any lost asset value associated with the stigma of failure. Owners could potentially be subject to a Directors and Officers (D&O) claim as well. In addition, the FDIC must pay the cost of administering insurance and preparing the resolution. From an economic standpoint, these costs should be considered when contemplating an increase in the PCA threshold.

16. Some of the bank's creditors could suffer losses if contracts are abrogated or if the receivership does not pay creditors as much as they would have received had the bank stayed open. In addition, if the bank was not located in a competitive market, the bank's customers (and others in the community) may not be able to obtain credit or make deposits at equivalent terms. These effects could in turn harm the local economy more broadly. This appears to be most likely for small, rural banks in situations where the acquirer has less interest in the local community than the failed bank. See Gilbert and Kochin (1989) for an analysis of these effects.

17. If crossing the 2% threshold did not cause any material change in strategy, the cost would probably be negligible. If there was a change in strategy that improved the allocation of capital, there could be an economic benefit; if the opposite occurred, there could be an economic loss. But these results relate to the PCA threshold only if the threshold (rather than the weak condition of the bank) was the true cause of the change. In addition, the owners would, for the most part, retain the freedom to control their assets.

18. Like owners that suffer from closure, they would lose the freedom to control their assets, and they would have to pay the transaction costs associated with transferring information to a buyer. They might also be required to sell the franchise for a below-market price because of the 90-day deadline.

19. There have been some receiverships with a surplus. However, a surplus can occur for reasons other than an avoidable closure. For example, it can occur because of positive developments in the markets after failure or because the FDIC was able to reverse or mitigate problems experienced at the bank (such as excessive employee compensation or self-dealing on the part of management). Shibut and Critchfield (2000) found no evidence of wrongful closure in their review of low-cost failures.

20. The tradeoff may also be influenced by the nature of the problems experienced by the banking industry. For example, the optimal PCA threshold for banks undergoing a regional recession may not work as well for stresses associated with high interest rates or subprime lending.

21. See chapter 5 in FDIC (1997). While it appears that the sudden application of PCA rules as the crisis mounted would have had terrible consequences, it is difficult to gauge the results if PCA triggers and the current accounting rules had been in place long enough to alter the banks' behavior well in advance of the crisis.

22. He states that the systemic risk exception in FDICIA allows regulators enough discretion to avoid excessive costs associated with the PCA thresholds. Thus concerns about extreme situations need not be considered unless they do not involve systemic risk. If, however, an unexpected event caused the PCA threshold to be inappropriate for a large number of banks at the same time, the systemic risk exception would become untenable.

23. The study concentrated on the pace of recovery and the implications for selecting an appropriate time horizon for Value-at-Risk (VaR) models.

24. Recovery was defined as reaching a leverage ratio of 5%.

25. The Meriden Trust and Safe Deposit Bank was eliminated from our analysis because it had no insured deposits and was part of a cross guaranty case. The First National Bank of Keystone, Keystone, WV and BestBank in Boulder, CO were eliminated because the fraud involved in these failures was large enough to seriously distort their financial reports.

26. We use the term Call Report as shorthand for both the Call Report and the Thrift Financial Report.

27. All but 7 of the 32 institutions that fell below the threshold failed within 1 year. There were 3 institutions that fell below the PCA threshold over 1 year before failure but before 3 years, and we decided to use the PCA date for our analysis. There were 4 institutions that fell below the PCA threshold over 3 years before failure and we decided to use their failure date because they fell below the PCA threshold before PCA was fully implemented. There were four institutions that fell below the PCA threshold over 3 years before failure. These dates ranged from 1990 to early 1993 (which was the very beginning of implementing the PCA rules).

28. Five institutions that fell below the 2% tangible capital level were excluded. (1) New Meridian Trust was excluded because it was a bridge bank created by the FDIC to operate a failed institution until a buyer could be found. (2) Valley First Community Bank of Scottsdale, AZ reported a capital level below 2% on its very first regulatory report after establishing its operations. (3) Chicago-Tokyo Bank of Chicago, IL was held by a foreign bank holding company and it reported virtually zero assets on its last report. (4) Suntrust Bankcard, National Association of Orlando, FL had one quarter during a downsizing that produced a low capital ratio because the denominator was based on average assets that did not reflect the end-of-period level of assets. 5) Continental Savings Bank of Seattle, WA filed a report with a missing value for capital in one quarter.

29. There were 14 institutions that were absorbed by mergers that eliminated their charters within one year of falling below the 2% threshold, and there were 7 institutions that were purchased by a holding company within one year of falling below the 2% threshold.

30. There were 6 institutions out of the 84 institutions studied that failed to file a financial report in the quarter after their last full examination before falling below the PCA capital limit.

31. To create a problem bank index we summarized the branch-level deposits of all FDIC-insured institutions that were rated CAMELS 4 or 5 for every market which was located in a metropolitan statistical area (MSA) or county for any county that was not in an MSA. We divided this sum by the total deposits for the MSA or county and then multiplied these percentages by the percentage of each institution's deposits located in each market. Then we summed the totals for each market that an institution had a presence in for the mid-year before the institution fell below the PCA limit of 2% or before failure.

32. This was calculated as of the middle of each year before the institution fell below the PCA limit using data from the annual Summary of Deposits. We calculated the percentage of an institution's deposit in each market in which it operated and then squared these percentages. Then we summed the squared percentages for all markets in

which an institution operated so that the results should range from 0 to 1. This measure was based on the work of Katherine Samolyk.

33. All parameter estimates were statistically significant at the 1% level. The R^2 was 0.33. The sample included commercial banks during the 1984–1989 time period.

34. Under GAAP, the allowance for loan and lease losses (ALLL) should cover probable estimated credit losses in the loan portfolio, not a specified number of years of expected charge-offs.

35. Of the 45 receiverships, 32 (71%) had terminated by year-end 2000. The remaining receiverships held $79 million in assets for sale as of year-end 2000, which was 6.8% of the assets held by these receiverships at failure.

36. In fact, comparisons of simple averages for analysis were unsatisfactory because of outliers, and comparisons of weighted averages were unsatisfactory because they tended to represent only the largest banks in the sample. Thus, we relied most heavily on medians, distributions, and the Wilcoxon test for analysis.

37. Throughout the results section, we use the terms significant and insignificant to mean statistically significant and statistically insignificant.

38. There are four classification levels used by examiners to indicate the level of impairment. The distribution of classifications across these levels has a strong influence on the Jones and King estimate.

39. Our results are consistent with those of Barakova and Carey (2001). They briefly compared the components of changes in equity of failed banks with those that recovered. The authors found no marked differences in performance between these two groups, although failed banks raised somewhat less equity and experienced higher cumulative losses than the banks that recovered.

40. All correlations and tests of significance are based on the Kendall's tau test and compare the FDIC loss rate to the item being discussed.

41. Eight low-cost failures and five high-cost failures did not breach the PCA threshold prior to failure. For these institutions, we treated the final Call Report date as the PCA failure date.

42. The correlation was 0.16 and insignificant. This could relate to idiosyncratic differences between banks (particularly the amount of loss attributable to fraud or mismanagement) and the small sample size.

43. McDill (2001) confirmed that a relationship exists. Using data from 1980 through 2000, she regressed the FDIC loss rates of failed banks against various business-cycle items and bank-specific characteristics. She found that loss rates were higher for institutions located in states with falling personal income levels – particularly if the reduction occurred after a "boom." She also found that loss rates increased for institutions located in states that had concentrations of problem banks. As an example of the effects, she used the results to estimate the loss rate for a typical Texas failure in 1988 and 1999. The loss rate in 1988 was six percentage points higher than the 1999 loss rate.

44. Capital is basically a measure of current condition and largely ignores the likelihood of future deterioration. Mailath and Mester (1993) developed a theoretical model on optimum bank closure policy and found that regulators should consider the future prospects and probable actions of a failing bank in order to minimize losses to the insurance funds. A more forward-looking measure of capital might mitigate losses during periods of stress, but it would introduce more subjectivity into the equation as well.

45. If regulators imposed extremely tight restrictions on risk (that is, narrow banking) or very high capital requirements, it might be feasible to largely eliminate insurance fund losses during periods of stress. However, there would probably be substantial costs in the form of tighter credit availability and higher credit costs for a large number of borrowers.

46. The market for deposits was strong throughout the period. There could be a different result during periods of lower demand.

47. We investigated the amount of foreclosure activity during receivership, but found that the median change in OREO (as a percentage of total assets) between closing weekend and the final receivership balance increased about the same amount (two percentage points) for both groups.

48. Appendix 3 provides more detail about the asset composition at failure and in receivership.

49. These loss rates were calculated as the difference between the gross book value recorded by the receivership and the sales proceeds. If the costs associated with selling the assets had been included, the difference between the two groups of institutions would have been larger.

50. There are several reasons why reserves may be sufficient under GAAP for an operating institution but still be smaller than the asset losses experienced at liquidation. Examples include changes in market conditions, changes in interest rates, and differences in the value anticipated for an asset held in a long-term portfolio vs. the value if the asset is sold relatively quickly.

51. Receivership income and expenses were calculated on a cash basis, and they excluded gains and losses from asset sales, asset write-offs, holding costs, income from the bid premium and other equity adjustments. Holding costs were defined as the FDIC's lost income from funding the deposits up front and waiting for recovery from the receivership. Appendix 2 provides more information on the composition of these items.

52. Because the level of activity and the duration (in time) of receiverships vary substantially, all income and expense items are reported as the total amount over the life of the receivership divided by total assets at failure.

53. One cannot merely subtract receivership income from receivership expenses and assume that the difference (as a percentage of total assets at failure) is the amount of loss in percentage points attributable to receivership operations. Many receiverships start with substantial amounts of positive equity (partly because reserves are reversed at failure). In addition, some losses and gains do not flow through the receivership income statement, and some receivership losses are borne by creditors other than the FDIC.

54. An acquirer is defined as the institution (or institutions) that purchased the deposits.

55. The simple average for the percentage of assets sold to the acquirer was 30.01% for the high-cost institutions and 65.73% for the low-cost institutions.

56. National vacancy rates for office space were 16.8% at the beginning of our sample period. They dropped to 13.8% at year-end 1995, and by year-end 1997 they had dropped to 9.9%. The changes in sales volume were larger. For Class A office buildings, there were only 18 sales made in 1996, 35 in 1997, but 238 in 1998. Source: Torto-Wheaton Research.

57. The results concerning changes in the FDIC loss estimates over time were also consistent with this theory. The FDIC loss estimates increased substantially between the

original estimate and the latest estimate for high-cost failures, but only a little bit for low-cost failures. This supports the theory that markets deteriorated during the life of the receivership, or it might indicate that asset valuation at closure was more difficult for the high-cost institutions that carried riskier assets.

58. See Shibut and Critchfield (2000) for details.

59. Regulators often use cease and desist orders to force troubled banks to use appropriate methods for setting reserves. Because we did not collect data on formal and informal actions, we do not know whether there was a relationship between such orders and coverage ratios. In addition, the heterogeneity of banks, coupled with the amount of subjective judgement inherent in reserve levels, may make the task of limiting bank discretion through industry-wide rules a daunting one.

60. This concept is not an original idea. See also U.S. Treasury (1990), Berger et al. (1991), and Jones and King (1995).

61. Based on our research, the formula might use a combination of classified assets, asset types, changes in and levels of noncurrent loans and OREO, and data about local market conditions. Given the results of the Jones and King estimate (discussed in Section 4.1), the appropriate formula for banks approaching insolvency may differ from the optimum formula for less troubled banks. Thus it would be important to match the regulatory usage of the formula to the methods and data used in its development.

62. A formulaic approach may not meet GAAP, in which case the regulatory burden associated with a change may rise. The regulatory burden could be mitigated by using the formula solely for setting regulatory capital standards.

63. If such a policy were adopted, it may be beneficial for a separate team of FDIC staff (including examiners) to be involved in such decisions. This might reduce the potential for inefficiencies stemming from the principal-agent problem, which is eloquently described by Mishkin (1997).

ACKNOWLEDGMENTS

The views expressed in this paper are those of the authors and not necessarily those of the Federal Deposit Insurance Corporation. The authors wish to thank Tyler Davis, Heather Gratton, Toni Holloman-Spinner, Terry Kissinger, Jennifer Merrill, and Katherine Samolyk for assistance, and Charles Collier, Robert Ferrer, Grovetta Gardineer, Alton Gilbert, Herb Held, James Marino, Rae-Ann Miller, Larry Mote, Dan Nuxoll, John O'Keefe, Bob Storch, Bob Walsh and Jim Wigand for valuable comments. All errors and omissions are our own.

REFERENCES

Aggarwal, R., & Jacques, K. (2000). The impact of FDICIA and prompt corrective action on bank capital and risk: Estimates using a simultaneous equations model. *Journal of Banking & Finance*, *25*, 1139–1160.

Barakova, I., & Carey, M. (2001). How Quickly do Troubled U.S. Banks Recapitalize? With Implications for Portfolio VaR Credit Loss Horizons. Working paper presented at the 2001 Financial Management Association meetings.

Benston, G. J., & Kaufman, G. G. (1997). FDICIA After Five Years. *Journal of Economic Perspectives, 11*(3), 139.

Barth, M. E., Landsman, W. R., & Wahlen, J. M. (1995). Fair value accounting: Effects on banks' earning volatility, regulatory capital, and value of contractual cash flows. *Journal of Banking and Finance, 19*, 577–605.

Berger, A. N., King, K. K., & O'Brien, J. M. (1991). The limitations of market value accounting and a more realistic alternative. *Journal of Banking and Finance, 15*, 753–783.

Carnell, R. S. (1997a). FDICIA After Five Years: What has Worked and What has Not? In: G. G. Kaufman (Ed.), *FDICIA: Bank Reform Five Years Later and Five Years Ahead* (pp. 11–16). Greenwich, CT: JAI Press, Inc.

Carnell, R. S. (1997b). A Partial Antidote to Perverse Incentives: The FDIC Improvement Act of 1991. In: G. G. Kaufman (Ed.), *FDICIA: Bank Reform Five Years Later and Five Years Ahead* (pp. 199–233). Greenwich, CT: JAI Press, Inc.

Dahl, D., O'Keefe, J. P., & Hanweck, G. A. (1998). The Influence of Examiners and Auditors on Loan-Loss Recognition. *FDIC Banking Review, 11*(4), 10–25.

Eisenbeis, R. A., & Wall, L. D. (2002). Reforming Deposit Insurance and FDICIA. *Economic Review, 87*(1), 1–16. Atlanta, GA: Federal Reserve Bank of Atlanta.

Federal Deposit Insurance Corporation (1997). *History of the Eighties: Lessons for the Future.* Washington, D.C.: FDIC.

Gilbert, R. A. (1992). The Effects of Legislating Prompt Corrective Action on the Bank Insurance Fund. *Federal Reserve Bank of St. Louis Review, 42*(4), 3–22.

Gilbert, R. A., & Kochin, L. A. (1989). Local Economic Effects of Bank Failures. *Journal of Financial Services Research, 1989*(3), 333–345.

Gunther, J. W., & Moore, R. R. (2000). Financial Statements and Reality: Do Troubled Banks Tell All? *Economic and Financial Review*, (3rd Quarter), 30–35. Dallas, TX: Federal Reserve Bank of Dallas.

Jones, D. S., & King, K. K. (1995). The implementation of prompt corrective action: An assessment. *Journal of Banking and Finance, 19*, 491–510.

Kaufman, G. G. (1997). FDICIA After Five Years: What has Worked and What has Not? In: G. G. Kaufman (Ed.), *FDICIA: Bank Reform Five Years Later and Five Years Ahead* (pp. 35–43). Greenwich, CT: JAI Press, Inc.

Mailath, G. J., & Mester, L. J. (1993). When Do Regulators Close Banks? When Should They? Federal Reserve Bank of Philadelphia Working Paper no. 93–10.

McDill, K. (2002). Federal Deposit Insurance Corporation memo on the loss rates of bank failures over the business cycle, January 28.

Mishkin, F. S. (1997). Evaluating FDICIA. In: G. G. Kaufman (Ed.), *FDICIA: Bank Reform Five Years Later and Five Years Ahead* (pp. 17–32). Greenwich, CT: JAI Press, Inc.

Peek, J., & Rosengren, E. S. (1996). The Use of Capital Ratios to Trigger Intervention in Problem Banks: Too Little, Too Late. *New England Economic Review*, (September/October), 49–58. Boston, MA: Federal Reserve Bank of Boston.

Peek, J., & Rosengren, E. S. (1997). Will Legislated Early Intervention Prevent the Next Banking Crisis? *Southern Economic Journal*, (July), 268–280.

Shibut, L., & Critchfield, T. (2000). An Analysis of Low Cost Failures. Unpublished manuscript. December 11.

U.S. General Accounting Office (1990). *Bank Insurance Fund: Additional Reserves and Reforms Needed to Strengthen the Fund.* GAO/AFMD-90-100. Washington, D.C.: Government Printing Office.

U.S. General Accounting Office (1992). *Depository Institutions: Flexible Accounting Rules Lead to Inflated Financial Reports.* GAO/AFMD-92-52. Washington, D.C.: Government Printing Office.

U.S. General Accounting Office (1996). *Bank and Thrift Regulation: Implementation of FDICIA's Prompt Regulatory Action Provisions.* GAO/GGD-97-18. Washington, D.C.: Government Printing Office.

U.S. Department of the Treasury (1991). *Modernizing the Financial System: Recommendations for Safer, More Competitive Banks.* Washington, D.C.: Government Printing Office.

APPENDIX 1

Summary of the PCA Provisions

The PCA provisions require that banking regulators take pre-specified actions whenever bank capital levels fall below established levels. Table A1-1 summarizes the capital requirements for each capital level, except for critically undercapitalized institutions (defined as institutions with a leverage ratio below 2%).

Table A1-1. Capital Ratio Thresholds Under PCA.

Capital Category	Capital Ratio		
	Total Risk-based	Tier 1 Risk-based	Leverage
Well capitalized*	10% or more, and	6% or more, and	5% or more
Adequately capitalized	8% or more, and	4% or more, and	4% or more
Undercapitalized**	Less than 8%, or	Less than 4%, or	Less than 4%
Significantly undercapitalized	Less than 6%, or	Less than 3%, or	Less than 3%

* An institution is not considered to be well-capitalized if it is subject to a formal regulatory action that requires the institution to meet and maintain a specific capital level.
** The leverage ratio can be as low as 3% if the institution has a CAMELS rating of 1.
Source: GAO (1997).

Table A1-2 provides a summary of the required actions and limits set by FDICIA. The limits are additive. For example, a significantly undercapitalized bank is under the restrictions for both the undercapitalized institutions and the significantly undercapitalized institutions.

Table A1-2. Mandatory Actions under the PCA Provisions of FDICIA.

Well capitalized and adequately capitalized
- None

Undercapitalized
- May not pay dividends or management fees.
- Subject to increased monitoring.
- Must implement acceptable capital plan.
- Asset growth restricted.
- Approval needed for acquisitions, branching, and new business lines.
- May not issue brokered deposits.
- Access to discount window restricted.

Significantly undercapitalized
- Subject to provisions applicable to undercapitalized.
- Compensation of senior officers restricted.
- Unless action would not further purposes of PCA, supervisor shall:
  - Require bank to raise additional capital or be merged.
  - Enforce Sec. 23A of F.R. Act as if exemptions in Act do not apply.
  - Restrict deposit interest rates to those prevailing in region.

Critically undercapitalized
- After 60 days, no payments on subordinated debt without approval.
- Must be placed in receivership:
  - Within 90 days, unless action would not achieve purposes of PCA.
  - Within 270 days, unless specific statutory requirements are met.
- Access to discount window restricted more than for undercapitalized.
- May not do the following without FDIC approval:
  - Undertake material transaction, except in usual course of business.
  - Extend credit for any highly leveraged transaction.
  - Make any material change in accounting methods.
  - Undertake a *covered transaction*, as defined in Sec. 23A of F.R. Act.
  - Pay excessive compensation or bonuses.
  - Pay interest on liabilities above prevailing market rates.

Source: primarily Jones and King (1995).

APPENDIX 2

Details on Selected Calculations

This appendix discusses selected calculations and accounting policies that influence the data sources used for this analysis. Some of the accounting policies inhibit the comparability of failed bank data across time. The more material items are discussed here.

2.1. The Calculation of FDIC Loss

At resolution, the FDIC generally bases its loss estimate on an Asset Valuation Review (AVR). The AVR estimate of loss is calculated as the difference between the FDIC's anticipated outlay and the net present value of the funds recovered from the receivership.[1] As the receivership progresses, the loss calculation (as published by the FDIC in the Failed Bank Cost Analysis (FBCA)) changes somewhat: it is essentially calculated as the FDIC's resolution outlays minus the funds recovered from the receivership and the estimated funds to be recovered from the receivership in the future.[2] Both cost figures exclude pre-closing expenses associated with preparing the bank for resolution and determining which deposit accounts are insured.[3] These items tend to be a relatively small component of FDIC losses.

The FDIC is required to fund the insured deposits at the time of failure; however, the receivership pays dividends to the FDIC and other creditors as assets are sold (after meeting expenses). Thus, the FDIC has working capital requirements during the interim period between the failure date and the dates when dividends are paid by the receivership.

Because funding costs are a real cost to the FDIC (in the form of lost interest income to the insurance fund) but are largely excluded from the FBCA, we estimated the funding cost for each bank where the FBCA figure was the most up-to-date published figure.[4] The estimate was made as follows. First, we collected the FDIC claim and dividend payments made through year-end 2000. For open receiverships, we assumed that the remaining asset value (based on discounted cash flow, net of expenses) would be paid to the FDIC on December 31, 2000. Then, we calculated the interest that the receivership owes to the FDIC on the portion of its claim that either had been paid or that we assumed would have been paid on December 31, 2000. We used the FDIC's average yield on its investments as the interest rate. We also treated two items included in the FBCA figure as holding costs: interest earned on the receivership's cash balances (which reduced holding costs) and interest paid to other creditors by the receivership (which increased holding costs). This allows for a more accurate comparison of the economic costs across receiverships, and of the initial cost estimate and the latest available cost estimate.[5] Across the full sample of banks, the median difference between the FBCA cost and the cost used in this paper was 3.75% of total assets as of the quarter-end date prior to failure.

2.2. *Differences Between GAAP and the FDIC's Receivership Accounting Policies*

While open banks normally prepare financial statements and Call Reports using accounting principles that are predicated on their being ongoing concerns, receiverships use cash-basis accounting. The primary difference between bank and FDIC receivership accounting policies relate to the treatment of accrued items, reserves for troubled assets, and intangible assets. Receiverships do not typically record accrued items or intangible assets, except in cases where certain intangible assets are recorded on the books at one dollar for control purposes.[6] Receiverships record loans at gross book value, thereby reversing partial charge-offs or reserves recorded by the failed bank.[7] These differences sometimes result in large changes in the equity ratio of a bank when the basis of accounting shifts at failure, at times resulting in a receivership initially showing more equity than the failed bank. As assets are sold, receivership equity inevitably declines, reflecting the asset recovery received.

At closing, the FDIC calculates the institution's closing balance sheet and then makes adjustments to conform to the receivership accounting policies. Although we collected both initial balances, we relied primarily on the institution's closing balance sheet for analysis because they are more comparable to the Call Report. Thus, all references to the bank's balance sheet at closing in Section 4.2.3 exclude the adjustments made to conform to receivership accounting policies unless an exception is cited.

The data on asset composition as of the failure date and during the receivership should be interpreted with care, partly because of differences in the accounting basis (discussed above) and partly because of different asset categories.[8] It appears likely that many – perhaps even all – of these banks used asset categories for their general ledgers that did not align closely to the asset categories used on the Call Report.[9] Differences in asset category may be quite small for securities and OREO, but appear to be much larger for loans. Other differences may occur due to limits in data availability and time over closing weekend. Therefore, the results should be interpreted with these caveats in mind.

Receivership financial statements differ substantially from those of an ongoing bank or thrift in other ways as well. For example, the liabilities are grouped according to claims that have been proven (or remain unproven) and the income statement does not include interest expenses for most classes of creditors.[10]

2.3. Asset Losses, Charge-offs and Reserves

Asset losses are a primary factor that determines the FDIC loss. There are substantial disparities in the information collected about asset losses of a failed bank over its life cycle. This section discusses certain adjustments made to the receivership loss figures to improve the comparability across the banks' life cycle and summarizes differences in policies and practices between the asset losses estimated at resolution and the asset losses recorded by the receivership.

In preparation for resolution, the FDIC prepares an Asset Valuation Review (AVR) that estimates asset losses for the entire portfolio. These losses are based on total assets – gross of reserves – per the Call Report.[11] To prepare the estimates, analysts review the available documentation, project all cash flows (including associated income and expenses), and discount the cash flows using a market-based discount rate. These estimates are made for various pools of assets, which are typically packaged to facilitate the marketing process. Because these packages do not always align with the asset categories recorded on the Call Report, we have largely omitted such comparisons.

Receiverships record asset losses as the difference between the gross asset balance (after reversing reserves and, to some extent, charge-offs) and the sales price. The receivership asset loss figures are not discounted, and they exclude sales expenses and net income (loss) received prior to the sale.[12] Because both the definition of asset loss and the asset categories differ between the AVR and the receivership, we made no attempt to analyze changes in loss estimates between resolution and year-end 2000 by asset category.

Receiverships record judgments (awards made in a court) and certain deficiency balances (charged off assets) at gross book value, whereas they are typically not recorded at all on the Call Reports. For this analysis, we exclude judgments and deficiencies (both balances and losses) recorded by the receiverships to improve the comparability of losses over the life of the failed bank.

Some of the receiverships had unsold assets as of year-end 2000. To facilitate comparisons across the full sample of failed institutions, we estimated future losses by asset type and incorporated these estimates into the asset loss rates for the receiverships. We relied upon supporting documents for the FDIC's year-end financial statements for 2000 to prepare the estimates.

In addition to differences in practices and policies, the asset loss data are difficult to interpret due to activity that occurs between the last Call Report and the failure date. Because no financial statements are filed during this period, we have no information about charge-offs, loss provisions, asset sales or realized losses. If a bank sells a substantive amount of assets during the period, we have no record of the transaction. We can merely make inferences based on balance sheet changes between these dates. Comparisons also become difficult when interest rates or the health of the economy change during the course of the resolution and the receivership.

In summary, comparisons of financial data across time are difficult to interpret because of differences in accounting policy and data collection over the course of a failed bank, changes in the economy, and missing data for a brief period of time. For a typical failed bank, the initial equity balance of the receivership is markedly higher than the closing equity found on the Call Report. Because many of receiverships begin with positive equity balances, losses recorded on the income statement of the receiverships usually exceed the FDIC's loss on its receivership claim.[13] Asset losses recorded by the receivership may be either higher or lower than the reserve levels recorded by the bank and the original AVR asset loss estimates because of different calculation methods – even in cases where original expectations are exactly met. Therefore, one must be careful when interpreting comparisons of results over the life of a failed bank.

APPENDIX 3

Comparison of Asset Composition: Call Report vs. Receivership

We collected high-level balance sheet data as recorded by the bank's general ledger on the date of failure, and the initial balance sheet of the receivership (that is, at failure), after adjustments made over the life of the receivership.[14] We also compared these to the final Call Report data filed by the institution. The comparison is found in Table A3-1. All figures are shown as a percentage of total assets.

The data on asset composition at receivership are difficult to interpret, partly because of accounting differences and partly because of different asset categories. Section 2.2 in Appendix 2 discusses these obstacles to straightforward comparisons. The results should be interpreted with these caveats in mind.

Both the low-cost and high-cost failures shrank between the final Call Report date and failure. The median shrinkage was 7.10% for low-cost failures and 9.34% for high-cost failures. Between failure and receivership, both groups experienced a small increase in assets (attributable largely to the reversal of reserves).

From the final Call Report date to failure, the median level of securities increased slightly for low-cost institutions and decreased slightly for high-cost institutions. A review of the individual institution results indicates that a few of the low-cost institutions apparently sold a material amount of loans during the intervening period.

The mortgage results were puzzling. From the final Call Report date to failure, the median percentage of mortgages to total assets increased: from 23.00% to 27.53% for low-cost failures, and from 17.58% to 22.09% for high-

Table A3-1. Comparison of Median Balance Sheet Composition Before and At Failure (as a Percentage of Total Assets).

	Low-Cost Failures			High-Cost Failures			All Failures		
	Call/TFR	Bank G/L	Recv.	Call/TFR	Bank G/L	Recv.	Call/TFR	Bank G/L	Recv.
Securities	10.82%	12.91%	18.01%	9.73%	7.55%	12.04%	10.06%	9.10%	12.56%
Mortgages	23.00%	27.53%	28.98%	17.58%	22.09%	30.25%	18.94%	27.27%	28.98%
C&I Loans	31.74%	26.31%	23.90%	33.95%	44.47%	36.36%	33.50%	32.62%	33.08%
Other Loans	3.07%	3.58%	3.54%	4.00%	5.18%	5.31%	3.92%	5.01%	4.97%
OREO	0.69%	0.91%	3.80%	3.64%	5.69%	5.33%	2.47%	4.15%	5.14%
Reserves	–2.76%	–2.58%	0.0%	–2.68%	–3.09%	0.0%	–2.72%	–3.04%	0.0%
Other Assets	16.21%	18.92%	7.04%	19.54%	14.24%	6.35%	19.33%	14.35%	6.51%

cost failures. The increase continued in the receivership. The change in median levels between the failure date and the receivership was negligible for the low-cost failures but large (22.09% at failure; 30.25% in receivership) for the high-cost failures. Reviewing the results by institution, it appears that the largest factor is differences in asset category definitions.[15] Some portion of the increase between the Call Report date and failure is probably attributable to reductions in other types of assets (thereby increasing the proportion of mortgages).

Like the mortgage results, the C&I loan results were characterized by substantial swings that frequently appear to be changes in asset type definitions at failure. The median percentages dropped for the low-cost failures. For the high-cost failures, they increased between the Call Report date and failure, but decreased during the receivership.

The OREO results appear to be untainted by differences in asset category definitions. Between the final Call Report and failure, there was a substantial change in the median ratio for high-cost failures (3.64% on the final Call Report; 5.69% at failure) but little change for the low-cost failures (0.69% on the final Call Report; 0.91% at failure). The median increase in OREO during the receivership, calculated in percentage points of total assets at failure, was similar (1.96% for low-cost failures; 2.19% for high-cost failures).[16] These figures include foreclosure activity.

There were few changes in reserves between the final Call Report date and failure. Reserves are reversed in receivership.

There were substantive changes in the median levels of other assets (including cash and fed funds). From the final Call Report date to failure, the median level of other assets increased slightly for low-cost institutions (16.21% to 18.92%) and decreased slightly for high-cost institutions (19.54% to 14.24%). Most institutions reduced their balances of other assets between the Call Report and failure, although a few institutions showed substantive increases because of apparent asset sales. We were unable to ascertain the underlying reasons for the persistent reductions shortly before failure. There were also large and persistent reductions in the receivership: the most likely cause was write-offs of intangible assets, accrued interest, and prepaid expenses.

APPENDIX NOTES

1. The steps of the calculations include:

(a) estimate the net present value of the assets;
(b) estimate the volume of creditors in each creditor class;

(c) estimate payments to each creditor class, given the discounted asset value estimates; and
(d) estimate the FDIC loss as the difference between the FDIC claim and its anticipated recoveries.

In addition, the interest due to the FDIC is calculated and placed on the receivership books in cases where the FDIC expects some or all of the interest to be paid in the near future. It is excluded from the cost reported in the FBCA even in cases where it is reported and/or paid by the receivership.

2. For terminated receiverships, all cash flows are undiscounted. For ongoing receiverships, actual recoveries to date are undiscounted, and expected future recoveries are discounted to the date of the estimate. For example, assume that a failure occurred in 1995. The FDIC loss as of year-end 2000 would be calculated as the 1995 outlay minus all dividends paid through year-end 2000 minus estimated future dividends (which would be based on the anticipated future recoveries from the receivership, discounted to year-end 2000).

3. Differences in the cost of insurance determination are considered when the FDIC determines the least-cost bid. The cost of preparing for resolution is a sunk cost that would not influence the selection of a winning bidder, and thus is excluded from the least-cost test.

4. Our estimates do not follow FDIC regulations and practices for the payment of interest to receivership creditors.

5. This adjustment still does not result in a fully consistent comparison of economic costs. The initial cost estimate uses risk-adjusted discount rates based on the asset composition of the bank, whereas the adjustment to the 2000 FBCA cost estimate effectively uses the FDIC's cost of funds for discounting.

6. For example, assume that a bank sells a portfolio of mortgages, but retains the servicing rights. The servicing rights may have real value but they are typically recorded on the books of the receivership at one dollar.

7. Gross book value was typically defined as the historical cost or unpaid loan balance minus any charge-offs that had been recorded by the bank. If there were partial charge-offs recorded by the failed bank that were identifiable at failure, they would normally be reversed; however, this is frequently not the case. Thus, the treatment of charge-offs is not always consistent across receiverships.

8. By asset categories, we mean types of assets grouped by loan purpose (such as single-family mortgages or C&I loans).

9. Banks frequently categorize assets on their general ledgers based on the sub-systems used in servicing the assets. For example, all fixed rate amortizing instruments may be boarded on one sub-system (regardless of loan purpose), and the general ledger may carry one set of accounts that is used for all such instruments. To prepare the Call Reports, information from both the general ledger and the sub-systems would be used. At failure, the FDIC attempts to align the general ledger categories to those used internally by the FDIC receiverships (stratified by loan purpose, similar to the Call Report), but time constraints and the discord in asset categories limits the FDIC's ability to succeed in this effort.

10. For many creditors, receiverships pay post-insolvency interest only after the principal is paid in full. The FDIC's current policy is to calculate and record the interest cost due to creditors when 95% of the principal balance has been repaid. Such costs are

treated as an adjustment to equity rather than interest expense, because the bulk of such claims are typically accrued but not paid and receiverships use cash accounting principles.

11. Charge-offs are not reversed.

12. While accounting policy excludes all asset sales expenses from these figures, occasionally certain asset sales expenses incurred at the time of sale are included.

13. This could also occur because of losses incurred by other creditors. However, most at-risk creditors flee banks before failure, so that the FDIC and the bank's stockholders typically bear almost all of the losses at failure.

14. Some of the adjustments made during the receivership relate to post-closing activities rather than the institution's asset balance at closing. We dropped all adjustments that we could identify as occurring after failure.

15. Unfortunately, we were not always able to determine which report provides the most accurate picture of the institutions. For some of these institutions, there was a change in receivership that appears to bring the institution's balance sheet into closer conformity with the Call Report. This type of change probably indicates that the asset types recorded on the institution's general ledger did not align well with the Call Report.

16. Ironically, the median percentage of OREO to total assets dropped from failure to the receivership for the high-cost institutions even though the median change in OREO was an increase. The increase did not occur evenly across the sample.

PRICING BANK DISTRESS: BEFORE AND AFTER PCA

Gerald A. Hanweck and Lewis J. Spellman

ABSTRACT

The early resolution of banks thought to be approaching insolvency is believed to induce more sensitive risk pricing of the bank's securities. However, we find that, if investors believe that a bank resolution will occur while the bank is still marginally solvent, this expectation will serve to mute the market signal for subordinated debt but not for equity. We have examined episodes of the pricing of the securities of five banks that have been publicly identified to be nearing insolvency to see if the pricing is consistent with a solvent resolution. There were a limited number of episodes for which PCA expectations were apparently priced though they appeared in a minority of the cases studied.

I. INTRODUCTION

Following episodes of bank forbearance that have been attributed to sizable deposit insurance losses, the policy antithesis of forbearance has emerged.[1] Early intervention, or in its legislated terminology, Prompt Corrective Action (PCA) is an activist policy to quickly resolve banks whose capital has been weakened but are yet solvent. PCA sets interventionist standards for both solvency (2% tangible capital) and speed of resolution (one to three quarters).[2]

Prompt Corrective Action in Banking: 10 Years Later, Volume 14, pages 203–225.

ISBN: 0-7623-0987-3

While PCA was legislated as an antidote to deposit insurance losses, its interventionist posture was also expected to serve as a warning to bank security holders that they will suffer swift losses in the event of a bank insolvency. Thus, PCA in addition to setting resolution standards perhaps more importantly redefines regulatory expectations by projecting an attitude that past forbearance or "Too Big to Fail" policies are no longer operative. The more risk sensitive pricing of bank securities that were anticipated to emerge also serve the duel purpose of providing disincentives for banks from risk taking but also serve as a real time market indication for regulators that the bank's capital has deteriorated.[3]

Implicit in this understanding of market discipline is the basic assumption that the prices of market traded bank securities will fall if regulatory intervention is imminent. This is reflected for example, in Flannery and Sorescu (1996) who attribute the statistical significance of subordinated debt yields to measures of bank risk for post PCA data from the 1990s in contrast to the lack of a relationship of market yields to bank risk found in their data and other studies (Avery, Belton & Goldberg, 1998; Gorton & Santomero, 1990) that covered the forbearance episodes of the 1980s.

Despite the general presumption that the new interventionist regulations will cause investors to be more risk sensitive in their pricing of bank securities, there are some that still question whether market discipline will occur. One question concerns the ability of investors to penetrate the opaqueness of the public reporting of bank conditions in order to determine the bank's asset quality. A second question follows from the fact that even if the investor's were aware of the bank's assets, markets for bank loans are so incomplete that pricing the individual loans in a bank's portfolio is not possible (Beaver, Datar & Wolfson, 1992).[4] Other questions have been raised as to whether early intervention would indeed follow early detection because regulatory incentives might be perverse to intervention (Kane, 1990). If that were true or expected by investors it would obviate the need to price the prospect of an imminent failure.

This paper explores another facet of questionable market discipline not based on opaqueness or incomplete pricing of bank assets but rather based on the possible perverse effects of "resolution while solvent" (the 2% solvent rule). The decline in market discipline could occur as a direct result of the PCA rule of quickly resolving banks while still solvent. This could occur because a policy designed to provide the asset coverage to retire the bank's senior deposit debt (so as to make the deposit insurer whole), might also provide the assets to retire the bank's junior debt and possibly some equity. If so, investors' belief in quick resolution while solvent will perhaps inadvertently blunt the early warning of bank insolvency. That is, the expectation of a solvent bank resolution is likely to be priced differently than the expectation of an insolvent bank resolution in a way that might reduce market price signals of bank capital impairment.

In Section II, we state the contingent claim model of bank securities prices in order to determine how subordinated debt and equity pricing will be affected by the expectation of resolution while solvent vs. resolution after becoming insolvent. In Section III, we show that the contingent claim model implies that if investors believe the bank will face early resolution with positive tangible capital this would increase the value of the bank's subordinated debt. In contrast, the bank's equity holders should price a more quickly approaching resolution while solvent with less enthusiasm. This is because the future stream of earning is cut off and will likely result in greater losses than their compensation in retirement proceeds. Thus a price divergence in subordinated debt and equity prices should result.

In Section IV, we examine some case studies of distressed banks both prior to and under PCA regulatory standards to see if the pricing of the bank's securities are consistent with resolution while solvent, or resolution while insolvent. We find that, with the exception of two periods for two banking companies, the pricing evidence is consistent with an investor belief that banks that near insolvency will not be resolved until after insolvency occurs. In Section V, we summarize and conclude that the pricing evidence gives but little evidence that investors believe a PCA resolution will occur.

II. A MODEL OF EARLY INTERVENTION AND BANK SECURITIES PRICES

The contingent claims model of bank securities prices contains explicit arguments for bank solvency and time until resolution. These are the variables necessary to examine the pricing effects of quick resolution while solvent vs. insolvent. The contingent claims model was developed by Black-Scholes and extended to subordinated debt pricing by Black and Cox (1976). The application of the contingent claims pricing to bank equity was pioneered by Merton (1977) and applied to deposit insurance pricing by Ronn and Verma (1986). The model was extended to the pricing of both bank equity and subordinated debt by Schellhorn and Spellman (2000) and Hanweck (2001).

The continent claims approach to pricing includes variables that correspond to the banks solvency (capital) ratio and the timeliness of resolution. The investors' perception of these variables is impounded into the prices paid for a bank's equity and subordinated debt. Hence it is useful for the analysis of the how PCA expectations of a quick resolution while solvent is priced as compared to a resolution after the bank is insolvent.

In the model, the bank's capital structure consists of equity and debt, with total debt having components of senior deposit debt and subordinated debt. The notation used in the following discussion will be:

V = the market value of the bank's assets.
E = the market value of the bank's equity.
D_j = the market value of the bank's subordinated coupon debt.
B_S = the maturity value of the bank's senior debt.
B_{Sub} = the maturity value of the bank's subordinated debt
B = the maturity value of the bank's total debt $(B_S + B_{Sub})$
σ_V = the standard deviation of the rate of return on the value of the bank's assets per year.
σ_E = the standard deviation of the rate of return on the bank's equity per year.
r = the risk-free interest rate per year.
τ = the investor's expectation of time until resolution
$N(.)$ = the cumulative normal density function.

A European equity call formulation results in the following two equations:

$$E = VN(g_1) - (B)\exp(-R_f\tau)N(g_2) \tag{1}$$

where:

$$g_1 = \frac{\left[\ln\left(\frac{V}{(B_S + B_{Sub})}\right) + (R_f + 0.5\sigma_V^2)\tau\right]}{\sigma_V\sqrt{\tau}} \quad \text{and} \quad g_2 = g_1 - \sigma_V\sqrt{\tau}.$$

Black and Cox (1976) and Smith (1979) showed that the market value of subordinated debt, D_j, equals the value of the difference between two call options:

$$D_j = VN(d_1) - B_S\exp(-R_f\tau)N(d_2) - VN(g_1) + (B_{Sub} + B_S)\exp(-R_f\tau)N(g_2) \tag{2}$$

where g_1 and g_2 are defined as above and:

$$d_1 = \frac{\left[\ln\left(\frac{V}{B_S}\right) + (R_f + 0.5\sigma_V^2)\tau\right]}{\sigma_V\sqrt{\tau}} \quad \text{and} \quad d_2 = d_1 - \sigma_V\sqrt{\tau}.$$

The time until resolution is a regulatory policy variable. Regulators do not reveal the time until resolution for a distressed bank, but the investor must evaluate this variable as it adds or detracts from the value of the bank's securities. Hence, the investor's prices are based on their expectation of how long the regulator will allow a bank to continue to operate.[5] Once a bank is resolved, the value of the claims on the bank, whether debt or equity, depend on the terminal value of the bank's assets. If the expectation is that a resolution will provide sufficient funds to pay off the subordinated debt holders after the senior debt is retired, this will no doubt be reflected in its pricing. Similarly, the equity value also reflects resolution time and solvency because a speedy solvent resolution might provide the equity holder with a partial recovery. On the other hand, a speedy resolution cuts off the income stream provided by the bank's assets and has a perverse effect on equity pricing in particular.

The model also contains investor-estimated value of total assets, V. The value of the total assets in turn directly lead to the bank's solvency ratio $(V - B)/V$ as the debt components are exogenously known. Values of E and D_j are influenced by the value of asset volatility or σ_V. This is a measure of risk that incorporates any cause of a change in the accumulated asset value either from current earnings or losses or asset appreciation or depreciation. In order to understand the effect of PCA expectations on the pricing of bank equity and subordinated debt, we also assume a σ_V of 0.05 in the simulations in the next section.[6]

III. THE PRICING EFFECTS OF AN EXPECTED SOLVENT RESOLUTION

The variables of interest are D_j and E, the prices of subordinated debt and equity. To see how they are priced in relation to solvency and the investor's expected time until resolution, τ, is our task. That is we examine the investor's pricing their expectation of a solvent resolution. Note that the fulfillment of those expectations is not relevant at the time the pricing takes place as investors price expectations. In Figs 1 and 2 we demonstrate the *ceteris paribus* response of D_j and E for reduced values of τ while the bank is still solvent. The pricing loci for a shorter τ for banks with a +2% solvency, zero solvency and –2% solvency are shown. We are most interested in the effect of a shortening of τ when the asset value V exceeds the sum of B_S and B_{Sub} by 2% which is the necessary condition to invoke early resolution under PCA.

In Fig. 1, the pricing loci make clear that when the investors expected time until resolution declines to less than a year, this will *increase* the price of the subordinated debt which approaches the full redemption value as the resolution time gets shorter. This occurs because the resolution for a still solvent bank will provide the funds to retire the subordinated debt closer to par whereas a longer

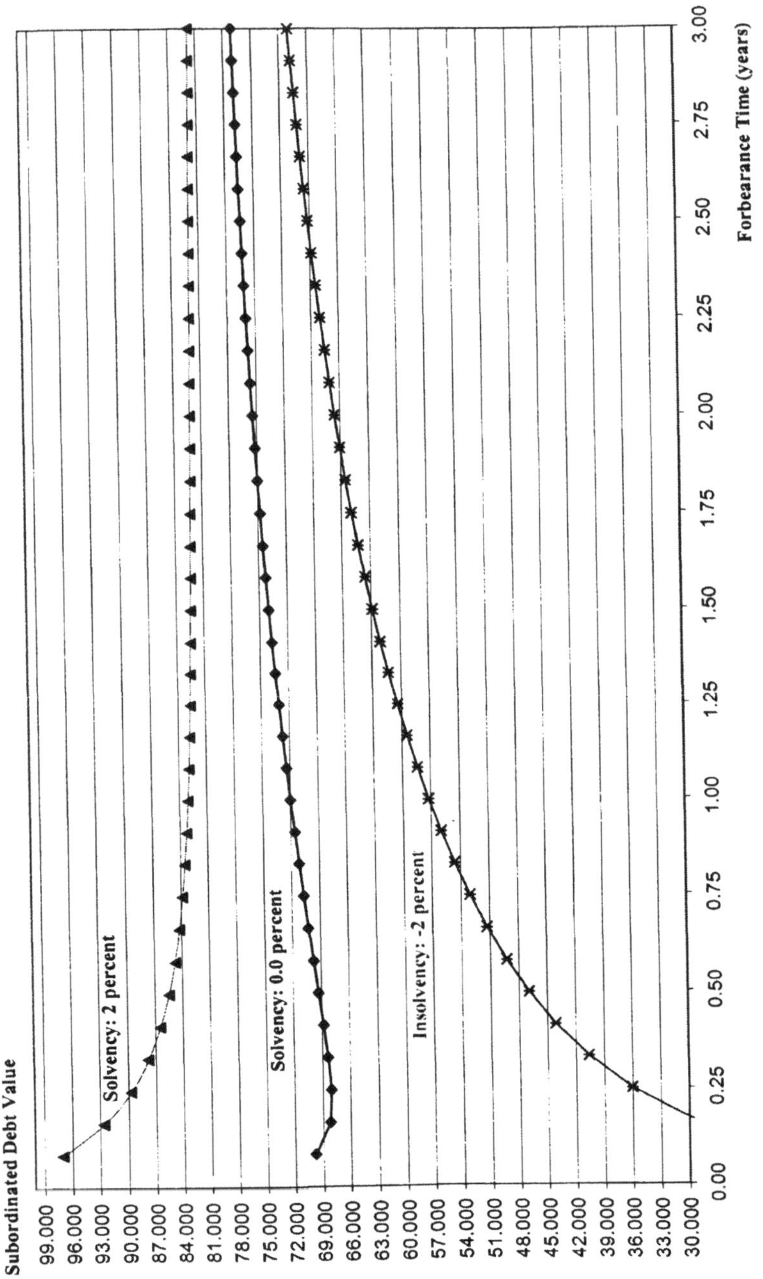

Fig. 1. Subordinated Debt Market Values By Forebearance Time at Different Insolvency Levels. (Solvency $=(V-B)/V$ at 2%, 0.0% and −2%, $\sigma_V=0.05$)

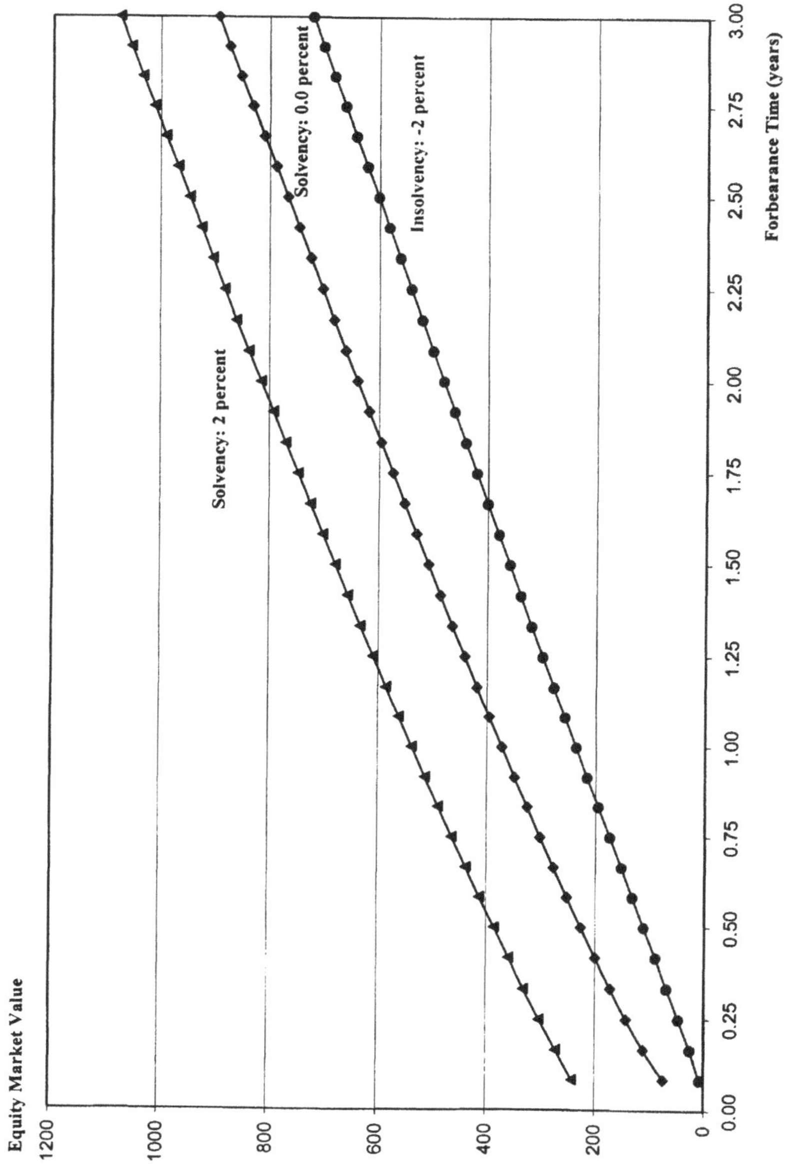

Fig. 2. Equity Market Values By Forebearance Time at Different Insolvency Levels. (Solvency = $(V - B)/V$ at 2%, 0.0% and −2%, $\sigma_V = 0.05$)

τ with a precarious leverage position introduces the possibility of an insolvent resolution. Thus if investors hold PCA expectations, higher subordinated debt prices and lower yield spreads should obtain.[7] The reverse is true for the equity price for the 2% solvent resolution because quickly resolving the bank while still solvent should provide only limited retirement value and the equity holders lose the future stream of income provided by the bank's assets (Fig. 2). *Hence, the pricing loci indicate that a negative correlation between the changes in the subordinated debt and equity price should occur if a quick solvent resolution is expected.* That is if information that the bank is distressed causes investors to believe a PCA resolution will occur, equity prices fall and subordinated debt prices increase. Hence, under PCA expectations, market discipline is confined to bank equity prices alone.

To examine whether investors have come to believe the legislated PCA standards will occur we examine the pricing data of banks that have been identified in the press as being distressed. Some banks eventually were resolved and some recovered. If the investors believe the warning is sufficiently early and if they believe that a PCA resolution will follow, we should find cases of divergence of subordinated debt and equity prices prior to or following the public news of bank distress. We examine price data for banks both pre- and post-PCA that became effective year-end 1991. The banking company cases are limited to five for several reasons. First, the banking companies needed to have a reasonably meaningful period of distress. Second, the banking companies needed to be of reasonable size to attract national media attention. Finally, data had to be available for banking companies for equity and debt pricing, in particular debt had to be traded so that at least weekly pricing could be observed.[8]

Table 1, panel A shows the banks that became insolvent or had a "near-death" experience for which market prices of both subordinated debt and equity

Table 1. Banking Companies in the Analysis.

Panel A: Banking Companies That Became Insolvent		
Bank of New England	January 6, 1991	Pre-FDICIA
Bankers Trust	Merged with Deutsche Bank January 1999	Post-FDICIA
Panel B: Banking Companies That Survived Financial Stress		
Citicorp	Late 1990	Pre-FDICIA
Bank One	Fall 1999	Post-FDICIA
First Union	Spring to Late 1999	Post-FDICIA

and yields to maturity are available.[9] Table 1, panel B shows the banks that have had severe financial distress, but have recovered. For each of these banks we determined the date of first public press mention of problems and then examine the pricing response immediately before and after. Using the concepts and terminology developed above these pricing responses are summarized in Table 2 showing periods when banking companies were experiencing stress and the corresponding pricing results for a significant period (at least 8 consecutive weeks). The criteria of price change are determined by periods of extended statistically significant positive or negative correlation of stock and subordinated debt prices. The periods must show significant correlation at the

Table 2. Summary of Results of Banking Companies under Financial Distress.

	Period	Correlation (Stock Price with Debt Prices)	Stock Price	Debt Prices	Solvency Condition	τ	PCA Consistent Pricing*
Pre-PCA							
Bank of New England (Failed)	Oct. 1989 Oct. 1990	+0.50 to +0.96 Average +0.80	(−)	(−)	Insolvent	(−)	No
	July 1989 Aug. 1989	−0.47 to +0.70 Average −0.58	(−)	(+, 0)	Insolvent	(−)	Yes
Citicorp (Survived)	June 1990 Nov. 1990	+0.68 to +0.92 Average +0.77	(−)	(−)	Insolvent	(−)	No
Post-PCA							
Bankers Trust (Acquired)	June 1998 Aug. 1998	−0.41 to −0.93 Average −0.84	(−)	(+, 0)[1]	Insolvent	(−)	Yes
Bank One (Survived)	July 1999 Sep. 1999	+0.50 to +0.96 Average +0.75	(−)	(−)	Insolvent	(−)	No
First Union (Survived)	May 1999 Sep. 1999	+0.51 to +0.93 Average +0.76	(−)	(−)	Insolvent	(−)	No

* Refer to Section III of the text for an interpretation of PCA consistent pricing.
[1] A (+, 0) means increase or no change and a (–, 0) falling or no change.

two-tailed 5% confidence level or better (±0.62 or better) over at least eight consecutive weeks or a two-month period based on 10-week rolling correlation coefficients.[10] We chose eight weeks because this was considered sufficient time for a meaningful correlation to be established if one were to occur. The shaded areas in Figs 3 through 7 represent time periods during which statistical significance occurred.

IV. A. PRE-PCA PRICING

A.1. The Bank of New England

The Bank of New England (BNE) failed on January 6, 1991 along with its major affiliate banks, Maine National Bank and Connecticut Bank and Trust. Following these events, the Bank of New England Corporation (BNEC) declared bankruptcy. According to the *History of the Eighties* (FDIC, 1997, pp. 374–378), the OCC became seriously concerned with BNE after an examination that began at year-end 1988 and was completed in May 1989. This examination resulted in a formal agreement with Bank of New England on August 10, 1989 to "correct the deficiencies the OCC examiners had identified in the bank's real estate lending practices." The OCC began having a continuous examiner presence in September 1989 and on September 30, 1989 BNE was downgraded to a CAMEL 5 from a CAMEL 3, having held a CAMEL 2 rating since at least late 1986 (FDIC, 1997).[11]

In May 1988, the Bank of New England Corporation was considered a banking company with substantial and sustainable growth prospects, but by July 1989, a Kidder Peabody analyst recommended to clients that the stock be sold (FDIC, 1997, p. 374). Although BNEC stock and debt prices continued to fall throughout 1990, prior to fourth quarter 1989 the debt market showed little concern over BNEC, but the stock market was indicating a loss of confidence in the continued high growth of BNEC (Fig. 3). From the perspective of our model, there was price divergence: stock price declines with debt price increase or stability – a PCA case (see Table 2). Beginning in the fourth quarter of 1989, there was a distinct change in market perception of the survivability of BNEC. By early December 1989, prices of debt and equity began to decline synchronously, with a brief increase in debt prices in late early December of 1990, until the closure in January 1991 (Fig. 3). The correlation of stock debt prices from October 6, 1989 to October 26, 1990 were significantly positive at between +0.49 to +0.96 and averaged +0.75, indicating a persistent pricing relationship. This suggests that the market considered the bank insolvent and in line for early resolution – a Non-PCA case. The brief debt price increases in

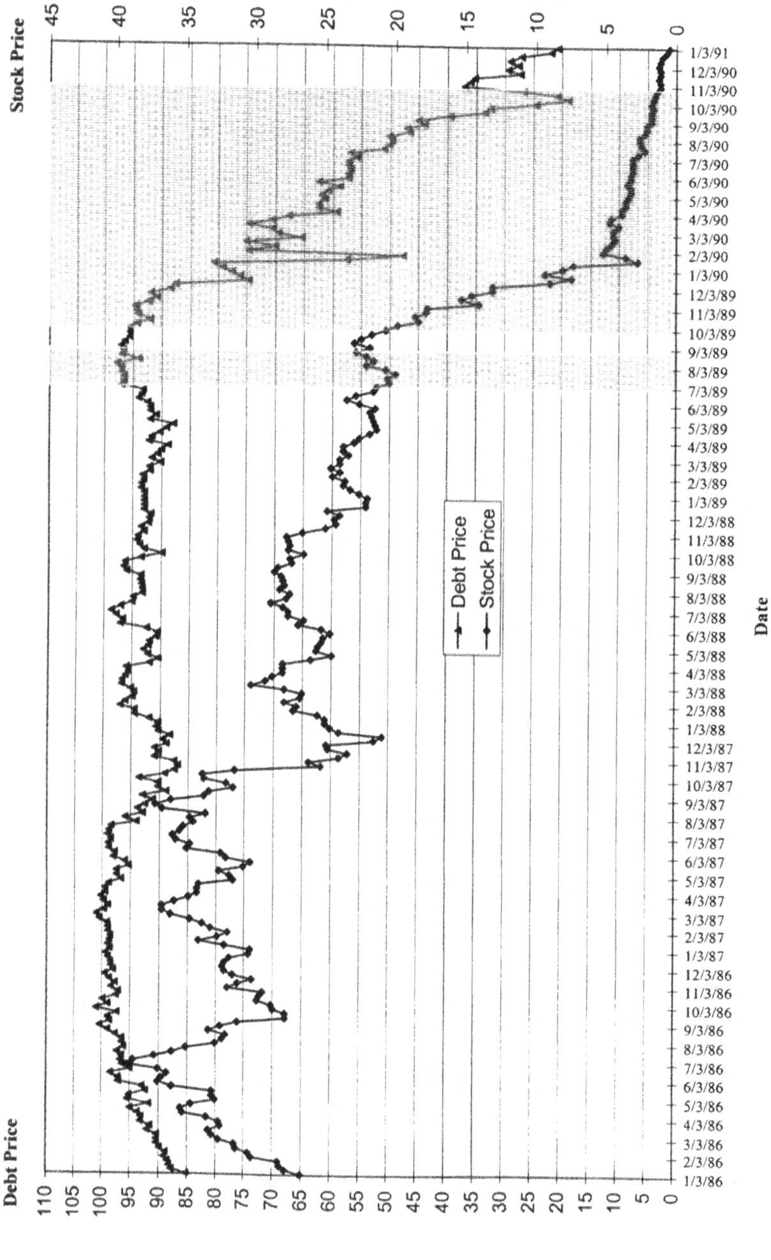

Fig. 3. Bank of New England: Subordinated Debt and Stock Prices. ($, weekly, January 3, 1986 to January 4, 1991)

December 1990 may be considered a meaningful price relationship since the spreads halved from their previous high of 40% while stock prices continued their downward drift. These changes followed cease and desist orders issued by the OCC and may have been associated with a period when investors changed their expectations that the BNEC might survive through a sale of assets or regulator forbearance.

A.2. Citicorp

By the third quarter of 1990 Citicorp's principal banking subsidiary, Citibank, was facing declining earnings growth and capital that had reached 3.62% of assets adjusted for risk.[12] Although not made public at the time, John Reed, CEO of Citicorp, had made significant concessions to the Federal Reserve Bank of New York to increase the capital of Citibank and Citicorp.[13] At the time of these efforts in the Fall of 1990, the financial market information revealed that Citicorp's stock price was falling and that prices on subordinated debt fell to 74.3 in early November 1990 from 94.1 in late June 1990 (Fig. 4). Over this same period, Citicorp's stock price fell 48%. In terms of our model, equity and debt investors in Citicorp, during periods of severe stress, experienced a fall in stock and subordinated debt prices. The correlation coefficient over the period from late June 1990 to early November 1990 averaged +0.77 (Table 2). This is evidence of a Non-PCA case over nearly a 5-month period until Citicorp's debt prices returned to pre-June 1990 levels in May 1991. This rebound in prices is evidence that the market considered the bank to be close to insolvency and a candidate for forbearance (Table 2). After this period, stock and debt prices rose, indicating that the market considered the bank in financial distress, but subject to a longer τ.

IV. B. POST-PCA

B.1. Bankers Trust

Bankers Trust (BT) stock prices began a downward trend in March 1998, as its stock price slid to $51 in early October 1998 from a high of $135 in March 1998 (Fig. 5). This decline preceded the Russian default and devaluation on August 21, 1998 and was due largely to losses from investments in emerging markets as a result of the ongoing emerging markets currency crises.[14] By the third quarter, Bankers Trust had posted a larger than expected loss of $488 million with few prospects of an immediate recovery.[15] Prior to this announcement, Fitch downgraded Bankers Trust debt to an A from an A-plus

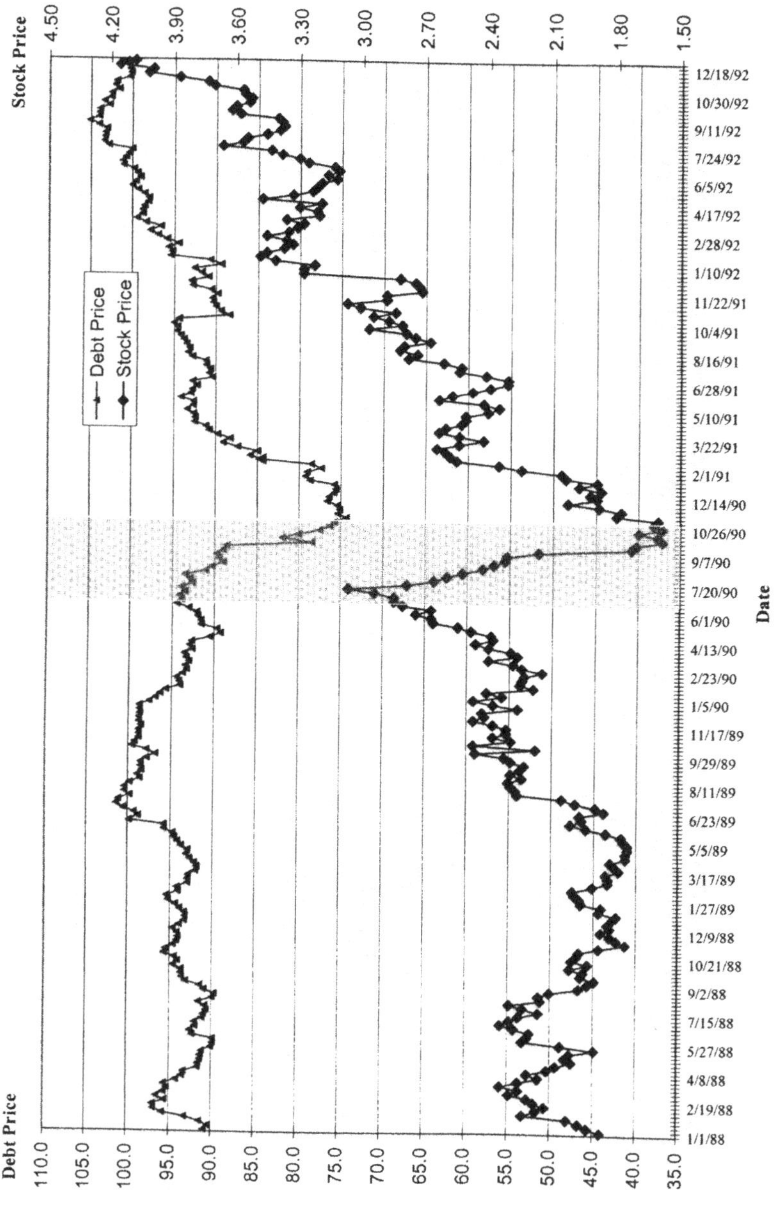

Fig. 4. Citicorp: Stock and Subordinated Debt Prices.
($, weekly, January 1, 1988 to December 25, 1992)

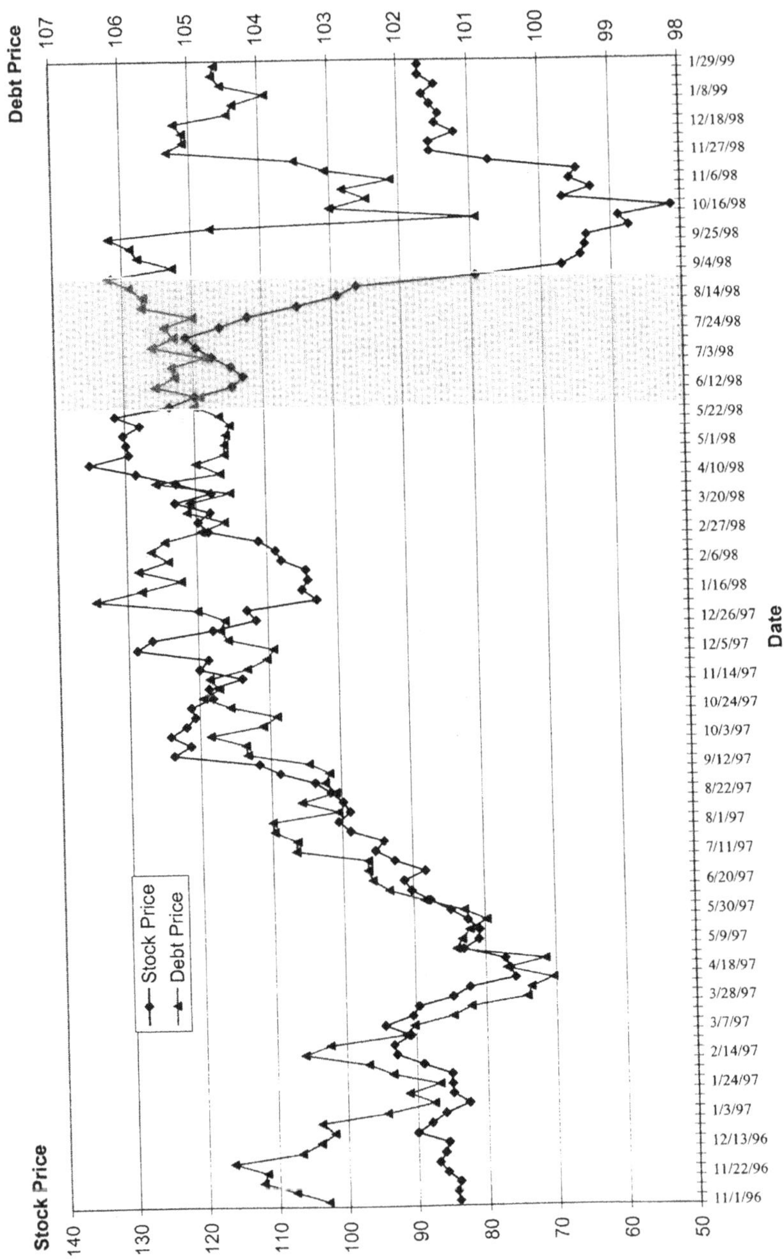

Fig. 5. Bankers Trust: Stock and Subordinated Debt Prices.
($, weekly, November 1, 1996 to January 29, 1999)

on October 12, 1998. Although Deutsche Bank had shown an interest in acquiring Bankers Trust during the Spring and Summer of 1998, this led to further increases in the spread on Bankers Trust debt to 307 basis points in mid-October from 81 basis points in mid-August. The period from June through August was a period of extreme financial stress for Bankers Trust. During this period stock prices fell and while debt prices remained almost unchanged or increased (Fig. 5). From early June through August, the correlation between BT's stock price and debt price averaged–0.84 and ranged from –0.41 to–0.93. In terms of our model, this period of stress showed equity prices and debt prices inversely related and investors' belief of an early resolution, a shorter τ – a PCA pricing episode (Table 2). A different pricing behavior occurred after the November 22, 1998 announcement that Deutsche Bank and BT had reached an agreement to merge. This time, stock and debt prices increased, a case of recognition of investors believing BT was nearing insolvency, but with a longer τ in the form of a merger agreement – possibly indicating forbearance since all would gain the full value of their investment (Fig. 5).

B.2. Bank One

From the summer of 1999 until early 2000, Bank One experienced a shrinking profit margin, a reduction in the rate of growth of its primary consumer lending subsidiary, First U.S.A, and a corresponding reduction in earnings.[16] The financial stress became so significant that on December 21, 1999 CEO and Chairman John McCoy took early retirement at age 58 from the bank.[17] For Bank One this was an extraordinary event because McCoy was the CEO for 15 years and the son of the previous CEO who built Bank One. From July through August 1999, stock and debt prices fell (Fig. 6). The correlation ranged from +0.50 to +0.96 and averaging +0.75with stock prices falling to $42 from $60 – a Non-PCA case (Fig. 6). Although bond prices continued to fall until May 2000, well after the change in senior management, stock prices rose moderately. This period after the resignation of McCoy may appear to be a period consistent with an investor upgrade of the company, however, the correlation of stock and debt prices was never negative and statistically significant for more than five consecutive weeks.

B.3. First Union

The acquisitions of CoreStates Financial Corp., a Philadelphia-based multistate bank holding company, in April 1998 and later the Money Store became very costly to integrate. In January 1999, First Union acknowledged that its

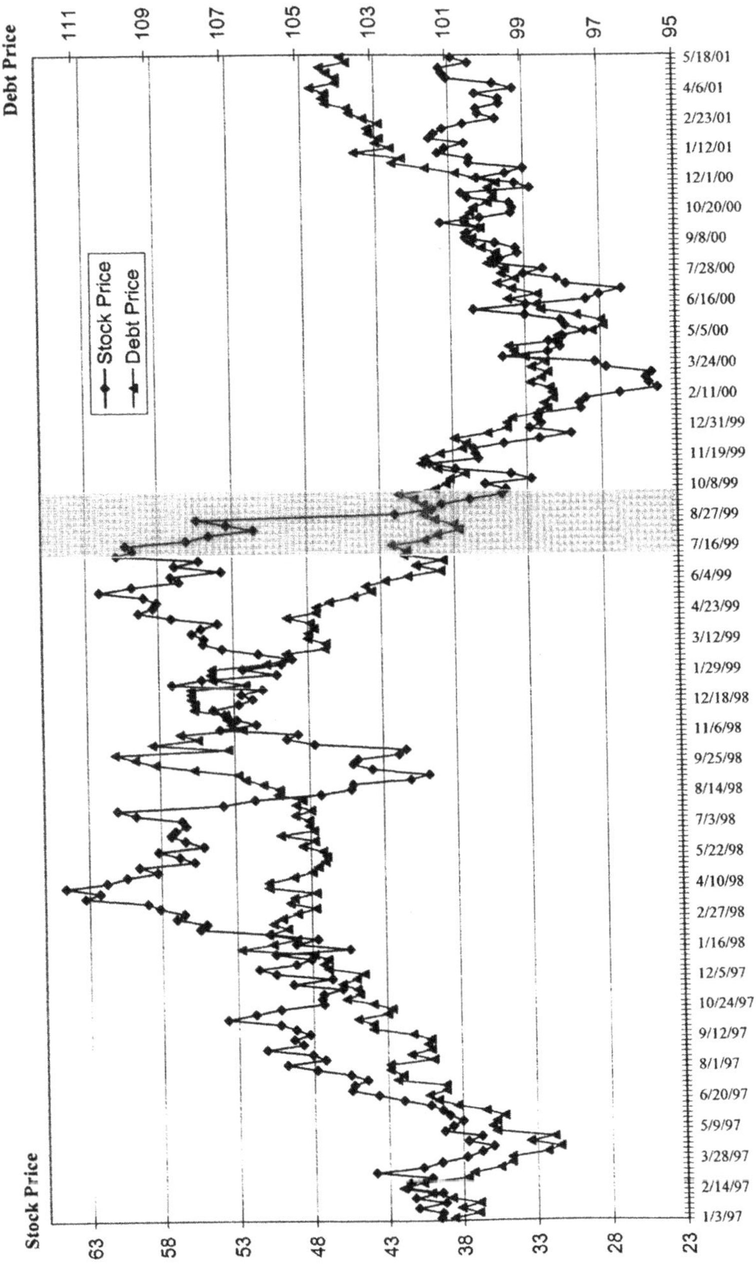

Fig. 6. Bank One: Stock and Subordinated Debt Prices.
($, weekly, January 3, 1997 to May 18, 2001)

profitability had fallen below its previously announced expectations (some two weeks prior) for 1998.[18] Banking industry analysts at this time began to question the credibility of First Union management to disclose accurate information about the company. By August 1999, First Union's president, John Georgius retired opening speculation that more management restructuring may be necessary.[19] From May 1999 to mid-September 1999, stock and subordinated debt prices fell and were significantly and positively correlated, with a correlation coefficient averaging +0.76 (Table 2 and Fig. 7). During this period of financial stress, stock prices were falling to $37 from $50 and debt prices were falling to $99 from $103 (Fig. 7). This relationship is consistent with a Non-PCA case or one where the market believed First Union should have been acquired. After mid-September 1999, stock and debt prices trended downward while yield spreads remained well above what they were a year earlier. However, there were no periods of persistent significant correlation of stock and debt prices when stock prices were falling.

IV. C. SUMMARY OF FINDINGS

Our findings are summarized in Table 2. Here we show, for identified periods of financial distress for our five banking companies, the correlation of yield spreads and equity price results, the direction of change of stock and debt prices, the expected solvency condition of the banking company, the implied τ and what these results imply about market expectations of regulatory action. As discussed above, the sub-periods were chosen based on media and published supervisory reports of financial stress for each of the companies. In order to qualify as a meaningful period for study, we used the criteria that the average correlation over each sub-period had to be statistically significant at the two-tailed, 5% level (±0.62 or better) based on 10-week, rolling correlation coefficients. With the exception of a period of a possible PCA case for Bank of New England and Bankers Trust, the average correlation for each sub-period and banking company was statistically significant at least at the 2% level with a correlation of at least ±0.75.

We find that for two periods, one for Bank of New England and one for Bankers Trust, there were pricing patterns of debt and equity that indicated PCA episodes. Furthermore, we also find no difference in the pricing response for our sample of banking companies' subordinated debt or equity during financially stressful periods before or after the adoption of PCA standards in 1991.

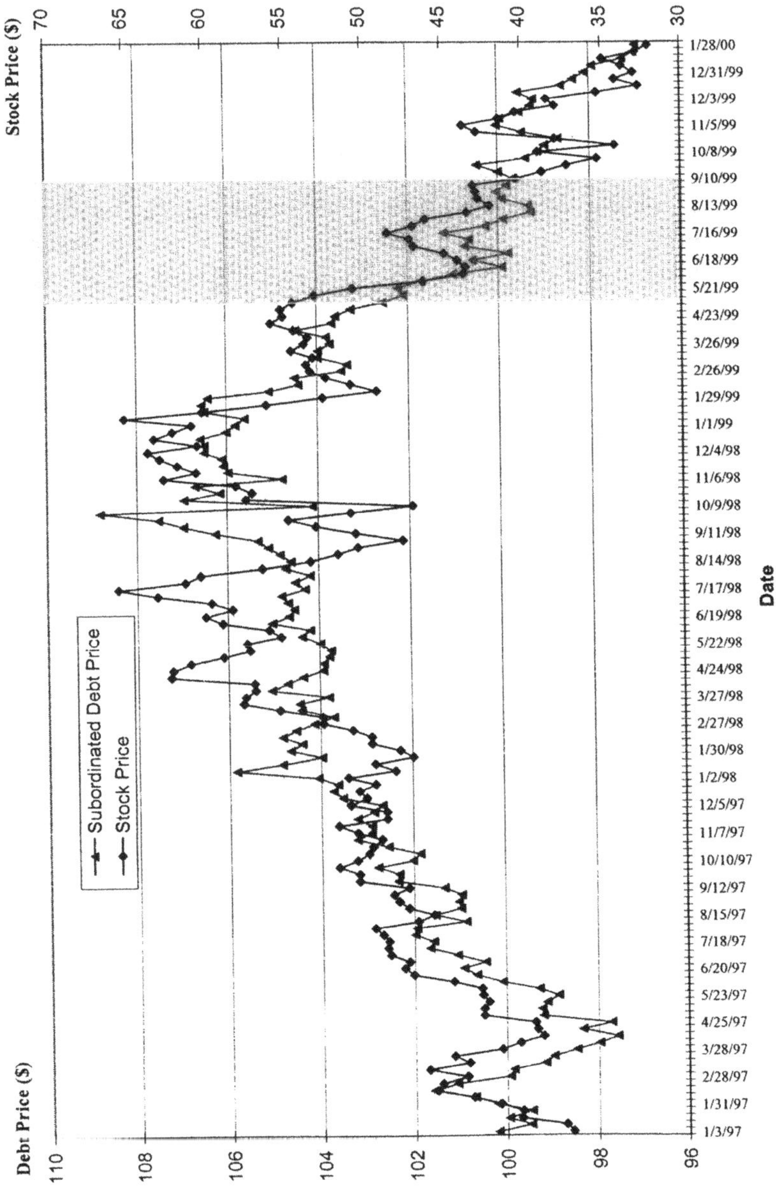

Fig. 7. First Union: Stock and Subordinated Debt Prices.
($, weekly, January 3, 1997 to January 28, 2000)

V. CONCLUSION

Early market detection of bank distress followed by a more rapid movement to resolution is now incorporated in PCA regulation. This is thought to provide for the defense of the insurer of a bank's senior deposit debt. Furthermore because of an implied willingness to fail banks more promptly it is generally thought that investors threatened with the resulting loss of value of their claims would price these claims with greater risk sensitivity and thus enhance the early detection system of market prices. That is, PCA is widely believed to enhance market discipline.

Using an options model to evaluate the bank's subordinated debt and equity, we find that, if PCA standards, of a shorter time until resolution while the bank is still solvent, is believed by investors, this will cause them to place a higher price on the bank's subordinated debt. This perverse market discipline effect will occur because a solvent early resolution designed to provide net assets to protect the senior debt claimants (depositors or the bank insurance funds) will also provide protection for the junior debt claimants, but little protection for equity holders. The net effect on equity holders still applying risk pricing is to reduce valuation because an early resolution on balance eliminates their claim to the future value of the bank's assets.

Given these divergent pricing reactions to anticipated PCA actions, we examined the pricing data for five distressed banks during both the pre-PCA era and post-PCA era to seek to detect pricing consistent with investor belief in the PCA regulations. To determine whether investors believed in early, solvent resolution we examined the data for a price divergence between subordinated debt and equity following an announcement or a series of announcements that questioned the bank's solvency.

To identify pricing behavior consistent with PCA expectations we examined the pricing of five banks that were publicly reported to be experiencing difficulties and in financial distress. There were two 8-week pricing episodes that corresponded to PCA expectations of declining equity and rising debt prices. For shorter time periods, following public disclosures of bank distress, we find some downward movement in equity prices along with stability in subordinated debt prices in a number of cases, but these were not inconsistent with a belief in a prompt solvent resolution. Hence, on a theoretical level and with limited empirical support, the early detection of banking company distress, while the bank is still solvent, is more likely to be found in equity prices than subordinated debt prices.

NOTES

1. FDIC (1997), *History of the Eighties*, p. 252

2. The Prompt Corrective Action contained in the Federal Deposit Insurance Corporation Act FDICIA, a bank is considered to be "critically undercapitalized" when the ratio of tangible capital to total assets is 2.0% or less (12CFR, Ch. III, Subpart B, section 325.103(c), FDIC 1992). If the bank is declared to be critically undercapitalized the Act calls for a receivership or conservatorship not later than 90 days after an insured depository institution becomes critically undercapitalized. However, the act explicitly allows receivership delays. Thereafter the bank is given the opportunity to restore capital for a time period of up to 270 days and possibly longer (FDICA, subtitle D, Section (3), subsection (h)(3)(c)(I)(ii)(I and II). After the expiration of the 270 days, additional delays are based on the Federal banking agency determination that the bank has positive net worth, the bank is in substantial compliance with an approved capital restoration plan, the bank is profitable or has an upward trend in earnings that agency projects as sustainable and the bank is reducing the ratio of non performing loans to total loans. See FDIC (1997, p. 454) for data on actual delays.

3. Investor signals of bank solvency can derive from a number of priced claims though most studies have examined bank deposits, whether insured or uninsured (e.g. Cook & Spellman, 1996), and subordinated debt (e.g. Flannery & Sorescu, 1996). Recently there has been an expansion in the investigation of other market signals to include market microstructure variables such as bid-asked spreads, trading volume and volatility in the pricing of bank stock (Flannery, Kwan & Nimalendran, 1998).

4. The efficacy of market discipline has also been questioned on the basis not of the signaling effect but rather on the basis of whether sufficient incentives exist to cause a behavioral adjustment to bank risk taking (Bliss & Flannery, 2000).

5. Forbearance expectations are the opposite of PCA expectations in that resolution delays are expected after the insolvency occurs.

6. Other assumptions need to be made. The maturity of the subordinated debt is 5 years, the risk free rate is assumed to be 4.0%, and the subordinated debt comprises 1.0% of the banks capital structure. The value of σ_V used in the study of 0.05 is on the low side of the mean estimated in Hanweck and Spellman (2002) of 0.068.

7. A higher subordinated debt price implies a lower yield to maturity. For a constant risk-free interest rate, lower yields to maturity imply lower spreads over comparable maturity risk-free (Treasury) yields to maturity.

8. Data on bank equity and debt prices, yields to maturity and other debt characteristics were obtained from Interactive Data Corporation, a Financial Times company. Constant maturity Treasury securities yields to maturity are from the Federal Reserve Board, H.15 release. All data are weekly and as of trading on a Friday or the last business day of the week.

9. Bankers Trust is included as an insolvent bank because of its serious financial condition just before being acquired by Deutsche Bank in 1998.

10. The statistical significance is determined by the Fisher z-statistic assuming a bivariate normal distribution. The z-statistic for a test of the null hypothesis of no correlation is where n is the number of observations (10 in our study) and r is the estimated correlation coefficient. The z-statistic is distributed as a standard normal (Freund, 1962, p. 311).

11. CAMEL is an acronym for the composite examination ratings of 1 (best) to 5 (worst) of Capital adequacy, Asset quality, Management, Earnings and Liquidity.
12. Bleakely, *The Wall Street Journal*, 10/11/1990, p. A4.
13. Fromson and Knight, *Washington Post*, June 1993.
14. *Wall Street Journal*, October 13, 1998, p. B12.
15. *Wall Street Journal*, October 13, 1998, p. A3.
16. *Wall Street Journal*, August 26, 1999, p. A2.
17. *Wall Street Journal*, December 22, 1999, p. A3.
18. *Wall Street Journal*, January 28, 1999, p. C24.
19. *Wall Street Journal*, August 2, 1999, p. A4.

ACKNOWLEDGMENT

All views are those of the authors and do not necessarily reflect those of the FDIC or its staff.

REFERENCES

Avery, R. T., Belton, T., & Goldberg, M. (1988). Market discipline in regulating bank risk: New evidence from the capital markets, *Journal of Money, Credit, and Banking*, *20*, 597–610.

Beaver, W. H., Datar, S., & Wolfson, M. A. (1992). The role of market value accounting in the regulation of insured depository institutions. In: J. R. Barth & R. D. Brumbaugh, Jr. (Eds), *The Reform of Federal Deposit Insurance* (pp. 259–276). New York: Harper Collins Publishers, Inc.

Black, F., & Cox, J. (1976). Valuing corporate securities: some effects of bond indentures. *Journal of Finance*, *31*, 351–367.

Bleakley, F. R. (1990). Citicorp Pursues Asset Sales to Bolster Capital Base; Loss-Reserves Boost Seen. *The Wall Street Journal* (October 11), A4.

Bliss, R. R. (2001). Market discipline and subordinated debt: A review of some salient issues. *Economic Perspective*, *XXV*(1), 24–45. Federal Reserve Bank of Chicago.

Bliss, R. R., & Flannery, M. (2000). Market discipline in the governance of U.S. Bank Holding Companies: Monitoring vs. influencing. Federal Reserve Bank of Chicago. Working Paper, No., WP-2000-03.

Cook, D. O., & Spellman, L. J. (1996). Firm and Guarantor Risk, Risk Contagion, and the Interfirm Spread among Insured Deposits. *Journal of Financial and Quantitative Analysis*, *31*(2), 265–281.

Evanoff, D. D., & Wall, L. D. (2001a). SND yield spreads as bank risk measures. *Journal of Financial Service Research*, forthcoming.

Evanoff, D. D., & Wall, L. D. (2001b). Measures of the riskiness of banking organizations: subordinated debt yields, risk-based capital, and examination ratings. Federal Reserve Bank of Atlanta. Working Paper 2001-25.

Evanoff, D. D., & Wall, L. D. (2000). Subordinated debt and bank capital reform. In: G. Kaufman (Ed.), *Research in Financial Services: Private and Public Policy*, *12*, 53–120. JAI Press.

Federal Deposit Insurance Corporation (1992). FDIC Adopts Final 'Prompt Corrective Action' Rule.*FDIC News Release*, (September 15). Washington D.C.

Federal Deposit Insurance Corporation (1997). *History of the Eighties: Lessons for the Future* (vol. 1). Washington, D.C.

Flannery, M. J., & Sorescu, S. M. (1996). Evidence of Bank Market Discipline in Subordinated Debt Issues: 1983–1991. *Journal of Finance*, *51*, 1347–1377.

Flannery, M. J., Kwan, S. H., & Nimalendran, M. (2000). Market Evidence on the Opaqueness of Banking Firms Assets. Working Paper 99-11. Federal Reserve Bank of San Francisco, San Francisco, CA.

Freund, J. E. (1962). *Mathematical Statistics*. Englewood Cliffs, NJ: Prentice Hall.

Fromson, B., & Knight, J. (1993). The Saving of Citibank. *Washington Post*, *16* (June), A1.

Gorton, G., & Santomero, A. M. (1990). Market Discipline and Bank Subordinated Debt. *Journal of Money, Credit, and Banking*, 22, 119–128.

Hannan, T., & Hanweck, G. A. (1988). Bank Insolvency Risk and the Market For Large Certificates of Deposits. *Journal of Money, Credit, and Banking*, *20* (May), 203–211.

Hanweck, G. A. (1999). The Issue of the Federal Safety Net Subsidy: Evidence From the Pricing of Banking Company Subordinated Debt. *The Financial Services Roundtable*, (September).

Hanweck, G. A. (2001). A Methodology for Using Market Information to Assess Banking Company Insolvency Risk: The Simultaneous Use of Subordinated Debt and Equity Market Values. Working Paper, FDIC, October 2001.

Hanweck, G. A., & Spellman, L. J. (2002). *Forbearance Expectations*, Mimeo.

Kane, E. (1990). Principal-Agent problems in S & L salvage. *Journal of Finance*, *45*, 755–764

Merton, R. C. (1974). On the Pricing of Corporate Debt: The Risk Structure of Interest Rates. *Journal of Finance*, *29* (May), 449–470.

Merton, R. C. (1977), An Analytical Derivation of the Cost of Deposit Insurance and Loan Guarantees: An Application of Modern Option Pricing Theory. *Journal of Banking and Finance*, *1* (June), 3–11.

Morgan, D. P., & Stiroh, K. J. (2001). Market discipline of banks: The asset test. *Journal of Financial Services Research*, *10*, forthcoming

Ronn, E., & Verma, A. (1986). Pricing Risk-Adjusted Deposit Insurance: An Option-Based Model. *Journal of Finance*, *41*, 871–895.

Ronn, E., & Verma, A. (1989). Risk-Based Capital Adequacy Standards for a Sample of 43 Major Banks. *Journal of Banking and Finance*, *13*, 21–29.

Schellhorn, C. D., & Spellman, L. J. (1996). Subordinated Debt and Forward-Looking Estimates of Bank Asset Volatility. *Journal of Economics and Business*, *48*, 337–347.

Schellhorn, C. D., & Spellman, L. J. (2000). Bank forbearance: A market-based explanation. *The Quarterly Review of Economics and Finance*, *40*, 451–466.

Smith, C. (1979). In: J. L. Bicksler (Ed.), *Handbook of Financial Economics* (pp. 79–121). Amsterdam: North-Holland.

The Wall Street Journal (1998). Bankers Trust Shares Decline 7.9% as Fitch Lowers Debt Rating (October 13, p. B12).

The Wall Street Journal (1998). Bankers Trust Corp. Was Approached By Deutsche Bank About Possible Deal (October 21, p. A4).

The Wall Street Journal (1998). Bankers Trust Is Hit by $488 Million Loss – Deficit Exceeds Forecasts Due to Volatile Markets; Firm to Cut Costs by 8% (October 23, p. A3).

The Wall Street Journal (1998). Deutsche Bank, Bankers Trust Near Pact – Deal for About $9.7 Billion Would Create Largest Financial-Services Firm (November 23, p. A2).

The Wall Street Journal (1999). First Union Stock Plunges 8.5% on Profit Warning (January 28, p. C24).

The Wall Street Journal (1999). First Union Corp.'s Friday Stock Close May Reflect the Need For More Changes (August 2, A4).

The Wall Street Journal (1999). Bank One Shows Drop of 23% on Forecast – Doubt Is Cast on Strategy of Consumer Lending As Profit Margins Shrink (August 26, p. A2).

The Wall Street Journal (1999). CEO McCoy Quits a Flagging Bank One – Credit-Card Bet Faltered; Stock Price Jumps 11%; Istock Is Acting Chief (December 22, p. A3).

COMMENT

Harvey Rosenblum

A little more than ten years have passed since the Federal Deposit Insurance Corporation Act of 1991 (FDICIA) became the law of the land in the United States. Among its many provisions, FDICIA sought to drastically reduce both the number of bank failures and their impact on taxpayers by forcing bank supervisors to practice prompt corrective action (PCA) at the earliest signs of trouble. PCA, it was thought, would eliminate forbearance, the dreaded "F-word" of the Texas savings and loan and banking crises of the late 1980s. Proponents of PCA believed that prompt intervention and resolution (or selling) of a bank while it was still solvent could potentially make federal deposit insurance redundant. With a decade of experience behind us, now is a good opportunity to evaluate how well FDICIA and PCA are working.

In this context, it was a pleasure to review the three papers presented at this session. Each paper contributed different and valuable insights on the successes and shortcomings of the PCA doctrine as practiced over the last decade.

I. THE POST-FDICIA ECONOMIC AND FINANCIAL ENVIRONMENT

The eleven year period that FDICIA has been in force can be described as a benign economic environment. By the time FDICIA became law, the comparatively short 1990–1991 recession was over. Prior to revisions to the GDP accounts released in July 2002, the economic data showed the U.S. economy to have expanded for ten years until March 2001, and, had it not been

---

The views are those of the author and not necessarily those of the Federal Reserve Bank of Dallas or the Federal Reserve System.

Prompt Corrective Action in Banking: 10 Years Later, Volume 14, pages 227–233.

ISBN: 0-7623-0987-3

for the 9-11 terrorist attacks on the World Trade Center and the Pentagon, it is possible that the U.S. economy would have avoided a recession altogether. (NBER, 2001). The GDP revisions changed the story somewhat. At the time of the WEA Conference (June 30–July 1, 2002), data indicated that the U.S. economy experienced only one quarter of negative economic growth, Q3 2002, in the period since Spring 1991. Subsequent revisions indicated that the economy experienced negative economic growth in each of the first three calendar quarters of 2001. While the recession turns out to have been longer and deeper than previously thought, it still was comparatively mild by historical standards. For example, the unemployment rate peaked around 6%, several percentage points lower, on average, than in the last few recessions.

This last decade has been a period of comparative interest rate tranquility, and one characterized by a downward trend in inflation and interest rates, all of which have helped to support banking profitability. Despite numerous international financial crises over the last decade, the U.S. banking system has been quite healthy and little affected by overseas turmoil. Even the bursting of the tech stock bubble seems to have had limited impact on the overall economy and the U.S. banking system. In short, any inferences about the effectiveness of PCA must be drawn against the backdrop of a banking system that has faced a very limited stress test over this period.

During late 2001 and the first half of 2002, stress on the U.S. banking system has been rising. As mentioned above, the economy weakened and fell into recession in 2001. In the commercial real estate sector, especially in cities that grew rapidly during the 1990s high tech boom, vacancies have risen sharply and rents have fallen accordingly. Bankruptcies of large, publicly-traded companies, in combination with corporate malfeasance and auditing/accounting scandals, are likely to add to the stresses and strains on the banking system stemming from weak economic growth. The banking system's real stress test lies ahead. Another acronym has to be added to the banking literature. We already have TBTF-to big to fail, and TSTC-too small to care. Given the fewness of bank failures and the benign economic environment in the decade of PCA, we have a situation of TSTG-too soon to generalize.

II. WHY THE NEED FOR PCA?

Banks are financial intermediaries that fund themselves to a significant extent with federally insured deposits. On the asset side, banks make a variety of loans that are idiosyncratic, illiquid, and difficult to mark-to-market. As a result, it is difficult, in real time, to estimate a bank's net worth position. Thus a bank can be insolvent and this situation might not be recognized promptly by its owners,

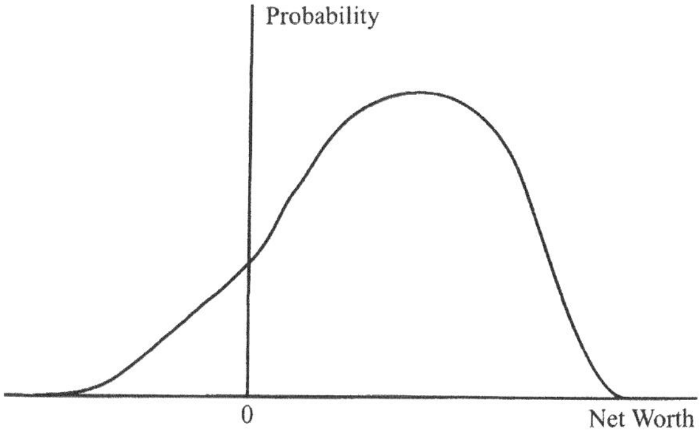

Fig. 1. Solvency Probability.

managers, or supervisors, in which case the FDIC, and ultimately, the taxpayers, may incur some losses. PCA is designed to require supervisory intervention before a bank becomes insolvent. Given the nature of a bank's assets, determining whether a bank is solvent is a blend of art and science. At any given moment, a bank's net worth has a probability distribution that may look like the example in Fig. 1.

An economic shock (a change in the price of a key commodity like oil, for example) or a financial shock (an unanticipated change in monetary policy, for example) can cause the probability distribution to shift to the left or right. The drop in oil prices from $28 in November 1985 to the low teens by February 1986 shifted the probability distribution for Texas banks sharply to the left and vice versa for banks in New England and California whose regional economies benefitted strongly from lower energy prices. Would PCA have altered the situation in Texas? Probably not. Nobody recognized how permanent the drop in oil prices would be, nor, even if the drop were permanent, how fast the ripple effects on the value of Texas real estate and other collateral values would take place. Like doctors, bank supervisors should have an oath of "do no harm." Translation, to paraphrase an old wine commercial: "We close no bank before its time." In other words, it would seriously undermine the financial sector in a free market economy to have supervisors closing (or selling) banks that are not clearly insolvent. What would be the implications for the nationalization of the rest of the private sector?

Why are banks in the situation where they are singled out for the special treatment of being subject to closure or involuntarily sale while still solvent? The answer is that the U.S., for nearly seven decades, has had a public policy that fostered (and sometimes subsidized) the persistent existence of a group of financial intermediaries that made illiquid loans funded by short-term, federally insured deposits. There is clearly a demand for this combination of payment and credit services provided by banks. In a $10 trillion economy, banking assets exceed $6 trillion and bank loans and leases are about $4 trillion. If bank assets were marked to market daily, we would automatically have PCA. But, as Fed chairman Alan Greenspan has noted on several occasions, we would have a banking industry that did not make idiosyncratic and illiquid loans and thereby, we would create credit gaps that would take some, perhaps substantial, time to fill.

In short, PCA can only do so much to control excessive risk-taking in banking and to get banking supervisors to close or resolve troubled banks at just the right time. I turn next to a review of three papers that evaluate the supervisory agencies' PCA record of the last decade.

III. HOW DO BANKS FAIL?

PCA would work well if banks tended to deteriorate slowly and in predictable ways for a narrow set of reasons. Unfortunately, that's not how the world works. Banks fail in a variety of ways, for a variety of causes, and over a variety of time frames. Just as bank loans are idiosyncratic, so too, bank failures are idiosyncratic. To complicate matters, many banks get into financial trouble, but not all financially troubled banks fail. In the early 1980s, many agricultural banks in the Midwest found themselves with CAMEL ratings of 4 or 5, the worst two ratings, when agricultural commodity and land prices fell. However, many of them recovered in the next few years. In contrast, banks in Texas that reached a 4 or 5 CAMEL rating were like the "roach motel;" once they checked in, they never checked out. Bank supervisors, like anyone else, cannot predict the size or persistence of the spillovers from economic shocks. Adhering to PCA is difficult in the real world.

One of the great strengths of the paper by Shibut, Critchfield and Bohn (2002) [SCB] is the way in which it deals with the idiosyncratic nature of bank failures and near-failures. SCB examined 48 bank failures and 44 near-failures of critically undercapitalized banks handled by the FDIC over the 1994–2000 period. SBC further divided these banks into four groups: low-cost failures, high-cost failures, near-failures that survived, and near-failures that were purchased. SCB rigorously analyzed the key characteristics and ratios of the banks in each of the four groups, and detailed how difficult it is to predict which group a bank belongs to based on traditional analysis of a bank's data one year before the PCA date, at the PCA date, or as of the date of the bank's resolution. Oftentimes, the economic conditions of the market in which a bank is located had as much to do with a bank's difficulties as did the characteristics of the bank itself. Another strength of the SCB analysis is their discussion of the costs of dealing with troubled banks, not just to the FDIC, but to *all* of the bank's stakeholders, including owners, managers, depositors, other creditors, and borrowers. As a result, the SCB paper should be considered "required reading" for all serious students of banking policy.

IV. HOW MUCH DISCIPLINE CAN BE PROVIDED BY MARKET DISCIPLINE?

For decades, economists have advocated that banks be subject to increased levels of market discipline as a means to control the excessive risk taking associated with the moral hazard provided by the public safety net. So how well is market discipline working? The answer provided by Hanweck and Spellman (2002) [HS] is that the market provides some, but very limited, discipline, at least to very large banks. HS examine five very large banking companies that experienced financial distress: Bank of New England and Citicorp in the pre-PCA period; and Bankers Trust, BankOne, and First Union in the post-PCA period. Interestingly, equity markets seem to provide a better signal of emerging difficulties and improvements than does the market for subordinated debt. In all five cases examined by HS, the signal from equity markets began flashing from two to six months prior to the signal from subordinated debt. Further, subordinated debt holders may exhibit different behaviors depending on whether there is a general belief that a bank will be resolved while solvent vs. being resolved after becoming insolvent. As a result, the risk restraining influence of subordinated debt has turned out to be much less than anticipated by advocates of mandatory issuance of subordinated debt. This calls into serious question whether the requirement of the Gramm-Leach-Bliley Act of 1999, that each of the 50 largest bank holding companies must issue publicly traded subordinated debt, may turn out in practice to have a perverse impact on banking risk.

V. IS GETTING SUPERVISORY INCENTIVES RIGHT THE RIGHT ANSWER?

FDICIA and PCA changed the rules the FDIC must follow in resolving failing banks. The FDIC was directed to revolve each bank in a way that would minimize the associated loss to the FDIC "fund." No longer would the goal be to simply minimize the number of bank failures. Eisenbeis and Wall (2002) [EW] examine whether this reform has been working as intended. They are discomfited that their analysis indicates that the FDIC's behavior suggests it is still trying to minimize the probability of bank failures rather than minimizing insurance losses. This finding is important and interesting, but definitely not surprising. The reason is simple. Changing the incentives faced by an institution or an individual is a necessary, but not a sufficient condition, to alter behavior. If I have any criticism, it is not with EW, but rather with the economics profession which so often seeks to change behavior by modifying some incentive at a very macro level, and without bothering to work through the details of how to incent-with both reward and penalty systems-people up and down the governance-management-employee chain. To develop a truly incentive-compatible reward system requires dealing with "the devil in the details." Economists eschew such details, believing them to be the realm of management consultants. The economics profession needs to become part of the solution, not just a player in the identification of the problem.

VI. SUMMING UP

All three papers seek ways to understand how much improvement in bank supervision, if any, has been provided by the PCA provisions of FDICIA and to make recommendations on how to tweak the system to work more effectively. In their own ways, each of the papers illustrate the difficulties and complexities of applying the rules of PCA. Given the uncertainty of the real time banking data that supervisory agencies must use, PCA still gives supervisors latitude and discretion that drives their action. As I read and interpret all three papers, PCA has constrained supervisory discretion over the last decade, and has likely been modestly successful in achieving its goals. But PCA is not a panacea; it will not make deposit insurance redundant.

If PCA is to work effectively, the behavior of bankers should also be different from what it was prior to FDICIA. To be sure, the penalties for bankers whose banks become undercapitalized are more explicit than they were in the 1980s. Bankers, on average, may be more cautious under PCA. None of the three papers sought to examine PCA from this perspective; all three focused on supervisory behavioral issues. Bankers' response to PCA is a fertile area for future research.

REFERENCES

Eisenbeis, R. A., & Wall, L. D. (2002). *The Major Supervisory Initiatives Post-FDICIA: Are They Based on the Goals of PCA? Should They Be?* This volume.

Hanweck, G. A., & Spellman, L. J. (2002). *The Pricing of Near Death Banking Experiences: Before and After PCA*. This volume.

National Bureau of Economic Research, Business Cycle Dating Committee (2001). *The Business Cycle Peak of March 2001*. Press release: November 26.

Shibut, L., Critchfield, T., & Bohn, S. (2002). *Differentiating Among Critically Undercapitalized Banks and Thifts*. This volume.

COMMENT

Larry R. Mote

I have chosen to discuss the last two papers on the session first, as they seem to me to precede logically the evaluations and conclusions in the paper by Eisenbeis and Wall, who might well draw on those papers in preparing their final draft. The paper by Lynn Shibut, Tim Critchfield, and Sarah Bohn of the FDIC is in many ways a model of the type of research the economic staffs of the banking agencies should be turning out. It uses reasonable statistical techniques and appropriate data to answer an interesting and important policy question, namely whether the 2% of assets capital threshold at which banks are currently required to be closed or quickly recapitalized or merged with a healthier institution should be raised substantially. The case for such an increase has been argued by a number of economists, most notably the chairman of this session, George Kaufman. As the authors note, however, the costs associated with intervening in banks incorrectly identified as troubled can be substantial. Therefore, the benefits of a higher threshold would have to be quite large to justify an increase.

The authors attempt to test whether the threshold and other financial data observed before and at the time of crossing the threshold or of failure are useful in separating failed banks, and particularly high-cost failed banks, from other troubled banks. To do so, they separate all the FDIC-insured institutions that crossed the threshold or failed between 1994 and 2000 into four groups – low-cost failures, high-cost failures, near-failures that survived, and near-failures that were purchased. Besides financial ratios for the two years before either failure or crossing the threshold – and, for surviving institutions, one year after – they looked at measures of classified assets from the last full examination before crossing the threshold, a measure of local bank distress, a geographic

Prompt Corrective Action in Banking: 10 Years Later, Volume 14, pages 235–240.

ISBN: 0-7623-0987-3

distribution index, an estimate of appropriate loan loss reserves, and data on the bidding for each failed institution.

Because of the small number of observations and the nonnormality of many of the financial variables, the authors' statistical analysis was limited to nonparametric univariate tests of differences in medians. In light of this restriction, it is disappointing, but perhaps not surprising, that very few variables proved significant in distinguishing between the four groups. The major exception was that the levels of nonperforming assets, particularly noncurrent real estate loans and OREO, were significantly higher in failed institutions than in near-failures. It was somewhat surprising that the failures had significantly higher core capital ratios in the quarter that they fell below the threshold and a higher net interest margin in the year before than did the nonfailures. However, both results may well have reflected inadequate loan loss provisioning for the higher risks in the loan portfolios of the failures.

In comparisons of low-cost failures with high-cost failures, most of the median condition ratios for the high-cost failure group were worse than for the low-cost group, although, again, few were statistically significant. As the authors note, the fact that low-cost failures tended to be represented in markets with less financial stress and to have more of their assets passed to acquirers than was the case for high-cost failures suggests that market conditions play an important role in determining the level of losses when banks fail. To the extent that this is true, it may not be possible to develop changes in regulatory treatment that will reduce losses to near zero, as the strongest proponents of PCA insist is feasible.

What limitations or deficiencies of the study might be changed to yield more conclusive results? One possible change would be to eliminate the arbitrary distinction between low-cost and high-cost failures. Collapsing the actual loss figures into a dichotomous variable throws away potentially valuable information. Moreover, there are other nonparametric statistics, such as rank correlations, that would allow one to keep more of the information in the individual bank loss ratios. After all, it may make an important difference whether a failed bank's losses are slightly or greatly above or below the arbitrary cut-off of 12% of assets.

It is also possible that some of the anomalous results in the comparisons of failed banks with non-failures that fell below the 2% threshold reflect the fact that some of the merged institutions were actually in worse condition than many of the formally failed institutions. Perhaps this problem could be remedied by using the prices at which the merged banks were sold to acquirers to reclassify some of them as failures.

Whether these suggestions are feasible or useful, the authors will have to judge for themselves. In any case, they have provided at least provisionally convincing evidence that no change in the 2% PCA threshold is warranted at the present time and that more attention needs to be devoted to loan loss reserves.

The second empirical paper, by Gerald Hanweck and Lewis Spellman, is an interesting application of option pricing theory to the question of determining whether the usefulness of market signals provided by subordinated debt and equity prices will be impaired if investors come to believe that regulators will resolve banks while they are still marginally solvent. As Hanweck and Spellman note, this idea contrasts with the conclusion of Flannery and Sorescu that PCA has enhanced the statistical significance of subordinated debt yields as measures of bank risk by weakening investors' reliance on the Too-Big-to-Fail policy to protect them from the consequences of bank failure.

The authors show that the value of subordinated debt, which they model as the value of the difference between two call options, would be expected to increase if investors come to believe that the bank would be resolved with positive tangible capital, thereby blunting the early warning signal provided by the price of the debt. On the other hand, investors would tend to reduce the price they would be willing to pay for the bank's stock, because early resolution would cut off the future stream of expected earnings. However, if it is believed that the bank is already insolvent, a reduction in the time to resolution will again lower equity prices, but it will also reduce prices and raise yields on subordinated debt, since debt-holders can no longer count on PCA to preserve the value of their investment. These predictions were tested, and generally supported, using data on five banking organizations for both the period before and the period after year-end 1991, when PCA was assumed to have become effective.

The most important point made by the paper is that the behavior of debt-holders depends not only on their predictions of the future status of an institution, but also their perception of its current condition. For example, only if debt-holders who are convinced that a bank will be insolvent when it is resolved also believe that it is already insolvent will they view it as good news that regulators are now going to take longer to resolve it. Unfortunately, the authors do not consistently specify for each of the four basic cases that they distinguish – "PCA intervention," "extended time," "forbearance," and "failure candidate" – both investors' perception of the current condition of the bank and their expectations regarding its condition at the time of regulatory intervention. They could greatly clarify the argument by the insertion of a table providing this information.

While the paper focuses on one possible shortcoming of a positive threshold for PCA, it fails to mention another one that has frequently been mentioned, namely the likelihood that moral hazard behavior, or "gambling for resurrection," will begin earlier with a positive threshold because the threat of closure appears earlier. Finally, the authors note that equity prices react more quickly to a public disclosure of distress than do debt prices, but fail to provide a convincing explanation for this difference in timing. But these are little more than nitpicks. The Hanweck-Spellman paper is an intriguing and valuable contribution to the analysis of PCA.

The paper by Robert Eisenbeis and Larry Wall is much different from the two other papers on the session. It is a broad overview of PCA that discusses the basic philosophy of bank regulation and draws heavily on the extant theoretical and empirical literature to assess how and for what purpose PCA should be implemented. It does so in the context of assessing what the authors identify as the three major safety and soundness initiatives since FDICIA: risk-based supervision, reform of the 1988 Basel risk-based capital regulations, and deposit insurance reform.

According to Eisenbeis and Wall, the goals of supervision have changed substantially since FDICIA. The goal of supervision was originally to prevent systemic failures and panics by preventing banks from failing. The authors assert that the bank regulatory agencies were effective in doing this for many decades. I would note, however, that by 1934, when deposit insurance was implemented, the worst banks had been weeded out. Most of the remaining banks were ultra-conservative in their lending behavior for several decades after the debacle. It was not until the 1960s that banks began to lend more freely and to compete more aggressively for deposits. Thus, it is difficult to isolate the effects of bank supervision per se in keeping the failure rate low between 1934 and the early 1980s.

The authors argue that FDICIA replaced failure prevention with minimization of losses to the insurance fund as the primary goal of bank supervision. While noting that the two goals are at least superficially related, they insist that there is a fundamental contradiction between them. For example, failure prevention puts the primary burden on supervisors. In contrast, minimizing losses means that when a bank fails, the role of the supervisors is simply to choose that means of resolution that results in the smallest long-term losses to the fund.

The paper cites externalities, primarily potential adverse effects on other banks, customers, and financial markets generally, as the reasons for preventing failures. However, with the apparent exception of disruption to the payments mechanism, they dismiss these as being either nonexistent or of little consequence. But, these same considerations have often been cited as the justification for having government-administered deposit insurance. If they are unimportant, the most straightforward way to minimize losses to the insurance fund would be to abolish deposit insurance. However, unlike such critics of bank regulation as George Benston, who has explicitly argued that both bank supervision and federal deposit insurance should be abolished, Eisenbeis and Wall – probably reflecting their assessment of what is politically possible – take the continued existence of deposit insurance as given.

The authors argue that minimizing losses should focus on problem institutions, not healthy banks. That may be so, but they do not provide convincing evidence that this is the case. Indeed, they do not make any effort to dispose of a statement that appears early in the paper: "Superficially, the goals of failure prevention and loss minimization appear to be related. If a bank does not fail then it cannot impose losses on the deposit insurer." I suspect that, if pushed on this point, they would argue that the prevention of all failures is an unattainable goal and that, in any case, it would be undesirable on efficiency grounds since it would restrict socially beneficial risk-taking. On the other hand, advocates of the narrow bank insist that other types of lenders would take advantage of the opportunities that banks were excluded from by strict limits on their risk-taking.

It can be argued that the paper overstates the change in supervisory goals intended by the language of FDICIA. The act requires supervisors "to resolve the problems of insured depository institutions at the least possible long-term cost to the deposit insurance fund." Clearly, this is a call for supervisors, conditional on a bank already being in trouble, to minimize losses to the insurance fund. But, while it does not specify failure prevention as the goal of the ongoing supervision of healthy banks, neither does it preclude it. As noted above, at no point in the paper do the authors dispose of the notion that a supervisory policy with the goal of unconditional minimization of losses to the FDIC would involve significant elements of failure prevention – i.e. it would try to prevent losses by preventing failures, and only when this policy failed in a particular case would it be faced with the problem of choosing the means of resolution that would minimize losses to the insurance fund.

The paper does provide convincing evidence that, in applying the PCA provisions of FDICIA, the agencies may have substituted their own preferences for failure prevention for the act's requirement of loss minimization. At the very least, it is clear that these provisions have not had the desired effect of reducing losses to near zero that was touted by the designers and advocates of early intervention.

In its discussion of the effort to revise the Basel risk-based capital regulations, the paper dates the beginning of the modern history of U.S. capital regulation with the announcement of numerical capital guidelines in 1981. I think this does a disservice to those at the Federal Reserve who devised the Form for Analyzing Bank Capital (ABC Form) in the 1950s. This is true despite the fact that the Fed stopped using the form in the early 1970s. The form was abandoned partly because of the perceived obsolescence of its risk weights, which were based on experience in the 1930s, but also because of the Fed's regulatory competition with the OCC, which had declared numerical capital guidelines arbitrary and unnecessary. In many ways, the ABC Form was more advanced than the Basel guidelines – e.g. in giving explicit weights to both the asset and liability sides of the balance sheet.

Despite the minor criticisms raised here, this is an extremely rich paper with arguments and conclusions on every page that are extremely interesting and provocative. It deserves a close reading by everyone concerned with the functioning and regulation of the financial services industry.

PART III:
PCA AND MARKET DISCIPLINE: THE NON-U.S. EXPERIENCE

DO DEPOSITORS DISCIPLINE SWISS BANKS?

Urs W. Birchler and Andrea M. Maechler

ABSTRACT

We examine whether depositors withdraw their savings deposits whenever the fundamentals of their bank are no longer satisfactory. By relying on a quantity indicator (uninsured savings deposits) rather than more standard price indicators (yield spreads), we are able to extend our analysis to a larger number of banks, including those that do not issue tradable debt. We find considerable evidence of market discipline. Depositors respond to bank-specific fundamentals, institutional differences across bank groups, and institutional changes in the Swiss depositor protection system.

I. INTRODUCTION

Market discipline is not only an important pillar for a sound banking system, but also for overall economic efficiency. In the absence of discipline, depositors (or their insurers) implicitly subsidize the risks taken by their banks. Such subsidies raise banks' incentives to take higher risks and hence, raise the probability of bank failures. Through contagion effects, a bank failure can have a negative impact on the entire financial system and thereby put at risk the country's economic stability. Furthermore, bank failures generally impose large costs to the banking system and to the economy as a whole.[1] Regulators have long recognized the importance of market discipline. The new proposals by the Basel Committee for Banking Supervision (2000) make market discipline one

Prompt Corrective Action in Banking: 10 Years Later, Volume 14, pages 243–275.

ISBN: 0-7623-0987-3

of three pillars of a sound financial architecture after sufficient bank capitalization and supervision.

While the importance of market discipline in banking is widely recognized, there is much less consensus among economists as to its actual *presence*. In theory, it has been argued that depositor discipline in banking is inherently insufficient. Small depositors have little incentives, and often high costs, to gain information on a bank's health.[2] Deposit insurance may further weaken monitoring incentives.[3] At the same time, large and uninsured lenders to a bank may still find monitoring worthwhile.

Researchers have thus spent considerable efforts to measure bank creditor discipline. Broadly, two different approaches have emerged from the literature. The most widely used approach is the price-based approach, which uses yield spreads (the difference between a market yield on bank debt and a risk-free asset such as government debt) as a proxy for the market's perception of bank risk. A good overview on this strand of literature is given in Board of Governors & U.S. Treasury (2000). European evidence on depositor discipline is examined in Sironi (2000).

Another approach, the quantity-based approach, examines the extent to which a bank is able to raise (uninsured) debt.[4] Goldberg & Hudgins (2002) find that failed thrift institutions exhibit declining proportions of uninsured debt prior to failure. Similarly, Jordan (2000) finds that, in the 1990's New England banks experienced a fall in uninsured deposits prior to failing. Covitz, Hancock and Kwast (2000) find that relatively weak banks are unwilling (or unable) to issue subordinated debt in bad times. While Gilbert and Vaughan (1999) find no effect on the behavior of uninsured savings deposits following a public enforcement announcement, Billet et al. (1998) find that a downgrade from Moody's increases a bank's reliance on insured deposits. Peira and Schmukler (1998) find for Argentina, Chile, and Mexico, that even small, insured depositors exert market discipline by withdrawing deposits from weak banks. Finally, some studies use a combined approach by looking at prices as well as quantities, see e.g. Park and Peristiani (1998).

In this paper, we examine the presence of market discipline in the Swiss bank deposit market using a quantity-based approach. As a proxy for the depositor confidence in a particular bank, we use the fraction of uninsured savings deposits to total savings deposits held in this bank. The main hypothesis underlying this study is that depositors monitor their banks and transfer uninsured deposits to a better bank whenever the performance of their bank is no longer satisfactory. To test this hypothesis, we use a panel with bank-specific variables for 247 banks over the period 1987–2001. We examine three particular aspects of market discipline, namely, whether:

(i) bank fundamentals influence depositors' willingness to entrust uninsured deposits to a particular bank;
(ii) institutional differences among bank groups affect the degree of market discipline in the banking sector; and
(iii) institutional changes in the Swiss depositor protection system alter the behavior of depositors.

The use of quantities, rather than prices, is justified on several grounds. First, economic theory argues that under asymmetric information a debtor is rationed by quantity rather than by price (see e.g. Stiglitz & Weiss, 1981). Differences in yields may thus underestimate the presence of market discipline. This is particularly true in the Swiss retail deposit market, where banks do not primarily compete via prices (i.e. via the rates they offer), but via quality criteria. Furthermore, Blum (2002) shows that, while prices (yield spreads) may indicate excessive risk-taking, they do not necessarily reduce banks' risk appetite. This suggests that market discipline is only enforced if investors make a quantity adjustment.

Second, the quantity-based approach is applicable to a much larger number of banks and bank categories, including those that are generally excluded from market discipline studies because they do not issue tradable debt. In contrast, the use of yield spreads limits the analysis of market discipline to banks with traded debt and thus to relatively big and sophisticated institutions. Such banks are a small minority in most countries, including Switzerland. The quantity-based approach thus allows us to complement the existing literature with empirical evidence for a country that has an important banking sector, albeit only a few global banks that issue tradable debt.

The recent empirical literature on market discipline has focused primarily on the price-based approach, namely, on the ability of movements in yield spreads to signal effectively changes in a bank's risk appetite. This form of market discipline requires the existence of tradable subordinated debt instruments, which are widely available in the U.S. But it is not clear that introducing such instruments in countries other than the U.S. would effectively raise market discipline. While the U.S. benefits from deep and highly liquid secondary markets, this is not true in the case of the European financial markets and even less so in the case of financial markets in emerging and developing economies. Thus, the quantity-based approach remains an important tool to understand the behavior of market discipline and its role in buttressing the stability of the banking sector.

Overall, we find considerable evidence of market discipline in the sense of uninsured savings depositors reacting to adverse information on their bank. In particular, we find that depositors are not only sensitive to the evolution of bank-specific fundamentals, but also to institutional differences across bank groups and to institutional changes in the Swiss depositor protection system.

The rest of this paper is organized as follows. Section II outlines the Swiss depositor protection system. The empirical methodology is presented in Section III. Results are provided in Section IV. Section V concludes.

II. PROTECTION OF DEPOSITORS ON SWITZERLAND

2.1. Protective Regulation

Switzerland has no explicit, government-run depositor insurance system. Instead, there are three different insurance schemes that protect depositors in the case of a bank failure:[5]

(1) The *state guarantee* offers an extensive guarantee for deposits held at a cantonal bank. The state guarantee is provided by the specific canton (i.e. the state) that has created a cantonal bank and typically protects all deposits held in this particular institution. Only two of the 25 cantonal banks have limited their guarantee to a particular type of deposits.[6]

(2) *Priority insurance* for savings deposits up to CHF 30'000 per depositor grants a priority status to savings deposits of up to CHF 30'000 (approximately U.S.$20'000) per depositor. This means that in the case of a bank failure, claims to savings deposits of up to CHF 30'000 are senior to all other claims.[7] Priority status "insures" depositors in the sense that it gives them a first claim against a failed bank's assets. It is comparable to "depositor preference" introduced in 1993 in the U.S. When introduced in 1934, priority insurance was limited to CHF 5'000 per depositor. In 1971, the limit was raised to CHF 10'000 and in 1997 to CHF 30'000.

(3) Private *liquidity insurance* protects savings deposits up to CHF 30'000 per depositor and, since 1993, for an aggregate amount ("cap") of CHF 1 billion per bank. Liquidity insurance assures the prompt repayment of savings deposits up to CHF 30'000 per depositor in the case of a bank failure.[8] This insurance is provided under a private agreement among the Swiss Bankers Association (SBA). In the case of a bank failure, the SBA pays out depositors and acquires in exchange their respective claims, including their priority status.[9] Thus, the SBA primarily guarantees the liquidity of savings deposits. It bears, however, the residual risk that the failed bank's assets may not be sufficient to honor the full amount of these deposits.[10] In 1993, in response to the Swiss loan crisis, the SBA imposed

a cap, which restricted the scope of liquidity insurance to an aggregate amount of CHF 1 billion per bank.[11] In practice, this limit implies that for approximately the 20 largest banks the insured amount effectively falls short of the theoretical limit of CHF 30'000 per depositor.

2.2. *Insured Liabilities: Some Stylized Facts*

The focus of this article is on savings deposits. Historically, these were the dominant source of funds for Swiss banks. After a secular decline, savings accounts still represent 27.3% of all deposits held by the public in 2000. With 2.2 savings accounts per capita, savings accounts outnumber by far any other type of account.[12] Furthermore, they remain the typical investment instrument of small depositors. Although some savings deposits exceed CHF 100'000 (about U.S.$70'000), in 2000 the average balance was around CHF 17'000, with a median around CHF 4'000.[13] Thus, a majority of savings accounts remain small.

Table 1 presents data on the evolution of savings deposits in Switzerland. The information is broken down into the fraction of deposits that is insured (by priority insurance in column (3) and by state guarantee in column (4)) and the fraction that is uninsured (column (5)).[14] This table highlights three stylized facts. First, nominal growth of savings deposits (column (1)) has led to a continuous decrease in the share of priority savings, except in 1971 and 1997, when the priority ceiling was revised upwards (column (3)). Second, cantonal banks have continuously lost market share in the Swiss deposit market (column (4)). Hence, the fraction of savings deposits covered by a cantonal guarantee has been falling continuously since 1945. Finally, the share of savings deposits that is covered by neither the priority insurance nor the state guarantee has risen steadily until 1997, at which time the upward revision in priority insurance brought it back to its 1970 level (column (5)).

Table 2 takes a closer look at the structure of savings deposits as of end of 2000. For illustration, figures under the old ceiling of priority insurance (up to CHF 10'000) are given on the first row, while figures under the current insurance ceiling (up to CHF 30'000) are given on the bottom row. Savings deposits are further broken into those that are insured (columns (3) and (4)) and those that are uninsured (column (5)). In terms of insured deposits, the table differentiates between fully insured savings deposits (those that are inferior to the insurance ceiling of CHF 30'000) and partially insured savings deposits (those that exceed the insurance ceiling).

Under the current ceiling of CHF 30'000, 31.6% of savings deposits have balances below the ceiling and thus are fully insured (column (2)). Another

Table 1. Structure of Savings Deposits, 1935–2000.

End of	Savings accounts balance: Total	Average percentage of total with: Per account	Priority insurance	State guarantee	Neither
	CHF bn.	CHF	%	%	%
	(1)	(2)	(3)	(4)	(5) = 100 − (3) − (4)
1935	5.8	1'385	n.a.	n.a.	n.a.
1940	5.2	1'342	n.a.	n.a.	n.a.
1945	6.6	1'495	39.0	50.1	10.9
1950	8.2	1'635	38.3	48.9	12.8
1955	11.1	1'956	36.2	47.8	16.0
1960	15.1	2'368	33.3	47.9	18.8
1965	22.7	3'081	30.0	48.0	22.0
1970	35.3	3'902	28.9	44.4	26.8
1975	64.8	5'977	33.8	41.1	25.1
1980	90.3	7'431	30.9	39.1	30.0
1985	113.7	8'692	28.2	36.2	35.6
1990	129.3	8'972	29.2	34.8	35.9
1995	210.3	13'655	22.4	34.8	42.9
2000	211.4	14'305	39.4	33.9	26.7

Source: Les Banques Suisses, 1935–2000.

Table 2. Structure of Savings Deposits, end of 2000.

Ceiling	Insured: Fully	Insured: Bottom part	Insured: Total	Uninsured
CHF	%	%	%	%
(1)	(2)	(3)	(4)	(5)
10'000	11.4	20.5	31.9	68.1
30'000	31.6	27.2	58.8	41.2

Insured and uninsured savings deposits (as a percentage of total savings deposits)

Source: SNB, Les Banques Suisses, 2000, Table 20.2-3.

27.2% of savings deposits is only partially insured, as only the bottom part (up to the CHF 30'000 priority insurance ceiling) is insured. In total, 58.8% of savings deposits are insured (column (4)), while the remaining 41.2% of the total volume of savings deposits are uninsured (column (5)). For comparison, the first row shows that under the pre-1997 priority insurance ceiling of CHF 10'000, only one third of savings deposits would be insured, while over two thirds would be uninsured.

III. EMPIRICAL METHODOLOGY

3.1. Hypotheses

The main hypothesis underlying this study is that depositors exert market discipline by monitoring their banks and by withdrawing uninsured deposits whenever the performance of their bank is no longer satisfactory. Bank fundamentals should thus help to explain the amount of uninsured deposits a bank is able to attract. This leads to our first general hypothesis:

> **Hypothesis 1 (General market discipline.)** The supply of uninsured savings deposits (as a fraction of total savings deposits) is related to movements in bank fundamentals.

Furthermore, we examine whether institutional differences or changes in deposit insurance affect the supply of uninsured savings deposits. First, we examine whether the presence of an extensive *state guarantee* lowers depositor discipline in cantonal banks.

> **Hypothesis 2 (State guarantee.)** The fraction of uninsured savings deposits (in total savings deposits) is relatively less responsive to movements in bank fundamentals at cantonal banks than in the Swiss banking sector as a whole.

Next, we examine whether the behavior of uninsured savings deposits responds *to changes in the deposit insurance system* during the sample period under study. The two relevant changes were:

(i) the 1993 introduction of an aggregate cap for liquidity insurance; and
(ii) the 1997 increase in the per-depositor limit of priority insurance from CHF 10'000 to CHF 30'000.

> **Hypothesis 3 (The liquidity insurance cap.)** Banks for which the 1993 liquidity insurance cap is a binding constraint exhibit a lower fraction of

(theoretically) insured savings deposits than banks for which the cap is not binding.

In practice, the introduction of the CHF 1 billion cap means that the largest 20 banks benefit from an insurance coverage that falls short of the CHF 30'000 theoretically guaranteed under the liquidity insurance. In the presence of market discipline, we thus expect to find relatively fewer (theoretically) insured deposits at cap-constrained banks.

Hypothesis 4 (The priority insurance ceiling.) In response to the 1997 upward revision to the priority insurance ceiling, depositors are more willing to hold larger savings deposits (i.e. above CHF 10'000).

The second institutional change we examine is the 1997 extension of priority insurance from CHF 10'000 to CHF 30'000 per depositor. We test whether this institutional change raises the depositors' willingness to entrust larger savings deposits (i.e. above CHF 10'000) to their banks, as a higher fraction of savings deposits are now insured in the case of a bank failure. To test these four hypotheses we use the reduced form model presented in the following section.

3.2. Model Testing

The fundamental hypothesis underlying this paper is that the presence of market discipline can be inferred from the extent to which the supply of uninsured savings deposits reacts to indicators of bank strengths. Our dependent variable is α^j_{it}, the ratio of uninsured savings deposits to total savings deposits of bank i at time t under insurance type j. The focus on savings deposits allows us to work with a homogeneous aggregate. Changes in the fraction of uninsured savings deposits are not likely to be distorted by shifts between different kinds of deposits as may, e.g. be induced by changes in the level of interest rates.

Our explanatory variables are a set of independent proxies for bank safety on which depositors may base their decisions. We use the following general reduced form:

$$\alpha^j_{it} = \mu_i + \delta' M_t + \beta' X_{it-1} + \gamma' D_{it} + \varepsilon_{it}, \tag{1}$$

where $i = 1 \dots N$ and $t = 1 \dots T$. On the right hand side μ_i stands for each bank's specific or fixed effect. M_t is a vector of macroeconomic variables. X_{it-1} is a vector of bank-specific variables. This vector is included with a lag to account for the fact that balance sheet information is available to the public with a certain delay. D_{it} is a vector of control variables that account for the revisions in the deposit insurance system. Thus, according to Eq. (1), a bank's ratio of uninsured savings deposits to total savings deposits, apart from bank specific differences, is determined by three main factors: general developments in the macroeconomy, the evolution of the bank fundamentals and revisions in the insurance deposit system.

To estimate Eq. (1), we use different specifications of a fixed-effects time series cross- section regression on our panel of approximately 250 Swiss banks. As usual, we assume that residuals have a conditional mean of zero, a finite variance and are uncorrelated across time and across banks.

3.3. The Data

We use panel data from the Swiss National Bank banking statistics on bank-specific variables for 247 Swiss banks. The annual data cover the period 1987–2001. The panel is unbalanced in the sense that the number of observations per bank (N) varies across banks.[15] To estimate Eq. (1), we combine bank specific variables with macroeconomic variables and deposit insurance control variables. We first introduce our macroeconomic variables.

Macroeconomic Variables

To control for the general conditions of the banking system, we include three macroeconomic variables, namely the Swiss GDP growth rate (GDPGR), the 3-month CHF money market rate (CHMM3M) and the consumer price index (CPINDEX).[16] As these variables reflect the relative strength of the economy, we expect each of them to have a *positive* relationship with the dependent variable α^j_{it}, the share of uninsured savings deposits.

Bank-Specific Variables

Bank-specific variables are derived from the CAMEL rating system of banks (Capital adequacy, Asset quality, Management, Earnings and Liquidity).

Capital adequacy. A sound capital base should strengthen depositor confidence. Thus, we expect a *positive* relationship between the ratio of capital to total liabilities (KTL) and α^j_{it}, the share of uninsured savings deposits.

Asset quality. We consider asset quality both in a narrow and in a wide sense. In a narrow sense, we use two proxies. First, we use credit growth (CRGR) as an indicator of credit quality. However, strong credit growth can mean either that a bank is in a flourishing condition or that it is (too) aggressive. Within our sample period, strong credit growth is most likely an indicator of bad lending until 1995 and of good lending thereafter. This is because Switzerland experienced a real estate bubble, which bursted in 1991 and which was followed by falling prices until 1994. A slow and sustained recovery started in 1995. To disentangle between these two different effects, we include a second variable (CRGR_B) for credit growth before 1995. We expect a *positive* sign for credit growth in the whole period (CRGR) and a *negative* sign in the bubble sub-period (CRGR_B). Second, we use the ratio of mortgage lending to total assets (MORTA) as a measure for the degree of collateralized, i.e. relatively secure, lending. We expect a *positive* relationship between this variable and the fraction of uninsured savings deposits, α^j_{it}.

To consider asset quality in a wider sense, we examine the quality of funding. To do this, we include three variables. First, we look at the ratio between customer liabilities and mortgage lending (CLTMO), which indicates the degree to which a bank can finance its mortgage lending, i.e. its core lending business, through customer deposits. As a strong customer base contributes to bank safety, we expect a *positive* relationship between this variable and our dependent variable, α^j_{it}. Second, the ratio of interbank borrowing to total liabilities (IBTL) measures a bank's overall dependence on relatively expensive, or fragile, funding. We expect a *negative* relationship with α^j_{it}. Finally, the ratio of non-savings deposits to total uninsured deposits (NSTUL) controls for substitution effects within uninsured deposits, i.e. between uninsured savings deposits and non-savings deposits (such as time or demand deposits). As the different types of uninsured deposits are substitutes,[17] we expect a *negative* relationship between NSTL and α^j_{it}, the share of uninsured savings deposits.

Management. To account for management quality, we include the ratio of non-interest expenditures to total liabilities (NIETL). This variable, which includes a variety of expenses (such as payroll, workers compensation and training investment), reflects the management's policy stance. In our sample, we have only a few number of banks with important private banking activities which create large expenses without a corresponding volume of liabilities. A high fraction of non-interest expenses to liabilities thus reflects a high level of spending in not-directly-productive activities, i.e. most likely an inefficient management. We thus expect a *negative* relationship with our dependent variable.

Earnings. To account for the bank's earnings profile, we include four variables. A high profit rate, measured by the ratio of net aggregate revenue to total liabilities (NARTL), should strengthen depositors' confidence. We thus expect a *positive* relationship with α^j_{it}, the share of uninsured savings deposits. The next two variables account for the degree of revenue diversification. These are the ratio of net commission revenues to total liabilities (NCRTL) and the ratio of net interest rate revenues to total liabilities (NIRTL). As diversification of revenue into non-interest income increases bank stability, we expect a *positive* (*negative*) relationship between NCRTL (NIRTL) and uninsured savings deposits. The fourth earnings-related variable is the growth rate of total liabilities (TLGR). Assuming that depositors interpret a high growth rate as a signal of the management's confidence in expanding its activities, we expect a *positive* relationship between this variable and α^j_{it}.

Liquidity. Finally, we account for the degree of liquidity by including the ratio of liquid assets to total liabilities (LIQTL). Liquid assets are defined as cash plus secondary liquidity (net of short term liabilities) in percentage of total liabilities (the definition follows articles 15–18 of the Banking Ordinance). The impact of liquidity is ambiguous. As a relatively liquid bank may be less prone to a bank run, one could expect a positive relationship between the liquidity variable and α^j_{it}, the share of uninsured savings deposits. However, as liquid assets normally have low yields, one would expect a negative relationship.

Insurance Control Variables

Market discipline also means that depositors know whether, or to what degree, their deposits are protected in the case of a bank failure. In particular, in the presence of depositor discipline, we expect institutional changes to the deposit insurance system to have an impact on depositors' willingness to withdraw their uninsured savings deposits from fragile banks. For example, we expect depositors to exert less discipline on cantonal banks, which benefit from an extensive state guarantee from their respective cantons. Similarly, we expect changes to the liquidity and priority insurance to affect depositors' behavior. Our sample permits us to test depositors' regulatory knowledge and the extent to which a change to the Swiss deposit insurance system affects their behavior. This is because the sample under study contains two important changes to the Swiss deposit insurance system, namely:

(i) in 1993, when the cap on liquidity insurance was introduced; and
(ii) in 1997 when the limit (per depositor) on priority insurance was raised from CHF 10'000 to CHF 30'000.

Liquidity insurance. First, we examine whether the 1993 cap on liquidity insurance has reduced depositors' willingness to hold their savings deposits in a cap-constrained bank, i.e. in a bank where the *effective* (cap-inclusive) liquidity insurance per depositor (as limited by the cap) falls short of the theoretical CHF 30'000. To do this, we include a dummy (DCAP), which equals one if the bank's volume of insured deposits was constrained by the 1993 cap, and zero otherwise. The impact of the DCAP on α_{it}^{LINC}, the share of savings deposits that would be uninsured in the absence of the cap, is a priori ambiguous. One the one hand, it can be *positive* if cap-constrained banks become relatively unattractive and risk-averse depositors move their previously insured deposits to banks where their small deposits (up to CHF 30'000) are fully insured. We may call this the "small deposits" effect. On the other hand, by reducing the effective level of insurance, the cap may not only induce depositors to move their previously insured savings deposits (i.e. up to CHF 30'000) but also their uninsured savings deposits (i.e. above CHF 30'000). This would have a negative impact on α_{it}^{LINC}, the fraction of savings deposits that would be uninsured in the absence of the cap. This may be called the "large deposit effect."

To disentangle the effect of the 1993 cap from any possible size effect, we include a size control dummy variable (DSIZE) which, over the whole sample period, is equal to one if the size of insured deposits is above CHF 1 billion and zero otherwise. The coefficient for DSIZE might be either positive, if bigger banks are believed to represent a lower risk (as in the case of too-big-to-fail), or negative, if bigger banks are believed to represent a higher risk (as in the case of too-big-to-be-purchased).

To test the robustness of our results, we control for the liability structure of banks. To do this, we introduce the ratio of savings deposits to total liabilities (STL). We expect a *positive* impact between this variable and the dependent variable, α_{it}^{LINC}. This is because savings deposits are typically cheaper than other deposits, as competition among banks is less fierce in the savings market than, say, in the internationally contested markets for time deposits. Furthermore, more sophisticated banks, which have a relatively small portion of savings deposits to total liabilities, may offer attractive alternative saving instruments to traditional savings deposits.

Finally, to test the robustness of our results, we introduce an interaction term between the cap and the fraction of savings deposits to total deposits, DCSTL. After the 1993 cap, we expect depositors to withdraw their savings deposits from cap-constrained banks. Again, as in the case of DCAP, we must differentiate between the small deposits effect (if depositors withdraw primarily insured savings deposits) and the large deposits effect (if depositors withdraw both insured and uninsured savings deposits). For example, a *positive* coefficient of DCSTL would support the small deposits effect in the sense that cap-constrained banks experience a flight of insured savings deposits.

To test the impact of the cap, we thus modify Eq. (1) to the following expression:

$$\alpha_{it}^{LINC} = \mu_i + \delta' M_t + \beta' X_{it-1} + \theta' DSIZE + \rho' DCAP_{it}$$

$$+ \phi' STL + \lambda' DCSTL_{it} + \varepsilon_{it} \tag{2}$$

where, as before, μ_i stands for each bank's fixed effect, M_t is a vector of macroeconomic variables, X_{it-1} is a vector of bank-specific variables, and DSIZE is a size control dummy variable, which equals 1 if savings deposits exceed CHF 1 billion and zero otherwise. The dependent variable $\alpha_{it}^{\mathrm{LINC}}$, is defined as the fraction of savings deposits that are not covered by liquidity insurance even in the absence of the cap (i.e. as the fraction of savings deposits strictly above CHF 30'000). The last three terms in Eq. (2) allow us to examine the impact of the introduction of the cap on depositors' behavior. As mentioned, DCAP is the "cap binding" dummy, STL is the ratio of savings deposits to total liabilities and DCSTL is the interaction term between STL and the cap.

The empirical results of Eq. (2) will be presented below in Section 4.4. But before discussing our findings, let us now turn to the second institutional change that affected the Swiss deposit insurance system over the sample period, namely, the upward revision of the priority insurance from CHF 10'000 to CHF 30'000.

Priority insurance. Second, we analyze the 1997 revision to priority insurance, which raised the level of insurance for savings deposits from CHF 10'000 to CHF 30'000 per depositor. A higher coverage should encourage depositors to hold larger (above CHF 10'000) savings deposits. To test this hypothesis, we include a priority insurance dummy (DPI), which equals one after the 1997 priority insurance revision and zero otherwise. We expect a *positive* relationship between this variable and $\alpha_{it}^{\mathrm{PIB97}}$, the share of savings deposits that are uninsured according to the pre–1997 definition.

In particular, after the 1997 revision, we expect to see a rise in the newly insured savings deposits (i.e. between CHF 10'000 and CHF 30'000), possibly at the expense of savings deposits above CHF 30'000. To test this hypothesis, we introduce the two variables NS30A and NS30B, measuring the number of deposits (as a percentage of the total number of savings deposits) above CHF 30'000 (NS30A), and below CHF 30'000 (NS30B), respectively. The two interaction terms, DPNS30B and DPNS30A link the two variables with the priority insurance dummy (DPI).

We expect a *positive* relationship between NS30A and the dependent variable α_{it}^{PIB97}. The higher the number of savings deposits in excess of CHF 30'000 (as a fraction of the number of total savings deposits), the higher we expect the fraction of uninsured deposits to be. For NS30B, *however*, the expected sign is ambiguous, as this contains both insured (below CHF 10'000) and uninsured (above CHF 10'000) savings deposits. Thus, a rise in the number of savings deposits below CHF 30'000 may either raise or reduce the fraction of uninsured savings deposits, depending on whether a bank attracts a greater proportion of small (insured) or large (uninsured) savings deposits.

For the sake of our study, the most interesting elements are the interaction terms. In particular, we expect a negative sign for DNS30B, as the 1997 upward revision in the priority insurance, which raises the insurance ceiling from CHF 10'000 to CHF 30'000, may induce depositors to entrust larger (up to CHF 30'000) savings deposits to their bank. We expect a much weaker impact of DNS30A, as depositors are less likely to split their (previously uninsured) savings into smaller (below CHF 30'000) savings deposits in response to the 1997 revision.

We consequently modify Eq. (1) to the following expression:

$$\alpha_{it}^{PIB97} = \mu_i + \delta' M_t + \beta' X_{it-1} + \varphi' DPI_{it} + \xi' NS30B + \upsilon' NS30A$$

$$+ \chi' DPNS30B_{it} + \tau' DPNS30A_{it} + \varepsilon_{it}(3) \qquad (3)$$

where, μ_i, M_t, and X_{it-1} are defined as above. The dependent variable, α_{it}^{PIB97}, represents the fraction of savings deposits strictly above CHF 10'000 (i.e. uninsured savings deposits according to the pre-1997 priority insurance definition), DPI represents the 1997 priority insurance dummy variable, and the last four terms represent, respectively, the numbers of savings deposits below CHF 30'000, the number of savings deposits above CHF 30'000 and their interaction terms with the priority insurance dummy variable.

Summary Statistics

The data set includes 247 (129) banks in 1987 (2001) and covers a wide range of bank categories, including big international banks, state-run (cantonal) banks and small regional banks. There are 27 (24) cantonal banks. We have an unbalanced sample, as between 1987–2001 the number of cantonal banks dropped by 10%. For some variables, we have no data for 1987 and 1988. Cross-sectional summary statistics are thus given for end of 1989 (rather than 1987) and 2001, respectively. These statistics are given in Table 7 in the Appendix.

IV. RESULTS

4.1. Overview

Empirical results are reported in Tables 3–6 below. First, we examine whether bank fundamentals affect depositors willingness to entrust their uninsured savings deposits to a particular bank. This is shown in Table 3, where the results of the general market discipline hypothesis (Eq. (1)) are presented using a fixed effects model. For a robustness check, we also estimate the model in first differences (Table 4). Second, we examine whether institutional differences among bank groups affect the degree of market discipline in the Swiss banking sector. In particular, the impact of the *state guarantee* on depositors' behavior in cantonal banks is presented in column (2) of Tables 3 and 4. Third, we examine whether institutional changes to the Swiss deposit insurance system alters the behavior of uninsured deposits. While the impact of the 1993 liquidity insurance cap on depositors behavior (Eq. (2)) is presented in Table 5, the effect of the 1997 upward revision to the priority insurance (Eq. (3)) is illustrated in Table 6.

4.2. General Market Discipline

The data seems to support our general hypothesis, that the fraction of uninsured savings deposits is related to movements in a bank's fundamentals. In Table 3 we report results for all banks and for the sub-sample of cantonal banks. According to our results for all banks, our explanatory variables explain remarkably well fluctuations in the dependent variable, the share of uninsured savings. All three macro variables are strongly significant and all have the expected sign. Thus, uninsured savings deposits clearly react to business conditions. They tend to be high during booms (high lagged GDP-growth, high lagged inflation), but low after high short-term interest peaks.

Among the thirteen bank-specific variables,[18] eight are statistically significant and most have the expected sign. In particular, all earnings and management quality variables have a measurable impact. The results for the asset quality variables are less pronounced. In particular, while the ratio of customer liabilities to mortgages (CLTMO) and the ratio of mortgage lending to total assets (MORTA) are statistically significant, credit growth, both in the full sample period (CRGR) and in the pre-bubble sub-period (CRGR_B), and interbank lending (IBTL) fail to be significant. Secondary liquidity (as defined in the law) (LIQTL) seems to bring banks more costs than benefits, as this variable consistently gets a *negative* sign across all estimations. One potential

Table 3. Standard Model.

	All Banks (1)	Cantonal (2)
$gdpgr_t$	0.487*** (6.259)	0.281 (1.459)
$chmm3m_t$	−1.309*** (−13.458)	−1.543*** (−6.499)
$cpindex_t$	0.460*** (9.277)	0.331** (2.503)
$ktl_{i,t-1}$	−0.056 (−0.893)	0.192* (1.954)
$morta_{i,t-1}$	−0.085*** (−2.988)	0.013 (0.138)
$crgr_{i,t-1}$	−0.002 (−0.414)	0.032 (1.151)
$crgr\_b_{i,t-1}$	0.0003 (0.052)	−0.042 (−1.210)
$cltmo_{i,t-1}$	0.006*** (8.765)	0.029 (1.069)
$ibtl_{i,t-1}$	−0.005 (−0.144)	−0.023 (−0.285)
$nstul_{i,t-1}$	−0.020 (−1.346)	−0.110* (−1.932)
$nietl_{i,t-1}$	−5.012*** (−4.254)	−9.017* (−1.793)
$nartl_{i,t-1}$	0.834** (2.371)	0.978 (1.124)
$nertl_{i,t-1}$	1.682*** (3.178)	1.047 (0.398)
$nirtl_{i,t-1}$	−0.199 (−0.521)	−0.399 (−0.398)
$tlgr_{i,t-1}$	0.011* (1.840)	0.031 (1.104)
$liqtl_{i,t-1}$	−0.104** (−2.351)	−0.277* (−1.809)
constant	0.064 (1.231)	0.206 (1.194)
No. of obs.	2014	302
No. of groups	244	29
R-square:		
within	0.704	0.826
between	0.421	0.218
overall	0.492	0.615
F-value	245.49	71.27
Prob > F	0.000	0.000
corr(u_i, Xb)	0.055	−0.052

surprise is the *negative* sign of MORTA, the ratio of mortgages to total assets. It seems that the relatively safe nature of a mortgage credit is dominated by the fact that, in the sample period, the real estate crisis hit mortgages harder than credits in general. It is interesting to note, however, that a high level of mortgage lending reduces depositors' confidence in their bank, unless this type of lending is covered by customer liabilities. This is shown by the significant and positive coefficient of CLTMO. Thus, while depositors do not seem to have changed their behavior in response to the Swiss loan crisis (CRGR_B is not statistically significant), they do care about the quality of their bank's lending.[19]

For a robustness test, we estimate the same model in first differences. Overall, the results given in Table 4 are similar to those we found using the specification in lagged levels.[20] The few important differences are mostly explainable. For example, the three-month interest rate (CHMM3M), while significant in levels, is no longer significant in first differences. This makes sense given that a small change in the interest rate typically has less impact on the dependent variable than the level of interest rates. The same is true for the inflation rate. It seems less clear, however, why the sign of net aggregate returns to total liabilities (NARTL) changes across specifications. One possible explanation could be that a big increase in returns is more likely if the initial level is low. The (negative) coefficient of non-savings in total uninsured deposits (NSDUL) is higher in first differences than in levels. This is because in first differences, this variable mirrors changes in the speed of uninsured deposits outflows, which translates directly into a lower fraction of uninsured in total savings deposits.

But perhaps the most interesting change between levels and first differences regards credit growth (CRGR). Only in first-differences does this variable become significant, with a *negative* sign for the whole period and a *positive* sign for the "bubble" sub-period (i.e. before 1994). This suggests that while depositors did not seem to worry about a bank's strong credit growth during the real-estate bubble, they became much more wary once the bubble had bursted. This points to some important limits of market discipline: The fact that investors use their information, does not imply that they use it correctly. Market discipline thus does not shield banks and depositors from irrational swings in general market sentiment.

We conclude that the Swiss deposit market is characterized by market discipline, in the sense that uninsured depositors monitor the fundamentals of their banks and respond accordingly. Yet, our results also suggest that not all CAMEL-based indicators are equally available to or used by all investors.

Macroeconomic variables, for example, are public information; not surprisingly, they are strongly significant. The same is true for earnings, which are periodically disclosed and reported in newspapers. Asset quality, in contrast, is mostly banks' private information (in Switzerland, non-performing loans were not subject to a disclosure requirement during the sample period). This may explain the somewhat weaker results for those variables. The clear impact of cost efficiency, however, may be somewhat surprising as it may be more difficult for depositors to observe this variable. Finally, our results on credit growth suggest that investors may be victims to herding behavior, in which case "depositor discipline" may benefit, in times of economic booms, the more risky banks, rather than the more prudent ones.

4.3. State Guarantee

Our results also confirm our second hypothesis, namely, that the presence of a state guarantee reduces the degree of market discipline. The fraction of uninsured savings deposits held at cantonal banks (which benefit from an extensive state guarantee) is indeed relatively less responsive to movements in bank fundamentals than that held in the banking sector as a whole. In Table 3, in the case of cantonal banks only four of the thirteen bank-specific variables are statistically significant (and only at the 10% significance level), as opposed to seven in the case of all banks. This result is consistent with the view that state guarantee weakens market discipline.

4.4. The Liquidity Insurance Cap

Our third hypothesis regards the impact of the 1993 CHF 1 billion liquidity insurance cap. In particular, we test whether banks, which are constrained by the insurance cap, experience a drop in (theoretically) insured savings deposits or, alternatively, a rise in uninsured savings deposits. Our results confirm this hypothesis. The first column of Table 5 shows that the insurance dummy, DCAP, is positive and statistically significant for the Swiss banking sector as a whole.[21] This suggests that the "small deposits effect" dominates: after the 1993 liquidity insurance cap, insured savings deposits held at a cap-constrained bank migrate to another bank, that offers the full extent of the liquidity insurance. Again, we find a weaker response in the case of cantonal banks, for which the coefficient for DCAP is not significant. Thus, the presence of an extensive state guarantee seems to weaken market discipline.

Note that the size dummy (DSIZE) has a negative and significant impact (see, for example, column (1)). This suggests that a bigger bank, which tends

Table 4. First Difference.

	All banks (1)	Cantonal banks (2)
$\Delta gdpgr_t$	0.055 (0.824)	0.057 (0.479)
$\Delta chmm3m_t$	−0.559*** (−6.050)	−0.104 (−0.587)
$\Delta cpindex_t$	−0.124* (−1.695)	−0.209* (−1.711)
$\Delta ktl_{i,t}$	−0.109 (−1.347)	−0.438** (−2.053)
$\Delta morta_{i,t}$	−0.210*** (−5.764)	0.397*** (3.396)
$\Delta crgr_{i,t}$	−009*** (−3.125)	−0.007 (−0.552)
$\Delta crgr\_b_{i,t}$	0.008*** (2.701)	0.002 (0.099)
$\Delta cltmo_{i,t}$	0.004*** (8.231)	0.196*** (4.995)
$\Delta ibtl_{i,t}$	−0.146*** (−3.138)	−0.059 (−0.651)
$\Delta nstul_{i,t}$	−0.333*** (−19.586)	−0.772*** (−19.594)
$\Delta nietl_{i,t}$	−4.926*** (−3.786)	−10.223** (−2.380)
$\Delta nartl_{i,t}$	−1.061*** (−6.996)	0.359 (0.714)
$\Delta ncrtl_{i,t}$	2.706*** (3.452)	0.188 (0.079)
$\Delta nirtl_{i,t}$	−0.185 (−0.474)	0.206 (0.246)
$\Delta tlgr_{i,t}$	0.006 (1.476)	0.028* (1.670)
$\Delta liqtl_{i,t}$	−0.004 (−0.106)	−0.124 (−1.165)
constant	0.010*** (5.439)	0.013*** (4.361)
No. of obs.	2011	302
No. of groups	244	29
R-square:		
within	0.393	0.734
between	0.217	0.257
overall	0.382	0.723
F-value	66.55	41.52
Prob > F	0.000	0.000
$corr(u_i, Xb)$	−0.059	−0.065

to be more sophisticated, generally offers attractive alternative savings instruments for large uninsured savings deposits. Alternatively, it could also mean that a bigger bank is believed to represent a higher risk of bankruptcy. This would fit the experience of the Swiss banking crisis in the early 1990s, when the smaller banks were typically absorbed by bigger ones. During this time, being small facilitated absorption and hence, provided additional safety to depositors. This does not preclude, however, that Swiss depositors believe that the big banks are protected by an implicit too-big-to-fail guarantee. But it does suggest that the small-enough-to-be-rescued effect dominates our sample.

To test the robustness of our results, we allow for an interaction between the cap and the fraction of savings deposits to total liabilities. The idea is that depositors may care about the savings structure of their banks. For example, we find that banks with a large ratio of savings deposits to total liabilities (STL) exhibit a relatively higher share of uninsured savings deposits. This suggests that large savings deposits are kept in less sophisticated and less diversified banks. This is shown in column (3) in Table 5, where the coefficient of STL is significant and positive. This phenomenon seems to be especially strong in the case of cantonal banks (column (4)).

In terms of the 1993 introduction of the liquidity cap, we find that cap-constrained banks experienced a flight of insured savings deposits. After 1993, insurance-sensitive depositors withdrew their (previously insured) savings deposits from cap-constrained banks, as these institutions offered a level of insurance that was much lower than the theoretical CHF 30'000 offered under priority insurance. This is shown in column (5), where the coefficient of DCSTL is significant and positive. Finally, the negative coefficient of DCSTL for the cantonal banks in column (4) suggests that these banks, which enjoy a substantial state-guarantee, benefited from the cap in the sense that they received the insured savings deposits that fled from the other cap-constrained banks. This is consistent with our hypothesis that cantonal banks mitigate the effect of market discipline.

We conclude that Swiss depositors responded to the 1993 cap by withdrawing their theoretically insured savings deposits (up to CHF 30'000) from cap-constrained banks.

4.5. The Priority Insurance Ceiling

Finally, our findings support our fourth hypothesis, namely, that the 1997 priority insurance revision, which raised the priority insurance ceiling from CHF 10'000 to CHF 30'000, induces depositors to hold a higher volume of savings deposits above CHF 10'000. This is shown in Table 6, where the

Table 5. Liquidity Insurance Model.

	Specification 1		Specification 2		Spec. 3
	All Banks	Cantonal	All Banks	Cantonal	All Banks
	(1)	(2)	(3)	(4)	(5)
$dsize_{i,t}$	−0.073*** (−5.810)	−0.001 (0.041)	−0.077*** (6.187)	−0.003 (−0.234)	−0.075*** (−5.866)
$dcap_{i,t}$	0.016** (2.504)	−0.010 (−1.036)	0.005 (0.392)	0.027 (1.392)	−0.001 (−0.046)
stl			0.125*** (5.228)	0.289*** (3.315)	0.124** (5.208)
stl_bb					−0.728*** (−2.872)
$destl_{i,t-1}$			0.0484 (1.139)	−0.130*** (−2.151)	0.071** (1.577)
$destl\_bb_{i,t-1}$					0.137 (1.017)
constant	0.077 (1.609)	0.164 (1.011)	−0.018 (−0.353)	−0.0252 (0.153)	−0.006 (−0.126)
No. of obs.	2014	302	2014	302	2014
No. of groups	244	29	244	29	244
R-square:					
within	0.710	0.824	0.714	0.833	0.716
between	0.304	0.170	0.275	0.150	0.229
overall	0.410	0.586	0.383	0.561	0.342
F-value	236.83	66.09	218.07	63.06	199.78
Prob > F	0.000	0.000	0.000	0.000	0.000
corr(u_i, Xb)	−0.067	−0.081	−0.149	−0.158	−0.235

dependent variable is defined as the fraction of savings deposits above CHF 10'000 to total savings deposits.[22]

Once we control for the structure of savings deposits, Swiss depositors seem to respond to the upward revision of the priority insurance. This is shown in Table 6, where the coefficient for the priority insurance dummy, DPI, is significant and positive, except for the cantonal banks, for which it is only borderline significant. This suggests that a higher deposit insurance level has raised depositors' willingness to entrust higher savings deposits (above CHF 10'000) to their bank.

To differentiate between a simple nominal growth effect and a change in depositors behavior, we examine whether the upward revision in priority insurance has raised depositors willingness to hold newly insured savings deposits (between CHF 10'000 and CHF 30'000), possibly at the expense of large savings deposits (above CHF 30'000). The results are shown in columns (3) to (5) in Table 6. First, we control for an increase in the number of savings deposits, both below CHF 30'000 (NS30B) and above CHF 30'000 (NS30A). Then, we examine the impact of the 1997 upward revision in priority insurance. Overall, we find that a rise in the number of savings deposits above CHF 30'000 translates into a relatively lower rise in uninsured savings deposits after 1997 than it did before 1997. This is shown in column (3) of Table 6, where the coefficient of DPNS30A is significant and negative. This means that after 1997, banks are able to attract more savings deposits that are closer to the new insurance ceiling (i.e. around CHF 30'000) than larger uninsured savings deposits (well above CHF 30'000).

As far as the big banks are concerned, they also attract a higher share of small and insured savings deposits (i.e. up to CHF 10'000). This is shown in column (5), where the coefficient for NS30B_BB is significant and negative. This supports our hypothesis that the higher priority insurance ceiling induces insurance-sensitive depositors to entrust newly insured savings deposits in their banks.

Finally, in response to the 1997 priority insurance revision, cantonal banks lost newly insured savings deposits (between CHF 10'000 and CHF 30'000) in return for receiving more uninsured savings deposits (above CHF 30'000). This is shown in column (4), where the coefficient of DPNS30B is statistically significant and negative. This suggests that the priority insurance revision reduced the comparative advantage of cantonal banks in attracting savings deposits that are now falling in the bracket of newly insured savings deposits (between CHF 10'000 and CHF 30'000). Nevertheless, cantonal banks seem to maintain their comparative advantage in attracting large (uninsured) savings deposits (above CHF 30'000) in the sense that the higher priority insurance does not seem to affect the coefficient of DPNS30A, which remains statistically significant (column (4)).

Overall, our results suggest that Swiss depositors seem to be aware of and to care about priority insurance. The upward revision of the priority insurance induces depositors to take advantage of the higher insurance ceiling by entrusting banks with a larger volume of newly insured savings deposits (above CHF 10'000) and a smaller volume of uninsured savings deposits (above CHF 30'000).

4.6. *Robustness of Results*

We find our empirical results to be robust across a broad range of specifications, including correcting for the presence of heteroscedasticity and first-order autocorrelation. While the Breusch and Pagan Lagrangian multiplier test favors the random-effects specification over the fixed-effects specification, the results remain consistent with those found under the fixed-effects specification, both in terms of coefficient signs and level of significance. Furthermore, the Hausman specification test rejects the hypothesis that the individual-level effects are adequately modeled by a random-effects model. These results suggest that either the current specification is not appropriate or the zero-correlation assumption between the bank-specific error term and the explanatory variables is violated. Overall, however, we feel confident with the latter interpretation, given the consistency of our results over a wide range of specifications.

V. CONCLUSIONS

In this paper, we examine the presence of market discipline in the Swiss deposit market. Overall, we find that the perceived "quality", or relative safety, of a bank clearly influences depositors' willingness to hold uninsured savings deposits in a particular bank. For example, our standard model (where savings deposits are insured up to CHF 30'000) explains more than 70% of a bank's variations in uninsured savings deposits over time and almost 30% of differences between banks (column (3) in Table 5). If we focus on the priority insurance (where savings deposits are insured up to CHF 10'000), our model explains up to 73% of variations within a bank and 66% of variations between banks (column (3) in Table 6). According to these results, depositors seem to exert considerable market discipline in the Swiss deposit market, in the sense that uninsured depositors monitor the fundamentals of their bank and respond accordingly.

Not all information is equally relevant or accessible by depositors. Macroeconomic variables represent public information and hence, are closely monitored by depositors. Depositors also care about asset quality. Yet, relevant variables are mostly part of banks' private information, which explains the somewhat weaker impact of these variables on depositors' behavior. In addition, depositors may exert discipline in the "wrong" direction by, say, interpreting a strong credit expansion as a sign of healthy bank performance during a period of economic boom. Finally, information on earnings and management quality, although only partially disclosed, seem to have a measurable influence on depositors' decisions.

Most remarkably, we find clear evidence that depositors care about protective regulations. First, depositors are aware of the extensive state guarantee that is enjoyed by cantonal banks. For example, the behavior of uninsured deposits in cantonal banks is relatively more responsive to changes in bank-specific fundamentals than that exhibited in the aggregate banking

Table 6. Priority Insurance Model.

	Specification 1		Specification 2		Spec. 3
	All Banks (1)	Cantonal (2)	All Banks (3)	Cantonal (4)	All banks (5)
$dpi_{i,t}$	0.012*** (3.399)	0.011 (1.230)	0.035*** (3.229)	0.060 (1.777)	0.036*** (3.284)
$ns30b_{i,t-1}$			−0.037 (0.620)	0.217* (1.958)	0.185*** (2.762)
$ns30b\_bb_{i,t-1}$					−3.186*** (−6.960)
$ns30b\_cb_{i,t-1}$					−0.046*** (−4.284)
$ns30a_{i,t-1}$			0.670*** (10.280)	0.658*** (4.704)	0.597*** (8.351)
$ns30a\_bb_{i,t-1}$					1.521*** (3.277)
$ns30a\_cb_{i,t-1}$					0.286* (2.236)
$dpns30b_{i,t-1}$			−0.109 (−1.555)	−0.393** (−2.029)	−0.130 (−1.747)
$dpns30b\_bb_{i,t-1}$					1.345*** (4.225)
$dpns30b\_cb_{i,t-1}$					−0.089 (−0.747)
$dpns30a_{i,t-1}$			−0.600*** (−0.936)	0.110 (0.906)	−0.080 (−1.086)
$dpns30a\_bb_{i,t-1}$					−1.188*** (−2.434)
$dpns30a\_cb_{i,t-1}$					0.164*** (1.123)
constant	0.153*** (2.927)	0.215 (1.342)	0.132*** (2.598)	0.321*** (02.061)	0.129*** (2.620)
No. of obs.	2014	302	2014	302	2014
No. of groups	244	29	244	29	244
R-square:					
within	0.706	0.827	0.731	0.846	0.749
between	0.434	0.231	0.661	0.555	0.284
overall	0.502	0.623	0.641	0.755	0.361
F-value	247.95	71.77	225.88	62.45	179.4
Prob > F	0.000	0.000	0.000	0.000	0.000
corr(u_i, Xb)	0.067	−0.045	0.168	0.062	−0.364

sector, where fundamentals have at best a weak influence on the supply of uninsured savings deposits. Similarly, we find that depositors in cantonal banks are less responsive to changes to the liquidity and priority insurances.

Second, depositors respond to changes to the deposit insurance system. Regarding liquidity insurance, we find that the introduction of the 1993 cap (which reduced effective insurance far below the theoretical CHF 30'000 per-depositor) discourages depositors to hold savings deposits with balances below CHF 30'000 at cap-constrained banks. Regarding the 1997 upward revision to the priority insurance, we found that it raised depositors willingness to hold newly insured savings deposits (between CHF 10'000 and CHF 30'000), sometimes at the expense of large savings deposits (above CHF 30'000). In either case, the cantonal banks, with their extensive state guarantee, act as a counterbalance to the rest of the banking sector. They gain from a reduction in the effective level of deposit insurance (as in the case of the 1993 cap on liquidity insurance) and lose from a higher deposit insurance coverage (as in the case of the 1997 upward revision to the priority insurance). All in all, these findings indicate that Swiss depositors care about deposit insurance and respond to changes to its application.

Overall, we conclude that, during our sample period, savings depositors responded to developments in bank-specific variables, to institutional differences across bank groups and to institutional changes in the depositor insurance system. Even though savings depositors are often regarded as relatively unsophisticated investors, they seem to contribute to discipline in the Swiss bank deposit market. It should be repeated here that these results are not driven by shifts from savings deposits to other types of deposits (say, demand or time deposits), but by shifts within savings deposits from the uninsured to the insured part. Our results are encouraging for supervisors, who want to rely increasingly on market discipline ("pillar 3" of the New Basel Accord). Since our study has focused on a quantity-based indicator (the behavior of uninsured savings deposits) as opposed to a price-based indicator such as yield spreads, our setup may be of interest to the study of market discipline in other countries, where the banking sector is dominated by a relatively large number of small and medium sized banks, which do not issue tradable debt.

Finally, two caveats regarding the interpretation of the term "market discipline" apply. First, in the context of our paper, market discipline occurs when depositors withdraw their funds from institutions that are deemed to be engaging in excessive risk-taking activities. This does not mean, however, that depositors necessarily help banks distinguish between fundamentals-driven increases in, say, real estate prices and bubbles. For example, according to our results, depositors did not consider a bank's asset quality with more suspicion in the wake of the Swiss loan crisis than in its aftermath. In such cases, market discipline only implies that depositors interpret new information and react accordingly upon it, regardless of whether their interpretation proves correct with hindsight.

The other caveat regards the chain reaction between deposit withdrawals and bank behavior.[23] While we find that depositors discipline their Swiss banks, our results do not allow us to infer anything about the effectiveness of this discipline in changing the banks behavior. If bank managers find it more difficult to raise uninsured debt in the form of saving deposits, they may look for alternative sources of funding or continue to run a risky (albeit smaller) bank. While this is a valid criticism to our approach, we believe that it applies to the entire literature on market discipline. To our knowledge, no empirical paper so far, whether based on a quantity indicator (such as uninsured deposits) or a price indicator (such as yield spreads), has been able to establish the role of market discipline in changing the banks behavior with respect to risk-taking activities. This is consistent with the results drawn from the theoretical literature, which suggest that although high yield spread may indicate excessive risk-taking, they do not necessarily induce banks to adopt a lower level of risk (Bliss & Flannery, 2000, and Blum, 2002). Thus, further research on the relationship between depositor monitoring, risk sensitivity of funds, and bank behavior is warranted before a definite conclusion can be drawn regarding the effectiveness of market discipline in reducing banks risk appetite.

NOTES

1. For example, while the budgetary costs of the 1997 Thai and Korean banking crises are estimated to have reached 30% of GDP, the cost of the Indonesian banking crisis is believed to have reached up to 50% of GDP. For more details, see World Bank (2001).
2. Dewatripont and Tirole (1985).
3. For excellent reviews on deposit insurance systems, refer to Demigürç-Kunt and Kane (2002) and Garcia (1999).
4. From a slightly different perspective, Kennickel, Kwast and Starr-McCluer (1995) look at a related question, namely, which investor groups are most inclined to hold uninsured deposits. Using U.S. consumer finance data and controlling for investors characteristics, they find that older, male white-collar workers are most inclined to hold uninsured (i.e. above USD 100'000) deposits.
5. For more detailed information, see Birchler (2000).
6. In particular, the cantons of Vaud and Geneva have limited, at least de jure, the state guarantee to savings deposits.
7. Federal Act on Banks and Savings Banks (Article 15, Section 2). The respective French and German expressions for this protection scheme are "privilège en cas de faillite" and "Konkursprivileg."

8. A thorough discussion on this private deposit guarantee can be found in Winzeler (1994).

9. Again, this very much resembles the 1993 U.S. depositor preference rules, under which the FDIC acquires priority of deposits when paying out insured depositors. Note that while depositor preference in the U.S. extends to all deposits, and not only to insured deposits, in Switzerland, the current definition of deposits covered by the priority insurance coincides with that of deposits covered by the SBA liquidity insurance.

10. In the fifteen years of its existence, the agreement was called upon in three cases (Banque de Participations et de Placements, Lugano; Mebco Bank SA, Geneva; Spar + Leihkasse Thun, Thun). In all three cases the respective bank's assets were sufficient to cover priority deposits.

11. After exhaustion of this aggregate amount, a new agreement among the SBA would have to be negotiated.

12. This relatively high figure is relevant for the present study, as it indicates that people diversify savings accounts across banks, perhaps to avoid holding uninsured savings.

13. By the end of 2000, 59.6% of saving accounts had balances below CHF 5'000, which makes the figure in the text a reasonable estimate for the median.

14. Unfortunately, no data are available on liquidity insurance. In order to estimate the fraction of savings deposits covered by priority insurance, we assume (somewhat counterfactually) that each depositor holds only one savings account per bank.

15. From 1991–1995 the Swiss banking sector experienced a real-estate related loan crisis which hit the regional banks most severely. The number of regional banks fell from 210 to 135.

16. The selection of our macro and bank-specific variables is consistent with similar studies on market discipline. We also draw from the literature on "leading indicators" of banking crises. See Bell (2000), and, for the U.K., Logan (2001).

17. Any complementary relation, dominating the substitute relation during a bank-run, e.g. is irrelevant here as we use fractions to total liabilities.

18. Here we count CRG and CRG_B as one variable.

19. Note that we have also tried to capture the effect of the bubble on mortgage lending by disentangling mortgage lending in the period before 1995 (MORTA_B) from that over the entire period (MORTA). However, as in the case of credit growth during the bubble period, MORTA_B remains statistically insignificant. Thus, depositors seem to have neither altered their behavior in result of the real estate price bubble, nor mitigated the effects of the bubble ex-ante.

20. If some variables are non-stationary, an estimation in first differences yields more reliable results. However, the interpretation of results does not necessarily carry over from levels to first differences.

21. For convenience, Table 5 shows only the coefficients of the liquidity insurance variables. A complete set of table, including macroeconomic and bank-specific coefficients, is given in Appendix 6.2.1.

22. For convenience, Table 6 shows only the coefficients of the priority insurance variables. A complete set of table, including macroeconomic and bank-specific coefficients, is given in Appendix 6.2.2.

23. We thank Curt Hunter for pointing our attention to this important point.

ACKNOWLEDGMENTS

We are grateful to Robert Bichsel, Jürg Blum, Curt Hunter, George G. Kaufman, Myron Kwast, David Llewellyn, Kathleen McDill, and Bertrand Rime for helpful discussions and suggestions. Comments from Suzanne Ziegler as well as from participants at the 2001 BIS Research Workshop on "Applied Banking Research", the 2002 WEA Meetings in Seattle and an IMF Institute seminar greatly improved the quality of the paper. For valuable research assistance we are indebted to Matteo Facchinetti, Jeannette Müller and Christian Spielmann. All errors are our own. The findings, interpretations and conclusions expressed in this paper are entirely those of the authors and do not necessarily represent the views of the Swiss National Bank or the International Monetary Fund.

REFERENCES

Basel Committee on Bank Supervision (2000). The New Basel Capital Accord. Consultation paper (http://www.bis.org/publ/bcbs04a.htm).

Barajas, A., & Steiner, R. (2000). Depositor Behavior and Market Discipline in Colombia. IMF Working Paper, No.214, December.

Bell, J. (2000). Leading Indicator Models of Banking Crises-a Critical Review. *Financial Stability Review*, Bank of England, December.

Billet, M., Garfinkel, J., & O'Neal, E. (1998). The Cost of Market vs. Regulatory Discipline in Banking. *The Journal of Financial Economics*, *48* (June), 333–358.

Birchler, U. W. (2000). Bankruptcy Priority for Bank Deposits: A Contract Theoretic Explanation. *Review of Financial Studies*, *13*(3), 813–840.

Bliss, R. R., & Flannery, M. J. (2000). Market Discipline in the Governance of U.S. Bank Holding Companies: Monitoring vs. Influencing Federal Reserve Bank of Chicago. Working Paper, No. 03.

Blum, J. M. (2002). Subordinated Debt, Market Discipline, and Banks' Risk Taking. *Journal of Banking and Finance*, *26*(7), 1429–1443.

Board of Governors of the Federal Reserve System (1999). Using Subordinated Debt as an Instrument of Market Discipline. Staff Studies Paper, No.172, December.

Board of Governors of the Federal Reserve System and U.S. Department of the Treasury (2000). The Feasibility and Desirability of Mandatory Subordinated Debt. Report to the Congress, December.

Caprio, G. (2001). Finance for Growth: Policy Choices in a Volatile World. World Bank Policy Research Report. Washington, D.C.: World Bank.

Covitz, D. M., Hancock, D., & Kwast, M. (2000). Mandatory Subordinated Debt: Would Banks Face More Market Discipline? Working Paper. Board of Governors of the Federal Reserve System.

Demigürç-Kunt, A., & Kane, E. J. (2002). Deposit Insurance Around the Globe: Where Does it Work? *Journal of Economic Perspectives, 16*(2), 175–195.

Dewatripont, M., & Tirole, J. (1994). The Prudential Regulation of Banks. *Walras-Pareto Lectures* (vol. 1). Cambridge and London: MIT Press.

Evans O., Leone, A. M., Gill, M., & Hilbers, P. (2000). Macroprudential Indicators of Financial System Soundness.Occasional Paper, No. 192, Washington, D.C.: International Monetary Fund, April.

Garcia, G. G. H. (1999). Deposit Insurance: A Survey of Actual and Best Practices. Occasional Paper, No. 197. Washington, D.C.: International Monetary Fund.

Gilbert, A., & Vaughan, M. (2001). Do Depositors Care About Enforcement Actions? *Journal of Economics and Business, 53*(2/3), 283–311.

Goldberg L. G., & Hudgins, S. C. (2000). Depositor Discipline and Changing Strategies for Regulating Thrift Institutions. *The Journal of Financial Economics, 63*(2), 263–274.

Goldberg L. G., & Hudgins, S. C. (1996). Response of Uninsured Depositors to Impending S&L Failures: Evidence of Depositor Discipline. *The Quarterly Review of Economics and Finance, 36*(3), 311–325.

Jagtiani, J., & Lemieux, C. (2001). Market Discipline Prior to Bank Failure. *The Journal of Economics and Business, 53*(2/3), 313–324.

Jordan J. J. (2000). Depositor Discipline at Failing Banks. *New England Economic Review,* (March/April), 15–28. Federal Reserve Board of Boston.

Kennickell, A. B., Kwast, M. L., & Starr-McCluer, M. (1996). Households' Deposit Insurance Coverage: Evidence and Analysis of Potential Reforms. *Journal of Money, Credit, and Banking, 28*, 311–322.

Logan, A. (2001). The United Kingdom's Small Banks' Crisis of the Early 1990s: What Were the Leading Indicators of Failure? Bank of England. Working Paper Series, No. 139, pp. 1–37.

Martinez Peira, M. S., & Schmukler, S. L. (2001). Do Depositors Punish Banks for Bad Behavior? Market Discipline, Deposit Insurance and Banking Crises. *The Journal of Finance, 56*(3), 1029–1051.

Morgan, D., & Stiroh, K. (1999). Bond Market Discipline of Banks: Is the Market Tough Enough? Staff Report No.95, Federal Reserve Bank of New York, December.

Ramos, A. M. (1998). Capital Structures and Portfolio Composition During Banking Crises: Lessons from Argentina 1995. IMF Working Paper, No.121, August.

Sironi, A. (2000). Testing for Market Discipline in the European Banking Industry: Evidence from Subordinated Debt Issues. Board of Governors of the Federal Reserve Bank System, Finance and Economics Discussion Paper, No. 40, July.

Stiglitz, J., & Weiss, A. (1981). Credit Rationing in Markets with Imperfect Information. *American Economic Review, 71*(3), 393–410.

Winzeler, C. (1994). Der Einlegerschutz für Bankgläubiger. *Schweizerische Zeitschrift für Wirtschaftsrecht, 66*, 57–69.

VI. APPENDIX

Descriptive Statistics

Table 7. Summary Statistics 1989.

1989		All Banks		Cantonal banks	
		Obs.	Mean	Obs.	Mean
Dependent Variables	alinc	246	0.281	27	0.293
	apip97	246	0.572	27	0.590
Macroeconomic Variables	gdpgr	246	0.043	27	0.043
	chmm3m	246	0.069	27	0.069
	cpindex	246	0.785	27	0.785
Bank-specific Variables	ktl	246	0.065	27	0.052
	morta	246	0.634	27	0.592
	morta_b	246	0.634	27	0.592
	ergr	245	0.123	27	0.121
	ergr_b	245	0.123	27	0.121
	eltmo	246	1.343	27	1.283
	ibtl	246	0.041	27	0.045
	nstul	246	0.603	27	0.738
	nietl	246	0.006	27	0.006
	nartl	246	0.003	27	0.003
	nertl	246	0.003	27	0.002
	nirtl	246	0.008	27	0.007
	tlgr	246	0.096	27	0.080
	liqtl	246	0.087	27	0.069
Liquidity Insurance Variables	dsize	246	0.081	27	0.519
	dcap	246	0	27	0
	stl	246	0.371	27	0.290
	destl	246	0	27	0
Priority Insurance Variables	dpi	246	0	27	0
	ns30b	246	0.155	27	0.168
	ns30a	246	0.083	27	0.099
	dpns30b	246	0	27	0
	dbns30a	246	0	27	0

Table 8. Summary Statistics 2001.

2001		All Banks		Cantonal banks	
		Obs.	Mean	Obs.	Mean
Dependent Variables	aline	129	0.427	24	0.427
	apip97	129	0.688	24	0.690
Macroeconomic Variables	gdpgr	129	0.013	24	0.013
	chmm3m	129	0.029	24	0.029
	cpindex	129	1.013	24	1.013
Bank-specific Variables	ktl	129	0.081	24	0.071
	morta	129	0.714	24	0.678
	morta_b	129	0	24	0
	crgr	129	0.034	24	−0.020
	crgr_b	129	0	24	0
	cltmo	129	267.731	24	0.899
	ibtl	129	0.045	24	0.096
	nstul	129	0.441	24	0.645
	nietl	129	0.007	24	0.007
	nartl	129	0.004	24	0.003
	ncrtl	129	0.004	24	0.004
	nirtl	129	0.017	24	0.016
	tlgr	129	0.064	24	0.028
	liqtl	129	0.082	24	0.056
Liquidity Insurance Variables	dsize	129	0.163	24	0.667
	dcap	129	0.163	24	0.667
	stl	129	0.391	24	0.260
	destl	129	0.041	24	0.167
Priority Insurance Variables	dpi	129	1	24	1
	ns30b	129	0.168	24	0.170
	ns30a	129	0.135	24	0.135
	dpns30b	129	0.168	24	0.170
	dbns30a	129	0.135	24	0.135

Complete Set of Tables

Table 5-A. Liquidity Insurance Model.

	Specification 1		Specification 2		Spec. 3
	All Banks (1)	Cantonal (2)	All Banks (3)	Cantonal (4)	All Banks (5)
$gdpgr_t$	0.521*** (7.040)	0.384** (2.034)	0.562*** (7.618)	0.505*** (2.675)	0.537*** (7.258)
$chmm3m_t$	−1.326*** (−13.774)	−1.787*** (−7.407)	−1.180*** (−11.874)	−1.703*** (−6.988)	−1.176*** (−11.867)
$cpindex_t$	0.445*** (9.058)	0.345*** (2.601)	0.472*** (9.629)	0.329** (2.514)	1.574*** (9.307)
$ktl_{i,t-1}$	−0.035 (−0.568)	0.476* (1.867)	−0.038 (−0.609)	0.435* (1.748)	−0.033 (−0.534)
$morta_{i,t-1}$	−0.060** (−2.097)	−0.004 (−0.037)	−0.056** (−1.984)	0.039 (0.404)	−0.046 (−1.612)
$crgr_{i,t-1}$	−0.002 (−0.487)	0.029 (1.046)	−0.001 (−0.251)	0.027 (0.988)	−0.002 (−0.292)
$crgr\_b_{i,t-1}$	0.001 (0.195)	−0.039 (−1.111)	−0.000 (−0.060)	−0.031 (−0.909)	0.000 (−0.006)
$cltmo_{i,t-1}$	0.006*** (7.677)	0.029 (0.979)	0.006*** (7.585)	0.024 (0.828)	0.005*** (6.445)
$ibtl_{i,t-1}$	−0.484 (−1.298)	−0.016 (−0.195)	−0.019 (−0.507)	0.046 (0.564)	0.043 (−1.124)
$nstul_{i,t-1}$	−0.024 (−1.452)	−0.071* (−1.721)	0.010 (0.573)	0.029 (0.565)	0.003 (0.143)
$nietl_{i,t-1}$	−5.017*** (−4.294)	−8.753* (−1.727)	−4.504*** (−3.873)	−8.897* (−1.752)	−4.398*** (−3.790)
$nartl_{i,t-1}$	0.904*** (2.585)	1.073 (1.217)	0.966** (2.779)	1.165 (1.352)	0.797** (2.276)
$ncrtl_{i,t-1}$	1.366*** (2.591)	1.148 (0.424)	1.562*** (2.980)	2.809 (1.047)	1.504 (2.872)
$nirtl_{i,t-1}$	−0.215 (−0.056)	−0.168 (−0.167)	−0.206 (−0.543)	−0.571 (−0.058)	−0.158 (−0.416)
$tlgr_{i,t-1}$	0.013** (2.167)	0.032 (1.064)	0.014** (2.302)	0.033 (1.191)	0.013** (2.270)
$liqtll_{i,t-1}$	−0.097** (−2.211)	−0.280* (−1.854)	−0.110** (−2.537)	−0.283 (−1.871)	−0.104** (−2.400)
$dsize_{i,t}$	−0.073*** (−5.810)	−0.001 (0.041)	−0.077*** (6.187)	−0.003 (−0.234)	−0.075*** (−5.866)
$dcap_{i,t}$	0.016** (2.504)	−0.010 (−1.036)	0.005 (0.392)	0.027 (1.392)	−0.001 (−0.046)
stl			0.125*** (5.228)	0.289*** (3.315)	0.124** (5.208)
stl_bb					−0.728*** (−2.872)
$dcstl_{i,t-1}$			0.0484 (1.139)	−0.130*** (−2.151)	0.071** (1.577)
$dcstl\_bb_{i,t-1}$					0.137 (1.017)
constant	0.077 (1.609)	0.164 (1.011)	−0.018 (−0.353)	−0.0252 (0.153)	−0.006 (−0.126)
No. of obs.	2014	302	2014	302	2014
No. of groups	244	29	244	29	244
R-square:					
within	0.710	0.824	0.714	0.833	0.716
between	0.304	0.170	0.275	0.150	0.229
overall	0.410	0.586	0.383	0.561	0.342
F-value	236.83	66.09	218.07	63.06	199.78
Prob > F	0.000	0.000	0.000	0.000	0.000
corr(u_i, Xb)	−0.067	−0.081	−0.149	−0.158	−0.235

Table 6-A. Priority Insurance Model.

	Specification 1		Specification 2		Spec. 3
	All Banks (1)	Cantonal (2)	All Banks (3)	Cantonal (4)	All banks (5)
$gdpgr_t$	0.312***	0.147	0.071	−0.121	0.166
	(3.303)	(0.674)	(0.770)	(−0.562)	(0.018)
$chmm3m_t$	−1.322***	−1.521***	−1.161***	−1.345***	−1.093***
	(−13.789)	(−6.395)	(−12.425)	(−5.774)	(−12.001)
$cpindex_t$	0.396***	0.319**	0.305***	0.185	0.261***
	(7.607)	(2.432)	(6.037)	(1.2430)	(5.319)
$ktl_{i,t-1}$	−0.024	0.428*	−0.017	0.299	0.065
	(−0.380)	(1.693)	(−0.271)	(1.218)	(1.057)
$morta_{i,t-1}$	−0.096***	0.006	−0.078***	−0.032	−0.033
	(−3.357)	(0.064)	(−2.852)	(−0.350)	(−1.221)
$crgr_{i,t-1}$	−0.001	0.032	−0.003	0.024	−0.004
	(−0.200)	(1.184)	(−0.521)	(0.884)	(−0.796)
$crgr\_b_{i,t-1}$	−0.001	−0.046	0.001	−0.028	0.002
	(−0.162)	(−1.333)	0.144)	(−0.843)	(0.473)
$cltmo_{i,t-1}$	0.006***	0.032	0.002***	0.005	0.002
	(8.442)	(1.182)	(3.117)	(0.174)	(1.566)
$ibtl_{i,t-1}$	−0.018	−0.034	−0.001	−0.015	−0.119***
	(−0.496)	(−0.424)	(−0.014)	(−0.189)	(3.216)
$nstul_{i,t-1}$	−0.032***	−0.105***	−0.017**	−0.084**	−0.299
	(−2.730)	(−2.836)	(−1.528)	(−2.354)	(−2.644)
$nietl_{i,t-1}$	−4.982***	−8.439*	−2.579**	−4.716	−1.375
	(−4.247)	(−1.712)	(−2.262)	(−0.988)	(−1.235)
$nartl_{i,t-1}$	0.856**	1.095	0.823**	0.8439	0.651
	(2.440)	(1.254)	(2.423)	(0.996)	(1.960)
$nertl_{i,t-1}$	1.545***	0.678	0.865	−1.293	0.451
	(2.929)	(0.258)	(1.691)	(−0.497)	(0.900)
$nirtl_{i,t-1}$	−0.733*	−0.871	−1.062***	−0.757	−0.408
	(−1.770)	(−0.821)	(2.644)	(−0.706)	(−1.028)
$tlgr_{i,t-1}$	0.010*	0.038	0.011*	0.025	0.102
	(1.688)	(1.328)	(1.935)	(0.925)	(1.815)
$liqtll_{i,t-1}$	−0.106**	−0.303**	−0.098**	−0.276*	−0.065
	(−2.418)	(−2.028)	(−2.314)	(−1.918)	(−1.567)
$dpi_{i,t}$	0.012***	0.011	0.035***	0.060	0.036***
	(3.399)	(1.230)	(3.229)	(1.777)	(3.284)
$ns30b_{i,t-1}$			−0.037	0.217*	0.185***
			(0.620)	(1.958)	(2.762)
$ns30b\_bb_{i,t-1}$					−3.186***
					(−6.960)
$ns30b\_cb_{i,t-1}$					−0.046***
					(−4.284)
$ns30a_{i,t-1}$			0.670***	0.658***	0.597***
			(10.280)	(4.704)	(8.351)
$ns30a\_bb_{i,t-1}$					1.521***
					(3.277)
$ns30a\_cb_{i,t-1}$					0.286*
					(2.236)
$dpns30b_{i,t-1}$			−0.109	−0.393**	−0.130
			(−1.555)	(−2.029)	(−1.747)
$dpns30b\_bb_{i,t-1}$					1.345***
					(4.225)
$dpns30b\_cb_{i,t-1}$					−0.089
					(−0.747)
$dpns30a_{i,t-1}$			−0.600***	0.110	−0.080
			(−0.936)	(0.906)	(−1.086)
$dpns30a\_bb_{i,t-1}$					−1.188***
					(−2.434)
$dpns30a\_cb_{i,t-1}$		46			0.164***
					(1.123)
constant	0.153***	0.215	0.132***	0.321***	0.129***
	(2.927)	(1.342)	(2.598)	(02.061)	(2.620)
No. of obs.	2014	302	2014	302	2014

PCA IN INTERNATIONAL PRACTICE

Aristóbulo de Juan

INTRODUCTION

1. May I introduce myself by saying that I am not an economist or an academician, but a Doctor in Law, who has worked in senior positions in banking for the past 40 years. First, as a private commercial banker, then, as a bank Supervisor and Restructurer with the Spanish Central Bank. Then, as a Financial Advisor with the World Bank on Financial Sector Reform in emerging countries. And, for the last 14 years, as a consultant on the above areas in over 30 countries, including practically all of Latin America and former Socialist countries.
2. Let me say, first of all that the comments in this paper do not mean to be specifically applied to the U.S.A, but to any country that may consider gradual and prompt corrective action based on poor or non verified information or on regulatory forbearance.
3. The structure of this paper will be divided into 3 parts:
   - The applicability of effective PCA to countries with poor supervision,
   - Supervisory preconditions for successful PCA and
   - Some qualifications on moral hazard.
4. My initial reaction when I learn about sophisticated legislation and mechanisms in the above areas is one of admiration. Such is the case of FDICIA and, to use a more recent and fashionable example, the current Basle Committee efforts to improve international standards on capital adequacy. Then, I usually have second thoughts: This is real progress but. . . . passing a final judgement on them will have better grounds once these schemes are put to a real test. Additionally, I tend to consider whether

Prompt Corrective Action in Banking: 10 Years Later, Volume 14, pages 277–292.

ISBN: 0-7623-0987-3

those schemes might prove valid only for a few developed countries or also for the countries I usually work on.

5. This paper will not dwell on the numerous praiseworthy elements of FDICIA, such as the technical and political efforts made by the author to have the act passed, their fight against dilution of some of its "beef", a detailed description of the enacted FDICIA features and mechanisms, or the relevance of its achievements for the soundness of the American financial system. All those present here know better than I do and my contribution in this respect would certainly prove both poor and redundant.
6. On the contrary, this presentation means to play the devil's advocate, by telling about the situation I see in many countries, which would make legislation like FDICIA and the resulting PCA difficult to apply there. I do not mean to be negative, but just informative, as an implicit message to encourage bank Regulators, in both emerging and industrialized countries to achieve real transparency, through strong supervision, as a prerequisite for market mechanisms to operate effectively and for any scheme of PCA to be suited to the real situation. My remarks may also prove useful as a general warning against possible temptations to export certain formulas to countries before they have reached an appropriate supervisory context.

Applicability of Effective PCA to Countries With Poor Supervision

7. In my view, transparency in financial systems worldwide is conspicuous by its absence. Except in a small number of countries and in healthy banks. Actually, transparency is only spontaneously displayed by bankers when their institution is sound. When this is not the case, transparency is avoided by them through a score of procedures that are well known to Supervisors. Cosmetics or imaginative accounting prevail. As a result, analysts, markets, rating agencies, investment banks and even regulators, if basing their function just on the information published by banks, are often lead to take wrong stands and make late and often wrong and harmful decisions. Let alone the bankers moral hazard element that is prompted by late or no identification of solvency problems, as well as by the absence of adequate or timely corrective actions.
8. Of course, this happens, unless government Supervision is strong or is strengthened as a first priority. And I mean Supervision, in its broadest connotation, to mainly include what I consider clear priorities:

   (a) Strict regulation and its application,
   (b) On-site verification, as a crucial element,

(c) Timely and thorough Resolution of insolvent banks and, above all,
(d) Political will, both at the Regulator and at the top Government level.

This view is perhaps a truism and is probably shared by many. But I feel you never overemphasize it. In any case, this will be the core of my presentation.

9. I wish to stress that this view is based on my international hands-on experience in Supervision for 25 years, both in Spain and in a number of countries, where governments disclosed to me – or allowed me to disclose for them – the real figures of their banks, including their best and worst ones, both big and small. I learned to identify the dramatic difference between a reality of thorough insolvency and the "fiction", shown in public figures, through fake – and often tolerated – accounting. In such cases, governments would not identify the depth of problems through verification work, but only when flagrant iliquidity or fraud occur. Particularly if these situations become public knowledge and thus trigger the need for government action. Actually, in over 80% of the countries I have worked on, I have often seen Regulators and market players rating banks as "excellent" or "good", on the basis of a declared capital adequacy "well above" the minimum standards and a "low percentage" of bad loans, with a "satisfactory" coverage for potential losses in the books. Then, overnight they jump to deep insolvency. Early and gradual detection of problems by way of implementation of strict regulations and, thorough onsite work is conspicuous by its absence.
10. In such cases, the actual room for any effective scheme of PCA proves rather limited. Of course, the Regulator may apply lenient and/or gradual sanctions, because he concludes that such banks are not insolvent, but just slightly undercapitalized. This proves to be the wrong treatment for deep insolvency. Kind of treatment of cancer with aspirin. It is not that those sanctions bother, but they do not solve the real problem. Worse, they leave the bad bankers in place and allow the spiral of deep losses to continue. Actually, while these measures are being applied, banks go deeper into their misery and both moral hazard and the eventual cost of resolutions skyrocket. This happens particularly in emerging countries. And it is easier to understand. But it also happens in industrialized countries.
11. The cases of Japan, Scandinavia and France (Crédit Lyonnais), to mention just a few developed countries, are notorious cases where PCA would have proved ineffective:

- Japan's banking system has been insolvent for about a decade and still is. The Government has been reluctant to recognize it and has put in place ineffective and insufficient recapitalization mechanisms, while gradually unveiling increasing stocks of losses that, as of to-day, are not yet realistic enough. Could PCA serve any purpose in the midst of unveiled insolvency?

- The Scandinavian countries suffered a systemic and dramatic crisis in the early 1990s. Bad loans were the main cause, but they had not been identified before the crisis blew out. Actually, on-site examination left much to be desired. And PCA could have hardly been applied to banks that were supposedly in good health.
- Crédit Lyonnais in France was also a dramatic case. A State-owned bank, with an accelerated growth policy, and a risky lending policy proved to be considered, sequentially, as a good bank, a problem bank, an undercapitalized bank, an insolvent but too big to fail bank and a deeply insolvent bank. Recapitalization and restructuring were first very modest and real losses were only unveiled gradually and slowly, which lead the bank to accumulate new losses. Only after six years of judicial investigation, Crédit Lyonnais was addressed as a problem bank and was thoroughly recapitalized, precisely to prepare it for privatization. The losses hit a record in bank history. Where was Supervision? Was there much room for PCA?

12. This scenario happens in contexts of poor regulation, of course. But it also happens in countries with just reasonable regulation or even with good regulation, when it is not properly applied. This may be mainly due to:
    (a) Lack of skilled human resources.
    (b) Lack of good supervisory or verification procedures.
    (c) Lack of effective resolution mechanisms, a situation that leaves "zombie" banks alive, while pretending they have been treated.
    (d) Lack of supervisory leadership or political will.
    (e) Pressure from lobbies or governments.

Some Supervisory Preconditions for Successful PCA

13. I have selected here a series of major flaws that are an obstacle for effective PCA, as I have seen them in numerous countries. I also give some hints to solve them. These hints refer to the areas of Regulation, Supervision, Resolution and Institutional strengthening. And they may be of use even if reasonable legislation and mechanisms in those areas are in place, but have serious gaps.
14. In the area of *Regulation*, four concepts are to be highlighted: Entry policy, Capital, Assets classification and Accounting systems.

14.1. Enhancing competition through the entry of new banks or new bankers in the market is a must. But a number of countries have applied too liberal policies of access to the financial market. As a result, a large number of new banks are shaky or have been set up by businessmen or enterprises as a treasury operation. This was typically the case of former Socialist countries, where banks were often created with a small capital. And were often used to collect deposits from the public and allocate them primarily to the businesses or enterprises owned by or related to the owners. When these kind of weak banks fail, they are seldom addressed by the governments and the market ends up crowded with "insolvent inviable banks", which, among other things, cause a serious damage to sound competition. Therefore, the standard key requirements for sound entry should be imposed: high initial capital, clearly identified origin of the capital, as well as fit and proper bankers. Also there needs to be a policy whereby proper symmetry is established between liberal entry, if this is the case, and tough exit, i.e. closure and liquidation, as a priority.

14.2. Having a good level of capital is also a must. Actually, most governments and banks have accepted the present Basle Committee guidelines, whereby a bank should have a minimum capital ratio of 8% of its risk-weighted assets. This allows for a reasonable degree of soundness and sets an equal footing for national and international competition. New guidelines are being worked out by the Basle Committee and are expected to come into force in 2006. The problem with whatever formal guidelines is that, in a number of countries, Regulators and bankers claim that their banks have capital ratios of 8%, 10% or even 15%, but pay little attention to the quality of their assets and to the subsequent need for additional provisions for losses. A situation that would erode or turn the equity capital in the books fictitious. Actually, what happens with a bank that claims to have a 10% capital adequacy, for instance, but has an undisclosed loss of 30% of its assets? Its real capital level would be minus 20%, the bank would actually be insolvent and should be recapitalised or closed. Gradual corrective action would prove highly insufficient if the situation is undisclosed, since the absence of flows from non performing assets would keep the stock of losses deepening. The need for thorough on-site verification is obvious.

14.3. Some regulators may be self-complaisant: "we do have a good system of asset classification and provisioning, according to international standards: it is based on service performance, i.e. if a loan is past-due, it is classified and provisioned for." Correct. But if loans are not classified according to the repayment capacity of the borrower, irrespective of whether the loan is past-due or otherwise, the above regulation is no good. Why? Because most banks in difficulties do not disclose their losses to the supervisors or to the public. And when they have large bad loans close to maturity and do not expect repayment, they roll them over, more or less indefinitely, and in a variety of modalities, in order to avoid the accounting treatment of past-due situations, which would disclose the borrowers default and, as a result, the bank's insolvency. Experience says that the worst loans, those that can make a bank go under, are most of the times classified as current loans, not as past-due loans. Supervisors should therefore examine thoroughly "good" loans on the books rather than bad loans, which are already being dealt. One could extrapolate this rule of thumb and say that "good" banks should be examined more closely that banks already classified as "bad". In this respect, softening supervision of "well capitalized" banks in countries with poor supervision might not be adequate. Regulations on assets classification and their application should not only classify loans based on the borrower's repayment capacity. They should also ignore ineffective or insufficient collateral and should also avoid accepting income recognition for capitalized interest in roll-over operations. Otherwise regulations may allow for banks to look solvent and profitable, through formal compliance of such legal context, while being insolvent and unprofitable in reality.

14.4. A prerequisite for a good assessment of solvency and a good asset classification is a good accounting system. Many countries do not apply consolidated accounting or supervision, ignore potential problems in off-shore establishments, do not require coverage of goodwill, consider fiscal credit as an asset even in situations of current losses, and so on. Without rigorous accounting standards and its proper application, the supervisory framework and bank analysis may become an exercise of "garbage in garbage out." Establishing a proper diagnosis of banks may prove impossible, both for the regulator and for market players. And, if ordinary regulations are satisfactory, forbearance through special regulations or suspension of their implementation should be avoided.

15. In the area of *Supervision* proper, the following aspects can be highlighted:

15.1. In practice, a number of supervisory mechanisms are off-site oriented, i.e. based on just the banks' reports. However, on-site verification is a key element for effective supervision. As said above, insolvent bankers will tend not to disclose their problems. And their reports, if unchecked, will be meaningless or even misleading. But if, additionally to off-site supervision, examination teams are also in place, the number of examiners should be sufficient, their skills satisfactory and their remuneration competitive, in order to prevent corruption. Contrary to what some say, my view is that, good supervision is seldom too costly, if compared with the distortions and disasters to be financed, when supervision does not unveil problems at an early stage.

15.2. External audits are necessary but not necessarily sufficient as supplementary supervisory procedure. In a number of countries, Governments may claim that their auditing system operates according to international practices. But auditors often work in a context of poor local laws and regulations they consider themselves obliged to apply, rather than international standards. Also, competition is such that core audit work is often ascribed to junior and low-cost auditors. Communication between external auditors and supervisors is not always allowed for or may not happen at all. Lastly, what if auditors are not independent? Enron and other recent or not so recent stories should not be forgotten. Worse, I have seen inaccurate or misleading audit reports be used by the previous owners in court, as a defense weapon against supervisors when the supervisor tries to apply its enforcement powers, for remedial action purposes, and the audit reports are more lenient than the supervisors'.

15.3. Last but not least, political will on the part of the government and a sense of realism to address the problems is perhaps the most indispensable precondition. Political or social reasons, lack of legal safety for the Regulator and lack of fiscal resources are typical obstacles. Vested interests handled by lobbies or directly by some bankers may also be present. In these cases, the problems are not solved, the system – which took a great effort to be set up – is discredited and, even worse, a certain complicity may develop between the bankers, the auditors and the government itself not to disclose the reality. Because doing so may prove costly, unpopular, contrary to strong interests or make political parties lose votes.

16. Effective mechanisms to deal with problem *bank Resolution* should be in place. If that is not the case, when problems are unveiled and brought to the desk of the Regulator, solutions will be delayed, unsatisfactory or not applied at all. As a result, those supervisory mechanisms will be discredited and sometimes even corrupted.
    16.1. Proper institutions and financial mechanisms for Resolution – be they ordinary or extraordinary – should also be in place. Otherwise, insolvency is likely to be addressed in an improvised manner and/or half-way. As a result, the same banks may have to be resolved several times, at a compound cost. Sometimes, after poor resolution, the message is sent by the government to the markets that full restructuring of the system has taken place. In these cases, governments become captive of their own message and are unable to act energetically for a few years, since their banks were supposed to be in good health. Bankers can even blackmail governments. Cosmetic accounting and further insolvency may be the outcome. PCA becomes unthinkable or even counterproductive.
    16.2. If a bank is deeply insolvent, the shareholders do not recapitalize it and the government decides not to close it, for fear of contagion, as is the case of T.B.T.F. banks, the bank should be thoroughly restructured, in terms of capital, change in management and change in ownership. Recapitalization through capital injection and/or carving out of bad assets, should be full, so as to cover the stock of losses and generate positive flows. This is very seldom the case in numerous countries. In this context, some recapitalization practices that form part of their conventional wisdom should be avoided. Let us elaborate briefly on the following policies.

    - Mergers of banks, for the sake of merger, without any other therapy. In actual practice, mergers are only a solution to insolvency, if and when the merging banks are well capitalized – or recapitalized, if need be – and one of them, at least, has a strong management team with the necessary skills and depth to take over the other partner successfully. Otherwise, the problems existing in those banks prior to the merger will compound. Let alone the fact that mergers, even between well capitalized and well run banks, undergo a cumbersome process of mutual adjustment and fight for power, that affects the banks and may even paralyze them in the initial years. An exception to this rule could be mergers where one of the banks is large and solvent and the other is insolvent but very small. In this case, the losses of the small bank could be diluted in the larger bank, without a major damage.

- Assets revaluation to build up new reserves. In inflation times, in a number of countries, banks are authorized to revalue their assets at market value and create the equivalent income and reserves, without any tax impact. This measure allows banks to increase their equity, accountingwise, but this proves an obstacle to enforcement of real capital increases, commensurate with the growth of the balance sheet in inflationary terms. Here also, if the bank is deeply insolvent, this policy does not improve the flows. Only real capital injection or replacement of bad assets with good ones will do.
- Lasting liquidity support – by way of last resort or special loans – should also be avoided. This is – treating a solvency problem as if it were a liquidity problem. In cases of deep insolvency, only huge and disproportionate amounts of liquidity, long-term and at a very low cost would allow the bank to obtain enough yield to write-off the past losses and generate new profits over time. Since this proves impossible in practical terms, the lasting liquidity support will keep the bank afloat but, all or a part of the new liquidity will probably be used to pay both financial and operational costs and the stock of losses will continue to accumulate, even if current losses diminish. In the end, if the bank is closed, the liquidity support will have been lost. If the bank is restructured, new amounts of money will have to be injected in terms of capital. Additionally, in the process of liquidity support, a negative incentive is being given to the bad managers that are being supported: the higher the losses you make, the higher the assistance you get.
- Simple debt rescheduling does not help out insolvent banks, but is a frequent regulatory proviso to avoid reserves on the original debt or even to allow for reserves to be reversed. Debt rescheduling postpones maturity and foreclosure and improves the liquidity situation of the borrower, but it does not improve its solvency situation, unless creditor banks and other creditors, such as suppliers, write-off their debt or part of it . . . And, also unless the borrowers undergo a serious simultaneous process of adjustment. If this is not the case, the bank does not improve its solvency or its liquidity situation, since it agrees to postpone foreclosure and may even extend new loans. Relying on this kind of regulatory

forbearance in the hope that the economy will recover often proves a serious mistake, since insolvency normally grows faster than the impact of potential economic recovery.

- Insufficient recapitalization is the most frequent case in the countries I know. Recapitalization may prove insufficient for several reasons:

  (a) The size of the loss is miscalculated,
  (b) The volume of capital or clean up injections does not suffice to make up for the past stock of losses,
  (c) The volume of assets cleaned up is adequate, but they are bought by the government at less than face value, thus leaving the stock of losses, or part of it, within the bank,
  (d) The capital injected or the funding of the purchase of assets is done through government securities with a low interest rate, that does not allow for the bank to make a spread that can generate positive flows.

These situations are very frequent. The bank has not been properly recapitalized and, again, gradual sanctions make little dent in the bank problems.

- Zero coupon bonds are often designed by government to postpone fiscal impacts. But they prove to be just a financial gimmick when provided to solve the serious liquidity problems of deeply insolvent banks. Banks are recapitalized through capital increases or through purchase of assets that are paid with zero coupon bonds. These securities, upon maturity, but not before, pay the total amount of interest accrued to cover the book value of the assets bought. But, how does this instrument improve the cash-flows that are deeply negative and work on a compound basis?. This financial instrument may prove interesting in other context, but not when dealing with deep insolvency.
- Swap of borrowers debt for equity. In a number of countries, some advocate for this arrangement, as a modality of financial restructuring. They argue that: (a) The bank improves its solvency situation, since it exchanges a bad loan for ownership rights; (b) The borrower reduces its debt; (c) The bank can participate in the restructuring of the borrower, as a co-owner, thus improving the quality of its asset. But these arguments do not necessarily prove true. Actually, if the borrower is in trouble and does not take any other adjustment actions, the bank's assets related to that

borrower, be them loans or shares, may have a similar quality and should be provisioned for, practically to the same extent. As to the banks' role in the borrowers restructuring, international experience says that most of the times, bankers do not necessarily prove to be good entrepreneurs or good managers of industrial or service concerns. Also, when a banker has a participation in the capital of a borrower company, it will find itself under strong pressure to increase the volume of loans to that borrower, even if the situation of the latter remains as difficult as or worse than before.

- Simple recapitalization without management change. If owners or governments recapitalize a bank, even fully, but leave in place the same management that caused the bank's insolvency, the problems are very likely to repeat themselves: best practices will not prevail, bad borrowers are likely to get further loans, recovery policies will remain ineffective, operational costs will remain uncut and internal controls will be as unreliable as before.

17. *Institutional strengthening* may prove no good in itself if it is applied to deeply insolvent banks without undertaking simultaneous or previous recapitalization action. The best systems, computer technology or sophisticated management practices will prove useless to reconstruct the bank's solvency. The best managers in the world would be overwhelmed by insolvency, which keeps growing deeper and deeper, if not treated financially.

Moral Hazard

18. One of the objectives of FDICIA enactment was to avoid moral hazard that had lead banks to take excessive risks and also avoid Regulators' delay to impose appropriate regulatory sanctions. Actually, there are cases where deposits are protected by high or no coverage limits, be it as per the existing legislation or by "de facto" treatment of insolvency. It is obvious that, in situations like that, moral hazard operates: depositors do not have proper incentives to escape danger and keep depositing their savings in their bank, whatever the quality. And those deposits ensure regular funding and facilitate the bankers' risky behavior. Agreed, no question about it. But, having said that, I would like to qualify the concept of moral hazard, from a practical viewpoint.
19. Logically, Regulators should do their best to avoid moral hazard or limit it to a minimum. But, sometimes, a general fear about the risk of moral hazard in the financial system sounds to me unrealistic, seen as a concept

that indiscriminately haunts a number of aspects of bank regulation and particularly of bank resolution. I feel that qualifying this topic may clarify when moral hazard is a real danger and when it is not. Or when it is just a lesser evil. And it may prove relevant for the treatment of banks with a capital adequacy below – or even far below – 2% as per FDICIA table, or in the very frequent case where Regulators have to face overnight the reality of deep insolvency and illiquidity. Almost taken by surprise. Actually, when decisions on bank resolution have to be made urgently in a government's board room late in the night, stemming "the bleeding" becomes a first and foremost objective and avoiding moral hazard tends to be a second priority. I will distinguish among several kinds of moral hazard: bankers', depositors', creditors', borrowers' and supervisors'.

Bankers' Moral Hazard

20. Bad bankers can be led to take excessive risks by making risky placements or risky off-balance sheet operations, to incur fraudulent practices or to remain "physically" liquid by paying high interest rates on their liabilities. Particularly so if they are in trouble and want to gamble for resurrection. This will happen if they are aware that the regulatory framework is weak and they have nothing to fear. Poor regulation and supervision make also possible for bank insolvency, connected lending and fraud to go unnoticed. And the damage will not be prevented or undone by fines, dividend suspension, mandatory capital write-offs, mandatory capital increases, closure of banks, etc., if these measures are untimely. To this effect, poor regulation and supervision – probably to a larger extent than full deposit insurance – do foster bankers' moral hazard. On the contrary, if the regulatory framework is strong, it will be possible for the government to identify and unveil problems early, to impose gradual provisioning and prompt and effective sanction, make transparency possible, close banks, write off capital and force the owners and managers to leave the bank. And bankers will feel a credible threat that all this may happen. They will know that they are likely to lose their investment, their financial instrument, their social pre-eminence and may even be taken to court or to prison. If this is the case, bankers' moral hazard would play no role. This is why this paper emphasizes strong supervision as a precondition for effective PCA.

- Full deposit protection certainly leads to moral hazard, especially if it is explicit. Ironically, this may also be the case when there is no deposit insurance at all, because such a situation often leads to full implicit protection. Be it explicit or implicit, full or high protection makes it difficult for Regulators to close banks. It proves too costly. In fact, in a number of countries with full insurance, there is a tradition that banks are never closed. Bad bankers do not care too much about depositors, but about staying in place and be legally safe. But, if they are aware that their bank is very unlikely to be closed, they will certainly be tempted to embark on risky practices. On the contrary, limited and explicit deposit insurance is no panacea, but it does not necessarily foster bankers' moral hazard, because it makes bank closure easy, and the threat of government intervention, as described above, becomes more credible to bad bankers.

- Does bank restructuring foster moral hazard? If restructuring consists of just recapitalization, while the old owners and managers are left in place, it certainly fosters bankers' moral hazard. If recapitalization is delayed, more or less indefinitely, for lack of funds or faulty institutional arrangements, moral hazard will also exist. But, if restructuring is timely and capital write-off goes hand-in-hand with the removal of owners, boards and managers, bankers' discipline will be reinforced. Bankers will be very careful about the way they run their bank. One can see no reason for moral hazard. The threat of government intervention, here again, becomes more credible. The "paper tiger" (the Regulator) becomes a real tiger This was clearly the case in Spain since 1980, where inception of a Deposit Guarantee Fund, with restructuring powers, became key to bankers' self discipline. Until today.
- As for last resort lending, if it is short term and moderate in size – just enough to cover occasional liquidity gaps which are normal in any banking system – there is no moral hazard in last resort lending. But if the size of this kind of support grows indefinitely and the maturity of the loans is indefinitely rolled over, there will be bankers' moral hazard. The bad banker knows that the Central Bank becomes more and more committed to bail him out, and his bargaining position becomes stronger. "Come on". "Close the bank now, if you dare", he may hint. The bad bankers and/or their subordinates may even be tempted to use those funds for their personal interests.

Depositors' Moral Hazard

If regulation and supervision are not capable of unveiling problems promptly, if deposit protection – "de jure" or "de facto" – covers 100% of deposits and if governments never close banks, depositors will be led to place their money in those banks that pay the highest interest, with no further investigation. These are normally the worst banks. This is moral hazard. But, if strong regulation and supervision unveils insolvency promptly, if deposit insurance is limited to modest depositors and if insolvency leads to either bank closure or bank restructuring, there may be no moral hazard. There is one exception: protected depositors may be led to make fragmented placements in different banks, just up to the protected limit. But this is probably a lesser evil. At any rate, are depositors ever in a position to tell a good bank from a bad bank? If we take into consideration that rating agencies, investment bankers, Multilateral Financial Organizations and even supervisors, who have access to tons of information, do make serious diagnosis mistakes, can we expect depositors to make the right judgement?

21. What about depositors protection in case of bank restructuring, through the continuity of the bank, a purchase and assumption or a bridge or good-bad bank arrangement? There might be some moral hazard. But, if restructuring is decided on a case-by-case consideration and closure remains a possibility every time insolvency is identified, moral hazard will be mitigated, because uninsured depositors are still at risk. At any rate, if restructuring is considered to be necessary in order to avoid contagion, this kind of potential moral hazard may also be the lesser of two evils.

Creditors' Moral Hazard

22. What is said about uninsured depositors is also valid for creditors in case of closure, when the creditors are protected through modalities of bank restructuring that allow for the continuity of banks. But if, as a rule, creditors are required to write off all or a part of their subordinated debt or their credits, as part of the restructuring package, or are forced to swap them for longer-term debt or capital, creditors' moral hazard will be clearly mitigated.
23. In systemic crises, particularly in large economies or regions, lending of last resort also may foster moral hazard for creditors, if given in large amounts and very long term. Creditors will probably end up recovering their loans with their high-risk premium and assume that next time the same mechanism will apply. They will keep making risky loans to risky banks in the hope that the risk premium will cover the risk. Eliminating moral hazard in this scenario seems very difficult. But some suggestions to limit it could be: make it clear that things may be different next time; try to make creditors take a certain hit; and do close banks, when you conclude that they are not viable even if they received last resort lasting assistance.

Borrowers' Moral Hazard

24. A good regulatory framework will lead bankers to properly classify and duly provision bad debts, as well as other bad assets or potential losses. This will force them, in turn, to stop lending to bad borrowers and reinforce recovery, which will constitute a moral hazard deterrent for borrowers. Limited deposit insurance, which facilitates bank closure, as well as judicial recovery or liquidation of bad assets, may also be a deterrent. Restructuring will also deter borrowers' moral hazard, if assets recovery and liquidation is left with the restructured bank under new and strong management or with a specialized, efficient and strong recovery institution.

But if loan concentration, assets classification, provisioning and income recognition requirements are soft, there will be borrowers' moral hazard. Also, if asset recovery, in case of restructuring, is left with previous bankers, with the Central Bank (often a poor recover) or even with a specialized institution with no proper staffing and incentives to recover, then, there will also be moral hazard for the borrowers. They will ask for more and more loans, even beyond their commercial or investment needs. High lending rates would not worry them, since they are in a strong position to avoid being seriously required to service their debt. Borrowers' moral hazard also occurs when political interference puts pressure on banks to be lax on recovery of certain loans, which happens very frequently – but not only – with state-owned banks, with state-owned enterprises or where cronyism prevails.

A most dangerous way to borrowers' moral hazard occurs when governments impose mandatory write-offs or moratoria on banks vis-à-vis their borrowers' debts, across-the-board. Uruguay in the 1980s and the 1990s and Argentina at present are clear examples.

Regulator's Moral Hazard

25. There is no reason for Regulators' moral hazard, in a context where they are – legally and de facto – independent, regulation is strong, examiners are skilled, enforcement action is effective and exit policies and mechanisms are realistic. But, if there is no legal safety for Regulators, no political will or no proper policies, no proper institutions or funding to "clean up the decks", no matter how good the rest of the regulatory and supervisory framework may be, Regulators will have negative incentives to identify and address problem banks or insolvency situations. This scenario

is very frequent in many countries. Because, if Regulators identify the real problems, "the baby" will remain in their lap with no solution ahead, and they will run very serious risks, including legal ones. There is also Regulator's moral hazard when they were associated with the problems in the past, because of forbearance, delayed action or just negligence. If so, they may be tempted to avoid unveiling the problems, for their mistakes will then become apparent.

OTHER PAPERS BY THE AUTHOR

His written material includes the following papers, published by different institutions:

From Good Bankers to Bad Bankers (describing management deterioration as a major element of financial crises). World Bank. E.D.I. (Economic Development Institute).

Does bank insolvency matter? and what to do about it. World Bank. E.D.I. (Economic Development Institute).

Financial Stabilization and Prudential Regulation. Westview Press (USA), sponsored by Yale University and the Ford Foundation.

Linkages between Bank Privatization and Bank Restructuring (C.E.E.P.). European Center of Public Enterprises, Brussels.

Linkages between Bank Privatization and Bank Restructuring in Spain. Pending Publication. World Bank.

False Friends in Banking Reform. B.E.R.D. (European Bank of Reconstruction and Development).

The Roots of Banking Crises: Micro-Economic issues and issues of Supervision and Regulation. I.D.B. (Interamerican Development Bank).

Clearing the Decks: experience in banking crises resolution. World Bank.

WHEN DOES FINANCIAL LIBERALIZATION MAKE BANKS RISKY? AN EMPIRICAL EXAMINATION OF ARGENTINA, CANADA AND MEXICO

William C. Gruben, Jahyeong Koo and Robert R. Moore

ABSTRACT

In the literature on systemic banking crises, two common themes are:

(1) lack of market discipline encourages risky lending; and
(2) financial liberalization or privatization leads to risky lending.

However, there is evidence to suggest that neither financial liberalization nor weak market discipline always precedes risky lending. We test for depositor discipline and, separately for post-liberalization or post-privatization risky lending in Argentina, Canada, and Mexico. In the countries without market discipline, lending risk increases significantly in the wake of liberalization. Where depositors discipline banks, banks neither behave riskily nor does their risk increase in the wake of privatization.

Prompt Corrective Action in Banking: 10 Years Later, Volume 14, pages 293–312.

ISBN: 0-7623-0987-3

I. INTRODUCTION

In the literature on systemic banking crises (viz. Calomiris, 1990; de la Cuadra & Valdés, 1992; Kaminksy & Reinhart, 1996; McKinnon & Pill, 1996), two of the most common themes are:

(1) Lack of market (depositor) discipline on the banking system – which is typically blamed on government guarantees including deposit insurance – encourages risky lending that ultimately disrupts the financial system.
(2) Financial liberalization or privatization often results in regulatory breakdowns and market share struggles that lead to risky lending that ultimately disrupts the financial system.

Nevertheless, while risky lending and financial disruptions occur from time to time in many countries, these events are neither continuous nor eternal components of most countries' financial landscapes. Blowups happen, but most of the time most bankers go about their business uneventfully. Similarly, not every financial liberalization in every country precedes a bubble and then a bust. Sometimes a regulatory transition is just a regulatory transition.

In sum, on the one hand there do seem to be connections of market indiscipline and of financial liberalization to what McKinnon and Pill (1996) call "overborrowing" or what – as bank regulators – we view as risky overlending. On the other hand, the sporadic appearances of these connections ought to suggest that they are conditional on something else.

This paper relies on what could be called circumstantial econometrics to suggest one type of conditionality. The econometrics are circumstantial in the sense that – with a sample of only three countries – we cannot unequivocally prove the conditionality we postulate. Nevertheless, in our model, risky bank behavior turns out to materialize just where and when we would expect it if it were indeed persistently conditional on the absence of market discipline.

We model market discipline during crisis periods in the Argentine, Canadian, and Mexican banking systems by relating depositor responses at such times to bank asset quality, capitalization and to other factors reflecting asset and liability characteristics. The degree of banking market discipline turns out to vary greatly among these three countries.

Having identified the degree of market discipline on banks in each country, we test for the proclivity of banks to take on risk in the wake of liberalization or privatization. We use empirical models of market contestability that can determine if and when financial institutions operate at output levels where marginal cost exceeds marginal revenue before or after regulatory or ownership regime changes. Running where marginal cost exceeds marginal revenue is a statistical result consistent with a struggle for market share. Indeed, we claim that banks run in this way when some present value calculation motivates them to countenance taking short-term losses in expectation of longer-term gains.

Our results suggest a negative and direct connection between the degree of depositor-imposed discipline on a nation's banks and their predisposition towards risky lending in the wake of liberalizations or privatization.

II. MARKET DISCIPLINE: THE ROLE OF DEPOSITORS

Although government guarantees are commonly blamed for breakdowns (or the simple absence) of discipline upon bankers by depositors, the use of direct measures of government guarantees to identify such breakdowns is difficult. The reason is, depositors may perceive implicit government guarantees even when explicit guarantees do not exist.

In the literature on moral hazard and depositor discipline, bankers are typically imagined to know beforehand how much depositors will (or will not) discipline them – punishing (or not punishing) the bankers with bank runs in retaliation for poor performance. Bankers' perceptions of the punishments they will receive for a bad outcome of risky lending is accordingly supposed to affect how riskily bankers will lend. If bankers do not expect any or much punishment, the good outcomes that can occur from risky lending will motivate them to lend more riskily, even though they know bad outcomes are possible. It follows that if lenders perceive that depositors believe implicit guarantees exist, lenders will lend more riskily in anticipation that depositors will not punish them for it, even in the absence of explicit guarantees.[1]

To test for depositor-imposed market discipline on banks in Argentina, Canada and Mexico, we apply an empirical model of depositor growth for each country during a period of financial stress.[2] The examination corrects for the effect of other links between deposit flows and asset quality. Consistent with a narrative in which depositors may or may not flee banks whose assets have begun to sour, this model uses bank-by-bank data to examine bank-by-bank characteristics that might aggravate or temper depositor reactions. These include a capitalization ratio to capture a bank's capital adequacy, a bank's share of total assets to account for too-big-to-fail perceptions, and a measure of liability composition.[3] However, very detailed analyses using numerous financial measures are not practical because of limitations on the number of financial institutions. Adequate data were available for only sixteen Mexican banks. In the case of Canada, a full set of data (particularly past-due loan data) was available for only the six largest banks (although it should be noted that they account for 90% of total Canadian bank assets).[4]

An examination of the results (Table 1) linking deposit growth rates and bank characteristics in Argentina, Canada, and Mexico offers large differences across countries. Depositors exerted significant discipline on Argentine banks but not on Canadian or Mexican banks. In all models, the dependent variable (DEPGRP) is the percentage change in inflation-adjusted deposits.

Recall that the examination period chosen for each country is one of financial stress. For Argentina and Mexico, the examination is performed for the *Tequila Effect* period of December 1994–June 1995. For Canada the percentage change is year-over-year for 1984, 1985 and 1986, so as to capture the stresses leading to the first Canadian bank closures (in 1985 and 1986) in more than six decades.[5] PDL_i/TA_i is past-due loans as a percentage of total assets, included to measure the quality of the asset portfolio. EQ_i/TA_i is equity capital as a percentage of total assets, which is included to measure the ability to maintain solvency in case of financial losses. $Ln(TA_i/TA)$ is the logarithm of the quotient of total assets for a given bank divided by the sum of all bank assets, so as to account for too-big-to-fail perceptions. DEP_i/L_i is deposits as a

Table 1. Deposit Growth and Asset Quality In Three Western Hemisphere Nations.

	Argentina	Canada	Mexico
Constant	–67.546**	–30.600	–54.999*
	(–2.17)	(–0.24)	(–1.82)
PDL_i/TA_i	–1.052***	–0.060	0.473
	(–3.43)	(–0.01)	(0.12)
EQ_i/TA_i	0.821*	–6.366	–0.888
	(1.90)	(–1.65)	(–0.25)
$Ln(TA_i/TA)$	2.978	–9.389	–8.376
	(0.63)	(–1.33)	(–1.27)
DEP_i/L_i	1.075***	0.504	0.386
	(4.20)	(0.38)	(0.66)
R^2	0.770	0.348	0.255
Prob(F-Stat)	0.0001	0.2027	0.4751
No. of Observations	20	18	16

Note: the dependent variable is the percentage change in the inflation-adjusted deposit growth rate of bank i. PDL_i/TA_i is bank i's past-due loan as a percentage of total assets. EQ_i/TA_i is bank i's equity capital as a percentage of total assets. $Ln(TA_i/TA)$ is the log of bank i's total assets over the sum of total assets of the banks examined. DEP_i/L_i is bank i's deposits as a percentage of total liabilities. *t*-statistics in parentheses, based on approximate standard errors (***: significant at 0.01 level, **: significant at 0.05 level, *: significant at 0.1 level).

percentage of total liabilities, which we include to control for the potential influence of liability composition on depositor behavior.

In the cases of Mexico and Canada, none of the explanatory variables is individually significant at the 10% level. They are also not jointly significant at the 0.10 level although, with an F-value level of significance of 0.2027, Canada's joint significance level is closer to an acceptable level than Mexico's 0.4751. In contrast, the model's explanatory power for Argentina is highly statistically significant at the 0.0001 level.

Despite our concerns about implicit guarantees, the degree of depositor discipline among the three countries turns out to be inversely related to the maximum level of deposits that are explicitly insured in each country. While Mexico's deposit insurance was virtually open-ended, that of Canada was limited to $60,000 (Canadian dollars), while Argentina's maximum was $10,000 or $20,000 (U.S.) depending on type of deposit.[6] Accordingly, in our model, a bank's asset quality least explains its deposit growth in Mexico (the country with the most explicit guarantees) and most fully explains deposit growth in Argentina (the country with the lowest level of explicit guarantees). Indeed, for Mexico the effect of asset quality weakness (PDL_i/TA_i, past-due loans divided by total assets) on deposit growth takes on a perversely positive value, although the t-value of 0.12 (0.904 level of significance) is far from significant. Canada's PDL_i/TA_i coefficient is also insignificant, but the negative sign is as expected. In contrast to Mexico or Canada, the relation between asset quality weakness and deposit growth in Argentina is not only negative but significant. That is, when asset quality weakens, depositors withdraw their funds.

Results for Argentina differ noticeably from those of Mexico and Canada not only because of the model's joint significance and because of the significance of the past due loans as a share of total assets variable (PDL_i/TA_i), but also because of the significance and signs of the equity and deposit-share-of-liabilities variables. If depositors are very sensitive to a bank's capitalization, and if they are more likely to remove their funds from a poorly capitalized bank than from a well-capitalized institution, the coefficient on EQ_i/TA_i (equity as a percentage of total assets) ought to be positive and significant. For Mexico and Canada, the coefficient was negative and insignificant. For Argentina, the coefficient was positive and significant at the 0.08 level. In sum, for Argentina but not for Canada and Mexico, the results support the view that depositors discriminated based on the financial condition of banks.[7] That is, during stress periods, depositors disciplined Argentine banks but did not significantly (if at all) discipline Canadian banks and did not discipline Mexican banks at all according to the present criterion.[8]

III. FINANCIAL LIBERALIZATION, MARKET SHARE STRUGGLES, AND RISKY BEHAVIOR

Having established that banks receive more market discipline in some countries than others, we now test for conditions under which banks lend more riskily in countries with less discipline than in countries with more discipline. Recall that, in testing for market discipline, we chose periods when each country's banking system was under stress. But in testing for risky behavior, we chose periods when there is reason to suspect that each country's banks might be particularly subject to temptations to take risks. Since the periods we chose immediately followed either a financial liberalization or privatization, it is useful to clarify why we think such temptations occurred then.

Large changes in legal regimes for banks can signify changed opportunities to develop various categories of markets. The liberalization or privatization of a banking sector is typically followed by a large increase in liabilities – as banks are permitted to take on liabilities at the rate the market will bear instead of at what the government permits – and by rapid increases in bank assets (Gorton, 1992). In a narrative that resonates particularly with privatization episodes de Juan (1995) notes that on a bank-by-bank level, when new owners take control of a bank, they commonly increase lending relative to the value of equity capital or the deposit base. Whether or not liberalizations and related rapid loan expansions are followed by large increases in loan defaults – as they typically are in Gorton (1992), de Juan (1995), Kaminsky and Reinhart (1996), and McKinnon and Pill (1994) – a common adjunct to financial liberalization is markedly increased competition in the banking system (International Monetary Fund, 1993).

As liabilities expand and banks seek to match them with new assets, not only the quantity but the *quality* of assets changes – and in more than one sense of the term. First, more assets sometimes means much more of certain types of assets. Mexico's newly privatized banks focused on consumer markets far more than when those same banks had been publicly owned.

But asset quality also often changes in the sense of the other meaning of the term *quality*. Under this same paradigm of financial liberalization, after a repressed financial system is liberalized, banks cannot supply intermediation services efficiently because they lack expertise and adequate technology (Kaufman, 1998). Banks' portfolios become riskier because banks cannot evaluate the riskiness of loans and higher real interest rates under the new regime. Lenders lack past distributions on which to base their assessments.

These depictions of post liberalization/privatization banking markets are consistent with a more general theoretical literature on strategic interaction among firms in growing markets where investment and growth of the firm are constrained by physical factors (which could include qualified personnel) or financial factors. In this literature, firms make pre-emptive investments as part of a struggle for market share (Spence, 1979). This struggle for market share in a suddenly new market environment may be seen as key to the onset of the high-risk bank behavior on which much of the current literature on financial and exchange rate crises is based.

These same depictions of post liberalization/privatization banking markets are also consistent with studies of consumer behavior in which, for example, a credit card holder typically develops a long-standing affinity for the first credit card he or she receives (Wall Street Journal, 1996). That is, banks fighting for market share may be willing to engage in riskier strategies in newly opened markets (for example, consumer credit markets in Mexico in the early 1990s), than they might in a more mature market, for the simple reason that the long-term stream of rewards might be correspondingly greater to survivors who practiced pre-emptive behavior.

At some point, or perhaps at several, since the beginning of the 1980s Argentina, Canada, and Mexico have all undergone significant changes in the role of government in banking. In probing for shifts in risky behavior in the banking system of each country, we focus on one such major regime shift for each country.

As of 1991 publicly-owned banks controlled 61% of all bank assets in Argentina. Beginning in 1991, at the same time as the initiation of Argentina's Convertibility Plan and of related financial liberalizations, Argentina initiated efforts to privatize its extensive government-owned provincial banking system.[9]

Nevertheless, by the onset of the Tequila crisis at the end of 1994, only three banks were actually privatized and only one more was effectively privatized in January 1995. However, from December 1995 through the first quarter of 1997 an additional eleven institutions were privatized so that by the latter date less than one-third of all bank assets were in publicly-owned banks. We model the period 1991.IV–1997.I to assess onsets of what may be construed as risky bank behavior. The discussion below focuses on efforts to find a structural break at 1995.IV, the onset of the massive privatization effort.

Canada's regime shift commenced with the 1980 Bank Act. The Act permitted a large increase in the number of banks and allowed nonbank financial institutions to clear checks – a practice previously prohibited. The Act was the beginning of a trajectory of financial liberalization in the 1980s that relaxed restrictions on commercial and consumer lending, allowed federally chartered financial institutions and foreign investors to own 100% of securities dealers, and more generally permitted fuller bank competition with nonbanks and vice versa.[10]

In contrast, Mexico's banking system was characterized by financial repression until the late 1980s (Bank of Mexico, 1996). The government had nationalized the banking system in 1982 and restricted interest rates on deposits and loans. The government forced the banks to lend to it, crowding out extensions of credit to the private sector.

The late 1980s saw profoundly market-oriented changes. In 1987, the government of Mexico sold to the private sector a total of 34% of the ownership in the publicly-owned commercial banks. In 1989, Mexico introduced reforms to eliminate controls on interest rates and on the term structure of traditional types of bank deposits, eliminated forced loans to the public sector at below-market interest rates, and eliminated governmental edicts on the industry-by-industry allocation of funds.

These liberalizations notwithstanding, the most profound regime change since the 1982 bank nationalization was the June 1991–July 1992 privatization, when Mexico auctioned off majority ownership in all eighteen-government owned commercial banks. We present a model of Mexico's banking system performance during the period 1987–1993, with particular attention to a structural break at the beginning of 1992, in the middle of the privatization process.

IV. THE MODEL

Although the purpose of the model, as we apply and interpret it, is to identify moves toward high-risk behavior in a banking system, the model was originally designed to assess the degree of banking system competitiveness. When the model is able to identify breaks at which the typical bank commences the high-risk tactic of producing where marginal cost exceeds marginal revenue, this identification is an adjunct to the original purpose for which the model was designed. We measure the degree of competition because one state of competition – the state that Shaffer (1993) has defined as *supercompetition* – is mathematically identical to the high-risk tactic of producing where marginal cost exceeds marginal revenue.

It is important to reiterate why we emphasize breaks in bank behavior. Our efforts are intended as examinations of an aspect of the current literature

(Kaminsky & Reinhart, 1996, for example) in which a trajectory beginning with financial liberalization, leading through subsequent risky bank behavior, and continuing with an onset of serious financial stress in a country can conclude with a financial and exchange rate crisis. We here focus on the portion of the trajectory that joins the financial liberalization to the risky bank behavior.

However, when seeking the bases for high-risk bank behavior, there is a second and equally important reason to focus on structural breaks. The paradigm we have presented so far involves banks' struggles for market share when liberalization and privatization have suddenly made new market opportunities possible. A market share struggle occurs when the present value of expected future return to the struggle looks consistent with the short-term stresses involved in a cost/revenue relation that cannot long be sustained, i.e. marginal cost exceeds marginal revenue.[11] We focus on breaks because high-risk bank behavior as we characterize it must be a temporary phenomenon. Because the type of high-risk behavior we attempt to characterize occurs as a struggle among banks for market share, it takes place across much or all of the banking system.

In order to characterize breaks into high-risk bank behavior, we present a simultaneous equation model that Shaffer (1993) introduced to the banking literature. This approach permits testing of the competitiveness of a commercial banking system through estimation of an index of market power (λ) and then identifying breaks in competitiveness by applying a dummy variable.

The test revolves around the idea that profit-maximizing firms would set marginal cost equal to what the literature calls their *perceived marginal revenue*. If the firm's perceived marginal revenue schedule and the firm's demand schedule are identical, then setting marginal cost equal to perceived marginal revenue is the same as setting marginal cost equal to demand price, yielding the classical conditions for a competitive equilibrium. Here, of course, firms behave simply as price takers.

In the collusive extreme, in which firms act as a joint monopoly, the firm sets marginal cost equal to a perceived marginal revenue that corresponds to the industry's marginal revenue curve (Bresnahan, 1982). Because the firm only perceives the marginal revenue schedule and the demand schedule as identical under competitive equilibrium, the index we use to gauge the competitiveness of a commercial banking system simply expresses the deviation of the average bank's perceived marginal revenue curve from the industry demand schedule. If there is no deviation, we have pure competition.

Following Bresnahan (1982) we write a demand function for commercial bank services:

$$Q = D(P, Y, \alpha) + \epsilon, \tag{1}$$

where Q is quantity, P is price, Y is a vector of exogenous variables, α is a vector of demand equation parameters to be estimated, ϵ is a random error term. Actual (as distinguished from perceived) marginal revenue is:

$$\begin{aligned} MR &= P + h(Q, Y, \alpha), \\ &= P + Q/(\partial Q/\partial P). \end{aligned} \tag{2}$$

The function $h(Q, Y, \alpha)$ is the semi-elasticity of demand, and $h(\cdot) \leq 0$. Firms' *perceived* marginal revenue is:

$$MR^{p} = P + \lambda h(Q, Y, \alpha), \tag{2'}$$

where λ is a new parameter to be estimated, $0 \leq \lambda \leq 1$. Here, λ measures the degree to which firms recognize the distinction between demand and marginal revenue functions. Let $c(Q, W, \beta)$ be the average firm's marginal cost function, where W is a vector of exogenous supply side variables and β is a vector of supply side parameters to be estimated. Maximizing firms will set *perceived* marginal revenue equal to marginal cost or, where η is a random error term,

$$P = c(Q, W, \beta) - \lambda h(Q, Y, \alpha) + \eta. \tag{3}$$

Price taking firms perceive no difference between their marginal revenue functions and demand function. For them, $\lambda = 0$. Firms acting as joint monopolies clearly perceive a difference between their demand and marginal revenue functions. They set output where marginal cost equals marginal revenue such that $\lambda = 1$. Intermediate values of λ correspond to other oligopoly solution concepts. A Cournot equilibrium is suggested when $\lambda = 1/n$.

An instructive detail of this estimating procedure is that (Shaffer, 1993) $-\lambda$ is also a local estimate of the percentage deviation of aggregate output from the competitive equilibrium level of output. Since actual price deviates from the competitive price by $-\lambda Q/(\partial Q/\partial P)$, and actual quantity deviates from the competitive quantity by $\partial Q/\partial P$ times the deviation in price, actual quantity will deviate from the competitive quantity by $-\lambda Q$. Thus, the percentage deviation in quantity is $-\lambda Q/Q = -\lambda$. If $-\lambda < 0$, then output is less than what would occur in competitive equilibrium, meaning that firms are behaving as if they perceived that they had market power.

Of greatest importance for the purposes of this paper, if $-\lambda > 0$, then actual output seems to exceed the competitive equilibrium output level, even though static allocative efficiency requires the marginal cost pricing outcome of $\lambda = 0$.

This bank behavior outcome is referred to as *supercompetition*. It signifies that the typical bank in the market is operating at an output level where marginal cost exceeds marginal revenue.

To estimate λ, it is necessary to estimate simultaneously specifications of both (1) and (3), treating P and Q as endogenous variables. The demand function is specified as:

$$Q = \alpha_0 + \alpha_1 P + \alpha_2 Y + \alpha_3 PZ + \alpha_4 Z + \alpha_5 PY + \alpha_6 YZ + \epsilon \qquad (2'')$$

where Q is output quantity, P is output price, Y is a measure of macroeconomic activity, assumed to be an exogenous variable, and Z is the price of a substitute for bank output, also assumed to be exogenous. The interaction terms, the products PZ, PY and YZ, are necessary to permit rotation of the demand curve as required to identify λ.[12]

Following Shaffer (1993), a translog cost function is used to estimate the average commercial bank's cost function as follows:

$$\ln C = \gamma_0 + \gamma_1 \ln Q + \gamma_2 (\ln Q)^2 + \gamma_3 \ln W_1 + \gamma_4 \ln W_2 + \gamma_5 \ln(W_1)^2/2 + \gamma_6 \ln(W_2)^2/2$$
$$+ \gamma_7 \ln W_1 \ln W_2 + \gamma_8 \ln Q \ln W_1 + \gamma_9 \ln Q \ln W_2, \qquad (4)$$

where C is total cost, W_1 and W_2 are exogenous input prices, as explained below. Equation (4) gives rise to following marginal cost function, $c(Q, W, \beta)$,

$$MC = (C/Q)(\beta_1 + \beta_2 \ln Q + \beta_3 \ln W_1 + \beta_4 \ln W_2) + \eta. \qquad (5)$$

Therefore, Eq. (3) is specified as follows:

$$P = -\lambda Q/(\alpha_1 + \alpha_3 Z + \alpha_5 Y)$$
$$+ (C/Q)(\beta_1 + \beta_2 \ln Q + \beta_3 \ln W_1 + \beta_4 \ln W_2) + \xi. \qquad (3')$$

However, Eq. (3′) is not configured to facilitate analysis of breaks in bank behavior. To allow for breaks, we rely on the following specification of (3):

$$P = -\lambda Q/(\alpha_1 + \alpha_3 Z + \alpha_5 Y) + (C/Q)(\beta_1 + \beta_2 \ln Q + \beta_3 \ln W_1 + \beta_4 \ln W_2)$$
$$- \beta_5 DQ/(\alpha_1 + \alpha_3 Z + \alpha_5 Y) + \xi, \qquad (3'')$$

where D is a dummy variable to be more fully explained below and ξ is a random error term. The system of equations represented by (2″) and (3″) is then estimated simultaneously.

It is not unusual in articles on the banking systems of any of the three countries we consider to disaggregate a banking system according to market scope. Banks are sometimes characterized as large national, small national, multiregional or regional. Out of appreciation for this bank-by-bank heterogeneity of market scope, it should be noted that the technique offered here does not rely on any particular definition of bank markets. As long as the data sample spans at least one complete market, then estimates of λ are unbiased. Where the industry comprises multiple markets, λ signifies the average degree of market power over the separate markets. Note that λ reflects the behavior of the average firm in the sample.

Another important detail is that, although this model assumes banks are input price takers, violations of the assumption do not damage the results in a way that would bother most modelers. If banks have market power over deposits, in violation of the assumption, it can be shown that the specification of λ overstates the overall degree of market power by misattributing any deposit power to the asset side.[13] Here a finding of perfect competition or supercompetition would be even more striking than if the input price-taking assumption were not violated.

V. DATA

So as to maximize degrees of freedom, we used the most often-reported data available for the applicable period for each country. This decision means that the number of observations per year is different in each of the three country models. For Mexico, the data were monthly and the period was April 1987 through December 1993. For Argentina, the data were quarterly and the period was 1991.I through 1997.I. For Canada, we ran a model using data presented in Shaffer (1993), which are annual and run from 1965 through 1989.[14]

It is important to reiterate that the latter portions of these time series capture events following major liberalizations and privatizations. These periods give us roughly two years (1992–1993) of monthly observations on the Mexican commercial banks during and after which the largest banks were privatized, six quarterly observations (1995.IV–1997.I) for Argentina during which most privatized banks there went through their privatizations, and a nine-year Canadian period (1981–1989) following Canada's Bank Act of 1980.[15]

The model applied here uses the intermediation model of a bank. This approach, developed by Klein (1971) and Sealey and Lindley (1977) and applied in Shaffer (1993) treats the bank as a firm that uses labor to acquire deposits and, then, uses labor and deposits to generate assets. The measure of output (Q) is thus total assets. The price of output (P) is total interest income divided by total assets, i.e. average rate earned on assets. It should be noted that this average rate of return will be affected not only by market lending rates but by changes in the past-due loan ratio. Since deposits and labor are the only production inputs, input prices for deposits (W_1) and labor (W_2) are required. In the marginal cost function, for W_1 the average interest rate paid on deposits (i.e. total financial costs/total liabilities) is used. For W_2 total personnel expenditures/total personnel is applied.

In principal, a particularly appropriate substitute for banking services would be the commercial paper rate in each country. Unfortunately, during the periods under study in each country, data on such instruments were not available. Accordingly, in the case of Mexico, the interest rate on 28-data *cetes*, or Mexican treasury bills was used. In the Canada model, rates on three-month Canadian government paper were applied. In the Argentine case, because of a lack of a series even for Argentine government paper rates for the period, three-month U.S. treasury bill rates were used because of their close correlation with LIBOR rates. Use of this series in the Argentine model provided the expected signs and hoped-for levels of significance in most cases.

As a measure of national output, an index of industrial production was used for Argentina and Mexico since less-than-annual observations for GDP were not always available. In the Canada model, annual GNP is used. All nominal variables were deflated using the consumer price index.

VI. ESTIMATION AND RESULTS

Table 2 presents the estimation results for the models of each of the three countries, with dummy variables for the relevant period of privatization or liberalization in each case. The results show that, after national liberalization or privatization regime changes, the average bank in the high-guarantee, low depositor-discipline nations of Canada and Mexico began to pursue statistically significantly riskier behavior than before these changes. In contrast, the average bank in the low-guarantee, high depositor-discipline nation of Argentina did not.

Indeed, our a priori expectations of the parameter estimates (a_i for α_i, b_i for β_i) were in general confirmed by the results, with the exception of a_2 in the cases of Argentina and Mexico. Since the demand curve is assumed to be downward sloping, the estimate of $\partial Q/\partial P = a_1 + a_3 Z < 0$ must hold, as it did in all cases. We also expected to find $a_2 > 0$ and $a_4 > 0$. As earlier noted, either a_3 or a_5 must be different from zero in order to identify λ, a condition that was always satisfied by a_3. Our estimate of the parameter vector β also met with a priori expectations, although we held no a priori expectation on b_5.

The systems of equations were estimated by the method of Full Information Maximum Likelihood. This method assumes normally distributed errors. Initial parameter values for the FIML estimation were supplied by first estimating the system by non-linear Three-Stage Least Squares. The interaction variable YZ had to be omitted in the estimation because it was nearly perfectly linearly

Table 2. Estimation of Equation (2″) and (3″).

	Argentina	Canada	Mexico
α_0	750979***	−12211	425690
	(3.86)	(−0.11)	(0.74)
α_1	−23857842***	−3020770***	−38456010*
	(−4.55)	(−5.25)	(−1.89)
α_2	−7342***	0.56925	−156
	(−3.89)	(1.27)	(−0.03)
α_3	−3373371***	61863	1828469***
	(−5.33)	(0.72)	(4.19)
α_4	133609***	9874	−186328***
	(5.38)	(0.76)	(−5.36)
α_5	243664***	13.869***	460617**
	(4.73)	(4.48)	(2.37)
α_6		−0.07015	
		(−1.69)	
β_1	6.89405***	0.71310	6.71503***
	(4.16)	(0.95)	(2.91)
β_2	−0.36894***	0.01034	−0.35608**
	(−4.09)	(0.26)	(−2.63)
β_3	0.01051	−0.06658**	−0.00144
	(0.17)	(−2.54)	(−0.02)
β_4	0.39261**	−0.00272	0.37083*
	(2.23)	(−0.03)	(1.83)
β_5	0.00620	−0.03563*	−0.32464**
	(1.25)	(−1.95)	(−2.57)
λ	−0.00053	−0.00183	0.45874
	(−0.24)	(−1.08)	(1.63)
Adj R^2 (2″)	0.770	0.971	0.700
Adj R^2 (3″)	0.959	0.995	0.969
No. of Observations	22	25	81

Note: t-statistics in parentheses, based on approximate standard errors (***: significant at 0.01 level, **: significant at 0.05 level, *: significant at 0.1 level).

correlated with the variable Z for both Argentina and Mexico. This was due to the small variation in industrial production that occurred over the period of the sample. Therefore, in the reported results, there are no estimates for α_6 for those two countries although there are estimates for Canada, where GNP was used for Y.

Problems with multicollinearity remain in this sample. In particular, ln W_1 is highly correlated with Z, causing difficulty in estimating and making inferences on the parameter vector β. Nevertheless, convergence of the estimates was fairly rapid in all cases. The estimates also appear to be robust relative to initial values of the parameter estimates.

For the purposes of this discussion, the most important results involve the coefficients of λ, the variable that measures level of competitiveness, and of b_5, the λ-related dummy variable coefficient for the liberalization or privatization period for each of the three countries. Recall that the value of $-\lambda$ represents a typical bank's percentage deviation of output from competitive levels. Thus, a $-\lambda < 0$ signifies output below the competitive level while $-\lambda > 0$ suggests that output for some reason exceeds the competitive level.

The null hypothesis that $\lambda = 0$ could not be rejected at a reasonable level of significance for any of the estimations. That is, the average bank in each of the three countries behaves consistently with the competitive paradigm. The inability to reject the null hypothesis means that in no case did the average bank operate for each *total* observation period where marginal cost exceeded marginal revenue. That is, the average bank in each country did not follow the high-risk tactic. The question remains, however, as to whether these countries operated at such levels during their post-liberalization or privatization periods.

In examining the results for the post-liberalization or privatization period, the sign and value of b_5, the dummy variable coefficient, deserve particular attention. For such periods, instead of equaling λ, the index of market power will equal $\lambda + b_5$ and b_5 is the difference of level of competitiveness between two periods. If b_5 is negative and significant, the period for which the dummy applies demonstrates a significant increase in the riskiness of bank behavior.

For both Canada and Mexico, b_5 is negative, significant, and takes on a modulus (absolute) value substantially larger than that of λ (where λ's value is insignificant in any case). The negative and significant value of b_5 suggests that the average bank in each of these two high guarantee countries significantly increased the riskiness of its behavior after liberalization or privatization. In the Argentine model, by contrast, neither b_5 nor λ were significantly different from zero. This signifies that neither did the average Argentine bank pursue the high-risk tactic of operating where marginal cost exceeded marginal revenue for the entire measurement period nor did banks increase the riskiness of their tactics in the wake of privatization.[16] That is, the post regime-shift operating behavior of Canadian and Mexican banks was at marked variance from Argentina's but pre-shift behavior was not.[17]

VII. CONCLUSION

Although the oft-alleged relation between market discipline and risky bank tactics is clearly demonstrated in the models we present here, of equal importance in our results is that this connection is not an eternal feature of banking systems. While a predisposition towards high risk tactics revealed itself in the low-discipline high-guarantee countries of Canada and Mexico and not in the high-discipline low-guarantee nation of Argentina, no country's banking system always operated where marginal cost exceeded marginal revenue. Although it would be hard to imagine a scenario in which any particular bank always operated where marginal cost exceeded marginal revenue (at least in the absence of both eternal stockholder optimism and eternal managerial optimism of the most extreme nature), the endless replacement of old banks with new and optimistic institutions would be possible. Neither phenomenon materialized.

Instead, banks in low-market-discipline, high-guarantee countries followed risky tactics when there were new markets that may have seemed to warrant new market-share struggles. Otherwise, high-risk tactics did not appear to be typical. While this additional conditionality for risky behavior may not be surprising, discussions of it are less common in the literature than are simple allegations of links between guarantees or low market discipline and risky lending without detailed consideration of how or when.[18] According to our results, the risky behavior and liberalization story is true and the risky behavior and guarantees story is true, but only when the two stories are told together.

NOTES

1. Gilbert's (1990) review of the literature suggests that it generally finds discipline where guarantees do not exist and does not find it where guarantees exist. The literature since Gilbert seems to derive similar results (see Park & Peristiani, 1998).

2. We focus on periods of natural financial stress because we think such periods are when depositors are most likely to consider whether they ought to leave their present banks for safer financial institutions or mattresses.

3. Rojas-Suarez and Weisbrod (1996) argue that suitable measures of capital may be unavailable for Latin American banks. Based on the rates offered on deposits, they conclude that bank liability holders in both Argentina and Mexico were able to identify risky banks, however.

4. Kryzanowski and Roberts provide detailed analysis of bank structure in Canada.

5. See Jayanti et al. (1996) for more on Canadian bank failures.

6. Fernandez and Schumacher (1998) note that, because the deposit insurance program was not fully funded, the de facto level of deposit insurance was in fact far lower than the $10,000 and $20,000 maxima. They also note that, by tying the size of monetary base to the size of foreign reserves, Argentina's Convertibility Law severely restricts the government's ability to finance assistance programs through money creation. See Caprio et al. (1996) for more extensive discussion of the constraints a currency board – as Argentina has – imposes on the lender-of-last resort function. Zarazaga (1995) provides further analysis of Argentina's currency board.

7. Note that the too-big-to-fail variable, the logarithm of the ratio of a banks assets to all sample banks' assets (Ln(TA_i/TA)), was not significant for any of the three countries. We used this ratio of assets in order to address the Canadian data problem, in which we had to use three years' data in order to have enough degrees of freedom to run the model. We were concerned that if we had simply used assets instead of a ratio, year-over-year growth in assets might distort our results. We also ran the models using simple logarithms of bank-by-bank assets instead of ratios. Neither the signs nor the significance of the coefficients changed as a result.

8. It may be said, however, that poorly performing Mexican banks were disciplined by having to pay higher interbank rates on the Mexican interbank market.

9. For a thorough and incisive analysis of the Argentine privatization process see Abad, Burdisso, D'Amato and Molinari (1997).

10. Amoaku-Adu and Smith (1995) note that, within a year after the passage of Bill C-56, the six largest banks in Canada had acquired control of most of the nation's large investment dealers.

11. The discussion above of consumer behavior with respect to credit cards offers a case in point. If credit cards have been little used in a country until a certain moment and if the first bank that presents a consumer with a credit card is likely to win the consumer for life, then some banks entering the suddenly new credit card market may be motivated to distribute credit cards as rapidly as possible and with less thought than otherwise to borrower creditworthiness.

12. As Shaffer (1993) explains, a necessary and sufficient condition to identify λ is that the demand equation not be separable in at least one exogenous variable that is included in the demand function, but excluded from the marginal cost function. This condition is satisfied if α_3 and α_5 do not both equal zero. This specification of the demand function, apart from the interaction terms, represents a first-order (linearized) approximation of the true demand function (Shaffer, 1993). Our results lead to the conclusion that α_3 and α_5 are not zero. Therefore λ is identified.

13. For a proof, see Shaffer (1994), 8–9.

14. In the case of Mexico, we stopped the model at 1993 because thereafter data reporting began to take place on a quarterly rather than monthly basis. We started with 1987 for Mexico and 1991 for Argentina because those were the earliest years for which data were available from each country's central bank. Recall that 1987 was an important year in the history of modern Mexican financial liberalization. In that year, the government sold off 34% of ownership in Mexico's publicly-owned banks. Thereafter, in the years prior to the 1991–1992 privatizations of the majority of bank ownership, substantial liberalizations included removal of controls on deposit and loan rates and considerable other changes. In Argentina, 1991 marked the inception of the Convertibility Plan and attendant financial liberalizations.

15. We also tested as Argentina's privatization period 1995.I–1997.I, so as to pick up twelve of the fifteen privatizations instead (as with 1995.IV–1997.I) of eleven. The results were not substantively different from characterizing the regime shift period as 1995.IV–1997.I.

16. D'Amato et al. (1997) also discuss the Argentine banking system's response to the tequila crisis.

17. We tried to test the robustness of the results for other specifications especially for log first differences. The results are qualitatively unchanged if iterations converge.

18. Another factor that might conceivably have influenced cross-country differences in bank risk is the strength or weakness of a country's banking supervision and regulation. Banks in a country with less prudential banking supervision and regulation might tend to behave more riskily. However, it turns out to be unlikely that banking supervision and regulation factors cause significant bias in the estimation of our model. In order to examine this problem, we need to have a single cross country index which measures a country's regulation and its ability to supervise its banks. The research to set up this cross country index is in progress (see Barth, Caprio & Levine, 1998; Caprio, 1998; Morgan, 1997) but is not yet refined enough for our purposes. An alternative method is to use proxies for banking supervision and regulation. La Porta et al. (1998) report the indexes of law enforcement variables during 1980–1995. Since prudential supervision depends more on the quality of supervision than on institutional elements, indexes of rule of law and of corruption can be proxies for prudential supervision. With the best law enforcement indexed to 10, the indexes of rule of law in Canada, Argentina and Mexico are 10.00, 5.35, 5.35, respectively. The indexes of corruption in Canada, Argentina and Mexico are 10.00, 6.02, 4.77, respectively. These proxies suggest that banking supervision in Canada would not be worse than Argentina and Mexico, and the difference between Argentina and Mexico may not be significant. Our results in Table 2 do not reflect these differences in the proxies of banking supervision.

ACKNOWLEDGMENTS

The authors thank Pierre-Richard Agénor, Jeffery Gunther, Ricardo Hausmann, Curt Hunter, George Kaufman, David Llewellyn, Kenneth Robinson, Eric Rosengren, Maria Soledad Martinez, Sherill Shaffer, John Welch, and the participants at sessions of the 2002 Research in Financial Services meeting in Seattle, 1999 Federal Reserve Bank of Dallas and World Bank conference on bank privatization, of the 1999 American Economics Association meetings, of the 1998 Jornadas of the Central Bank of Uruguay, and of the 1998 meetings of the Network of Central Bank Researchers of the Americas. The opinions expressed in this paper do not necessarily reflect the opinions of the Federal Reserve Bank of Dallas or the Federal Reserve System.

REFERENCES

Abad, M., Burdisso, T., D'Amato, L., & Molinari, A. (1997). Privatización de Bancos en Argentina: El Camino Hacia Una Banca Mas Eficiente? Central Bank of Argentina.

Amoako-Adu, B., & Smith, B. F. (1995). The Wealth Effects of Deregulation of Canadian Financial Institutions. *Journal of Banking and Finance*, *19*, 1211–1236.

Barth, J. R., Caprio, G., & Levine, R. (1998). Financial Regulation and Performance: Cross-Country Evidence. World Bank Discussion Paper. No. 2037.

Bank of Mexico (1996). *The Mexican Economy*. Mexico City: Bank of Mexico.

Bresnahan, T. (1982). The Oligopoly Solution Concept Is Identified. *Economics Letters*, *10*, 87–92.

Calomiris, C. W. (1990). Is Deposit Insurance Necessary?: A Historical Perspective. *The Journal of Economic History, 50*, 283–295.

Caprio, G. (1998). Banking on Crises: Expensive Lessons from Recent Financial Crises. World Bank Discussion Paper. No. 1979.

Caprio, G., Dooley, M., Leipziger, D., & Walsh, C. (1996). The Lender of Last Resort Function Under a Currency Board: The Case of Argentina. World Bank Discussion Paper. No. 1648.

De la Cuadra, S., & Valdés, S. (1992). Myths and Facts About Financial Liberalization in Chile: 1974–1983. In: P. E. Brock (Ed.), *If Texas Were Chile*. San Francisco: Institute for Contemporary Studies Press.

De Juan, A. (1995). The Roots of Banking Crises: Micro-Economic Issues and Issues of Supervision and Regulation. Paper prepared for the Conference on Banking Crises in Latin America, Inter-American Development Bank, Washington, D.C.

D'Amato, L., Grubisic, E., & Powell, A. (1997). Contagion, Bank Fundamentals or Macro-economic Shock? An Empirical Analysis of the Argentine 1995 Banking Problems, Central Bank of Argentina.

Fernandez, R. B., & Schumacher, L. (1998). The Argentine Banking Panic After the 'Tequila' Shock: Did 'Convertibility' Help or Hurt? In: S. S. Rehman (Ed.), *Financial Crisis Management and Regional Blocks*. Boston: Kluwer.

Gilbert, R. A. (1990). Market Discipline of Bank Risk: Theory and Evidence. *Economic Review*, 3–18. Federal Reserve Bank of St. Louis.

Gorton, G. (1992). Comment. In: P. E. Brock (Ed.), *If Texas Were Chile*. San Francisco: Institute for Contemporary Studies Press.

International Monetary Fund (1993). *International Capital Markets, Part II: Systematic Issues in International Finance*.

Jayanti, S. V., Whyte, A. M., & Do, A. Q. (1996). Bank Failures and Contagion Effects: Evidence from Britain and Canada. *Journal of Economics and Business, 48*, 103–116.

Morgan, J. P. (1997). Latin American Banks: How Conservative Regulations Help Create Profits. In: J. P. Morgan (Ed.), *Equity Research*.

Kaminsky, G. L., & Reinhart, C. M. (1996). The Twin Crises: The Causes of Banking and Balance-of-Payments Problems. Federal Reserve System International Finance Discussion Papers, No. 544.

Kaufman, G. G. (1998). Structuring Prudential Bank Regulation to Promote Efficiency and Safety. Paper presented at a conference on Regulation in Post-Privatization Environments: The Latin American Experience. Buenos Aires, Argentina, May 21–22.

Klein, M. (1971). A Theory of the Banking Firm. *Journal of Money, Credit, and Banking, 7*, 205–218.

Kryzanowski, L., & Roberts, G. S. (1992). Bank Structure in Canada. In: G. F. Kaufman (Ed.), *Banking Structures in Major Countries*. Boston: Kluwer.

La Porta, R., Lopez-de-Silanes, F., Shleifer, A., & Vishny, R. W. (1998). Law and Finance. *Journal of Political Economy, 106*, 1113–1155.

McKinnon, R. I., & Pill, H. (1996). Credible Liberalizations and International Capital Flows: The Overborrowing Syndrome. In: T. Ito & A. O. Krueger (Eds), *Financial Deregulation and Integration in East Asia*. Chicago: The University of Chicago Press.

Nichols, M. W., & Hendrickson, J. M. (1997). Profit Differentials Between Canadian and U.S. Commercial Banks: The Role of Regulation. *Journal of Economic History, 37*, 674–696.

Park, S., & Peristiani, S. (1998). Market Discipline by Thrift Depositors. *Journal of Money, Credit and Banking, 30*, 347–364.

Rojas-Suárez, L., & Weisbrod, S. R. (1996). Towards an Effective Regulatory and Supervisory Framework for Latin America. Inter-American Development Bank Discussion Paper No. 336.

Sealey, C. W., & Lindley, J. T. (1977). Inputs, Outputs, and a Theory of Production and Cost at Depository Financial Institutions. *Journal of Finance*, *32*, 1251–1266.

Shaffer, S. (1993). A Test of Competition in Canadian Banking. *Journal of Money, Credit and Banking*, *25*, 49–61.

Shaffer, S. (1994). Evidence of Monopoly Power Among Credit Card Banks. Federal Reserve Bank of Philadelphia Working Paper No. 94–16.

Spence, A. M. (1979). Investment Strategy and Growth in a New Market. *The Bell Journal of Economics*, *10*, 1–19.

Wall Street Journal (1996). *Business Bulletin* (July 25, p. 1).

Zarazaga, C. M. (1995). Argentina, Mexico and Currency Boards: Another Case of Rules vs. Discretion, Federal Reserve Bank of Dallas. *Economic Review*, 14–24.

COMMENT

W. Curt Hunter

Let me first congratulate the authors on writing an interesting set of papers. I found all three papers to be well done. They all address important questions and issues in banking and have real policy relevance. Let me first note that my comments are formally directed to the papers by Birchler and Maechler and de Juan. However, after briefly reading the Gruben, Koo, and Moore paper, I believe that some of my general comments on the Birchler and Maechler paper regarding its ability to actually confirm the presence effective depositor induced market discipline can also be directed to the paper by Gruben, Koo, and Moore. The two papers employ similar methodologies. Furthermore, given that the Gruben, Koo, and Moore paper concludes that in countries without market discipline, lending risk increases significantly in the wake of liberalization while it does not in countries with market discipline, my general comments on the de Juan should be relevant to the Gruben, Koo, and Moore paper as well.

The goal of the paper by Birchler and Maechler is to test for the presence of market discipline in the Swiss bank deposit market. The main hypothesis underlying the paper is that Swiss depositors exert market discipline by monitoring their banks and reducing the level of uninsured deposits whenever the performance of their bank is "no longer satisfactory". The interpretation is that adverse changes in bank risk characteristics induce depositors to withdraw their deposits (at least the uninsured portion). Four basic hypotheses are tested:

(1) The *general market discipline hypothesis* – the supply of uninsured deposits is related to movements in bank fundamentals

Prompt Corrective Action in Banking: 10 Years Later, Volume 14, pages 313–319.

ISBN: 0-7623-0987-3

(2) The *state guarantee hypothesis* – the supply of uninsured deposits is more responsive to movements in bank fundamentals at regional banks than at cantonal banks due full coverage at the latter
(3) The *liquidity insurance cap hypothesis* – banks facing a binding cap on the total level of deposit insurance coverage will have fewer uninsured deposits than banks where the cap is not binding
(4) The *priority insurance ceiling hypothesis* – depositors are willing to hold more deposits at their institutions in response to an increase in the ceiling level of insurance coverage

These hypotheses are tested using a reduced form regression equation where the dependent variable is the ratio of uninsured saving deposits to total savings deposits and the independent variables are: a set of macroeconomic control variables, a set of lagged bank specific control variables (allowing for delays in the release of such data), a set of control variables that account for revisions in the insurance program, and a variable accounting for bank specific fixed effects.

OVERALL ASSESSMENT

I found the paper to be well written and enjoyed reading it. It addresses an interesting and important issue. The authors do a fine job in setting up their hypotheses, organizing their sample, and conducting their econometric tests. The overall findings are consistent with a priori expectations, that is, each hypothesis is more or less confirmed by the data and the results hold up under a full battery of robustness tests. Thus, the authors conclude that Swiss depositors do discipline their banks by rationally withdrawing deposits in response to increases in perceived bank risk or changes in the level of insurance coverage. While it would be easy to quibble with various aspects of the paper (for example, the authors' choice of macro and bank specific control variables), I will forego such quibbles and instead focus the remainder of my comments on what I see as more substantive issues.

The authors test for the presence of market discipline by examining the responsiveness of deposit levels to adverse changes in bank fundamentals. However, it is not established in the paper that the withdrawal of uninsured deposits actually causes the banks in question any hardship . . . or, stated differently . . . enough hardship to actually change their behavior with respect to risk-taking activities. As noted by Bliss and Flannery (Market Discipline in the Governance of U.S. Bank Holding Companies: Monitoring vs. Influencing,

WP2000-03, Federal Reserve Bank of Chicago, 2000), the concept of market discipline requires that investors (depositors in the B&M paper) be able to evaluate a firm's (bank's) true condition, take actions that actually become impounded in equity prices and that managers actually respond to these actions in the desired manner. While the paper does find that uninsured deposits are responsive to changes in bank conditions, it does not demonstrate that the responsiveness is impounded into equity prices (or profits for that matter) or that bank managers actually change their behavior in response to the actions of depositors or profits or equity prices.

It would be useful for the authors to provide some information on the economic significance of the magnitude of the (typical/average) withdrawal observed in the market or implied by their empirical results. Are we talking about withdrawals that are of minor economic significance or withdrawals on the order observed in bank runs (as is probably the case in some of the banks in some of the countries studied by Gruben, Koo & Moore)? Along the same lines, do the banks simply replace the uninsured deposits with additional insured deposits? Do they replace them with elastically supplied higher cost deposits and if so what is the impact on equity prices (or profits) and do managers change their behavior as a result? In other words, it is not clear to me that the observed withdrawals actually lead the banks to reduce their overall risk. Indeed, one could argue that if the answers to these two questions are in the affirmative, then the banks could actually increase their overall risk levels in response to the withdrawal of uninsured deposits (via substituting insured for uninsured deposits that are not risk sensitive, allowing managers to take on additional risks with even less monitoring or by substituting "hot money" for stable cheaper core deposits). This possibility should be examined.

While I agree with the authors that small depositors are essentially price takers in the market under study, controlling only the quantity of deposits that they are willing to supply, the price approach to detecting the presence of market discipline may be a more attractive approach. This is because it more directly captures the increases in costs associated with a deterioration in underlying risk conditions that flow through to the bank's bottom line and equity prices (the direct effect) and also has the additional benefit of providing reliable signals to supervisors regarding changes in the risk profile of the banks. This allows supervisors to intervene in a timely manner or step up their monitoring activities. While changes in deposit levels may also lead to increased costs, there is no guarantee that this will happen and it is not clear that changes in the level of uninsured deposits produce robust signals about changes in underlying risk.

OTHER COMMENTS

The authors test their hypotheses using a reduced form equation. It would be instructive to see the structural model (demand and supply functions) of the deposit market that generates this reduced form equation. In particular, on the supply side, what role do factors like the bank expenditures on advertising, the number of branches, the length of business hours, availability of on-line banking, etc. have on the supply of deposits and why are these factors not included in the reduced form model.

It would be useful to the reader if the authors provided some history of the loss experiences of depositors in the Swiss banking industry. This would better allow the reader to assess the importance of the various forms of depositor protection available in Switzerland.

While I understand the role of the ratio of non-interest expenses to liabilities in the empirical analysis, I found it curious that the authors consider worker compensation (wages) and training expenditures as indicator of inefficient management. Presumably, higher wages should reflect higher productivity. Likewise, investment in worker training should also lead to a more educated and more productive workforce. Perhaps the authors could select other activity or efficiency ratios to proxy the quality of management.

I remain suspect regarding the presumption that small depositors really actively monitor macroeconomic variables as well as bank financial statements in making their deposit supply decisions. I view the relationship between the macro economy and deposit supply as simply reflecting household employment and income prospects. When the economy is growing soundly, household employment prospects and income tend to rise and so do savings deposits. When the economy sours savings deposits fall.

The paper by de Juan provides a nice overview of the difficulties of implementing prompt corrective action in countries with poor and inadequate bank supervision and the supervisory preconditions for effective and successful prompt corrective action. The paper also discusses issues related to moral hazard. I am very sympathetic to the basic proposition put forward in the paper: that a good infrastructure (economic and legal broadly defined) is the key prerequisite for the effective functioning of market mechanisms and programs of prompt corrective action. The author notes that transparency and effective supervision are key ingredients for any scheme of PCA to be suitable. I wholeheartedly agree with the author.

Indeed, it is my belief that one of the key lessons that policy makers have learned from recent global banking and financial crises is that countries with strong financial infrastructures including good operational (and not just theoretical) systems of supervision and regulation, legal frameworks, and private property rights (including bankruptcy laws) have tended to be more immune to financial shocks and have tended to enjoy more stable rates of growth. Such stability in the financial system breeds the necessary trust that the Federal Reserve considers essential to a well functioning competitive financial system. Recent research (e.g. Simon Johnson from MIT) has shown that weakness of legal institutions for corporate governance had an important effect on the extent of currency deprecations and stock market declines in the Asia crisis countries. Measures of legal protections, enforceability of contracts, corruption, and judiciary efficiency were all shown to be important in determining the depth of the crisis. Thus, it seems clear to me that an effective financial infrastructure, defined broadly as above, is a prerequisite for promoting market discipline in banking markets.

Banking supervisors have also learned the importance of ensuring that incentives induced by capital regulations are compatible with supervisory objectives. In this regard, efforts to enhance public disclosures of the scale and scope, results, and risks of bank trading activities have been motivated by a desire to bring greater market discipline to bear on banks. In addition, supervisors have begun to attempt to build better financial incentives into regulatory capital requirements. The recent proposed amendments to the Basle Capital Accord are designed to provide incentives for accurate risk measurement by allowing banks to select that approach which best reflects underlying risks and associated capital levels.

As the complexity of institutions, instruments, and markets – highlighted by increased interconnectedness driven by advances in technology (both, information processing technology and financial technology or financial engineering) increases, the probability of market surprises and the need for coordinated supervision and regulation will almost surely increase. In this regard, another lesson regulators and supervisors have learned is that direct measures of risk-taking can provide misleading assessments of overall exposure in an environment characterized by complex interconnections among policies, institutions, instruments, and markets. These interactions almost always produce non-normally distributed outcomes (the "so called fat tails" problem) or surprise correlations in situations where outcomes were thought to be ex ante independent. For example, direct lending exposure of global depository financial institutions to Thailand, Malaysia, and South Korea were limited at the time of the Asia financial crisis. However, proxy hedging of these risks in other more liquid and deep markets – including those in Hong Kong, Australia, Brazil, and Mexico proved costly when these markets were adversely impacted by the evolving events and their spillover effects.

The possibility of the need for increased regulatory and supervisory coordination has been taken by some as grounds for supporting the case for a single global financial regulator. It is my belief that this growing desire for centralized regulation must be tempered with caution, given the inherent difficulties associated with the design and implementation of socially optimal regulation. As is well known, inappropriate implementation of even well designed regulation tends to create more problems than it solves. This is because regulation does not occur in a vacuum . . . firms and agents react to changes in regulation in ways to affect the effectiveness of the regulation. In essence, regulators must know exactly how economic agents will react in order to implement optimal regulatory rules. However, given that regulators are generally looking from the outside in, such understanding is difficult and elusive. This is why enhancing market discipline is so important to the overall process of international harmonization of regulation. Market discipline compliments regulators' efforts allowing for more effective supervision. As an example, the importance of market discipline is demonstrated by the results offered in the Gruben, Koo, and Moore paper.

To be sure, regulators have learned that there is no way to ensure a fail-safe financial system. I believe that the de Juan paper acknowledges this fact. Regulators need help and market discipline provides a partial solution as argued in the Gruben, Koo, and Moore paper. Enhancing market discipline through dynamic incentive compatible approaches is the next challenge confronting regulators more generally. From the perspective of the Federal Reserve, we must respond to the recently passed financial modernization legislation (the Gram Leach Bliley Act) which allows full affiliation of banking and securities and insurance activities creating large complex banking organizations which have to be effectively supervised and regulated. Clearly, that regulation must be adaptive. Similarly, in the case of emerging markets and transitioning economies, regulation must be dynamic and adaptive. This makes sense since these markets/economies are in fact emerging and/or in transition.

The Chicago Fed has long pushed for more market discipline through increased disclosure and transparency and through such schemes as mandatory issuance of subordinated debt by large complex banking organizations. In our view, mandatory subordinated debt is incentive compatible in that it aligns the incentives and risk preferences of bondholders with those of bank supervisors. Being subordinated to other liabilities, the debt holders would be risk sensitive and would monitor and discipline bank behavior. They would demand higher rates from riskier banks (a direct effect) and have stronger incentives to quickly resolve problems and avoid forbearance and its associated costs. In addition, increases in interest rate spreads provide signals to supervisors that risk is increasing (an indirect effect). A recent issue of the Chicago Fed's journal – *Economic perspectives: a review from the Federal Reserve Bank of Chicago* (Spring, 2000) contains a comprehensive article on subordinated debt and its advantages as a tool for regulators in supervising large complex banking organizations.

COMMENT

David T. Llewellyn

I. THE ROLE OF MARKET DISCIPLINE IN A PROMPT CORRECTIVE ACTION REGIME

The topic of the session ("Prompt Corrective Action in Banking: 10 Years Later") is well chosen both for its analytical interest and its topicality in the context of the proposed Basel 2 Capital Accord. The new Accord contains (albeit rather weak) elements of PCA proposals, and its Pillar 3 gives emphasis to the need to strengthen market discipline as part of an overall regime for the safety and soundness of banks. It is topical also in the context of current controversies over the accuracy of accounting data as, to work effectively, PCA and the related requirement of market discipline need all potential monitors to be able to make accurate assessments of the financial position of banks: asset quality, capital, creditworthiness, and their behaviour. The requirement for accurate data is particularly emphasised in the paper by de Juan, though it permeates each of the papers.

While the topic of the session is PCA, the papers focus more on the general role of market discipline which is appropriate as the two are closely linked and, properly constructed, reinforce each other. For instance, market signals can induce corrective action by supervisory agencies and, if market discipline works effectively, it should induce corrective action by the banks themselves and before danger levels are reached. As the three papers relate mainly to the role of market discipline, the comments that follow will also focus predominantly on this issue.

Prompt Corrective Action in Banking: 10 Years Later, Volume 14, pages 321–334.

ISBN: 0-7623-0987-3

II. PRE-REQUISITES FOR EFFECTIVE MARKET DISCIPLINE

There is almost universal agreement that the role of market discipline in regimes for systemic stability should be enhanced. This is reflected, for instance, in Pillar 3 of the Basel 2 Accord. However, its precise meaning and the necessary requirements and pre-requisites for it to operate effectively are not always clear and are seldom made explicit. It is something of a "black box". In order to set the context of the papers, and before the three papers are discussed, a brief analytical framework is suggested which outlines necessary conditions for market discipline to work effectively: i.e. to make explicit the mechanisms within the "black box". Seven such conditions are required:

(1) Relevant and accurate information about the status of banks needs to be publicly available on a timely basis to all *stake-holder monitors* (SHMs). Stake-holder monitors are all those agents who have an interest in the outcome of the monitoring process: supervisory agencies, market participants, depositors, shareholders, debt-holders, etc.
(2) There needs to be a sufficient number of SHM groups who are capable of analysing the information made publicly available.
(3) SHMs need to have clear incentives to monitor the behaviour of banks and to incur the costs of doing so. The potential benefits of monitoring need to exceed the costs
(4) A sufficient cohort of SHMs need to adjust their behaviour on the basis of relevant information about the status of the banks in which they have an interest.
(5) SHMs need to respond rationally to relevant information which, for instance, implies that they are not subject to the same errors or misperceptions as the banks being monitored. In a world of herding this can be a demanding requirement as, under some circumstances, the euphoria that leads banks into hazardous positions may also be shared by those undertaking monitoring. There is a hint of this in the paper by Birchler and Maechler.
(6) Such rational responses need to lead to equilibrating changes in market quantities and/or prices (e.g. the supply and pricing of debt available to banks).
(7) Finally, bank managers need to have incentives, and the ability, to respond to these market changes, or must be conscious of the potential threat of such changes because, for instance, they would affect the competitiveness of the bank with respect to the business it is undertaking with depositors,

other suppliers of debt, shareholders and borrowers. In particular, managers need to respond to actual or threatened rises in the cost of deposits, debt and equity capital.

In essence, market discipline ultimately works through price and quantity signals as in any other market. However, there may be impediments to the signalling process and insufficient incentives to respond to those signals that do emerge.

Two immediate conclusions follow from this simple paradigm. Firstly, market discipline will not work effectively if any of these seven routes are impeded (sometimes as the unintended consequence of regulation of one sort or another) or, for any other reason, do not operate. Secondly, the role and power of markets can be enhanced by various mechanisms to strengthen each of these seven routes. In this latter respect, three examples can be cited: a high priority can be given to the timely publication of relevant information about the status of banks; factors that reduce the incentives of SHMs to conduct monitoring can be removed or eased, and mechanisms need to be in place to ensure that there is a sufficient number of SHMs who know they would lose in the event of a bank failure. One of the central challenges in regulatory and supervisory arrangements is to improve the conditions under which market discipline can operate effectively and efficiently which implies addressing each of the seven components within the "black box".

There are several reasons why, in practice, market discipline may not operate effectively with lack of transparency and of relevant, accurate and timely information being the starting point. A perception that a bank will be rescued in the event of distress (perhaps because it is judged to be TBTF) diminishes the incentives for effective market monitoring. The moral hazard attached to badly-constructed deposit insurance schemes has been well established: if it is (or is perceived to be) total, or is mis-priced, banks have an incentive to take excessive risk because risk-taking is effectively subsidised, and depositors may have an incentive to seek high-risk banks offering a higher expected rate of return on deposits. Similarly, the perception that official agencies conduct effective monitoring and intervention (perhaps based on an assumption of superior information and the benefits of economies of scale) may also weaken the incentives for others to conduct costly monitoring in the belief that they are only duplicating monitoring which is already being undertaken by an official agency.

Several contributions can be made to enhancing the effectiveness of market discipline including more demanding and relevant disclosure requirements. The incentives of SHMs to conduct monitoring can be increased through, for instance, a mandatory subordinated debt capital requirement, and limits set on deposit insurance. Also, a regime of credible PCA within a SEIR framework (and most especially a credible commitment to no bail-outs) can contribute to several of the routes within the paradigm outlined above. The requirement for behaviour to be influenced by information includes arrangements for effective corporate governance mechanisms. The requirement that behaviour leads to changes in quantities and prices can be addressed by, for instance, a mandatory subordinated debt rule. Whether bank managers respond to market signals depends inter alia on competitive conditions in the banking industry and the internal incentive structures within the bank.

III. PROMPT CORRECTIVE ACTION

Within this paradigm there is a strong and direct case for a credible PCA regime. A key component of any set of regulatory and supervisory arrangements is the nature, timing and form of intervention by supervisory agencies in the event of financial distress with banks. A key dimension in this is the impact interventions have on future incentive structures of banks and their appetite for risk. The central issue is when intervention is to be made. The experience of banking crises in both developed and developing countries indicates that there should be a well-defined strategy for responding to the possible insolvency of financial institutions.

In this regard, a major consideration relates to rules vs. discretion in the event of bank distress, i.e. the extent to which intervention should be circumscribed by clearly-defined rules (so that intervention agencies have no discretion about whether, how and when to act), or whether there should always be discretion. The obvious prima facie advantage for allowing discretion is that it is impossible to foresee all future circumstances and conditions for when a bank might become distressed and close to (or actually) insolvent. It might be judged that it is not always the right policy to close a bank in such circumstances.

There are, nevertheless, strong arguments against allowing such discretion and in favour of a rules approach to intervention including those embodied within a PCA programme. Firstly, it enhances the credibility of the intervention agency in that market participants, including banks, have a high degree of certainty that action will be taken. Secondly, allowing discretion may increase the probability of forbearance which usually eventually leads to higher costs when intervention is finally made. Thirdly, with discretion there are potential hazards associated with risk-averse regulators who might be disinclined to take action for fear that it will be interpreted as a regulatory failure, and the temptation to allow a firm to trade-out of its difficulty. This amounts to the regulator "gambling for resurrection." Fourthly, and this was relevant in some countries which recently experienced banking distress, it removes the danger of undue political interference in the disciplining of banks and regulated firms. Experience in many countries indicates that supervisory authorities face substantial pressure to delay action and intervention. Fifthly, and related to the first, a rules approach to intervention is likely to have a beneficial impact on ex ante behaviour of financial firms. A rules-based approach, by removing any prospect that a hazardous bank might be treated leniently, has the advantage of enhancing the incentives for bank managers to manage their banks prudently so as to reduce the probability of insolvency or distress.

Put another way, time-inconsistency and credibility problems can be addressed through pre-commitments and graduated responses with the possibility of over-rides. The case for a graduated and structured response is that there is no magical capital ratio below which an institution is in danger and above which it is safe as potential danger gradually increases as the capital ratio declines. A policy of Prompt Corrective Action may specify graduated intervention by regulators with pre-determined responses triggered by capital thresholds. Several countries have such rules of intervention (Basel Committee, 1999).

The need to sustain the credibility of supervisory agencies creates a strong case against forbearance. The overall conclusion is that there should be a clear bias (though not a bar) against forbearance when a bank is in difficulty. While there should be a strong presumption against forbearance, and that this is best secured through having clearly-defined rules within a PCA framework, there will always be exceptional circumstances when it might be warranted in the interests of systemic stability. However, when forbearance is exercised the regulatory agency should, in some way or another, be made accountable for its actions.

IV. THE ROLE OF MARKET DISCIPLINE

Monitoring is not only conducted by official agencies whose specialist task it is. In well-developed regimes, the market has incentives to monitor the behaviour of financial firms. The disciplines imposed by the market can be as powerful as any sanctions imposed by official agencies. The disciplining role of the markets (including the inter-bank market) was weak in the crisis countries of South East Asia in the 1990s. This was due predominantly to the lack of disclosure and transparency of banks, and to the fact that little reliance could be placed on the quality of accountancy data provided in bank accounts. This is not an issue for less developed countries alone. For instance, market discipline has not operated efficiently in Japan due largely to insufficient financial infrastructure (weak accountancy rules, inadequate disclosure, etc.).

Several parties are potentially able to monitor the management of banks and other financial firms: owners, bank depositors and customers, rating agencies, official agencies, and other banks in the market. In practice, excessive emphasis has been given to official agencies. The danger in this is that a monopoly monitor is established with many of the standard problems associated with monopoly power. There may even be adverse incentive effects in that, given that regulatory agencies conduct monitoring and supervision on a delegated basis, the incentives for others to conduct costly monitoring may be weakened.

The merit of increasing the role of market discipline is that large, well-informed creditors (including other banks) have the resources, expertise, market knowledge, and incentives to conduct monitoring and to impose discipline. A further advantage to having agents other than official supervisory bodies monitor banks is that it removes the inherent danger of having it conducted by a monopolist with less than perfect and complete information with the result that inevitably mistakes will be made. A monopolist supervisor may also have a different agenda than purely the maintenance of financial stability. It has been noted that "Broader approaches to bank supervision reach beyond the issues of defining capital and accounting standards, and envisage co-opting other market participants by giving them a greater stake in bank survival. This approach increases the likelihood that problems will be detected earlier ... [it involves] broadening the number of those who are directly concerned about keeping the banks safe and sound," (Caprio & Honahan, 1998). Strengthening the role of market discipline may also limit the danger of official forbearance. In addition, Caprio (1997) argues that broadening the number of those who are directly concerned about the safety and soundness of banks reduces the extent to which insider political pressure can be brought to bear on bank regulation and supervision. As neither the market nor regulatory agencies are perfect, the obvious solution is to utilise both with neither having a monopoly of wisdom and judgement.

V. LIMITS ON MARKET DISCIPLINE

While market discipline is potentially powerful, it has its limitations. This means that, in practice, it is unlikely to be an effective complete alternative to the role of official regulatory and supervisory agencies:

- Markets are concerned with the private costs of a bank failure and in principle reflect the risk of this in market prices. The social cost of bank failures, on the other hand, may exceed the private cost and hence the total cost of a bank failure may not be fully reflected in market prices;
- The private cost of market monitoring and information collection may exceed the private benefits to those undertaking it;
- Market discipline is not effective in monitoring and disciplining public sector banks;
- "Free-rider" problems may emerge if individual private monitors are unable to appropriate the full benefits of their costly monitoring for themselves. The benefits of monitoring must be evident to private agents which again implies that they need to be seen to lose in the event of failure;
- The market is able to efficiently price bank securities and inter-bank loans only to the extent that relevant information is available, and in many cases the necessary information is not available. Disclosure requirements are, therefore, an integral part of the market disciplining process;
- It is not self-evident that market participants always have the necessary expertise to make risk assessment of complex, and sometimes opaque, banks. In addition, there are some areas within a bank (e.g. its risk analysis and control systems) where disclosure is not feasible;
- In some countries, markets in debt of all kinds (including securities and debt issued by banks) are limited, inefficient and cartelised;
- When debt issues are very small it is not always economic for rating agencies to conduct a full credit rating on a bank' subordinated debt;

The conclusion, therefore, is not that market monitoring and discipline can effectively replace official supervision, but that it has a powerful role which should be strengthened within the overall regime.

VI. THE THREE PAPERS

The three papers consider various aspects of the role of market discipline and PCA programmes. Four general conclusions emerge from the papers:

(1) market discipline does work when the conditions are propitious and when it is allowed to work;
(2) conversely, market discipline frequently does not work when the required conditions are not met and when regulatory intervention has perverse effects on the required conditions for market discipline to play its role;

(3) deposit insurance has the effect of lowering the incentives for market discipline to operate; and
(4) the absence of market discipline imposes avoidable costs.

The paper by Gruben et. al. (GKM) considers two related issues: the extent to which the absence of market discipline (often due to the existence of deposit insurance) induces banks into risky behaviour; and the difference that the existence of market discipline makes in determining the impact that financial liberalisation has on banks adopting higher risk profiles. The analysis is based on an empirical investigation of three countries with different deposit insurance regimes: Canada, Mexico and Argentina. This is only a limited sample of countries and, therefore, care is needed when generalising to other countries. Nevertheless, subject to this reservation, the analysis is instructive and yields useful insights. The paper has three main conclusions. Firstly, in countries where market discipline arrangements are weak (Canada and Mexico) lending risks rose significantly in the post-liberalisation period. Secondly, when market discipline is imposed by depositors, banks did not behave hazardously and risks did not rise in the post-liberalisation period (the case of Argentina). In this respect, the results are in line with those of Demirguc-Kunt and Detragiache (1995) who find that, while financial liberalisation increases the probability of a banking crisis, the probability is reduced the stronger are the institutional pre-conditions for liberalisation and market discipline. Thirdly, there is a correlation between depositor-imposed discipline and the predisposition of banks towards risky behaviour. The overall conclusion is that liberalisation increases risk when market discipline is weak.

In the case of Mexico there also seems to be a perversity in that, with the one-way-bet option of deposit insurance, weakness in asset quality seems to have induced more substantial deposit growth. What is not clear in the paper, however, is what the causal mechanism is. The normal model of the moral hazard associated with deposit insurance operates through interest rates in that banks are able to finance high-return and risky loans by inducing a higher deposit inflow by offering a slightly higher rate of interest on deposits but without the incorporation of the full risk premium which is unnecessary as depositors are protected. It would be helpful if the paper were to make the mechanism clear and considered the explicit role of interest rates: in other words, the question arises as to what is happening within the "black box".

While the paper is persuasive, two qualifications are made: first, about the nature of increased risks in the post-liberalisation period, and second, a distinction needs to be made between the *stock-adjustment* effect and the *steady-state* effect of liberalisation. With respect to the nature of risks in the post-liberalisation period, the subsequent rise in the risk profile of banks may not be a reflection of ex ante intentions to take more risk, and banks may not necessarily be aware they are taking more risk. One of the characteristics of liberalisation (though it depends upon the precise nature of the liberalisation process and the nature of the controls that were previously in force) is that it is often followed by a period of rapid bank lending and a herding instinct towards balance sheet growth as a business strategy following the abandoning of regulatory-imposed restraints. This has been found in many countries including in the Nordic region prior to the Scandinavian banking crises of the early 1990s. Higher risk profiles ex post may simply reflect the same behaviour as in the past becoming more risky when all banks undertake the same behaviour simultaneously and on a larger scale than previously. Unanticipated changes in either the banking or economic environment following liberalisation (such as a sharp acceleration in asset-price inflation) can make given bank portfolios inherently more risky than was previously the case.

This means that a distinction needs to be made between liberalisation that induces banks to choose to take more risk, as opposed to liberalisation which makes the environment more risky and banks to under-estimate the risks they take. In this way, the risk profile of banks may increase either because they knowingly choose to take more risk or because, for various reasons, they underestimate and under-price the risks they are taking. Simply because risks are observed to rise after a period of liberalisation does not in itself mean that liberalisation raises the risk appetite of banks. Here is a second "black box": what are the precise mechanisms that operate between liberalisation and subsequent bank distress. In particular, to what extent is subsequent bank distress the result of banks adopting a greater risk appetite, the environment becoming more risky, or simply banks underestimating and under-pricing risks perhaps because they misunderstand the new market environment.

A second reservation about the conclusion of the GKM paper, and one that applies more generally to the many papers that identify a relationship between liberalisation and subsequent banking sector fragility, relates to the nature of the liberalisation process itself. In this regard a distinction is made between the *stock-adjustment* effect of liberalisation (the impact on behaviour as the banking system moves from a controlled to a more liberalised environment – the transition period) and the *steady-state* characteristics of a liberalised financial system. There are many reasons why the risk profile of banks might rise in the transition period: banks expand their loan portfolio very sharply in the immediate aftermath of liberalisation and risk analysis systems are often not suited to the new environment; a balance sheet growth momentum develops in a phase of generalised euphoria following liberalisation; rapid asset growth appears to be very profitable in the short-run; as all banks expand loans simultaneously, and herd behaviour emerges, behaviour that might involve acceptable risk for individual banks acting alone, becomes excessively risky when all banks behave in the same way; liberalisation usually implies more competition and the erosion of economic rents which in itself may induce banks into more risky behaviour than in the pre-liberalisation period.

In the stock-adjustment phase (i.e. during the period immediately following the liberalisation process) uncertainty is created as financial firms are unfamiliar with the characteristics and management requirements of the new regime. Previously protected institutions need to adapt behaviour though this may occur only with a time lag. New behaviour patterns need to be learned. Some mistakes during the process of liberalisation occur because banks do not adjust quickly enough to the requirements of the new regime. Behaviour which is appropriate under one regime may be inappropriate in another (see Llewellyn, 2000; Benink & Llewellyn, 1994 for a more formal discussion). At the same time, official supervisory arrangements may not adjust sufficiently to the new environment. Bisignano (1998) argues that this represents a combination of "excess momentum" by the private sector (banks) and "excess inertia" on the part of supervisory authorities.

The reservation about the conclusions that fragility follows liberalisation is that the characteristics of the immediate stock-adjustment phase (the transitional phase of moving from one regulatory environment to another) do not necessarily apply once the new steady-state has been reached. Many of the banking crises that have emerged following a period of liberalisation have been associated more with the uncertainties and mistakes during the transition phase rather than the inherent characteristics of a liberalised financial system. This can be seen in the now profitable banking systems in Scandinavian countries following the extreme distress experienced in the immediate post-liberalisation period.

VII. A CASE STUDY OF SWITZERLAND

The paper by Urs Birchler and Andrea Maechler presents an interesting case study of the discipline imposed by bank depositors in Switzerland. The main hypothesis underlying the empirical tests is that "depositors exert market discipline by monitoring their banks and by withdrawing *uninsured* deposits whenever performance of their bank is no longer satisfactory. Bank fundamentals should thus help to explain the amount of *uninsured* deposits a bank is able to attract." (italics added). The paper proceeds by testing three specific hypotheses. The methodology uses quantity indicators (supply of bank deposits) rather than price indicators. The three hypotheses are well constructed and the results are robust. The key conclusions may be summarised as follows:

- contrary to conventional wisdom, depositors do seem to monitor their banks;
- uninsured savings deposits react to business conditions and deposits are withdrawn when the fundamentals of the bank deteriorate;
- depositors responded to changes in the Swiss deposit protection system;
- depositors were found to be sensitive to institutional differences across banking groups; and
- state guarantees have tended to weaken market discipline.

While the conclusions of the paper suggest that market discipline does work when the conditions are propitious, one of the conclusions also suggests that depositors do not always respond rationally (see condition (5) in the paradigm outlined at the outset). The episode concerns how depositors responded in the event of a sharp rise in bank lending in a bubble period. Depositors did not seem to be concerned about the banks' strong credit growth during the real-estate bubble before 1994 though they became concerned once the bubble had burst. This is a reservation to the efficiency of this form of market discipline as there is ample evidence that problems build up during a period of sharp asset growth most especially when this is associated with real-estate euphoria. As put by the authors: "The fact that investors use their information, does not imply that they use it correctly." Again as stated in the paper: "Market discipline thus does not shield banks and depositors from irrational swings in general market discipline." This, of course, is not an argument against creating an enhanced role for market discipline in the overall regulation and supervision of banks. It does, however, suggest that total reliance cannot be placed on it, and that all the mechanisms within the paradigm outlined at the outset of this Comment need to be strengthened.

The encouraging aspects of the conclusions are that, contrary to conventional wisdom, depositors are in a position to monitor banks and to respond to bank-specific risks, that quantity indicators rather than price signals have a role in potentially disciplining banks, and that, when conditions are conducive, market discipline can be a viable disciplining mechanism on banks.

VIII. PCA IN PRACTICE

The paper by Aristóbulo de Juan ("PCA in International Practice") considers the applicability of PCA to countries with poor banking supervision, and the necessary conditions for PCA regimes to be feasible and effective. While accepting the case for PCA, and welcoming the FDICIA arrangements, the author argues that final judgement must be suspended until they have been put to a real test. The author judges that care is needed when transplanting models such as PCA and FDICIA to other countries where the conditions are different and the necessary prerequisites for success might be absent. Country-specific considerations always need to be taken into account when considering the relevance and suitability of such regimes. The author judges that these regimes may be suitable only for a small number of developed countries. In many other countries the necessary prior conditions for a FDICIA and PCA regime are not in place.

The paper argues that a major constraint in practice is that in many countries the availability and reliability of data are insufficient for PCA. This is judged to be an important issue as, in the author's view, PCA will not work effectively when supervision is inadequate and unreliable and when, in other ways, supervisory arrangements are weak. Emphasis is given in particular to the accuracy of data on the true value and quality of bank assets (and hence of capital) which in many countries is weak. The author judges that in many countries the stated value of bank assets (and hence capital) is something of a fiction. This is often the result of questionable accounting procedures and norms.

In particular, the author argues, a major pre-condition for effective PCA is that bank supervisory arrangements, and the practice of bank supervision, are sufficiently robust and are implemented rigorously.

On the basis of experience in many countries, the paper outlines several pre-requirements and pre-conditions for an effective PCA to be implemented:

- accurate and transparent data on the true position of banks and, in particular, on the quality of their assets;
- as strong supervision is a precondition for effective PCA, there need to be rigorous supervisory arrangements including on-site inspections;
- a prerequisite for an efficient assessment of solvency and good asset classification is a good and properly implemented accounting system which, according to the author, is conspicuously absent in many countries;
- sound authorisation conditions for banks;
- effective reporting to supervisors;
- adequately resourced and suitably remunerated supervisory agencies;
- a political will to be realistic about the status of banks and their true financial predicament coupled with a political willingness to act decisively and timely;

- institutions and mechanisms in place for effective resolution of problem banks.

These are demanding conditions and, for this reason, the author concludes that PCA may in practice not be feasible at the current time for a large number of countries. Given the potential value of PCA, the outline in the paper of the necessary conditions for effective PCA makes a constructive contribution.

IX. ASSESSMENT

The three papers consider a range of issues relevant for market discipline and a regime of PCA. Drawing some of the disparate threads together from each of the papers several conclusions emerge:

- there is an overwhelming case for both enhanced market discipline and PCA in creating conditions for stable financial systems;
- PCA regimes need to be viewed as part of a more general policy of enhancing the role of market discipline;
- the evidence is that, if the conditions are appropriate, market discipline can be an effective part of an overall regime designed to bolster systemic stability;
- conversely, if the necessary conditions are absent, market discipline fails to work effectively;
- as recognised in the proposed Basel 2 Capital Accord, information disclosure and transparency are key requirements for market discipline to operate effectively;
- there are, nevertheless, limits to what can be expected from market discipline and hence it is not an alternative to effective regulation and supervision by official agencies.

While the proposed Basel 2 Capital Accord makes reference to the need for early intervention in the event of bank fragility or potential fragility, and Pillar 3 focuses on the role of market discipline, it remains to be seen how much emphasis will be given to these in practice. There is also a danger that some aspects of Pillars 1 and 2, and most especially the detailed and prescriptive nature of some of the rules in Pillar 1, might in practice weaken market discipline mechanisms.

REFERENCES

Basel Committee (1999). A New Capital Adequacy Framework. Consultative Paper, Basel Committee on Banking Supervision, BIS, Basel, June.

Benink, H., & Llewellyn, D. T. (1994). Fragile Banking in Norway, Sweden and Finland. *Journal of International Financial Markets, Institutions and Money*, *14*(314), 5–20.

Bisignano, J. (1998), *Towards an Understanding of the Changing Structure of Financial Intermediation*. SUERF Study No. 4, Amsterdam

Caprio, G. (1997). Safe and Sound Banking in Developing Countries: We're not in Kansas Anymore. Policy Research Paper, No. 1739. World Bank, Washington.

Caprio, G., & Honihan, P, (1999). Restoring Banking Stability: Beyond Supervised Capital Requirements. *Journal of Economic Perspectives*, *13*(4), 43–64.

Demirguc-Kunt, A., & Detragiache, E. (1998). The Determinants of Bank Crisis in Developing and Developed Countries. IMF Staff Papers, March.

Llewellyn, D. T. (2000). Regulatory Lessons from Recent Banking Crises. De Nederlandsche Bank Discussion Paper. Amsterdam, May.

Printed and bound by CPI Group (UK) Ltd, Croydon, CR0 4YY

16/09/2026

14963402-0001